this must be the place

The Adventures of TALKING HEADS in the 20th Century

David Bowman

HarperEntertainment

An Imprint of HarperCollinsPublishers

A hardcover edition of this book was published by HarperEntertainment, an
imprint of HarperCollins Publishers, in 2001.

HarperCollins books may be purchased for educational, business, or sales
promotional use. For information please write: Special Markets Department,
HarperCollins Publishers Inc., 10 East 53rd Street, New York, NY 10022.

First paperback edition published 2002.

Designed by Jo Obarowski and Jeannette Jacobs

The Library of Congress has cataloged the hardcover edition as follows:

Bowman, David
    This must be the place: the adventures of Talking Heads in the 20th
century / by David Bowman.—1st. ed.
        p. cm.
    ISBN 0-380-97846-6 (hardcover)
    1. Talking Heads (Musical group). 2. Rock musicians—United
States—Biography.   I. Title

ML421.T27 B6 2001
782.42166'092'2—dc21
[B]   00-046082

ISBN 0-06-050731-4 (pbk.)

02 03 04 05 06 RRD 10 9 8 7 6 5 4 3 2 1

This history is for my good friends Brian Breger and Bucky Wunderlick.

With grateful thanks to my wife, Chloe Wing.

Also by David Bowman

Let the Dog Drive
Bunny Modern

Baba Baba Baba

Gadung gadung gadunt

Uma childa nobo

Distiptics in wine

Insane today

I was born with all language in my mouth.
Don DeLillo, Great Jones Street

fa fa fa fa fa fa fa fa fa fa
David Byrne

tracks

BOOK THREE
the big suit

BOOK FOUR
shrunken heads

introduction

Facts are never what they seem to be.
"Crosseyed and Painless," lyrics by David Byrne and Brian Eno

Forming a rock group is a mythic American tradition. It's Huck Finn and crew rafting down the Mississippi. Mickey Rooney and Judy Garland puttin' on a play. It's teenage boys hunkering down in a suburban garage, strumming electric guitars over the grease spot left from Dad's Mustang. David Byrne's garage band was called the Revelation, and they covered the Rolling Stones and Beatles. Drummer Chris Frantz's high school band was named the Hustlers. They played the Stones and Beatles as well. The Walkers was Jerry Harrison's first band. He played keyboards. His band only covered the Stones.

Tina Weymouth was never in a garage band. Chicks didn't do that in the 1960s. Tina did what girls did—sat cross-legged on her bed with a wooden guitar in her lap strumming Joan Baez. But after a year, she gave it up when, as she put it, she "discovered boys." Years later, Chris and David taught Tina how to play bass guitar.

It was in New York that these kids formed Talking Heads, a group that was completely of its time and totally outside of it. Talking Heads was a product of Art School America circa 1970. Painting was dead, so why not form a band? Talking Heads began as New Wave art rockers who understood soul music. They were accepted and thrived in the Bowery punk scene, although they were total outsiders. No torn T-shirts or black leather for them. They dressed prep-school casual. Little alligators over their hearts. The band's leader, David, was about as sexy as Norman Bates. The doe-eyed Tina played her huge bass with the fearful look of a blond Joan of Arc about to be burned at the stake. Talking Heads seemed too odd and original to ever be signed to a record company. One night in the early days, Chris overheard two music critics talking in the men's room of a club:

"Whaddaya think? You think the Talking Heads are gonna get signed?"
"I don't think it's gonna happen. I think they're just a downtown thing."
"Yeah. No one outside of New York City is gonna get it or even want it."

Not so fast, gentlemen. Talking Heads was signed, of course. Their first effort, *Talking Heads '77,* was a perfect platter of pristine electric minimalism produced by a disco carpetbagger. Its standout track was the lyrical musing of a serial killer sung partially in French. Then the band hooked up with the Svengali of avant-garde pop, Brian Eno, and released the absurdly titled *More Songs About Buildings and Food.* Against cultural logic, this album contained their first bona fide hit, a cover of Al Green's "Take Me to the River." Talking Heads' third album, *Fear of Music,* forever etched the psyche of underground Manhattan into the national vocabulary with Byrne's declaration, "This ain't the Mudd Club, or CBGB. . . ."

On three perfect albums, the band had pushed artiness to the brink before fulfilling Dylan's example of pop metamorphosis by adding five new members and becoming an integrated psychedelic funk troupe. Talking Heads' monster hit "Burning Down the House" was inspired from a chant heard at a Funkadelic concert. Their extraordinary pair of funk albums, *Remain in Light* and *Speaking in Tongues,* weren't just another example of whitey ripping off the 'hood. They were the products of delighted anthropologists that transcend global pop.

The band began charting back in the days of MTV's conception. Talking Heads made use of their art-school credentials to shoot surreal state-of-the-art eye candy that blatantly mocked the lip-sync clichés of the new genre of music video.

Talking Heads didn't stop with conquering video. They borrowed from New York avant-garde theater and toured an elaborate rock 'n' roll performance piece that documented their progress from funky art music to artful funk. The show climaxed with David Byrne dancing onstage wearing a monstrous white business suit, singing, "Who took the money? Who took the money away?" A celebrated Hollywood director filmed the show and created the best rock on celluloid since *A Hard Day's Night.*

Then the band changed direction yet again and recorded a "simple" pop album of Americana called *Little Creatures*. Although Talking Heads was satisfying the Beatlesque tenet that a band change directions several times in its career, *Little Creatures* was not the way musical evolution was supposed to work. It was as if the Fab Four had recorded *Revolver* first, then *Help!*

David Byrne once said, "I think Talking Heads can be as popular as the Carpenters." Before his band completed rock mythology by breaking up acrimoniously, they were indeed almost as big as Karen and Richard. This band that should never have been understood outside of New York City was a hit in Ohio and New Brunswick. They got them in Hollywood. They got them in Sheboygan. The Brits got Talking Heads. So did the Krauts and Danes. The last live Talking Heads performance happened on a New Zealand stage with Maoris in the audience.

Facts don't do what I want them to.
David Byrne and Brian Eno

Talking Heads starts with David Byrne. What I can tell you about meeting the man is that he doesn't just look like himself, he looks like a movie star. He's handsome enough to carry a picture. Interestingly though, it wasn't until the early eighties that Byrne became photogenic. In those first publicity shots he appears hollow-eyed and stricken—an American Artaud. A few years later, in photographs by Richard Avedon and Helmut Newton and Robert Mapplethorpe, Byrne has come into himself as a figure and an artist. He no longer has the face of an animal searching for a home.

In person, Byrne is very low key in a paradoxical jittery sort of way—although he is no longer excruciatingly shy like the early days. He's soft-spoken, but laughs often. And he has this little Scottish speech thing going, leaving the "g" off words endin' in "ing." Byrne talks and acts and looks like a big kid who has just stolen something good out of the cookie jar.

I once asked him about rock histories: "Should these things be written?" David Byrne answered that he hadn't read any rock histories lately— "But I read quite a few at one point and, yeah, I think they are a good thing. I was wonderin', 'How do you do this? How did this person do this? What's their attitude toward living? How do they make life decisions in this kind of work?' It's not like a nine-to-five job. You have to figure it out yourself. They

3

don't teach it in school. They get you started with the rudiments, but then you're on your own. Yeah, I derived tremendous inspiration from reading how other people got through it."

You have everything wrong. Everything in here is wrong. That's why I said I have to rewrite your book for you. It's all wrong, David. You know nothing about us.
Tina Weymouth

4

Tina Weymouth had played the thing for less than a year when the *Village Voice* called her "the queen of the bass players." In the early days of Talking Heads, Tina was treated like royalty while the press treated David Byrne like a carny geek. Ex–Velvet Underground member John Cale says Tina was queen because "she had a Jean Seberg thing going," that short-haired look of the actress who played Joan of Arc for Otto Preminger. The New Wave tomboy who hawked the *Herald Tribune* in Godard's *Breathless*. Both Jean Seberg and Tina Weymouth seemed adorably feminine because, to paraphrase Seberg's lover Carlos Fuentes, "To get to those two you had to negotiate the twists and turns of androgyny and homoeroticism."

Month by month, as Talking Heads conquered the small network of Manhattan nightclubs, Tina's "twists" began to matter less and less. David Byrne overshadowed his bandmate in the pages of the *New York Times* as well as the *Soho News*. Talking Heads became his group, not hers. Tina didn't stay quiet about it. She began what would become a career-long technique of using the press to send messages to David. She complained about him in newspapers and rock magazines. Cut him down to size. Long after the group finally broke up, Tina continues to rail against Byrne. She once said to me, "I'm going to become a hysterical woman. I'm going to become a hysterical woman if you keep me talking about the story of the band."

Tina said this in a Greek coffee shop near Columbus Circle. It was late afternoon in winter. It was already dark. Our table sat in a draft, and the joint was half empty. The vibe was pure 1940s film noir. I could imagine her as a figure in an Edward Hopper painting. She is attractive, but she no longer has her Jean Seberg going. She seemed a little brittle. She had the vibe of a Catholic saint. Or maybe a tragically lame prima ballerina. Or maybe Valerie Solanis, the woman who shot Andy Warhol.

Just as the story of the Beatles can be reduced to a tale of the love/hate relationship between John and Yoko and Paul, the story of Talking Heads can be reduced to a similar equation between Tina and David. Only Tina is complicated enough to fill the roles of both John and Yoko.

"I always lived in the world of imagination," she told me as she paid for our coffee. Then she said, "I thought that David Byrne was like me."

She paused.

"I made a mistake."

According to John Cale, the incredible thing about Talking Heads was no one could figure out what kept them together. A chronicle of the band and their times will provide some answers. As I was writing this book I asked David Byrne, "Does truth matter in rock 'n' roll?"

"No," he answered. "What's that quote? 'Between a truth and a myth, print the myth.' "

Talking Heads is composed of four very neat-looking individuals whom any parent would introduce in polite company without a trace of nervousness. When they freak out, it's in a much more complicated way.

Frank Rose

memories can't wait
BOOK ONE

the secret
life of
tina weymouth

In the summer of 1973, Chris Frantz was trimming Tina Weymouth's hair. They were both art students at Rhode Island School of Design, aka RISD, pronounced RizzDee. They were both in their early twenties. Tina was born in 1950, Chris the next year.

Chris Frantz had come into masculine beauty early. He was thin with a Lancelot intensity about him. As he snipped away at Tina's hair he was so taken with her that his hands trembled.

Young men's hands didn't usually tremble like this in the early seventies. Certainly drummer's hands didn't shake around chicks. Chris was a rock 'n' roll drummer who had shared an art studio with Tina for more than a year. But he had a girlfriend and Tina had a beau. When their respective college flings crashed in winter, Chris and Tina decided to start dating. Now Chris's hand was shaking. "You know. I feel like we could be married," he said.

"You know," Tina answered. "So do I."

Tina believed from that moment on that she "was already a married woman in the eyes of God." We could consider the story of Talking Heads as their private love story. That's one way to look at it.

Tina was born Martina Michèle Weymouth on November 22, 1950, in Coronado, California. Coronado is part of San Diego, a navy town. Her father, Ralph Weymouth, was a navy lifer who would eventually become an admiral. Tina's mother was French. Tina had a nine-year-old brother, Yann, and a seven-year-old sister, Nanu. Both had been born in Santa Barbara during World War II. Two years after Tina's birth, sister Danielle was born.

Ralph Weymouth then moved his family to Hawaii where Tina was schooled by Hawaiian nuns. Her parents gave her two more sisters, Lani and Letita—-Hawaiian names. Then Tina's father moved his family again. He was stationed in France, Belgium, Switzerland, and Washington, D.C. Tina was taught by French, Belgian, and Swiss nuns. During this time, she was given yet another sister, Laura, in 1957. Three years later, a second brother, Lawrence.

Tina's first mention in the *New York Times* occurred on November 29, 1964, in the wedding announcements section. Her brother Yann had married Elizabeth Morris "Lally" Graham, the Radcliffe-educated daughter of the *Washington Post*'s Katherine Graham, on the previous afternoon at the Naval Chapel in Washington, D.C. A photo of Mr. and Mrs. Yann R. Weymouth after their marriage appeared next to the story. The bride gave a toothy Gloria Vanderbilt stage smile while her taller husband stood beside her with a stunned and equally goofy look. *Holy cow. What have I done?* The paper didn't mention that the marriage "was horribly rash." Those would be the bride's words twenty years later.

The paper did report that Martina and her younger sister Danielle were junior bridesmaids. They wore similar gowns as well as wreaths of small peach chrysanthemums, and they carried bouquets to match. Tina's two other younger sisters were flower girls. The paper mistakenly called Tina's father a captain, but he was actually a rear admiral assigned to the Pentagon. The paper didn't mention the bride's father—newspaperman Phil Graham, publisher of the *Washington Post*. The year before, he had shot himself dead. The last note Phil Graham sent his daughter read, "I'll keep trying and before long I'll be doing better."

The January after Lally and Yann's wedding, Tina's father was sent to Iceland. It was there in frigid Keflavík that Tina pushed the boundary of vice. She had always been taught that marriage was holy and "prolonged kissing" was a mortal sin. After Tina made out with a boy in the Icelandic mountains, she was consumed by guilt.

Thankfully her father moved the family yet again to Los Angeles. She tried to forget her Icelandic sin by becoming the captain of the high school cheerleading squad. "It was so unreal," she would tell a reporter. "But this didn't make me any happier. I still always felt really left out and different. I would try to sneak into Whiskey-A-Go-Go because that was one place you could get in if you were underage. I'd see Paul Revere and the Raiders jumping in the swimming pool at Marineland and I felt they had such extraordinary, exciting lives. The radio was playing really good songs. When I was sixteen one of the big hits was 'Love Is All Around' by the Troggs."

Love *was* all around. Tina's parents would arrange dates for her with the sons of other military officers. When Tina was seventeen, she was escorted to Whiskey-A-Go-Go by a general's nineteen-year-old son. This was the summer of '68, and gunsmoke still hung over the L.A. shooting of Robert Kennedy. "Not wishing to look as weird as I felt," Tina recollected, "I wore the uniform of a California girl on a date: a bright pink A-line jersey knit mini dress with chunky white patent leather high-heeled sandals."

The general's son wore wheat jeans and a madras button-down shirt. The two drank soda, danced to top-forty songs. This was Tina's first nightclub. It was no big deal. "The experience was novel and yet thoroughly banal. I thought, 'So what's the big deal, why do adults like this?' "

On the drive home, the boy mentioned that Vatican II had just banned the use of contraceptives. He asked if a "good Catholic" girl like Tina would ever consider having an abortion. Tina turned red. "Embarrassingly, I had to ask my date what was meant exactly by 'abortion' and 'contraceptives,' because these things were never defined for us by the innocent little nuns at my school. I was not prepared for a sexual confrontation with a nineteen-year-old boy, let alone a moral confrontation with Mother Church. I was still feeling pretty guilty about those 'prolonged kisses' I had enjoyed two years earlier in Keflavík. As it was, I sensed that my ignorance struck my date as perhaps rather 'uncool,' but my innocence seemed to turn him on, a truly weird double standard." If this seems rather weighty for a girl in the mid-sixties with the Summer of Love just around the bend, keep in mind that Tina always saw herself as a nun inside her own interior.

"I was very, very shy," she said. "That was because we moved all

11

the time. I had my own inner world. Have you ever read Frank O'Conner's 'The Ugly Duckling'? It's a story about a girl who becomes a nun. He describes so beautifully what happened to her. She became a raving beauty sometime in her teens and had a lot of suitors. And the narrator moved to Dublin because of her and became a writer in order to impress the girl. She ended up dumping him for another guy, and in his pain and everything the narrator just forgets about her. Years later he found that she had gone into a nunnery. So he went and talked to her and eventually realized why she'd done what she'd done. She explained that she had been so long ignored and left to her own devices that she had created her own very, very rich emotional world. When finally the world was offered to her on a silver platter—when finally the boys took notice of her, when finally the boys were nice to her—they didn't compare. What they had to offer was so shallow it didn't compare to the inner world she had created in her mind. That's why she became a nun. She didn't need that extra baggage. As a nun she could continue in her world."

Rather than sequester herself in a nunnery, Tina got a summer job working for the Department of Health, Education and Welfare in the naval shipyard in Washington, D.C. Then she went up to Barnard College in New York where she had a double major in French literature and art history. She transferred to Old Dominion University for half a year, went back to Barnard for half a year, then dropped out.

These were the 1960s. Previously college had been a privilege. Now it was an expectation that could always be put off if one lost one's mooring. The chronology of this portion of Tina's life is confusing to dig up if the subject stops cooperating with the biographer.

I don't want you to get all personal so I'm not going to answer any more personal questions about my family. Talking Heads is one thing. My personal history is another thing, you know. . . .

Tina Weymouth is difficult, but needs no apologist. Gary Kurfirst, Talking Heads' future manager, explains the woman's psyche this way: "Tina is very intelligent, and has always had her own way of seeing things. Tina can look at a picture that's painted red and she'll tell you that it's green. But she's not putting one over on you. Tina sees things. You and I could look at something and go, 'God, look at that dog,' and she'll go, 'It's a fox.' And we'll go, 'No it's a dog.' And she'll go, 'No it's a fox—can't you see?' And it's not that she's putting one over on you. In Tina's eyes she saw a fox."

Before Tina clammed up, she talked about staying several months down in Tulsa, Oklahoma, with her sister Nanu and Nanu's husband. Tina hated Tulsa, there was nothing but "foxes" everywhere. Tulsa was Oral Roberts's town. Everyone knew Roberts was estranged from his son solely because his progeny grew a beard. Tulsa drove Tina nuts.

During her exile from college, Tina's brother Yann had become an architect while her sister-in-law Lally wrote for the *Boston Globe*. Then a daughter was born. And another. Then after six years of marriage, Yann and Lally divorced. Lally kept the family name of Weymouth and became an author and newspaper columnist. Soon she began to move in what Tina called the "very rarefied atmosphere" of Manhattan high society. Lally would become a cohort of Jackie Onassis and Truman Capote. The latter wrote that Yann's ex-wife had a "first-class mind, which she sometimes tries to disguise." Capote felt that this trait was common to intellectual women "who are very attractive."

According to Tina, Yann flipped out after the breakup. One afternoon he rode his bicycle into a tree and was knocked into a coma for three days. Tina saw this as his "unconscious" death wish. He soon recovered and did his younger sister a great favor by asking her to come to New York to help him paint his new bachelor apartment.

Tina's shyness flared again when she arrived in New York. She found that she couldn't bear to talk to the operator in order to make a collect call to her parents. If she got lost on the streets, she wouldn't ask strangers for directions. "I'd rather wander around lost for hours." But little by little the edginess of New York cured her. "New York opened me up," she said later. "In New York, somebody is going to say terrible things to you or not say terrible things to you. It doesn't matter. You have no choice. You can't escape it."

Tina left Yann and New York and enrolled at Rhode Island School of Design in Providence in 1970. New York may have indeed skinned the girl of shyness. Apparently Tina showed up at an art orientation meeting stark naked and covered with green paint. This wasn't unusual RISD behavior in the early 1970s. That said, Tina the nun had decided to become a painter. One fellow student remembers her work as "gray." She was doing gray aircraft-carrier paintings. She'd take strips of canvas and paint the whole thing gray. Another student remembers Tina's studio full of "huge canvases that she'd lay on the floor and do quite a bit of splattering around. Swirls of color. They weren't Jackson Pollock drips. Tina was using a tremendous amount of paint and smearing it around. She'd keep bending over and splattering all over the place."

Within a year, Tina's parents retired to Providence, buying a beautiful home up on the hill near Brown University. Two or three of Tina's younger sisters were living there. Fellow student Jean De Segonzac remembers, "The mother was having some problems with some of the younger girls because of Tina going to college. This meant the younger girls were also hanging out with college kids. I remember Tina's mother screaming, 'You can't see that girl anymore, she's a lesbian!'"

An understandable concern for a Catholic mother back in the early 1970s. The Weymouths did not seem overtly Catholic to outsiders, but De Segonzac, himself the son of a French mother, gives this testament: "A French mom is going to take you to church. This is very much a trait of French mothers. Doing what is *supposed to be done*. Acting the way *you're supposed to act*. Very much concerned about *what the family would think*. My mom dragged us to church every Sunday. She said that it's better to keep going to church *just in case*."

Tina's studio mate, Chris Frantz, painted differently. His work was colorful. He could get layers going. You could see through a chunk of color—a yellow area with red coming through. Chris's paintings were hard-edged. They had drips coming down. A little bit like Rothko, but not as soft. They had a rhythmical feeling to them. Which made sense, because Chris was a drummer.

He had been born Charlton Christopher Frantz at Fort Campbell, Kentucky. He had a high-ranking military pop just like Tina, a general. Chris grew up in the south. Then Pittsburgh. He drew as a kid. In fourth grade, he tried to play trumpet but his embouchure was too big, so the band leader made him switch to trombone. Chris couldn't blow that either. The band leader gave him some drumsticks and a little pad to beat.

It has been said that white people have no sense of rhythm, and this is frequently true. Imagine seeing a band play at Madison Square Garden with the massive audience clapping along to the rhythm of the music. In a white audience, thousands and thousands of people will all clap on the upbeat, sounding like dull robots. In an audience of people of color, most will clap on the downbeat. This is the beat that syncopation demands. Chris Frantz had the ears to hear this.

The boy loved beating his pads. Soon he even got to smack a real drum. After the Beatles appeared on *Ed Sullivan,* he got a drum kit. A tom-tom. A snare. The bass drum. He even got a charleston cymbal, which you could clank with a foot pedal. Like most of the kids in America post-Beatles-on-*Ed-Sullivan,* Chris went out and joined a garage band. He'd also excelled in art class. He found himself winning interscholastic arts festivals around Pittsburgh. One garage band Chris was in, the Beans, took him for an extended gig to the Electric Circus in New York City in the summer of 1970. When the Beans failed to become the next Steppenwolf, Chris returned to the world of art and enrolled at RISD.

During Chris's freshman year, many intellectuals in America declared that painting was dead. Painting was nothing more than decadent picture making for the bourgeoisie. But Chris didn't care. He loved dabbing paint on his brushes, then smearing it on canvas. He loved painting and loved the drums. Jean De Segonzac remembers seeing a performance piece at school during which Chris sat on the top of a metal cage and provided rhythmic beatings.

De Segonzac also remembers hearing that Chris Frantz dropped acid every day. That was probably just a rumor. Witnesses generally remember Chris as spacy at times. But he was also taciturn. Chris Frantz was a good listener.

Mark Kehoe was one of the crazier characters on campus. He and his girl-friend, Naomi, knew every Italian soap opera star from the dubbed shows they'd watch late at night. Kehoe himself knew Tina and found her abrasive at times. "We used to smoke pot and be miserable. Tina would be talking half in French." Chris and Tina once served Robitussin cough syrup at a dinner party.

Kehoe asked Chris to make some music for a film he'd completed. It was about a guy's girlfriend getting run over by a car. Chris said, "Oh, sure." The soundtrack was to be recorded at Tina's attic room in the garage behind her parents' house in Providence.

If Tina's French mother was worried about lesbians corrupting her daughters, Tina's father was reportedly cool and relaxed. The admiral was always happy to see ten kids in the house. He wasn't square. He wasn't bothered by boys with long hair. Tina's younger brother was always seen out in the driveway taking cars apart.

"Here I'd been living away from home for two to three years," Tina said. "But to save money, my parents didn't want me to have an apartment. So they fixed the garage. I ended up spending most of my time at other people's apartments. I did do work in the garage. And we kept Chris's drums there. He could play without bothering anybody. It was right next to the Brown tennis courts, which always had balls going back and forth."

Tina showed up at the garage to watch the recording of the sound-track. It was there she first met an intense young man face-to-face. He was a musician like Chris. He played guitar. "I had seen him around and thought, 'That's one guy to give a wide berth to,' " Tina recalls.

The kid's name was David.

byrned to a crisp

It's 1973 and David Byrne is twenty-one years old. He has a short Sigmund Freud beard and is playing "Pennies from Heaven" on a violin. A tiny feathered fake bird is attached at the end of his bow. A woman's high-heel shoe is strapped heel up on his head. The accompanist, Mark Kehoe, squeezes his accordion like the second coming of Myron Floren, Lawrence Welk's old wind box player. Kehoe's girlfriend, Naomi, stands at an easel and displays Russian words written on cardboard. The audience is enthusiastic but puzzled. Now David lowers his violin and produces a razor from his pocket. He raises it to his chin and begins shaving. If he'd been a real man—say, a real Russian—he'd have used a straight razor. Instead, he uses a Gillette safety razor.

Still the boy winces. Someone from the audience hands him a can of Narragansett beer. He splashes the brew on his face and begins hacking away in earnest. Naomi now passes out photocopies of Lenin signed, "Sincerely Yours, Walter Kaputski." Kehoe grunts over his squeeze box. Blood is running down David's neck. Lots of blood. Nobody in 1973 has seen anything like this before.

"Performance art"—what a strange cultural animal. Not a play. Not a dance. It's an art form for people who can't paint. David Byrne was a performance artist like German Fluxus artist Joseph Beuys, whose seminal 1965 piece was titled "How to Explain Painting to a Dead Hare." For the piece, Beuys wandered through a gallery in Düsseldorf with his head covered in honey and gold leaf, explaining his art work to a dead hare he cradled in his arms. Byrne's bleeding was a rougher, cruder affair.

His shaving was also distinctly masculine (discounting bearded ladies at freak shows). It was as gender specific as Shigeko Kubota painting pictures with a brush up her vagina. And a safer method of drawing blood than that of Californian Chris Burden, who several years before instructed a pal to shoot him in the arm. Most Americans would have called that homicidal insanity. Burden called it art. He even gave the performance a name: "Shoot."

Performance art was a new animal to the twentieth century. It began in Swiss coffeehouses during World War I, where the renegade art movement Dada was invented. Dadaists with names like Richard Huelsenbeck and Tristan Tzara and Hans Arp would read nonsense poems composed of words cut randomly from newspapers, while someone beat a drum with a riding crop. Men would pound on tables, then turn and pull down their trousers, mooning the audience. Had anyone thought of it, the Dadaists would have been quite comfortable shaving their beards while playing violins with small birds attached to the bow.

As with all performance art, from Dada to Fluxus, the mythology of David's shave was more important than the details of the actual occurrence. Maybe the shave didn't quite happen the way it was described. Thirty years later, David himself didn't remember whether or not he shaved with beer. A member of the audience claimed Kehoe actually played Cole Porter while David shaved. When the incident was later mentioned in *Rolling Stone*, the performance was said to have taken place at the Mercer Arts Center in Manhattan.

But reality isn't the point in performance art. Who knows what Joseph Beuys really said to the dead hare in his lap. In 1960, Yves Klein, a wild French conceptual artist known for using naked women as paint brushes, did a swan dive onto an empty Parisian street. The only witness appeared to be the photographer who recorded the dive on film. What a wondrous image that was: Klein's arms outstretched. His back arched. The empty pavement—looming. Looming. It was a perfect symbol of the arc the 1960s took. Perhaps the twenty-first century really began with Klein's leap.

But the photograph is doctored. The shot is a combination of an empty street and Klein diving onto a trampoline, surrounded by friends. The heart of performance art has always been fraud.

David Byrne was born on May 14, 1952, in Dumbarton, Scotland, the son of an electrical engineer, Thomas Byrne, and his wife, Emma. They moved to Hamilton, Ontario, around 1956 at the expense of a company that was recruiting engineers and semi-scientists from Europe. Young David chipped his front tooth chasing a girl on the boat coming over to Canada.

His sister, Celia, was born in 1957 in the New World. Tina would later say that this was the most traumatic event in David's life, that David never recovered from not being the only child.

After his sister was born, David and his parents would sit at the dinner table and eat baby food with Celia. When David was seven or eight, his father moved the family to the American town of Lansdowne, six miles from downtown Baltimore, where he had become an engineer for Westinghouse. Every so often in the middle of warm summer nights, David and his sister would sneak out of their house completely naked and sit on the neighbors' porches. Sometimes David would cover his sister with postage stamps.

The most generous description of the town that David and his sister would haunt is "lower-middle-class." Most everybody in that town during the 1960s lived near the train tracks. There were no bad or good parts of town. Everything was mostly the same—row houses or two-story industrial buildings. David didn't stay there long. "Lansdowne was on the fringes of suburbia—there were woods and farms on one side of us. We had to leave one house there because the new improved I-95 between Baltimore and D.C. was going through . . . right over our house, it turned out. I have a pretty good second sense of where the house was when I pass over it now on the highway. After moving out of there, we moved to a home on the main street of the little town of Arbutus—one movie theater (25¢), one A&P, a five-and-dime, and, of course, a gas station. We eventually had to leave there, as well. The house and yard were to be the site of a new parking lot. My friends and I got to see our house get compacted into its own cellar. . . . Amazing that it fit."

Baltimore was a place where the 1960s never happened. Screenwriter Bradley Paul gave this historical perspective on his hometown: "Baltimore is not Manhattan! I mean, from the 1820s to the 1940s, Baltimore was actually quite an urbane, happening place, supposedly a somewhat more Southern version of NYC, with a happening jazz scene. Billie Holiday was born here and cut her teeth with the likes of Duke Ellington and Eubie Blake in West Baltimore. And lots of writers—F. Scott Fitzgerald, Gertrude

Stein, and others. Herman Melville mentions the city as a center of sophistication in *Moby Dick*, but these facts are decades or even a century old. In the sixties and seventies, Baltimore was a charismatic but bleak, depressed town that had long since fallen from glory. Places like Lansdowne had an even more distant notion of culture."

This was the American environment in which David Byrne grew up. Everyone would remember this immigrant kid as a little withdrawn, a little weird. He tried to take after his old man. Byrne senior was an "electronics whiz." The man allegedly once "fixed a submarine with a coat hanger." Young Byrne thought science was a "noble calling."

David Byrne was not a brave kid. The first film he saw without his parents was *Godzilla*. At the beginning of the film, when the monster makes his debut and the ocean starts to bubble, David froze with his hand in his popcorn, suddenly convinced that whatever he was about to see was going to scare him out of his wits.

David was a nervous kid but he was also musical. He played violin and accordion. He later took up guitar. Although he was left-handed, he learned to strum with his right. "A teacher, of course, tried to get me to write with my right hand in fifth grade I think," David Byrne remembered. "I wrote like a real psycho killer for a couple of months before giving up. I didn't realize when I got my guitar that there might have been options to play it with my left hand. You know, turn it around, seek out a lefty guitar. Those ideas were well outside my field of vision. Maybe this helped me be a stronger rhythm than lead player."

As musical as Byrne was, he was denied a spot on the Arbutus Junior High choir because the choirmaster found him "off-key and withdrawn." When he was fifteen, he wrote his first song, "Bald-Headed Woman." He wore his hair in a Beatles mop top, a style that had taken a year to filter down to suburban America. He formed a garage band called the Revelation. The drummer was the singer, not Byrne. The latter saved his voice for a local coffeehouse near the University of Maryland campus where he strummed and piped out Dylan songs on a ukulele. He knew all ten verses of "Desolation Row." He also began making cut-up *musique concrète* experiments with an old reel-to-reel, influenced by the Stockhausen records he checked out from the library as well as John and Yoko's "Revolution #9" from the *White Album*.

The Vietnam War played itself out as the background of Byrne's youth. He went to one of the Nixon inaugurations. As Nixon went by, little D.B. inexplicably held up a banana. In high school, Byrne's peers considered him an oddball. He smoked a little pot. He had a girlfriend named Wendy. Her parents didn't dig David, but they didn't forbid their daughter to see him either. Young Byrne was flamboyant enough to attempt a run for student council president in his senior year. His platform was built around his desire to return the jukebox to the cafeteria.

He lost.

He performed at the senior talent show singing a corny old song on the ukulele. If there is an instrument that designates Byrne, this is the one. From a young buck to middle age, Byrne would retain a love of this toylike mini-guitar. "I've always liked the idea of a portable music-making device," Byrne said. "A take-anywhere, always-ready instrument. The ukulele has unfortunate associations—Tiny Tim—but if you listen to *Smiley Smile* and some of the other cool nutty psychedelic Beach Boys tracks, their use of the ukulele is subtle and sweet. It doesn't have to be campy."

In May 1970, David bought the new Beatles album, *Let It Be*. The depth of Beatles mythology is so vast that minor aspects are overlooked. We knew all about their major business. How John said the Beatles were bigger than Jesus. How George found the Maharishi. How John found Yoko. But it's often forgotten that many Americans assumed that 100 percent of every song written by Lennon/McCartney was actually written by *both* John Lennon and Paul McCartney, when it was just a convention they used both for songs they actually collaborated on ("A Day in the Life") and the numerous ones they wrote individually ("Hey Jude," Paul; "Come Together," John; etc.). Publicity photographs several years before, during the time of *Sgt. Pepper*, showed the Beatles playing brass instruments. Many American suburbanites, both children and their parents, assumed that these photographs were for real, that the Beatles were so gifted they actually played all the instruments that were recorded on their psychedelic albums. We hadn't yet heard of studio musicians. With thirty years' perspective, David Byrne would say, "The Beatles were the first group where it was assumed that the band members were all more or less equal. Wrote and performed their own songs. Had a certain amount of self-determination. It became a very important item— the band as a whole stood for something. Everybody more or less said the same thing—as if the group was on a mission."

Back in 1970, these things seemed eternal: Tang. The USSR. The Beatles. On April 10, a Friday, the British papers announced, "Paul has quit the Beatles." Today bands break up as often as Slavic countries, but in 1970 the Beatles' split was unthinkable. From that moment on, rock 'n' roll followed this drama:

Act 1 *Form a band.*
Act 2 *Take over the world.*
Act 3 *Break up.*

The possibility of a fourth and final act will haunt this present story—the ghost of a chance that the group would get back together.

When eighteen-year-old Byrne graduated from high school, he was eligible for the draft—Uncle Sam didn't care that he was not a citizen. But David Byrne didn't go to Vietnam. Instead, he donned the white uniform of a Good Humor man and pedaled a little cart around the neighborhood selling ice cream sandwiches to the kids.

Byrne claims he was accepted at both MIT and RISD.

Science. Art.

Dad's direction pointed to MIT. Byrne's heart pointed differently. In later years, Byrne quipped that he chose RISD because "the graffiti looked the best."

Gus Van Sant, director of the first "grunge" cinema classic, *My Own Private Idaho*, met Byrne at RISD. In *My Own Private Idaho*, the late River Phoenix plays a hustler in Portland, Oregon. Van Sant saw similarities between Portland and Providence. "They were very big in the twenties and thirties. Somewhere in the forties, they fell off. In Providence it was because of the textile industry. The population was bigger in the twenties than it is today. In our society that rarely happens because populations increase not decrease. S. J. Perelman came from there. Spalding Gray. H. P. Lovecraft, too. But I always think of it as a city that imploded. When we were there in the early 1970s, it was probably the bleakest time."

"I knew Providence was weird," David remembered. "It didn't feel like a real town. It seemed totally fragmented as a city. The worlds of the university and the city were totally separate. A lot of American towns are like that. The center is just completely vacated. They try blaming it on the car and suburbia, but they have cars in Europe and it doesn't seem to happen."

When David lived there, the Providence River flowed underground like the River Styx. "It was channeled through pipes and tunnels. So you never saw it. There were a couple of spots where you could go and there would be a space between some of the road and you could look down and go, 'Oh, look. It's a river. There it is.' Where did it come from? There was no evidence of it anywhere."

David's first dorm mate at RISD covered his side of the room with big pictures of Charlie Manson and the devil. "They were beautiful drawings actually," David Byrne remembered. "He was tripping a lot of the time he was there, but eventually had to drop out halfway through the year when his junk habit got too serious."

Sometimes you heard rock music blasting out of David's room, but just as often you'd hear the bell and gongs of Balinese gamelan music. This would prove to be a lifelong love. Called "World Music" today, it was more accurate in David's era to call it "Library Music." His interest in offbeat music was first sparked by all those peculiar records he used to check out of the library. He wasn't interested in global culture. He was just looking for weird sounds.

At RISD, David also studied Bauhaus theory and conceptual art. Some say he let his hair grow long. Other say he choose to cut it unfashionably short like John Lennon. He might also have grown a scruffy beard.

David soon abandoned painting for statistics. He wanted to develop a Neilsen rating system for visual arts. He also made Xerox art. Took Polaroids. He gave readings of lines from TV quiz shows. "Come on down!" he would shout, echoing Johnny Olson's familiar cry from *The Price Is Right*.

David dropped out of RISD a year later because, as he claimed, "the students were all rich kids." During the next few years, David would tell anyone who'd listen about his "working-class" background. He probably embellished a bit. Although he came from a lower-middle-class background, his pop was never a union man. Old man Byrne never worked in a factory, drove a truck, or pumped gas. His father and mother were more antisuburban than working-class. David would later admit that he was copping a typical 1960s attitude: *The poor are better than anyone else.*

• • •

23

David Byrne left Providence to join ex–high school girlfriend Wendy on a commune in Kentucky called the Flying Frog Farm. Communes have a long tradition in America, from the Amana colonies—a utopian religious community that flourished twenty miles northwest of Iowa City in the late nineteenth century—to Woodstock host Wavy Gravy's Hog Farm Commune out in Tujunga, California. By the early 1970s, there were perhaps a thousand such American-style kibbutzes across the country. David recollected that this particular commune had no apparent philosophy "except to get away from 'society' and smoke as much dope as you wanted." One could also aspire to "be free and read cool stuff." David was not a big doper and spent his days reading a vast amount of *Fantastic Four* comics (someone had a huge collection). He also played saxophone "à la Beefheart . . . noisy amelodic animal-like sounds." He was expected to do a few farm chores. Milking the cows was fun. He spent a few hard days lifting hay bales onto wagons. Other days he cleaned and sorted tobacco, a task that got him high after a couple of hours. "The nicotine must seep in through the skin," David hypothesized, finding it "a rather strange euphoric dizzy feeling to associate with work." He also had to cook now and then—"God, I can't imagine anything worse than these poor kids having to eat my cooking!"

A quickie paperback on Talking Heads published in the 1980s states that David now met commune leader Jim Brown's brother David. This second David—David Brown—was a science student. They both dug *The Fantastic Four*. When David Brown returned to Baltimore to continue his research with monkeys, David Byrne followed and crashed with him and tended to the monkeys. The two species took to each other. All the monkeys loved David.

David Byrne claims this never happened. But it is such a winsome detail—Byrne among the primates, especially in light of the monkeyshines contained on the last studio Talking Heads album, *Naked*—that it deserves mention even if it's legend.

During the summer of 1971, men were still being sent to the moon. The Twenty-sixth Amendment was ratified, which would have allowed David, had he been an American citizen, the right to vote. At summer's end, Defense Secretary Melvin Laird announced that for the most part the Vietnam War was over. David started school again. A new art school, the

Maryland Institute, located in Baltimore, the quiet town where Edgar Allan Poe died of drink or possibly rabies.

Mark Kehoe was not yet an influence in young David Byrne's life. He was just a student at the Maryland Institute. David had met Kehoe once or twice at RISD, and he wrote him a letter saying, "I heard you had a huge space. Could I come live with you?"

Kehoe wrote back, "Sure." Kehoe was nineteen. Born in Pittsburgh, raised in Metuchen, New Jersey. His father was an office worker for RCA's appliance division in Bayonne. The boy was a hippie who had applied to be a conscientious objector. He lucked out and drew a very high lottery number.

In those days Kehoe had such a compelling personality that he was the one other kids would phone after their suicide attempts failed. He spent a lot of time in hospital emergency rooms while someone had their stomach pumped.

The lad had rented a floor of a house north of North Avenue. It was a bad neighborhood, but a big space. When David showed up that fall, Kehoe discovered that the owner of the house had rented out all the rooms on his floor, so David and Kehoe were stuck in a tiny L-shaped maid's room. David didn't have a bed. He built one out of a door, some cinder blocks, and a bedroll.

Out back was an alley where packs of wild dogs lived. The newspapers were always saying the dogs had eaten small black children. David and Kehoe fell into the habit of daring each other—"Smoke that cigar we just found on the street."

"Walk on that ledge!"

"Pet that dog!"

The house was filled with other art students and everything was communal. A group refrigerator. Voting every week on new rules. Kehoe discovered that many residents thought David was retarded. When parents visited they shook their heads behind David's back. *There's something really wrong with that kid.* David was jerky and ungainly. He would get very quiet and then burst out laughing.

Kehoe saw the other side of David. He was very smart and particular and very single-minded. David knew what he wanted to do. He wrote free-form poems about the glory of fame. He could seem edgy because he kept to himself, didn't tell other people what he was doing. David could make the whole house feel uncomfortable. But it was a house full of artists, and everybody knows artists are very insecure people.

Neither David nor Kehoe really gave a hoot about the Maryland Institute. They started spending most of the week hitchhiking to and fro to Providence, crashing there with Kehoe's girlfriend, Naomi. David did stick around Maryland Institute long enough to take a course on realism, the school's specialty. Kehoe remembered David coming home with a painting of a playing card. Kehoe thought it was "pretty good." David also experimented with sculpture. One Saturday morning, he baked some bread but forgot to watch the oven. Seven hours later, the kitchen was filled with smoke, and the bread was baked into a dense nugget the size of a baseball. David brought the burnt object to an art show at the institute and set it among various small sculptures, along with a white card that said, BREAD, DAVID BYRNE. When the show closed a week later, the curators returned David's bread in a small box filled with packing paper.

Although the two didn't make much art, they still talked about it constantly. Kehoe loved smoking dope with David because David could really appreciate it. David revealed to Kehoe that he had the soul of an old California wino crossed with a moonshiner. He taught Kehoe how to brew "balloon juice": Place Welch's frozen grape juice in a jug; add yeast and water; seal it with a balloon; when the balloon goes up and down and up a second time, the balloon juice was done. Sweeten with sugar. Drink—but be careful, it ends up being more potent than wine.

David always had a guitar. He'd strum good jerky versions of Beatles songs as well as Smokey Robinson and the Miracles. Kehoe had been forced to play accordion by his mom as a kid. One night David asked, "Why don't you get it?" Kehoe did. David got out a violin. They decided to learn corny songs like "Pennies from Heaven" and "Dancing on the Ceiling" from Kehoe's fake book. They formed a duet called Bizadi and played "Pennies from Heaven" on the commons and for people standing in movie lines. They would play in the dark, with candles attached to the bow of David's violin.

The American pursuit of corny taste has been examined by eggheads, although not extensively. Clement Greenberg was the first highbrow to look at kitsch. In 1938 he wrote, "Kitsch was the epitome of all that is spurious in the life of our time." Tap dancing was kitsch. Hollywood was kitsch. And so was Norman Rockwell. The point of his essay was that kitsch was the only culture available in fascist countries like Hitler's Germany and Stalin's Mother Russia. How was Greenberg to know that at various moments after we won World War II, the avant-garde would embrace kitsch with a vengeance?

In 1964 one of the post-Eisenhower era's most prominent cultural critics, Susan Sontag, would exalt kitsch, calling it "camp." "Camp asserts that good taste is not simply good taste," she wrote in her seminal essay "Notes on Camp"—a collection of fifty-eight numbered ruminations on the subject. Number 54 states, "There exists, indeed, a good taste of bad taste."

David Byrne and Mark Kehoe were glorious examples of "a good taste of bad taste," fiddling and squeezing out "Pennies from Heaven" on the streets of Baltimore. Kehoe got the idea they should play these songs on the street wearing papier-mâché dog heads. "David's looked like Anubis." Kehoe remembers his mom shooting eight-millimeter footage of the two boys wearing dog heads and playing "Pennies from Heaven" in his parents' living room up in New Jersey. They also played a high school gig in Baltimore and brought David's sister along. The black kids in the audience witnessed Bizadi's camp in dead silence. A James Brown cover band followed. The moment the guitars started to play, knives were pulled and metal chairs started flying.

During this time David got a new girlfriend, a chick a little older than him named Joan Lobell—one of those perpetual students with a couple of degrees. Joan was of medium height, with creamy skin and red-blondish hair. She'd been to Europe. She seemed sophisticated.

And she had a car.

Joan lived in an old mansion in downtown Baltimore. David soon left the room above the Alley of the Dogs and moved in with her. Kehoe moved in as well, taking a vacant room above Joan and David. Gypsies lived in the basement. One night another tenant—a hippie—deliberately burned his worldly possessions in the fireplace. Kehoe and Joan and David awoke to a house filled with smoke, firemen with big rubber coats pounding through their bedroom. Later the gypsies surfaced and began rummaging wildly through everyone's apartment.

One of the things the three loved to do was wander through Bolton

Hill at dark. This was the neighborhood surrounding the school. Wild dog packs did not swarm through Bolton. There were no gypsies. A slum belt extended from Boston to Washington, D.C., but Bolton Hill had remained intact and classy. Ten years later, you'd call the residents of Bolton Hill yuppies.

David and Joan and Kehoe liked to walk across the darkened lawns, dodging sprinklers and watching people inside their homes before they'd seal up the windows for the night.

"Shhh, don't laugh!" Joan would scold. "This is normal life."

Joan could afford to admonish the boys. She was familiar with the Bolton Hill lifestyle. She had money in her background—her father was president of the Cavalier Shoe Polish Co. He considered himself the "Shoe Polish King."

Kehoe and David could only compare what they observed in Bolton Hill with the circus that was their own experience. They'd watch a mother unloading sacks of groceries and know that those bottles of Welch's weren't for balloon juice.

And everyone's kitchen was so clean. One night back in the old place, Kehoe went down to the communal kitchen and the walls were covered with undulating bugs. He took that as a sign. Soon after, he went back to his parents' house in New Jersey and cut his hair. He left his locks in a paper bag on the kitchen table. When he woke up in the morning, his parents had placed the bag of hair on the kitchen floor and were dancing around it.

You didn't see anyone's parents dancing around bags of hair in Bolton Hill. You didn't see the general chaos of David's old home either. Kehoe had gone home with David to his folks' house in Columbia. Very strange. They had two televisions, but little other furniture. In the morning there would be all these televisions and radios blaring. David's mother yelling, "Get up. Get up." Mr. and Mrs. Byrne seemed cool enough, but their accents were so thick the boy couldn't understand a thing they said, except David's pop's cry of "Emmah, brrringh me a cop-ah!"

Kehoe and David split up in the fall of 1972. Kehoe went to live with Naomi in Providence. David wrote lots of letters to Kehoe. David was a mail freak. When he was a kid he had wanted to be a mailman so he could read everyone's postcards as he made his delivery rounds.

• • •

Around Thanksgiving, Kehoe got a letter from David posted from California. David and Joan had gone there to meet up with a kid named Michael who was building a pinecone-shaped dome on a parcel of land north of San Francisco. By December, when Kehoe hadn't heard any more, he thumbed out west himself. There are no official records of young hitchhikers in the 1970s, only personal ones. Psycho killers might inhabit the hills of L.A. and Death Valley, but back then the rest of the country truly seemed like an extension of the Woodstock Nation. Hitchhiking was relatively safe—you were picked up by either Kerouacian working-class folk, older hippies, or hippies who'd gone straight. A boy didn't need a car or a ticket or even money to travel the breadth of America.

Kehoe met up with David at someone's parents' house in Sausalito. Joan had become disgusted with the scene and already returned to Baltimore. The house turned out to be a Frank Lloyd Wright building. None of the rooms were square—they were all rhomboid. The mother was all raged up because these kids were crashing in the rhomboid rooms. The family's black maid was named America.

Soon after Kehoe arrived, the mother kicked everyone out of the rhomboid house, but David had a car. He had bought it in New Mexico. It was a two-tone black 1956 DeSoto with a bullet hole by the inspection sticker. David and Kehoe decided to live in the DeSoto and play "Pennies from Heaven" on the streets of San Francisco for spare change. Some days they would make enough silver to get food. Other times the two would only come up with a buck-fifty. This was needed for gas. Those nights the two were forced to survive on the curried popcorn the Hare Krishna gave out. By the early 1970s, the Summer of Love was long dead and buried. Kehoe remembers Haight-Ashbury as a terrifying slum, its streets filled with crazy burned-out speed freaks.

The streets were almost as terrifying as David's driving. "His mind is always in another world," Kehoe said. "You'd have to sit and really watch."

The two would spend the night in gas station parking lots or places with views. Kehoe would flip for which one would get to stretch out in back and who was stuck up front with the steering wheel.

Imagine creeping up to the car and viewing the sleeping boy in the front seat. How far from Scotland David Byrne was. This was the wrong ocean. Californians were the wrong people. Instead of frugal, they were indulgent. Instead of honest whiskey, they drank wine. Instead of Macbeth, they had Charlie Manson.

The next day, David wised up. He sold his car for $150, and he and Kehoe hitched back east. They leapfrogged rides for three days before one ride reached the outskirts of Baltimore on Christmas Eve. David commanded the driver to pull over. "I have to get out here," he said.

And he did. He hopped out of the car and disappeared in the snow without so much as a wave good-bye to Kehoe.

But that was David. And after Kehoe rode farther north to his parents' house in New Jersey, he crashed for a monstrous eighteen hours. When he woke up, the television was on. Hitchock's *Vertigo* was being broadcast. There on the screen was the San Francisco that Kehoe had just left, Jimmy Stewart driving a ghost version of David Byrne's 1956 DeSoto.

During the winter of 1973, David returned to Joan Lobell. The two began hanging out with the Fells Point underground film crowd who gathered around John Waters, a twenty-seven-year-old Baltimorian who cultivated a Gomez Adams look.

Number 51 of Sontag's essay "Notes on Camp" acknowledges gay culture's strong identification with camp. "Not all homosexuals [*gay* wasn't in the popular lexicon in 1964] have camp taste. But homosexuals, by and large, constitute the vanguard—and the most articulate audience—of camp." Sontag postulates this, but her answer to *why* is thin: "Camp is a solvent of morality. It neutralizes moral indignation, sponsors playfulness." Actually, gay camp serves as a method to both embrace and dismiss the "normal" American culture that exiled gays to begin with. Sontag mentions that these citizens value camp items such as Tiffany lamps, *Swan Lake*, and the drawings of Aubrey Beardsley. Sontag never envisioned the taste of John Waters, a gay man who did not see swish art in art nouveau, let alone any goddamn Tiffany lamps. Instead he pursued his own vision, which included perhaps the single most grotesque act of the twentieth century—him filming a fat transvestite named Divine scooping up dog poop and eating it.

This was art to Waters. To hell with Susan Sontag's stereotypes. Waters became a cultural saint to both culturally exiled Americans as well as citizens who never outgrew the devilish joy of playing in their doo-doo.

Waters will admit to knowing the contemporary David Byrne, but doesn't remember him from the old days. Baltimore expert Bradley Paul explained Waters: "Everyone claims to have a John Waters story. Even in his early career, he was revered in Baltimore. Most of these tales are probably invented or embellished. I think one reason he's so popular, besides being a hometown success story, is that he speaks to the many intelligent Baltimorians who have realized that they live in a weird, insulated, pervasively idiosyncratic city."

John Waters may not remember David Byrne from other hangers-ons, but David and Joan became closer friends with Edith the Egg Lady, the obese woman Waters had filmed sitting in a crib in her underwear worshiping eggs in 1972's *Pink Flamingos*.

David and Joan would drive Edith around in Joan's car. When the Elgin Movie Theater up in Manhattan began showing the film, David phoned Kehoe (who was working again at the Revlon factory in Jersey) and told him, "Joan and I are taking Edith to the Elgin—we're going to stop by."

Kehoe's mother had never seen *Pink Flamingos*, but she assumed Edith was a movie star. Mrs. Kehoe prepared a platter of salami spread out like a deck of cards. Her son reported that when Joan and David appeared with Edith, complete with bad teeth and three hundred pounds' worth of girth, "My parents took one look and ran upstairs and slammed the bedroom door."

Right after this visit, Kehoe returned to Providence. David followed. Tina Weymouth said that David was clearly Kehoe's *sidekick:* "Mark would have these ideas and say, 'David, why don't you do this.' And David would do it. And sometimes David would misunderstand, and it would be cute. When David misunderstood, he misunderstood in a big way."

David moved with Kehoe and Naomi into a five-room apartment on Brown Street, in the Italian section of Providence. It was the top floor of a big house, with huge ungainly rooms and sloping ceilings. The rent was forty bucks a month. With twenty-five years of perspective Tina remarked: "Kehoe and Naomi were the Chris and Tina before Chris and Tina."

Naomi was physically quite different from Tina. She was about five-foot-four. She had big eyes, big lips, looked a lot like Laura Nyro. Kehoe described Naomi as an "earthy outspoken deeply emotional person." Her mother had been a painter and an opera singer. Before Kehoe had gone to

31

work for Revlon, Naomi had been a chubby Jewish hippie girl. When Kehoe returned to Providence, she met him at the bus station slimmed down and wearing an animal-print dress and thrift shop high heels, with a blond streak in her hair and heavy makeup. She even had a fake beauty mark.

Naomi was still actually enrolled at RISD. She showed Kehoe her new work—portraits of screaming women and depictions of Jackie Onassis in bondage. The first thing Kehoe decided to do was make a super-8 movie with Naomi titled *The Private Secrets of Liz Taylor*. The two proceeded to joyfully embrace kitsch glamour together. Naomi wore rhinestone sunglasses. They both wore black nail polish. Their clothing got wilder and wilder. A store in downtown Providence sold platform shoes really cheap. Kehoe himself had eight pairs. They were overjoyed at the revival of leopard-skin fabric. They wore matching leopard-skin coats. Kehoe even wore a leopard-skin pillbox hat. After David's arrival, the three became photo hounds. There was a photobooth sitting in a corner at the all-night train station in Providence. They'd go down there at three in the morning with wigs and hats and a roll of quarters. The three also took millions of Polaroids. Black and white. The peel-off kind.

"Somewhere I did an art photo of David Byrne without his shirt," Kehoe remembered. "I drew a diagram of male TV stars of the early 1970s, like the guy from *Adam-12*, on David's chest."

The three formed a mini–Jayne Mansfield cult. They listened to her rock 'n' roll album as well as her record reciting Shakespeare. Jayne Mansfield definitely fit Susan Sontag's definition of camp like a glove. In note number 9, Sontag claims the camp relish for androgyny is balanced by a contradictory enjoyment of "exaggerated sexual characteristics." However, in light of the practitioners of Queer Aesthetics' late-breaking attempts to claim camp as a solely gay concern, there is an alternate term to consider, *cheese*. As in the word *cheesy*. Professors Kevin Dettmar and William Richey wrote, "Cheese is a highly rhetorical embrace of those things that many would consider to be in bad taste." Thus David, Kehoe, and Naomi were into cheese as much as camp.

The big rock 'n' roll band at RISD was called the Motels—although they can only be called that for convenience. The band changed its name from year to year: Electric Drive Way. Iron Grandmother. Each concert was an elaborate singular performance. They rehearsed for months. They were accompanied by their own troupe of costumed dancers called the Tampoons.

Gus Van Sant remembered the Motels as RISD's version of Frank Zappa and the Mothers of Invention. The first time Mark Kehoe saw the band, the musicians were surrounded by a ring of lava lamps and were playing a song called "She's an Albino."

"It all looked too good not to be a part of," Kehoe said. He and Naomi ran up on stage and started dancing alongside the Tampoons. Soon he and David were booked as Bizadi between sets. It was at a Motels concert that David Byrne played violin and shaved while Naomi wore a blue cocktail dress. Mary Clarke, one of the Tampoons, remembered, "Yes, yes, yes. There was lots of blood. All running down David's face. I remember being worried that this person was hurting himself."

down normal

David had met Chris Frantz two years back during David's freshman year. After his violin shave in the fall of '73, the two got reacquainted when they began working on a soundtrack for the Kehoe film about a girlfriend getting run over by a car.

Chris was attracted to David's screwy musical vision and suggested they form a band. Not a performance group like the Motels, but a garage-style rock 'n' roll band. David went along with this. Chris scouted up the other musicians, even came up with the group's obvious art school name, the Artistics.

Along with Chris on drums and David on rhythm guitar and vocals, there was a kid named Hank Stahler on bass. Tim Beal honked sax. Another RISD student named David Anderson, who knew Chris from summer trips to Kentucky, played lead.

Little is known about Hank. Tim Beal was a film student. According to De Segonzac, "Beal's flicks were always about naked people." He had a party trick. He'd jump up and suddenly leap out of his third-story window as if he thought he was Yves Klein. Shocked witnesses inside the apartment would scream and dash to the window, only to see Beal laughing on the fire escape one floor down.

David Anderson wasn't as extravagant. He was a strangely soft-spoken painter from some backwater in Tennessee.

David Byrne was the unofficial band leader. Everyone would just jam and see what came out. David might then make suggestions. The band practiced for two hours a day, real loud. When they finally got gigs, they played real loud at the Pub, the RISD student bar. And Sam's in downtown Providence. And a few parties.

Artistics lore says the band all wore black. David Byrne played a leopard-skin guitar. The band did mainly covers. Al Green's "Love and Happiness." Smokey Robinson's "Tears of a Clown." The 1910 Fruitgum Company's "1-2-3 Red Light," a song whose lyrics were a repetition of "One, two, three red light . . ." It was the kind of lyric that David could appreciate, because he was very interested in a peculiar philosophy called cybernetics.

An egghead named Norbert Wiener coined that word in his 1947 book, *Cybernetics, or Control and Communication in the Animal and the Machine*. Cybernetics is a mind game that believes that all human structures can be more or less delineated as a series of mathematical functions. When this book was translated into French in 1948, Parisian newspapers used the term *cerveaux mécaniques*—"mechanical brains"—to describe cybernetics. This resulted in the average Frenchman concluding that Wiener was writing about robots (HAL hadn't been imagined yet). This misconception filtered back to America, where it morphed into bionic—the turning of people into mechanical men.

David Byrne didn't make the French mistake. He was familiar with Wiener's book. "I thought cybernetics made beautiful and intelligent insight about how the mind and perception and social organizations work," he said.

The linguistic branch of cybernetics was interested in the statistical possibilities of meaningful sentences being constructed at random, compared to pure gibberish. Although Norbert Wiener would never admit this, he was a brother to the Dadaists who created poems of words cut randomly from the *Zurich Times*. Many of the songs David was writing seemed cybernetic—such as "Warning Sign," a song that resembles a random rewriting of Creedence Clearwater Revival's "Bad Moon Rising." In David's song, he alerts us that a warning sign is coming, although he doesn't tell us what form this sign will take. Neither does he inform us what exactly this sign will warn us about. Instead, he mentions his hair. He moves it around a lot. He likes its design. Perhaps his hair is in fact the warning sign. David later said this was the most decadent song he had ever written. He imagined a Fellini-esque swarm of naked people all overdosing on drugs. Indeed, in the song the singer looks at his girl and she has glassy eyes and her mouth is gaping.

The song's most memorable lyrics would prove to be David's declaration, "I've got money now/I've got money now." Perhaps the warning sign will occur when someone takes his money away? A week after the Artistics' first gig, David was in despair because he *didn't* have money now. Gus Van Sant sat over lunch with the sad sack in a restaurant where David was a dishwasher. The two were "pretty good friends" according to Van Sant, but this was the first time David had ever opened up to him, muttering dramatically, "Something's got to happen. Something's got to break. Or I'm just going to kill myself."

David was in despair because he wasn't making any money from the Artistics. Van Sant was silent for a moment. He felt sorry for the guy. Van Sant was under the impression that David Byrne wasn't an actual RISD student because his parents couldn't afford tuition. Van Sant tried to say something hopeful. "Maybe the pain of not getting paid will add to your art."

David looked up, "No, no, no—that's sick! That's not how it works!" He was fervent that the myth of suffering for art was a cultural lie. Van Sant didn't defend his position. "I felt bad for Byrne," Van Sant recalled. "While he was complaining about his band, I was being consoling, but at the same time I was thinking, 'His singing is way off. His guitar playing is weird. If I ever met anyone on the planet who isn't going to make it, it is this guy.' "

After David spilled his guts to Van Sant, he realized how tired he was of washing dishes. He saw that he needed "that degree." David tried to get back into RISD. He showed admissions his conceptual art questionnaire projects—his "Do you believe in UFOs?" polls (Choose one: Definitely False/Probably False/Probably True/Definitely True), his collection of "objective" accounts of car accidents. The admissions department was outwardly sympathetic, but basically said, "We don't teach this kind of stuff. You should move to New York and make a go of it."

New York was definitely Oz. David wasn't ready for the tornado to take him there, so he did the next best thing. He began working at New York Systems, a Smith Hill hot dog joint modeled on forties/fifties New York nostalgia. The climax of the New York Systems eating experience involved the wiener boy delivering hot dogs balanced on his bare arms to your table. David was stuck as a grillman. His arms were too hairy to deliver hot dogs.

During the winter of 1974, David didn't have time for Bizadi, but he invited Kehoe and Naomi to perform in between sets for the Artistics at an art show he was organizing at RISD's Woods-Gerry Gallery. The show would be full of nude Polaroid collages as well as Naomi's portrait of Jackie O. in bondage. Cocktails would be served. Kehoe and Naomi would show up wearing gorilla suits and sing "My Baby Must Be a Magician." But the school canceled the show. Not because Jackie was in bondage, but because David wasn't a student.

Just as things were going to hell at RISD, things were starting to go to hell all over. There was a terrible gasoline shortage. Kehoe remembers driving with David to Boston to return the gorilla suits, then getting stranded there because Beantown had no gas. The two spent the day sitting in gas lines. Every time they finally got up to the pumps, the gas jockey would shake his head. "Sorry. No more."

David kept writing songs. A lot of them. In the beginning of 1974, he wrote what would prove to be his signature song, "Psycho Killer," a song that could serve as an underground national anthem for the America that has always produced the world's most compelling amateur killers. Charles Manson. Richard Speck. Leatherface.

David Byrne's voicing of America's passion for homicide was inspired by a twenty-four-year-old girl named Barbara Conway, one of the Tampoons dancers. Fellow Tampoon Mary Clarke called Conway a cross between Nancy Sinatra and Tina Turner. Barbara took the stage name Simone Cuc. She had a facile tongue when it came to language, inventing dozens of pet terms.

"Down normal," she would say. "In the Twinkie zone."

She called cool people and situations "psycho killer." For example, "Rosemary Woods is real psycho killer." Or she'd shorten the two words to PK, as in "Rose is real pee-kay." In a bit of American irony worthy of any Dadaist performance art, Barbara Conway would herself be shot by a psycho killer—a female stalker—in 1985.

Around Thanksgiving '73, David heard Barbara say "psycho killer" for the zillionth time and finally thought, "There's a song here." He tried to write a tune that could have fit on Alice Cooper's *Billion Dollar Babies,* which was all over the radio. David also tried to duplicate the dark sophistication of Randy Newman, maybe even the more populist wit of the Kinks' Ray Davies.

As David begins singing, his killer addresses the listener directly, revealing that he is in denial ("I can't seem to face up to the facts"), that he's wired, an insomniac. In case we miss the point, the killer announces, "Don't touch me I'm a real live wire." Then the psycho killer begins speaking French, *"Psycho killer, qu'est-ce que c'est?"*

Paul McCartney speaks French in "Michelle" to give the song a fake sophistication. One version of history says David's psycho speaks in French because the maniac imagines himself as very refined. Another because of his split personality. A third story says David originally wanted the guy to speak Greek, but was convinced that French was a more suitable language for someone who was disturbed.

Chris told David, "Hey, Tina speaks French. She'll help with the lyrics."

Tina remembers visiting David at his apartment to work on the song. His room was the proverbial pigsty, clothes strewn everywhere—including a corset and a pair of white shiny Nancy Sinatra vinyl boots.

"Whose are those?" Tina asked.

David answered, "Mine."

"Oh, really," Tina said. "Prove it to me. Okay?"

"Okay," David said. "Don't look."

The boy went behind a wall. He took off his clothes and put on the corset and boots.

"You never knew what to expect with David," Tina said later.

Tina never seriously questioned David's sexuality. The corset was Kehoe's kitsch influence. She had once seen David at a party with peroxide hair, wearing a red chiffon dress with high heels. Tina remarked, "To me, back then, David was kind of fun."

Tina contributed more than French to the song. Both she and Chris were Otis Redding freaks. Redding was a Stax recording artist best known for his '68 hit, "(Sittin' on) The Dock of the Bay." Two years before he released a single called "Fa-Fa-Fa-Fa-Fa (Sad Song)." It's a relaxed song. Otis tells us that he keeps singing sad songs. They're all he knows. But this particular sad song is a sweet song as well. Anyone can sing it. *Fa-Fa-Fa-Fa-Fa.*

The story goes that after Chris and Tina played it for David, he incorporated a string of *fa*s in his psycho killer song. He sang that short syllable *fa*—a simple exhalation of breath, with upper teeth pressed against lower lip, ten times:

fa fa fa fa fa fa fa fa fa fa

Otis Redding may or may not have been an influence, but there is a problem of pronunciation. The real influence of the *fa*s in "Psycho Killer" probably came from the Kinks' song "David Watts," which begins with Ray Davies singing:

fa fa fa fa fa fa fa fa

David would pronounce his *fa* the same as Davies.

This slight one-symbol word has a maddening mystery connected to it. When the song was released in 1977, the printed lyrics appeared with only six *fa*s. But on the actual record, as well as in concert, Byrne sang ten *fa*s. Bootlegs reveal that David Byrne experimented constantly with the rhythm of his *fa*s in the early days. A few times he sang seven *fa*s. Other times he did a kind of speeded-up string of them, sputtering his *fa*s like Porky Pig's famous line, "Tha-tha-tha-that's all folks." But he never sang six *fa*s. The mystery may never be explained.

David first sang "Psycho Killer" at RISD's St. Valentine's Day Masquerade Ball in 1974. *I've got money now.* The band was paid $200.

He would end up playing this song at almost every concert he did from then on. The song became David's personal hurl toward glory. It is less a Warren Zevonish "Werewolves of London" novelty number and more a Macbethian reflection on deranged violence. Splatter-film fans should note that the narrator doesn't actually mention shooting or choking or going chop chop chop to anyone. The fellow's only misanthropic remark is "I hate people when they're not polite."

John Douglas, the FBI agent who invented the art of profiling serial killers as well as being the man Thomas (*Silence of the Lambs*) Harris based his fictional profiler on, was both impressed and made nervous by David's take on psychosis, from the killer speaking in French to his aversion to rudeness. "Is that what Byrne really thinks?" Douglas said. "He could be walking the line. How is Byrne normally? Could he find himself in the position where he could whack somebody?"

Of course it's ridiculous for Douglas to make such assumptions based on a few song lyrics, but the story of Talking Heads is similar to any American history—be it artistic, political, or financial. Everything in the land is occasionally touched by blood. Murder is the American way.

find yourself
a city to live in

By spring 1974 the Artistics had acquired a new nickname—the Autistics. Rumor had it that David Anderson was autistic. At least Tina Weymouth assumed he was. But then, she assumed David Byrne was autistic, too. Tina says, "Watch out for the autism. It might be something much more complex. Psychics say he just has a firewall around him. He's only going to show you what he wants. He's not someone you can have a perception about."

David Byrne only remembered that David Anderson was "pretty mentally disconnected . . . as was I to a lesser degree."

Mark Kehoe has a conclusive word on the subject of autism. Neither of the Davids were autistic. David Anderson was "an interesting character." Strange, soft-spoken, almost to the point of being a nerd. One night he went out and walked up Angel Street and across Thayer Street and Waterman Street completely naked.

"What do you think you're doing?" a police officer shouted.

Anderson stood there naked and said, "I'm a RISD student."

The cop rolled his eyes. "Then you better get back to your dorm."

Tim Beal did something only slightly less outrageous. He got real stoned one night and did his leap-out-the-window trick. Except he missed the fire escape. He was suspended in the air like Yves Klein, then fell three stories to the pavement and broke both his arms. The saxophonist was laid up in a hospital for three or four months.

But it wasn't just the Autistics/Artistics who were strange. Mark Kehoe would occasionally stand on a street corner screaming at traffic lights. He would stand at the door of the cafeteria and try on everyone's clothes as they went in for lunch. He would put on people's hats and dance. Gus Van Sant thought Kehoe was "like an insane person you would see on the street."

Kehoe eventually calmed down. Whenever Van Sant asked him about his behavior, Kehoe would say, "I was going through an experiment."

Then there was the twenty-seven-year-old RISD video artist Jamie Dalglish. He was older than the other students. He was a Vietnam vet. Rumor had it that Dalglish went nuts inside a submarine. Jean De Segonzac found Dalglish pretty flipped. "Jamie would do things like stand on his head and everything would fall out of his pockets."

Jamie Dalglish made videos. One of his videos consisted of a continuous shot of him walking back and forth on a beach until his feet dug a trench in the sand.

Dalglish went to RISD on the Vocational Rehabilitation Act of the Veterans Administration. "I served in the navy from 1967 to '69," Dalglish explained. "I was on a diesel submarine. We'd listen to Janis Joplin on the submarine. When you're in a submarine fifty-five days underwater, a lot of shit happens. And you're suppose to take it all. Our mission at the time was secret. If we were blown up or taken prisoner, the U.S. wouldn't have acknowledged us. We had to go into Chinese waters. We had to study the movements of the Khmer Rouge. I didn't want to get behind a gun and shoot people. We were headed back to Japan. We hit a typhoon. The engine room was really messed up. When we got back to the port, I was ordered to clean up the engine room. I didn't want to go down and clean. 'They' were trying to frame me. So I went and threw a fit. The captain of the boat took me to the naval hospital in Japan. I spent my time next to another guy on a cot who claimed he had seventy-seven ears in a seabag. He kept reassigning to Vietnam so he could shoot people. He claimed you got a prize if you cut an ear off. I had a collection of submarine letters that my mother gave to Dennis Hopper for Christmas. Then video took the place of writing for me."

Near the end of the school year, Dalglish found a 1,200-square-foot loft in Manhattan, on Bond Street, for $225 a month. There was talk about David going to New York with him. Graduation had broken up his band. He got into a car with Dalglish and they drove to New York for the summer of 1974.

Just as Tina Weymouth's brother had given her room and board in New York in exchange for painting his floors, Dalglish let David live with him for as long as it took to sand the floors and paint the walls and build a loft bed. Et cetera, et cetera. In New York City terms, Dalglish now possessed *raw* space. There was still raw space in Manhattan to be had.

Girls dug Dalglish because he was tall and wore a big cowboy hat and had just come to Providence from Colorado. Mark Kehoe said that Dalglish looked like Clint Eastwood. Tina Weymouth disagreed. "Jamie didn't look like Clint Eastwood. Jamie was very tall and lanky and good looking." She paused. "All those Dalglish boys are." Gus Van Sant said, "Jamie was a pretty-looking guy. He looked like a young William Hurt."

Dalglish not only did videos, but he also painted. He had a wife at RISD who did ceramics and was referred to as "Mrs. Jamie." Her name was Nancy. People remembered her as very tall. And very, very uncomfortable with people. The last thing that Dalglish did in Providence before he left for New York was to divorce Mrs. Jamie.

David Byrne heard all of Dalglish's stories, but he didn't tell his. David rarely talked. The two would smoke a little dope, then Dalglish would yack. He'd talk about the submarine. He'd talk about art. Dalglish told David that when Matisse visited New York in the autumn of 1930, the Frenchman loved Gotham's light because it reminded him of home, as New York was located on the same meridian as Nice.

David could have cared less about Matisse or the light in New York. Painting was dead—all those mediocre works of abstraction, accompanied by a great deal of tedious terminology. Performance art was the art that was real. Dalglish called it all "conceptual art" and said, "Conceptual art is only as good as its ideas. And ideas are found in newspapers. Then they're thrown away." Dalglish believed it was the painter who truly revealed his soul.

Whatever David revealed through his artistic hijinks, Dalglish certainly didn't think it was the kid's soul. Of course, Dalglish's perceptions have to be taken with a little bit of salt because during this time he was taking various psychopharmacological remedies to stave off submarine craziness.

It was difficult to tell who was the bigger kook. One afternoon

43

Dalglish opened the door to his loft and found David lying on his back on the floor with a radiator on his chest as if it had fallen from the floor above. Was this a joke? Or performance art? Dalglish would play cards with David and find aces stuck everywhere. Was this conceptual art or conceptual cheating? After Dalglish's girlfriend, Susan, moved to the city from Providence, Dalglish came home and found David plucking her eyebrows and carefully arranging each strand in a row on a napkin in a perfect replica of the arch of her brow. This could have been art. But if it was, how could you sell it? David later said that during this time he considered himself an artist, but he knew that he wasn't doing the kind of work he could bring into a gallery on a slide.

Jamie's new girl, Susan, was a Providence townie. She was a lot of fun. Susan got drunk at parties and did a striptease. Susan had a very deep voice because of cigarettes. Dalglish planned for her to move in proper when he and Byrne finished fixing up the loft. Later he'd marry Susan and start selling paintings. In those days, Dalglish painted rather undistinguished abstracts. But they got better. It was still abstract, but now the swirls of colors were divvied up into grids or panels. He titled his work quaintly—*The All-American Pumpkin Patch* was a long painting of greenish stripes augmented by abstract strips of de Kooning–like chaos done with acrylic and gold powder. Dr. Lee Salk would buy Dalglish's work one day. So would Armand Hammer. But back in 1974, Dalglish spent most of his energy on his ideas about video as a replacement for language. At year's end, Dalglish would undertake a massive seven-and-a-half-hour video consisting of more talking than images. It would be composed of fifteen static shots of fifteen different people sitting in a chair listening to David Byrne.

David was talking—jabbering actually—performing a stream-of-consciousness dialogue off camera. Tina said, "The tape was David spouting off what other people thought. Memorizing anecdotes and advertisements from TV. Things that he'd heard other people say. David Byrne has this photographic memory. He's like this idiot savant. He just hears what you say and boom, before you know it—'I wrote this!' We once had to stop him from using a T. S. Eliot line from *The Wasteland*. David didn't even know it was T. S. Eliot. It was something he saw. Then he regurgitated it. 'I wrote this!' That's how he is. He doesn't understand because he didn't go to college. He doesn't realize the seriousness of the crime, which is academic fraud." Academic fraud? "David is like Jerzy Kosinski—but at least he paid the ghost writers and stuff. The translators. He wrote the stories."

The point of Dalglish's video wasn't what David said, but the body language of the listeners. Dalglish also made this video for revenge. Byrne wouldn't talk? Well, Jamie Dalglish would make that tight-lipped son of a bitch talk for seven-and-a-half fucking hours. To Dalglish, the silent David had become insufferable.

Like Andy Warhol.

Dalglish felt both David and Warhol were enigmas without a sphinx. Warhol had become more than a cultural reference point to Dalglish. The wigged artist was an unseen presence in the building on the next block uptown. He owned a building on Great Jones Street, although he no longer lived there. One warm summer night in 1974, Dalglish and David came across a box of old *Life* magazines that had Warhol's address label on them.

Yes. Andy Warhol subscribed to *Life*. Didn't this seem so American? So suburban? David and Dalglish flipped through them as the traffic sped by on the Bowery.

In 1974 the street's citizens were for the most part old black winos with TB, and even older white ones. The Bowery itself resembled the main street of a Midwestern town. The average building was just four stories tall, and traffic moved both up and downtown—unlike most other avenues in Manhattan, which are one-way. The year before, novelist Don DeLillo's fictional rock 'n' roll star Bucky Wunderlick fled what he called "the tropics of fame" and holed up in an apartment near the Bowery on Great Jones Street (thus the novel is titled *Great Jones Street*). Bucky would gaze out the window on a cityscape of "warehouses, trucks and rubble." He contemplated all the wild men down on the Bowery cleaning the windows of cars for chump change to score Thunderbird or Black Cat.

A bar called CBGBs—just two blocks down from Great Jones, one block down from Bond Street—was droll enough to have been created by Don DeLillo, but that joint was real. CBGBs was located on the first floor of the Palace Hotel building, the biggest flophouse in New York. The Palace could hold 400, 500 people. People out of jail. Out of something. "Lost souls," Hilly Kristal called them. He owned the then–Hell's Angels bar called CBGB—a small "s" added to the name by those in the know. The joint's complete name was CBGB+OMFUG, short for: Country, Blue(G)rass, Blues & Other Music for Uplifting Gourmandizers.

"Every once in a while a bum would dive out of the window or stagger in here with a knife," Kristal remembered. "Every once in a while things dripped down and you never knew if it was wine or pee. The Angels? I'd never known a Hell's Angel in my life. They just came in. I think I was on crutches then. They took a liking to me."

Kristal at the time was a sort of leprechaun ex-Marine with curly long hair and a beard. On bad mornings, he wouldn't necessarily look out of place up in the Palace Hotel instead of crashed out below, there in the back of his bar where he lived. "The Bowery had once been a farm lane," Kristal explained. "It started in the aftermath of the Civil War. A lot of people came here after Gettysburg and Shiloh lost, out of their heads. People hung out here. First they had stables. Then it became a railroad street. It was dark and dingy from the third story down, and trains went by every few minutes. The place was lined with derelict bars in the early 1900s. So you had the Confidence Bar. The Last Mile. My place used to be called the Palace Bar."

David and Dalglish would drift catty-corner across the Bowery at night to play a little pool at CBGBs. David often wore a white plastic raincoat and shades. He was experimenting with his look. Neither of the two were any good at eight-ball, but David remembered, "We were posing as hard as we could."

CBGBs was no longer just a dive with a pool table. It was a place to hear bands—bands that weren't just cover bands or boogie bands. The music blaring through that 167-by-25-foot room was unwieldy. Raw. Unschooled—the antithesis to Yes and Emerson, Lake and Palmer. The Artistics would have felt at home. People called this music Street Rock. The big band of the early summer was Television. It was fronted by a kid guitarist name Tom Verlaine. Kristal had actually "created" CBGBs the year before. In a story that's become to rock legend the equivalent of Washington crossing the Delaware—or at least the Beatles at the Top Ten Club in Hamburg circa 1961—young Tom Verlaine, aka Tom Miller, walked past CBGBs just as Kristal was on a ladder hanging a sign. Verlaine, an intrepid lad, tugged on Kristal's pants cuff and asked if his band could play there some Sunday. Kristal was reluctant. Then he wasn't.

And Verlaine's group Television—although neither country nor bluegrass nor blues—had a gig.

Television played a version of electric Dionysian ecstasy. "I didn't like them at first," Kristal recalled. "They were very raw. I was used to hearing a different kind of music. I liked classical music. I studied opera. I liked folk singing and stuff. I had managed the Village Vanguard for three years. I saw the best jazz groups in the worlds. All my favorites are not alive anymore. Miles. Monk. Mingus."

Kristal and most everyone else immediately dug Verlaine's lover, Patti Smith. She was a tough Jersey broad who played music that was the incarnation of a Baudelaire vision. Smith and her small band would do a set that segued from Smokey Robinson's "The Hunter Gets Captured by the Game" (which she might dedicate to actress Charlotte Rampling) to an insane Wilhelm-Reich-returns-to-his-son-in-a-flying-saucer song, "Birdland"—both numbers sung in a slow Billie Holiday tempo. Smith yapped as if she'd just invented the idea of singing poetry. *Who the hell is Bob Dylan?*

Smith didn't play only at CBGBs. That summer she opened upstairs at Max's Kansas City for John Lennon's new backup band, Elephant's Memory. Max's was the once legendary Union Square haunt of Andy Warhol/Velvet Underground fame.

To get to Max's from Dalglish's on Bond Street, you'd saunter north on Bowery, cut over to Lafayette at Cooper Square, the Cooper Union lit clock staring down like the Cyclops of Time. You could almost hear the voice of Abraham Lincoln giving the speech that won him the Republican Party's nomination for president. Now head up Third Avenue. Cut by the Con Ed clock tower. Walk across the street from desolate Union Square—dark, trees, loitering junkies under a statue of General Grant. Then there was Max's.

47

If you hadn't been mugged or met any Civil War ghosts, it was only a fifteen-minute walk. Did Kristal feel he was competing with Max's? "I didn't compete with anybody," he said. "I just did what I did. I felt it was easier that way. I just wanted to do what I wanted to do. I just picked the bands I wanted. I wished they only played here. But they played here and they played there. When Max's reopened in late 1975, they copied CBGBs."

On the other hand, if you cut west on Bond Street to Broadway, walked a short walk to Fourth Street, then a couple of blocks west, you'd be at the

Bottom Line. An upscale club. "The Bottom Line was a record club," Kristal said. "You didn't come there when you were a nobody. You came there when you had a record deal."

That summer a promising Jersey rocker named Bruce Springsteen had a gig at the Bottom Line. On a different night, Jobriath tried to burn up the stage. Jobriath was the corporate attempt to capitalize on David Bowie's glam-rock image—Bowie himself playing Madison Square Garden that summer to promote *Diamond Dogs*, an album whose cover portrays the singer as a Great Dane with large hairy balls.

David was too broke for Max's, let alone Madison Square Garden. He did manage to see the New York Dolls somewhere uptown. What made the biggest impression on young Byrne was that this mock-transvestite band all wore red in front of a huge Soviet flag. David felt obligated to follow the rock scene because he was writing opaque little songs for his white electric guitar. What he cleverly did was plug it into a reel-to-reel tape recorder that served as a tiny PA. (Remember, David Byrne was the son of a man who could "fix a submarine with a coat hanger.") This setup gave his guitar a clean sound, and it wasn't so loud that it would bug Dalglish. He found himself writing songs against the concept of compassion. He wrote a song that declared, "I'm not in love." As a last resort he'd fool around with "Psycho Killer."

It was summer. David, poor fellow, didn't have a girl.

Andrea Kovacs was a wild photographer from RISD. But David hadn't met her in Providence because she left RISD for Yale graduate school. She, in turn, never saw David front the Artistics.

In Andrea's days at RISD she was the queen of the scene. She was a really beautiful girl. Great figure. Tina described her as "Rubenesque." Guys described her curves the way guys speak to each other out of the earshot of women. Andrea dyed her hair jet black and wore kohl. Jean De Segonzac believed the RISD rumor that she had actually tattooed the tops of her eyelids black. The girl was from Queens and looked like a refugee from a Warhol movie—she wore all black clothes. Lots of cigarettes.

She would be eternally remembered for her acerbic nature. Her frown. Her love of putting people down, going for the jugular. She was given to wild rages. Finally, Andrea was also reportedly a great photographer. Black-and-white pictures.

She met David when she came down to hook up with Jamie Dalglish. In fact, Dalglish was under the impression Andrea would be his girl (nothing heavy, just fooling around). Everyone including David ended up at someone's apartment in the mid-Village. Someone produced an envelope of thin glass ovals. They looked like communion wafers. No one knew what they were for. Perhaps Andrea goaded David to do what he did or maybe he goaded her, but the two of them placed glass wafers on their tongues. David had a new song called "Sugar on My Tongue" but glass is not sugar. David would one day write, "Sing into my mouth," but he hasn't yet written a song about swallowing glass. This is what Andrea and David both did. Perhaps the act of swallowing wafers of glass is performance art. Probably it was just misdirected hormones and two horny kids during the summer of 1974.

"I was prepared to die," David remembered.

They went back to Dalglish's to spin records. David listened to a lot of different records that summer. He especially loved the Kinks. But he listened to weird things, too, like a female impersonator who sang and played piano. Dalglish found that David could make a performance out of listening to radio, twirling the dial. David put on Lou Reed's new live album, and he and Andrea ended up making love on Dalglish's kitchen floor while "Sister Ray" poured out.

49

The climax of the summer of '74 was when four amateurs called the Ramones debuted at CBGBs on August 16. David Byrne was there. This new group was more to his liking than Television. They were no opium dream. They were speed. No, they were airplane glue. Powerful cartoon pop. After the show he said to Dalglish and Andrea: "Those guys were Del Shannon and the Beach Boys playing chainsaws."

Kristal found the band too loud for his ears—"Getting off on volume was a way to cover your bad playing." But CBGBs was the only venue in the city, let alone the country, where the Ramones could have played songs like "Blitzkrieg Bop" and "Now I Wanna Sniff Some Glue." Not because of any particular music aesthetic. Because CBGBs was the only place that insisted a band play their own compositions. It's been forgotten that in the early 1970s, a new act started out as a cover band and tried to sneak two or three of their own songs into the set. "My policy was: You have to do your own music," Kristal said. "This seemed strange to some people, but musicians were thrilled and excited."

The Ramones made their chainsaw debut eleven days after the president of the United States resigned from office. The Ramones were exciting in a downtown way that the fall of Richard Nixon was not. "Watergate was a bore," David later said. "It was all so obvious the minute the break-in was reported. Geez, that happened months before Nixon was reelected. I couldn't believe that the public couldn't see what he was up to. Forget the war. Forget his policies. He was a crook and it was so plain." David sighed. "But I guess the people got what they wanted, which makes me feel sad and sort of alienated."

Most downtowners had similar views. The *Village Voice* crowd was rabidly liberal, but everyone else was "Ugh. Who cares?" Composer Philip Glass was familiar with the apolitical nature of downtown Manhattan. He drove a cab in the summer of 1974. If you yourself had visited New York during that summer *and* could afford cabs (unlike David and Dalglish, who had to hoof it everywhere), this curly-haired composer might have picked you up. Glass would have told you, "Most New Yorkers consider politics the dumb-dumb version of Middle America. Stupid stuff. None of the people I know have ever been inspired by politicians. JFK was an inspiration only in retrospect. People forget about the Bay of Pigs and other stupid stuff that was going on. It's true New Yorkers were unhappy about Vietnam, but it affected our lives—politics crossed into the real world. But a lot of politics doesn't cross into the real world for New Yorkers."

Everyone knows Philip Glass today. But in 1974, few New Yorkers had heard his name, yet alone actually heard his repetitious music—organ arpeggios played over and over—unless they were among the thirty-odd people who'd show up at his loft on Elizabeth and Bleecker for Sunday nights concerts. "Social issues, those were another matter," Philip Glass continues. "The civil rights movement was a social movement, not a political one. That's a very important distinction. It didn't belong to a party. It belonged to classes of people. It wasn't owned by anyone. Europeans are much more political. You go over to Europe and they're talking about Mao and Che and all that crap. I was able to think through this. In New York City we had become disillusioned because we saw the corporation so clearly. In Europe, the corporation wasn't so clear. It was always a bit loftier. The French could talk about art. In America if you talk about art the people will laugh their heads off."

During that Watergate summer, David accompanied Andrea to visit her parents in Babylon, Long Island. Her stepfather couldn't stand David. He railed that the boy was a failure. Perhaps later, David had to admit that in the context of most of America, he was. Andrea went back to Yale. David moped a bit.

uh-oh, love
comes to town

Back in Providence Chris Frantz and Tina Weymouth graduated from RISD in August. They had both applied to graduate school at Yale, but neither made the cut. They had talked to David on the phone. He seemed to be having a ball. They thought they'd check out the city as well.

During the fall of 1974, however, Manhattan was no longer Oz. The city discovered it was $4.5 billion in debt. Mayor Abraham Beame figured the feds would bail him out, but President Gerald Ford stretched out his arm and went thumbs down.

Money was on everyone's mind. Chris and Tina needed to pull together a stake to get to NYC. Chris went home to Pittsburgh and painted murals for hotels. Tina stayed in Providence and shined shoes for two hours a day. She also painted some signs. At summer's end, she had only made sixty bucks, but then the cliché "times are hard" is true. Only the Sunbelt had money—Ford and Congress were happy to shovel funds their way at the expense of everyone else. This was looking like the worst economic collapse since the Great Depression.

Thank God Chris pulled through. He had amassed $2,000 in Pittsburgh. He and Tina drove her old 1964 Plymouth Valiant to New York where they camped out at her brother Yann's loft in Long Island City—an artists' neighborhood that was growing across the East River in Queens. Yann lived there with his girlfriend, Julie McFarland. He had met her at an anti-war march in D.C. back in '71. "Together they formed part of the new thing that was happening with young people who were enjoying New York without any money," Tina said. "They came up with low-tech high tech."

David was pleased when Chris showed up at Bond Street. Even more pleased when, after the two saw the Ramones play across the street at CBGBs, Chris brought up the idea of forming a band like the Artistics in New York. Chris thought about art a lot while he was painting murals in Pittsburgh. He'd thought it out. Painting did seem dead. And besides, you can't be acknowledged as a painter until you're forty. On the other hand, rock 'n' roll was a young buck's game. "Let's at least try it," Chris said. "If we fail, we fail. But we'll kick ourselves forever if we don't at least try."

David allowed himself to be swept up. He didn't have a brilliant career ahead of him making art of plucked eyebrows. But before they could form a band, other things had to happen. Like money. They needed jobs. Chris and Tina needed a place to live. Then they needed a bass player.

Byrne became an usher at the Murray Hill Cinema on Thirty-fourth Street. He made minimum wage, but "I was so excited just to be living and working in New York City. And I got to see *Young Frankenstein* over and over." Chris scored a gig in the packing department of Design Research, a store that sold chic, high-end furniture, lamps, dishes, and decorative housewares from Italy and Scandinavia—as well as then-fashionable Marimekko clothing from Finland. Jackie O. shopped there. As did Robert Redford, James Taylor, Carly Simon, Art Garfunkel, and other wealthy New Yorkers. Tina sold stationery at Henri Bendel, just as hoity-toity. After a few days, she switched to selling shoes because she'd get a commission. She later told a journalist that she had budgeted herself five bucks a day to buy cigarettes, newspapers, books, transportation, and food.

All over America, people were budgeting themselves on five bucks a day. President Ford had just given his State of the Union speech. He mentioned the economy. He advised Americans to "wait awhile" before "buying that new automobile." He then told how a one-legged Korean veteran was refusing to use credit cards. He told an anecdote of a California teenager who stopped listening to rock 'n' roll in order to save electricity.

Stop listening to rock 'n' roll?

Not in our lifetime!

Anyway, living downtown in Manhattan was cheap. Whether the recession was the cause or the effect, the fact that a recession was happening almost didn't matter. Downtown apartments were only $80 a month. CBGBs' downtown rent was $700. Admission was a dollar at the door on weekdays—three on weekends. On a Saturday night, CBGBs could gross one to two thousand bucks. Kristal says that CBGBs benefited from the recession because there were no juke joints on the Lower East Side. "St. Marks still had remnants of the 1960s, but it had become very dingy. The Fillmore had closed down in '72 or '73. In '74, you had Max's. You had me."

54

Just a few blocks down from CBGBs and one block east on Rivington was 195 Chrystie Street. There Chris discovered a loft was available for $250 a month. During the Christmas season, Chris and Tina and David moved their meager possessions into the space and commenced to follow the tribal ritual of many rock groups—living together and making music. Perhaps the most prototypical Lower East Side coupling was when John Cale and Lou Reed lived together farther east circa 1965 in an apartment at 56 Ludlow Street (rent $25) where the two shot heroin and wrote songs like "All Tomorrow's Parties."

Who could have guessed what events would transpire at 195 Chrystie Street? It was just a block east of the Bowery, bordered by Sarah D. Roosevelt Park, a narrow row of basketball courts, and trees that started at Houston Street and ended farther downtown than a human being would ever want to go. The park itself was a place to shoot hoops, score drugs, and get or give cheap blow jobs.

The loft itself was located on the top floor of a nine-story building. The northeast corner faced uptown and Chrystie Street. The building was filled mostly with sweatshops—although trumpeter Don Cherry was said to have a loft there.

All Chris and Tina and David's loft had was space. Raw space.

It was huge. A row of windows made of some kind of industrial safety glass, and you couldn't see though them. If you opened them, however, you had a superb view of the Empire State Building.

Although the place had a view, what it didn't have was twenty-four-hour heat. Like most working buildings, the heat went on at 6:00 A.M. and off at 7:00 P.M. The space also lacked a bathroom or kitchen or even a refrigerator. So Tina got them a hot plate. They'd get a mini fridge come spring, but for now it was cold enough to just stack food on the window ledge.

At least they had a sink. The communal bathroom was down the hall—four stalls and a couple of sinks. Everyone could bathe over at Dalglish's. As for heat, a floor below the loft was a foundry. The place was completely illegal, but what a godsend. The constant heat kept Chris and Tina and David's cement floor warm. Once Chris and David found a bass player, this would be the perfect space for the new band to practice. As for Tina, she could paint here—she had as much space as any SoHo artist.

SoHo was a neighborhood that began half a dozen blocks farther west. SoHo is short for "south of Houston." Technically, the Chrystie Street loft was south of Houston, but it wasn't true SoHo. That neighborhood was composed of beautiful nineteenth-century cast-iron buildings. Back in the 1960s, urban guru Robert Moses intended to raze the whole neighborhood for a freeway. Landlords were only too glad to rent raw space in the doomed neighborhood to artists. So painters moved into industrial space and set up homes much the way Chris and Tina and David had.

In fact, the artist population became so great they stopped the neighborhood from being razed. During 1972, the city's Parks, Recreation and Cultural Affairs Administrator, August Heckscher, even proposed that SoHo's main street, West Broadway, be renamed Jackson Pollock Place. But many SoHo artists were contemporaries of Pollock and felt like they were still competing with that son of a bitch. The street remained West Broadway.

In the late fall, Tina went up to the Museum of Modern Art to see a show by an artist named Brice Marden. Painter Francesco Clemente had said there was "magic" in Marden's paintings. Tina looked at Marden's work—simple paintings of abstract squiggles and blocks of Aegean greens and browns and just gave up inside. "He's beaten me to the punch," she told herself.

Tina went back downtown and almost threw out her paints and brushes. She thought about video for about an hour, but rejected it. Dalglish had come over to the loft on Chrystie Street with Susan (who had moved in from Providence) to make a video with Byrne. Susan slipped into a leotard and they went out into the hall, where Dalglish had leaned a row of eight foot-long poles against the wall. He filmed Byrne spraying deodorant on the sticks while his girlfriend danced between them.

This was ridiculous. Tina had no interest in video.

Meanwhile, David and Chris were having no luck finding a bass player. They didn't want to be a boogie band or a dance band or go glam. They knew they wanted a crisp modern sound. David hated bands that sounded "mumbly." "Got mumbled" he'd say. They never wanted to do the musical equivalent of a dramatic trick. They'd avoid sensuous rhythms. David would never play a guitar solo. No drum solos either.

They never ran into a lone bass player who thought this sounded interesting. At least Chris never did. "Chris is the one who organized the band," David said later. "I might have been too shy to put a band together to play my songs." Chris would claim that he asked Debbie Harry of the Stilettos (which would later morph into Blondie) if she would be his group's singer. She rolled her eyes. *You guys.* Tina supposedly began putting down five dollars a week on a bass at We Buy Guitars on Forty-eighth Street. Midwinter, she brought it back to the loft. "I'll be the bass player," she said to David. "Teach me."

Listen, anyone can learn to play bass guitar. Anyone with two arms and two hands. Especially if she already knows guitar. Tina learned guitar back in high school. The only difference between guitar and bass is that a bass player does not strum chords, but plucks individual notes.

A bass is a bass is a bass.

Gertrude Stein was one of David's favorite writers. Gertrude Stein would have had a ball writing instructions for playing bass. It's likely Gertrude Stein could have even learned to play bass herself, providing Ernest Hemingway or Pablo Picasso or even David Byrne had been there to teach her.

Gertrude Stein could have bottomed the band. To bottom the band, both Tina and Gertrude would play the basic note of each chord the guitarist—say, David or Pablo—plays. If bass playing can be compared to reading, Tina and Gertrude would never need to advance beyond the linguistic complexity of Dick and Jane. The rhythms of Dick and Jane were only slightly simpler than those of Gertrude Stein.

Give each note its full value, girls!

Hold each note until you play the next.

Do not leave gaps in the music.

Do not leave gaps unless David wants gaps. Unless David wants nervous spaces. It doesn't matter whether the music is nervous and lean, you are playing pop music. Pop music uses simple rhythms. The drummer and bass play these simple rhythms for two or four bars. Then, either the drummer or bass player varies the pattern. Varies it for just a moment. These variations are called *fills*.

David taught Tina how to play bass and how to play fills. David taught Tina other tricks. Like a *thumb slap*. These are used in funk. Thumb slaps sound more sadistic than they really are. Tina's thumb didn't need to do any slapping. She just had to strike the string in such a way that it slapped against the upper frets of the neck. To do this, Tina kept her thumb straight but loose and brought it down on the string while twisting her forearm.

Within a few months, Chris and Tina and David felt confident enough to invite friends and coworkers to see them perform up at the loft— nicknamed "End of the World" by Patty Martin, who worked with Chris at Design Research.

"I'm thinking about my friends," David sang. "Come up and see me, my friends are important."

All these friends piling in the room. Brian Breger was from Design Research. So was Patty Martin. Tina's fellow shoe girls from Bendel's. Jamie Dalglish.

Then the band would start to play. Raw. Stark. Jittery. The prominent sound was the sound of Tina's bass. Tina's bass was the stake. The root. The six-level basement. All this while Byrne sang jittery nonsense about boys and girls and tentative decisions. Girls want to be with other girls because these other girls understand *abstract analysis*. These other girls make *intuitive* leaps. They make *plans that have far reaching effects*. These peculiar songs weren't exactly catchy, but were still weirdly melodic. David sang his peculiar lyrics as if he were a deaf boy, unaware of the pathos and inappropriateness of his own voice singing, "Come up and see me, my friends are important."

The friends of Chris and Tina and David thought the music they were hearing was really special. It was really out there. But then it wasn't like the three ever planned to be on *American Bandstand* or anything.

Or did they?

As spring came to Chrystie Street, pedestrians stopped bundling up. Chris and Tina and David decided to focus on the band's look. So many of the groups at CBGBs were into black. Tough cuts. Torn shirts. Slutwear. Chris and Tina and David decided they would try to look as neat as the Brady Bunch. They would have nice hair cuts. The straight look was in the air. A few months later in summer, a group called the Modern Lovers would release their first album. Their leader, Jonathan Richman, looked like he still built model airplanes and said, "Neat!" a lot. In England, a singer-songwriter named Declan McManus had begun cultivating a Buddy Holly crossed with Charlie Starkweather look; he'd later change his name to Elvis Costello. As for the rest of American men, they were all into the blow-dry look of Warren Beatty, who had starred in Hal Ashby's *Shampoo* the winter before.

It's easy to imagine that Byrne was premeditatedly checking out the downtown scene in 1974, deciding the correct look his band should have. The kind of songs they'd write. Deliberating, debating, and then staking out the Talking Heads niche. At century's end, Byrne said, "At that time in your life, it was never like this gnashing of teeth. 'This is it. It's all or nothing. This is the shot at the big time.' It just felt like, 'Let's rehearse some songs and let's see if we can get a gig.' We all loved the performances of Patti Smith and Television, but we had no desire to go in that romantic direction. We felt like it wasn't in our nature. I was thinking I loved it and it was in the rock 'n' roll tradition and I thought, I'm going to find another way of expressing things in popular music that owes something to another kind of language. Not the language of French poetry or whatever. That was a conscious thought. Other bands were hanging out together all the time. So it was as much the idea came out of an organic life experience as a prearranged formal thing of 'Here's a song. We need a bass line for this.' I'd spent hours improvising little guitar riffs. I'd type down little stanzas. At some point I'd started putting them together. It was sort of a DNA thing. See how many of them would hold together. If they would stick." He'd give the new song to Chris and Tina. "We'd start working on it. Things could be missing. It would evolve from there."

Chris Frantz really functioned as the band's de facto leader. When they decided the time was right to perform, he convinced CBGBs owner Hilly Kristal to let them audition.

"They played very precise," Kristal said later. "They knew what they were doing. They had obviously practiced much more than other bands. They had it down. They were an ensemble."

Kristal thought that Tina played well. It was no surprise to him when he learned she'd only played bass for six months. "Somebody goes to college, they learn to do it correctly."

As for David Byrne, Kristal knew he wasn't a true rock 'n' roller. "Byrne was very shy. Very quiet. He just did his thing, so to speak. He didn't communicate very much. He seemed almost embarrassed by it all." But Kristal loved Byrne's attitude. He loved the band's pure sparse sound. They were smart, but not Baudelaireans like Tom Verlaine and Patti Smith. Their sound was basic like the Ramones, the difference being that the Ramones were ham-handed, while this band sounded like knitting needles dipped in honey.

Now all they needed was a name.

in vogue at CBGBs

The group that eventually would call themselves Talking Heads might have been called the Vogue Dots. Or the Tunnel Tones. The World of Love. The Portable Crushers.

David would write these names on scrap paper and attach them to Chris's bass drum. Tina claimed that an old RISD buddy named Wayne Zieve got the term "talking heads" from *TV Guide*. Wayne Zieve also wrote the lyrics for one of the band's best songs, "Artists Only." It was such an art-school song. "I'm painting again!" David would sing over and over. He announces that pretty soon he will be bitter. Then a line whose poignancy is best felt by art-school students, "You can't see it 'til it's finished." Finally, David declares that he doesn't have to prove that he's creative.

Zieve's lines exist only to be sung in David's deranged howl. As for naming the band, there was no television at 195 Chrystie Street, but "talking heads" was the technical term for a head-and-shoulder shot of an interviewer or interviewee.

This was either an unconscious or conscious challenge to the group named Television. As for that group, certain members of the band believed that Tom Verlaine chose that name after his initials.

Two weeks before their first show, it was reported that Tina and Chris were walking down Bleecker Street wearing matching T-shirts that said TALKING HEADS. Some guy stopped them and said, "Is that the name of a band? That's a terrible name." A week before the show, Chris and a friend from work, Chuck Wachtel, were walking around the corner from CBGBs when a wino leapt out of the window of his flophouse. Chris was sure this was a bad omen. Chuck tried to convince him, "It wasn't. It wasn't."

Two nights before the show, Chris, Tina, and David plastered promo fliers on every wall and lamp post. Then came June 5.

Talking Heads were opening for the Ramones. Think of the Ramones as a band composed of four Fred Flintstones. The members, Johnny Ramone and Dee Dee Ramone and Joey Ramone and Tommy Ramone, were not brothers. Or cousins. Johnny and Dee Dee and Joey and Tommy were Mr. Cummings and Mr. Colvin and Mr. Hyman and Mr. Erdelyi. What they had in common with Mr. Frantz, Ms. Weymouth, and Mr. Byrne was electric music that was spare, short, and simple.

There were maybe twenty people there that night to see Talking Heads. But that was okay. CBGBs is a long narrow room. Twenty people would be all crowded together. Twenty people would feel like an audience. Byrne stood onstage before those twenty people, gaunt. Looking stricken. Tina had her little blond mop, clutching her bass guitar like it was a bazooka. Chris was happy and wired—a professional.

"We're Talking Heads," David choked out. They began playing.

No tape or set list exists for that first show, but research indicates the band opened with "The Girls Want to Be with the Girls." This song was brilliant. Loud. Simple. Modern. The members of the audience had to think about it. This was a song about boys who just want to talk about problems and the girls who can't follow their logic. These were not the lyrics any other band sang at CBGBs. Other bands' songs were influenced by the Velvet Underground. David was influenced by cybernetics, even though he had begun to waver in his enthusiasm for its concepts. If you asked him, he'd tell you that he felt describing reality as a computer mode was "sad."

Sad or enthusiastic, David sang "With Our Love" next. This was not a Frank Sinatra love song. This was not "I Want to Hold Your Hand." "Forget the trouble," David kept insisting. "*That's* the trouble. . . ."

Then the trio lit into a song called "I Want to Live." David declared that he wanted to live to see a face that isn't there. Tina's bass really carried this number. She pumped slick fat notes up and down the scale while David did some mumbling scat singing, his acoustic guitar sounding as metallic as the cymbal on Chris's kit. Speaking of the drummer, at some point during the set, Talking Heads played a Chris Frantz–written instrumental titled "Atom à Bomba," a song soon dropped from the group's repertoire.

The journalist Timothy White described all these songs as playful "but poker-faced." They combined "two or more simple melodic lines while maintaining the rhythmic independence of each." Their nervous sound was accented by David doing his deer-caught-in-headlights thing, while Tina's stage presence was restricted to boring a hole into the back of David's head with her stricken eyes.

At mid-point in the set, Tina took a slight step forward and began thumping out, *bum, bum, bum*. David moved to the microphone and confessed that he just couldn't face up to the facts. His eyes were now wide as Ping-Pong balls. He started speaking French. Then, "Fa fa fa fa fa fa fa fa fa fa."

David sang the bridge of "Psycho Killer" entirely in French. Actually, he shouted it. Tina Weymouth hadn't been the only one who helped him with the bridge the year before when he wrote "Psycho Killer" for the Artistics. She got stumped on some lines and called Jean De Segonzac. He wasn't much help. He suspects that Tina's mother, Mrs. Weymouth, came up with the bulk of it:

> *Ce que j'ai fait ce soir-là*
> *Ce qu'elle a dit ce soir*
> *Realisant mon espoir*
> *Je me lance vers la gloire.*

> *The things I did on that night,*
> *The things she said on that night,*
> *Realizing my hope*
> *I hurl myself toward glory.*

David was too wired to judge the performance. He was not having fun. It's not like this was the first gig he'd ever sung; he'd performed in front of dozens and dozens of people before. More people than were in CBGBs that night. But this was his first New York performance. He'd never practiced so hard to accomplish anything before. When the show was over, they hauled their gear out of the club into the trunk of Tina's car. It was the middle of the night. David felt wrung out. Friends said they were good, but he didn't feel like celebrating. There was no cathartic release, no *There, I got that out of my system*. At least he could sleep late. The first screening of *Young Frankenstein* wasn't until 12:30.

Talking Heads played for four nights. "What's a socially handicapped person doing getting onstage?" David asked himself. It was a paradox. Perhaps the reason he went onstage was to compensate for his shyness, the exhibitionism that he couldn't allow. The honesty and emotion that he couldn't reveal in a social context. He remembered stories of Tina showing up naked at RISD painted like the Jolly Green Giant. That's why she did it. What was the alternative for either of them? Living in a cabin in the woods building bombs?

As for the entire band, many in the audience couldn't figure Chris and Tina and David out. Some fantasized that they were a hip ménage à trois. Others figured Chris was gay. Chris thought of himself and his bandmates as Jesuits.

What was important was that the Ramones approved of Talking Heads. Talking Heads had a sympathetically bare sound, yet there was no testosterone in their performance. Talking Heads wasn't competition. And so a week later, Talking Heads played another three-day gig opening for the musical Flintstones. David loosened up a bit. He found himself moving. He didn't do the pelvis thrust or the jump-around or the Baudelaire drugged-out sway. Kristal said David moved more like a "chicken without a head." David would shake from the neck up and hold the rest of his body stiff. A newspaper article said David was a "crazed marionette."

As for his vocals, the newspaper said that the crazed marionette spit-out vocals that seemed to defy the melody. Someone else thought David's voice sounded like he had spent the last half hour whirling around in a spinning dryer. Another wrote that David sounded as though he was about to yell at his mother. But what he really achieved with his freak-show voice was the embodiment of the suppressed inner discomfort most of his audience felt about themselves and life. Listening to David was cheaper than analysis.

With each concert, Tina continued to give the back of David's head the *stare*. If asked, she'd say, "I want to anticipate any improvisation and to indicate support." The truth was, she stared at David with the determination of Lot's wife.

● ● ●

John Cale of the Velvet Underground, the man who would eventually produce Patti Smith's first album, *Horses*, went to CBGBs and saw the band. "The best thing about cinema," Cale explained, "is when the audience thinks the plot and story line are so incredulous that you say, 'This can't possibly be true.' But you follow it and you believe it and you buy it. The charm of Talking Heads was the same way. *This can't possibly be true.*"

Cale thought he figured out why Tina was staring at David. "It was her way to concentrate on what she was playing," he once said. "I think that amorphous thing trying to figure out what David was doing. Trying to stare through his head." He paused. "Stare *into it,* as it were."

When Jean De Segonzac saw Talking Heads that summer, he was floored by how good they sounded. He thought Tina was fantastic. Chris was fabulous on the drums. But what was most amazing was the whole thing David was doing: "He was buckling at the knees—doing all kinds of stuff. Afterward, Tina came up and asked, 'So how were we?' I immediately started talking about David. I was going to get to what I thought about her, but I was so excited about David's whole performance. I was halfway into my reactions of David when Tina got pissed off and just said, 'Okay. Thanks.' And walked away. Tina was already angry at David. Pissed at his whole success."

When the actress Anne McEnroe, wife of film producer Ed Pressman, first saw Tina Weymouth, she fell in love with the girl. Tina Weymouth was as cool as Emma Peel. "Did you ever see a female bass player?" McEnroe asks. That made other girls love her.

And just what was cool in 1975? Cool was still James Dean walking down Times Square in dungarees and his hands in his pockets circa 1953. Cool was still Bob Dylan in his amphetamine days. *Blonde on Blonde.*

James Dean. Bob Dylan. Tina Weymouth.

What's wrong with that picture?

In the late sixties with the release of *Self Portrait*, Dylan's coolness factor bottomed out, but by 1975 Dylan was hip again. At the end of June he showed up backstage at a Patti Smith concert. Smith wore a Keith Richards T-shirt. Richards was at least as cool as Dylan. Patti Smith was also cool— she was *this* cool and she hadn't even put out a record yet. *Village Voice* reporter James Wolcott described the "sexual excitation" in the room as Dylan met Smith. "Fuck you!" she yelled to the news photographers. "Take my picture, boys." Smith later commented that she and Dylan were like two electric chairs.

Who would sit on them? Certainly not Tina—she was no Ruth Snyder. Tina was just as androgynously cool as Patti Smith. Tina had her Jean Seberg thing going, plus she hoisted that huge bass. Boys could turn electric guitars into big phalluses, but Tina held her bass like she respected it. That little pixie chick then bottomed the band so intently it was as if all the nuns of her childhood had risen up as one and commanded her to the task.

Andrea Kovacs returned to New York at summer's end. She had a loft in Chinatown. She and David slept together now and then. They were on again. Off again. By her own admission, Kovacs treated David pretty badly. Tina observed that "Andrea was tantalized by someone who'd do whatever she said." When Andrea saw Talking Heads perform for the first time at CBGBs, she decided that Tina and David were obviously lovers.

"Yes," Tina admitted, "Andrea thought I was in love with David." She rolled her eyes after saying that.

When Andrea left David for good that fall, she placed a photograph of herself on his bedroll. It was a self-portrait of the girl sleeping.

There was another character at CBGBs as square-looking as David Byrne. But more sophisticated. For example, David wore double-knit pants for awhile, until he took them to the Laundromat instead of the dry cleaner and "they shrank up real small." John Rockwell, music critic for the *New York Times*, would never have made such a mistake. During the mid-seventies, he'd written mainly about opera. He'd gotten the bug for it when he was just a little kid. Rockwell was born in Washington, D.C., and at the age of five in 1946, his military father moved the family to Berlin. Two years later, the family moved back to the States—San Francisco. Rockwell grew up in Frisco and came of age during the Summer of Love, grooving on the Grateful Dead and sitar music, as well as opera.

After the Vietnam War, he lived in L.A. for awhile working as a music critic. "I would do things like *Tommy. 200 Motels. Jesus Christ Superstar,*" he says. When Rockwell moved east to review classical music for the *New York Times*, the paper had just hired a critic to pass judgment on rock. Rockwell stepped in while that critic was on vacation. He went down to CBGBs to hear Talking Heads after reading a rave in the *Voice*.

Rockwell loved what he heard. "I'm not embarrassed to tell you I'm a formalist," he later said. "The Heads were kind of structurally formal in a way that a lot of rock bands weren't. The Heads, pre-Harrison, were completely original."

Rockwell tried to be original himself. He always showed up in a suit and tie because he'd come downtown from some function at Carnegie Hall or Lincoln Center. His fellow members of the press were either self-consciously punky or sloppy bohemian along with a few proto-eighties black minimalist types. Rockwell got off cross-dressing against the norm. In the same way, he loved that the Heads were part of the CBGBs scene but not of the scene.

Rockwell appreciated Talking Heads because they didn't try to do the whole *thud thud thud* thing of rock 'n' roll. "They have a kind of nervous energy, but it's not *slug it out* rock. Instead of *strum strum strum strum,* they go *strum* once with five bars of silence. Then another *strum*. And off-beat accents. This music is really, really interesting." Rockwell appreciated the formal oddities of the songs and the group's almost Japanese austerity, much more than he liked David's singing. ("I *tolerated* Byrne's singing," he said.) Rockwell felt that Chris was the one most responsible for the sparseness of the sound. Rockwell believed most drummers were dopes. They thought a big macho display is what they should be doing. But Chris was a really interesting drummer. He had developed a style that was light.

Finally, everything returned to Tina. And the fact that she was cute when she played the bass. Really cute. He intuitively knew they both had upper-crust military childhoods.

Talking Heads wasn't loved by all of the other CBGBs bands. Punk historian Clinton Heylin reported that Alan Vega, of the duo called Suicide, went to CBGBs one night to check out "the talk of the town." Vega felt they were a bunch of pretenders. "It was all studied, the songs were all there, all his moves were all plotted, Byrne wasn't performing up there. He was just going through the motions. . . . He didn't make any twitchy gestures without in his head saying, 'Make a twitchy gesture now.' " Talking Heads turned Vega off.

If asked, Tom Verlaine of Television, that "rock-and-roll Gary Cooper man-child, stunned into an electric metaphor by the shock of city life" (so said the *Village Voice*), had no use for Talking Heads either. That trio and their sports shirts with little alligators on them must have gone against everything he stood for—drugs/electric guitar solos/ecstasy/Gary Cooper man-child indulgence. Certainly Verlaine seemed most destined for glory. Television was lining up to be the eternal rock band. Never in a million years Talking Heads. But then explain this: Tina was being called the "Queen of the Bass Players" in the *Village Voice* after just six months of practice. "There was a lot of jealousy from the scene that this little woman would get up there and dare to play the bass," Dalglish reported. "And she did."

Vega and Verlaine may have been thumbs-down on David, but Fred Smith, Television's bass player, adored Tina's simplicity so much that he reportedly went out and bought a Mustang bass just like hers.

The *Village Voice* remarked that David was now moving graceful and snakelike on stage. "The distance between his head and his body seems just right. A very sexy neck, that." Tina now stared as if she wanted to lob a brick at the back of Byrne's skull. Ignatz Mouse and Krazy Kat.

67

seymour stein

In August 1975, Mayor Beame had called for "Austerity Measures" to take place in the city. Garbage workers staged a wildcat strike. Soon 58,000 tons of garbage was sitting on the streets. "I came home one day in this record heat," Tina recalled. "It was the tenth day or second week of the garbage strike. The kids had opened up the fire hydrants and were playing in the spray. It had formed these torrents that began floating all the garbage on the street. It was a flotsam of every kind of thing: detergent cartons, Coke bottles, cardboard boxes, and the whole carcasses of dried-out, desiccated cats. And rats. And all kind of dead creatures. And the kids were lighting it all on fire. It was like the RISD art show where every year they have this thing called 'Waterfire,' which consists of permanent sculptures built into the river. Just like an Olympics, people light these bowls. And then people on gondolas and barrages keep stoking the fire with wood. It's beautiful. You got water. You got fire. But this apocalypse isn't beautiful in New York City. The stench is unbelievable. And then I looked at the wrought-iron fence that went down the avenue of Chrystie Street. All the dogs that I had been feeding scraps to on the roof had all been skinned. I saw their skins drying on the fence as all this burning garbage floated past. I even recognized individual dogs. I flipped out. . . ."

On October 11, *Saturday Night Live* premiered and soon turned out to be the *Laugh-In* of the 1970s. Eternally hip and sardonic, it didn't have canned laughter like *Laugh-In. Saturday Night Live* was broadcast before a live audience of New Yorkers. In one early skit, a comedian named Chevy Chase played a "Weekend Update" newscaster who reported that Gerald Ford's new campaign slogan was "If he's so dumb, how come he's president?"

As October progressed, Bruce Springsteen released his seminal album, *Born to Run*. A week later, Vice President Nelson Rockefeller broke with Republican ranks and urged Ford to save New York City. At the end of the month, Springsteen appeared on the covers of both *Time* and *Newsweek*. Ford dropped Rockefeller from his reelection ticket. The next day, Ford stood before the National Press Club and said that New York City should just go belly-up. The federal government could occupy the city. The *New York Daily News* banner headline screamed, FORD TO CITY: DROP DEAD.

Around this time at 195 Chrystie Street, Chris and Tina and David heard gunplay in the park. A bullet shot through the loft window and left a hole like the one in the window of David's old 1956 DeSoto. Around the same time, a girl named Squeaky Fromme shucked on a wild red dress and waved a .45-caliber pistol at Gerald Ford during his presidential visit to Sacramento. "This country is in a mess!" she shouted. "This man is not your president!"

Three weeks later a woman named Sara Jane Moore squeezed off a shot at Ford down in San Francisco. *Psycho killer, qu'est-ce que c'est?* Sara Jane Moore missed. *Fa fa fa fa fa fa.*

This was the local climate when the weird little trio Talking Heads met Seymour Stein, president of Sire Records.

"I'm a song guy," Stein stated. "It's the songs that excite me." He was an authority on R&B. Country. Many in the record industry recognized the man's great ear. He had toiled in the vinyl empire his whole life. When he was just a teen, he worked for Sid Nathan and King Records in Cleveland. Next, Stein went to Redbird Records. Between labels, he worked with James Brown. Hank Ballard. Cowboy Copus. Dixie Cups. The Shangri-las. Then he went to *Billboard*, putting together the "Hot 100." In 1966 he founded Sire with Richard Gottehrer, the producer who'd cowritten the classic "My Boyfriend's Back." Sire's early records include the American edition of the first incarnation of Fleetwood Mac.

Gottehrer eventual bailed out of Sire. Seymour's peculiar musical vision flourished when in 1973 he signed an out-to-lunch prog Dutch group, Focus. Against all logical or illogical odds of pop music, Focus scored a novelty hit with a song called "Hocus Pocus," an instrumental that moved from heavy-metal riffs to Tiny Tim–ish yodeling to a breathy imitation Jethro Tull flute solo. It made Sire a bundle. "When I made fifty thousand dollars in one chunk, I bought a place in London," Stein later said. "A year later I opened an office." Stein found himself spending much to most of the year in England. He'd heard about the CBGBs scene. He was intrigued. But he was never in town long enough to get downtown. He signed the Ramones to Sire because their manager, the notoriously hip Danny Fields, beat him over the head with their demo tape. Other friends raved about Talking Heads. Stein tried to see the trio, but they were never playing when he was in town.

One day, Danny Fields called him: "The Ramones have some new songs. Wanna hear them at the loft or down at CBGBs?"

Stein went down to the club.

Seymour was not typical of the CBGBs crowd only because he was a few years older than everyone else. He could pass for a downtowner with his unruly curly hair and unhealthy-looking droopy eyes. He usually wore a leather jacket so he didn't look like any button-down executive. On this particular evening, he stood outside the club taking in the night air.

"It was a very warm November night," Stein said. "I knew there wouldn't be very many more nights like this for this year. The opening band was the Shirts, led by a girl singer, Annie Golden, who later played a lead in the movie *Hair*. I had seen the Shirts. I had no interest in signing them. I was leaning outside in front of CBGBs with Lenny Kaye standing next to me."

Lenny Kaye was Patti Smith's right-hand man. David had always believed that Smith thought Talking Heads was arty and pretentious—"We didn't have that rock 'n' roll romantic thing that she had." But Kaye was very supportive of the band. He had called people to come see them after their first few shows.

As Seymour remembers, "All of a sudden I heard, 'When my love stands next to your love. . . . ' I actually felt like I was being moved by the music into the door. I was like a speck of dust with a vacuum cleaner. As I was moving I said to Lenny, 'My God, this doesn't sound like the Shirts.' 'It's not,' Lenny told me. 'They got a paying job in Brooklyn. This is Talking Heads.' "

"When my love stands next to your love . . ." was the beginning of a great new David Byrne song. It contained the most conventional melody that he had ever written. You might even call it a hook. The lyrics were typically

Byrne-style screwball yet with conventional resonance. Being in love was compared to a building on fire.

Stein rushed into the barroom on fire as well. "I was mesmerized," he said. "I saw this girl and she looked like a Keane painting come to life because her eyes were so blown-up transfixed on David. She was watching his every move. I thought mistakenly that they were together. Not that I gave it much thought because it was the music and David standing there—great guitar player, that quirky voice—and those lyrics one after another and everything."

On the bridge of the song, David claimed he had two loves and they go "tweet tweet tweet tweet tweet tweet tweet tweet tweet like little birds." It was an amazing performance. David sang the word "tweet" with complete wholeheartedness, not tongue-in-cheek. He repeated the word nine times as if he were reciting a scientific equation. This was probably the most sincere lyric David ever sang. Only a true innocent or young man completely out of his mind could *tweet* this way.

After the song—after the set—Stein was so taken with David and the group that he actually got up on the stage and offered to help cart their gear. "I never did anything like that before."

That night Stein taxied uptown with nothing but David Byrne on his mind. Stein lived in a doorman building on Central Park West. He had two kids, a wife, a live-in nanny from Barbados. He had all this, but on that night he could have been Brian Epstein after he first set his eyes on John Lennon. Stein couldn't get David or his music out of his mind. It wasn't just that the boy was handsome, poetic, and vulnerable. It was also that he was so white and funky. Seymour Stein had worked with James "Say it loud, I'm black, and I'm proud!" Brown, and he recognized that the whole band had an undercurrent of funk.

It took a week but Stein finally scored an audience with David and Tina and Chris down in their loft on Chrystie Street. He wanted to sign them immediately, but they held out. Tina explained the group wasn't ready to sign yet. "We don't want to be a collector's item or a tax loss. We want to sound more confident. Then we'll make a record."

Many years later, Stein said, "This was the beginning of the longest courtship that I ever had with a band."

In December 1975, Talking Heads did a Manhattan Cable TV show called "Rock from CBGBs." They shared the bill with Television.

"The three bands that I really loved were the Ramones, Talking Heads, and Television," Seymour Stein recalled. "And I very much wanted to sign Television. But I also saw the tension that was there from the onset between the guitarists Richard Lloyd and Tom Verlaine. Dee Dee Ramone told me, 'I think that band is going to break up.' His evaluation was that Tom Verlaine was a bully—Dee Dee's view was slanted, of course, because of his close relationship with Richard."

Verlaine has never been described in the press as a bully. The *Voice* called him "pallid and gaunt." The same paper thought David Byrne was just "skinny," a "neurasthenic Roy Orbison with the voice of a psychotic fifteen-year-old and he isn't even fifteen." Verlaine's "expressiveness rested on a very fragile dynamic between the ethereal quality of his poetic imagination and the sturdy craftsmanship of his lyric structure." As for David, there were moments when his remoteness seemed "ominous and real, and his homilies and clichés seem like the least threatening way for the troubled guy to communicate his feelings."

Seymour Stein disagreed. But then, he was a little lovestruck. "I was thirty-three years old. My days of being fanatical about music were when I was thirteen years old—Fats Domino, Elvis, Moonglows. But I had the same kind of fanaticism in regard to David and his band." Stein stayed in New York and attended Talking Heads gigs religiously. When he couldn't go he sent his wife, Linda.

With her owl face and Natasha eyes, Linda was just as curious and striking as her husband. She also stood out in the CBGBs audience because she dressed the part of a record mogul's wife—designer clothes and French leather jeans.

Together and separately, Stein and his wife were the biggest groupies of David's band.

"I loved that band," Linda Stein recalled. "Tina had those big eyes. They were always looking at David. She couldn't play the bass if she didn't look at David. It was very interesting. It was part of the look. Straight bangs." She thought that all the Talking Heads were eloquent in a "very rumpled way." They never used an iron. But most special was David. "Even in the CBGBs days, David was one of the most exciting artists alive. Period. Full stop. He was magnetic."

A majority of the audience was following Tina's big eyes, not what they were staring at. A *Voice* article compared David to Tina by making the observation that David was "Linus" clutching his guitar like a "security blanket," while Tina—with her "guttural bass which sometimes seems bigger than her arms"—was the "fulcrum" of Talking Heads.

New York City was "saved" on December 9 when President Ford reluctantly signed legislation to roll the city back from default. Lefty Jack Newfield compared New York to the Vietnam village of Ben Tre. During the war, that village had been given a peculiar epitaph by the U.S. Army: "We had to destroy it in order to save it." Such was Gerald Ford's deranged logic. Ford had seen to it that Consolidated Edison, Citicorp, Solomon Brothers, and the clubhouse hacks were saved. The rest of the city—from public works to the Morlock subhumans living in the Bronx—were given euthanasia.

In this climate, consider a new Talking Heads song, "Don't Worry About the Government." This bouncy number ends with David peculiarly contemplating his favorite legislation in Washington. He considers civil servants. He feels as close to some of them as if they were "loved ones." He admires how hard they work, their attempts to be strong. David tried hard not to sound ironic. He was singing a sincere song. He was sure most of the civil servants in Washington, D.C., didn't really hate New York City. He wrote this song influenced by Maoist philosophy. He couldn't see much difference between a Washington bureaucrat and one from Peking. He believed that "uniformity and restriction don't have to be debilitating and degrading."

Of course, an odd duck like David would have been sent to a work farm the moment he set foot in Red China.

73

Despite Tina's rejection of Debbie Harry sexuality, Richard Goldstein wrote in a February issue of the *Village Voice*, "Tina Weymouth [is] slight, pale, lascivious in a Fassbinder way." This year, 1976, was the beginning of a big cultural awareness of the German filmmaker Rainer Werner Fassbinder. The German film renaissance would be the last gasp of interesting cinema for the rest of the century, as Hollywood began its global dominance with *Rambo* and *Star Wars*. Commercial video tapes didn't yet exist in 1975. The idea that someday you could actually own a foreign film or rent it whenever you wanted wasn't even a viable fantasy. Cinema-conscious New Yorkers went to see Godard and Truffaut films at the Bleecker Street Cinema or old 1940s film noirs at a curious Upper West

Side theater called the Thalia—where the seats all slanted downhill from the movie screen. David says in those days he found going to the movies as exciting as hearing rock 'n' roll for the first time.

Walking to the loft one night in late December, Chris and Tina saw signs everywhere saying PUNK IS COMING! They didn't pay much mind. It was the name of some band. *Punk. Punk. What was that?* In Humphrey Bogart movies, a punk was a green hoodlum. In Depression boxing terminology, a punk was a lousy fighter. In pool halls, a guy who couldn't cue. In the circus, a baby elephant. Jack London called bread punk. But as William Burroughs was fond of telling everyone, a punk was a boy who took it up the ass for an older man on the road or in prison.

"Punk is coming" had nothing to do with baby elephants or sodomy. It was an announcement of Legs McNeil's forthcoming music magazine. Hilly Kristal's term for the CBGBs sound—"street rock"—was just too indistinct. By January 1976, CBGBs music was called "punk." In February, John Rockwell objected and wrote this music was not "punk rock." He pointed out that "New York rockers are cool, detached, alienated—even in the profession of passion. Long gone are the explicitly political enthusiasms of the sixties or summer-of-love sentimentality, or folk-based humanism or even the glitter outrageousness of just a few years ago." What the bands were, especially the Ramones and Talking Heads, was minimal.

"Minimal" was fast becoming a cultural buzzword. The term was coined by English composer Michael Nyman in his book *Experimental Music*. A number of like-sounding composers were all being lumped together under the "minimal" label. Steve Reich, a downtown minimalist ("Music for Mallet Instruments, Voice and Organ"), thought the term was "more pejorative than descriptive." Philip Glass, a man Reich considered his rival, says, "I don't think 'minimalism' adequately describes it. I think it describes a very reductive, quasi-repetitive style of the late sixties. But by 1975, everyone had begun to do something a little bit different."

A new hit on the radio—a *disco* song by Donna Summer—"Love to Love You Baby" was definitely minimal. All you hear on the track are the mechanistic duo sounds of a great robotic fucking machine (obviously retuned since it had been defeated by Barbarella's loins in 1968) mounting Donna Summer. Her repeated moans of pleasure. Who said minimalism had to be boring? As for Talking Heads, a better word to describe their music during this time might be *austere*.

Talking Heads' take at the door at CBGBs was austere, Mayor Beame–style. The band usually made $80 a night. They began playing other venues, such as the Second Avenue Theater, where witnesses saw Andy Warhol sitting in the audience, slowly stroking the necks of the boys sitting on either side of him. Soon Warhol began showing up at Talking Heads gigs at CBGBs. Dalglish was always in the audience. One night, he took a Polaroid of David smiling with his chipped tooth. Dalglish then took the Polaroid to Warhol, who signed it, turning the work into a counterfeit Warhol.

Later, Warhol would have the group over to his new Factory. This Factory was at 860 Broadway, on the northwest corner of Union Square, a few blocks up from the old Factory at 33 Union Square West, where Valerie Solanis plugged Warhol with a .32-caliber pistol on June 3, 1968. The new Factory surprised Talking Heads. This was definitely not the Factory anyone had seen in the press. There were no glamorous New York lowlifes hanging around. The boys were all preppy—preppier than Talking Heads. David later complained, "What a mind-fuck!"

When the group returned to the loft on Chrystie Street, they opened the window and tried to see the Empire State Building not as King Kong's jungle gym, but as the phallic star of Warhol's 1964 eight-hour film *Empire*.

Warhol was not the only celebrity admirer. There was also Lou Reed. He had just released *Coney Island Baby*. Plans were being made that summer for him to record an album called *Nomad* with his new label, Arista. Andy Warhol would do the cover. (Andy, of course, had designed the peel-off banana on the Velvets' first album cover.) Lou Reed hung out at CBGBs and talked to the Heads as elder statesman of the scene. He even had the band up to his sublet on the Upper East Side. During this time, Reed was hanging out with Rachel, the transsexual that Reed would live with for a few years.

Reed liked to hand out advice. "Get a lawyer," he stressed. He criticized David's and Tina's dress. One night they were all at Reed's apartment, going through their own individual tubs of Häagen-Dazs, when Reed suggested that they should slow down "Tentative Decisions," the song about girls wanting to talk about their problems. David was willing to eat ice cream and entertain the idea, but then, forget about it.

On another night, after the group had eliminated a song from the set, Reed confronted them: "That was a great song. Whydya drop it?" David told him that he didn't feel what the song said anymore. Reed rolled his eyes. "That's the stupidest reason I've ever heard. No matter what you feel, it doesn't have anything to do with you anymore." Then Reed glanced at David's arms and wrinkled his nose. "And your arms are too hairy. You should never go onstage in short-sleeve shirts."

Later, according to Tina, Reed quoted her a proverb: "A band is like a fist of many fingers. Record companies like to ego-massage one fin-ger . . . and break it off."

Reed influenced a larger sphere than recommendations about David's arm hair and aphorisms about broken fingers. He got Clive Davis interested in the band. Then Reed tried to get Chris and Tina and David signed to a production deal with his new booking agent, Johnny Podell, who was allegedly a skin-and-bones coke-head.

The three Heads met with Reed and Podell. Lines of nose candy were laid out. The Heads may have sniffed, but they wanted nothing to do with Podell.

Talking Heads felt like such innocents.

No one remembers the order of the Talking Heads' two demo ses-sions. One story goes this way: Talking Heads never knew exactly how sparse they sounded. The three had recorded songs on David's Dictaphone cassette recorder, but the quality was so poor they really didn't have any realistic sense of their sound. In early January '76, an A&R man from CBS named Mark Spector took a liking to the Heads and said, "If you hear your-self on tape you might be able to sort things out better." He offered them two hours at a CBS studio with sixteen tracks.

The Heads jumped at this chance. They went uptown and found the Columbia space impressive. Big. But then the bigness became very *Twilight Zone*. Chris and Tina and David set up the band in the middle of a vast floor. A guy David would remember as a "very uninterested geezer" miked each of them and then began recording. David was tense. He got more tense as the afternoon progressed. He wasn't used to the "dead" sound of a studio. Or hearing the lousy mix in his headphones. He blew his voice out.

That winter, the Heads recorded another session of demos for Beserkley Records, a small California label run by Matthew King Kaufman, whose most notable release was the first record by a new group, Jonathan Richman and the Modern Lovers. In those Emerson, Lake and Palmer days, the Modern Lovers had been the only act that seemed sympathetic to what bands were doing at CBGBs—short direct songs. No artifice. No obsession with technique. It made sense that Beserkley was interested in Talking Heads.

Kaufman took Talking Heads out to a studio in Long Island. Tina was told this was where "1-2-3 Red Light" had been recorded. The Heads' Long Island sessions went well. The studio was more intimate than Columbia. The band played "Psycho Killer," "Artists Only," and "First Week, Last Week/Carefree." That last song had a kind of fake innocence skewed with Mediterranean beach vibe to it—Gidget cast as one of the characters in F. Scott Fitzgerald's *Tender Is the Night*. When the sessions were over, the three seriously considered signing with Beserkley.

If, on the other hand, David and Tina and Chris went into the Long Island studio for Beserkley Records first, their experience would have been colored slightly differently. The Heads liked Kaufman. They seriously considered signing with the Californian. But then Mark Spector made an offer to record at Columbia in New York City. The Heads found this uptown studio far more impressive than the one in Long Island. But it was too corporate. The space was too big. David was completely alienated. The "geezer" who engineered the session never asked, "How do you want to sound, your voice, your guitar, et cetera." The band did two takes of fifteen songs. They played two songs that would be lost for many years, "Sugar on My Tongue" and "I Want to Live." The bass is the most prominent instrument and the tracks reveal how much Tina carried the band, provided the drive and the diversity. The basic simplicity of the sound is reminiscent of Waylon Jennings when he began his outlaw days. In fact, if you substituted Waylon Jennings for David Byrne, "Sugar on My Tongue" and "I Want to Live" could have been country hits.

77

The Beserkley sessions were mentioned in an article John Rockwell wrote on March 24, "Talking Heads: Cool in the Glare of Hot Rock." "I don't like to think of myself as an artist playing at having a band," David is quoted as saying. "It's gotten to the point where I think of myself as a performer—almost an entertainer. We take it very seriously, but it is entertainment."

David Byrne as an entertainer? This is the same man that the *Village Voice* describes as singing in a high somber voice, "somewhat like a seagull talking to its shrink."

At the end of the piece, Rockwell asked the "group" if they would be willing to compromise their music for commercial success: "Mr. Byrne looked dubious."

Miss Weymouth said, "We think we're commercial just the way we are." According to Rockwell, the girl was smiling as she said it.

Seymour saw the article and freaked. What were they doing with Beserkley Records? Tina had to calm him down. "We're going to the woodshed for a while," she told him. "We're not going to talk to anybody. When we think we're ready, we promise that we will notify you. This is not a plan to avoid you. We genuinely don't want to deal right now. We're not ready."

a former modern lover

The one thing Talking Heads heard on the demos was that their sound was too thin. Too minimal. They'd suspected this all along. When they took the stage, Byrne could never stop playing. Neither could Tina. If they did, the song fell apart and it became just a sketch. They needed a fourth Head. Maybe a cello? That didn't work. It sounded too highbrow.

A keyboard made sense. But the few keyboard players they practiced with tried to impress them with Keith Emerson finger-technics. Finding a fourth Head became as difficult as finding a bass player had been back in '74. Then the three ran into Andy Paley at the old Buffalo Roadhouse on Seventh Avenue, right above Sheridan Square. Paley was a twenty-four-year-old Bostonian singer in a group called the Sidewinders, who also did session work and jingles in New York. He was sitting with punk photographer Roberta Bayley. Paley vaguely knew Chris, David, and Tina, who had her sister Laura in tow. Paley had a conversation with Laura once. "She told me her father was an admiral. I remember thinking how neat that was."

The Heads asked him if he knew any keyboard players. He suggested they call Jerry Harrison, the keyboard player for the Modern Lovers.

"Oh, man!" Chris said. "Do you think we can really get him?"

Paley said, "Jerry is not doing anything. Far as I know."

Paley met Jerry because Paley was good friends with Ernie Brooks. They played together for a time in Elliot Murphy's band. "Jerry Harrison and Ernie

Brooks were inseparable. They both had girlfriends who had kids already. I think they lived in the same apartment building. They were like the Bobbsey twins. They both dressed alike. They both had curly hair." Back in Boston, Paley told Jerry Harrison, "There's this trio that's getting a lot of attention."

"I don't know if I want to be in another band ever again," Jerry said.

Jerry Harrison was twenty-seven. He had a mop of particularly curly hair and he was handsome, but in a peculiar way. There was something both cruel and mischievous about his eyes. If a painter or movie director wanted to portray the Devil as a young man, Jerry Harrison fit the part.

He was at Harvard to finish his degree in architecture. Jerry was a Milwaukee boy. An only child. He grew up taking piano lessons and building things out of wood in the backyard. In junior high school he played saxophone in a Dixieland band and a surf band. He went to Harvard to study architecture and dropped out from 1971 to 1974 to play keyboards in the glorious rock 'n' roll train wreck called the Modern Lovers.

The Modern Lovers became the genesis for every future band that missed the boat after them. The band was formed in Boston during 1970 by an uncool anti-hippie straitlaced geek named Jonathan Richman. He was one of the dozen Americans at the time who listened to the Velvet Underground and then went out to form his own band. In fact, when Richman was a kid, he traveled from Boston to New York to be the Velvet Underground's unofficial waterboy.

The Modern Lovers played original Richman compositions like "(When You Get Out of the) Hospital" and "I'm Straight"—a song about drugs, not sexuality. They sounded spare like the Velvets. Sometimes the audience threw cans at them. In the winter of 1971, Richman met Jerry Harrison and played him *Loaded,* the new Velvets album.

This is the stuff of friendship when you're young.

By spring, Jerry was the keyboard player for a new lineup of the Modern Lovers that included his bud, Ernie Brooks, on bass. They would play for children, hospitals, and old-folks homes.

In 1972, two record companies, A&M and Warner Bros., did flips over the Modern Lovers and flew the band out to Los Angeles. The band's champion at Warner was John Cale, who was working as a suit for the company during this time.

For a year, the Modern Lovers recorded demos in Los Angeles and San Francisco. The band was considered one of the most promising acts in rock 'n' roll. "But the more success was possible, the more difficult Jonathan made it to achieve," Cale remembered. "This is where the contrary side of his nature sort of came into full play. In the end, it prevented anything from really happening."

The "contrary" side of Richman's nature manifested itself when he began demanding that the other Modern Lovers play softer. He next had his band play for audiences of children and encouraged the kids to bang rolled-up newspapers in time with the music. Jerry's last performance with the Modern Lovers was in February 1974. Richman told him one time too many to play softer and Jerry gave up rock 'n' roll to return to Harvard.

Now, in the spring of 1976, here was an offer from Talking Heads. Tina phoned Jerry directly. She told him Talking Heads would be playing Boston. Could he check them out? Jerry didn't tell her that he'd seen them when they played a joint in Central Square called The Club. He didn't tell her that he was impressed, but felt they were still a work in progress. Instead he said, "Sure. I'll come." A few days later, Talking Heads performed. Jerry showed. He wasn't that much more impressed.

Earlier the *Village Voice* had made an unpleasant comparison between Richman and David: "If Jonathan Richman plays the kid who ate his snot, David Byrne plays the kid who held his farts in." With twenty-five years of hindsight, Jerry says, "Both David and Jonathan had an arrested presence, There was a certain uncomfortable quality they were able to portray."

Although Jerry didn't say no to Talking Heads, he didn't say yes. Seymour Stein was waiting to sign Talking Heads. Talking Heads had to wait to get Jerry.

Stein and his wife still came to Talking Heads shows as regularly as the devout go to church. In a private moment, Tina asked Danny Fields, the Ramones' manager, about Seymour. According to punk historian Clinton Heylin, Fields told them that Seymour was fine, but there wouldn't be any money in it. "There wouldn't be suitcases full of dollar bills on the doorstep." Talking Heads would have artistic control over the record jacket.

Fields probably didn't tell them that Seymour liked—as David himself would put it years after—"a pretty face."

Meanwhile Stein had intensified his Epsteining-out with David. He detected a vast fragile side to the kid. He found himself feeling protective of that innocence.

At the beginning of April, Talking Heads did not have Jerry Harrison. They did not have a record contract. They did not even have a manager. On April 6, 1976, they typed the following letter to John Rockwell. The shift key on their typewriter was locked permanently down.

82

Dear Mr. Rockwell:

The purpose of this letter, primarily, is to thank you for the immense encouragement your interest and articles have inspired in us. We sincerely appreciate your help and commentary as a critic.

Also, you might know that we have no manager and are seriously interested in connecting with the "right" one. Is there anyone you know of or personally could suggest to us? We feel fairly certain that we will be signing with a record company within the next few months (perhaps sooner) and we will need to work with someone extremely "competent"—we have been advised— who like talking heads alot. If you have any ideas, we would be very glad to hear from you.

Thank you again.

Sincerely,
Martina Weymouth
David Byrne
Chris Frantz

Rockwell had no one to recommend. Many groups didn't have managers or had managers who were lacking. A group called the Dead Boys was managed by Hilly Kristal, but Kristal had limited experience in the rock 'n' roll world outside of the sphere of CBGBs. This was a detriment, because a manager oversees every part of an artist's career (as opposed to an agent who just books the live shows).

On April 17, 1976, President Ford appeared in an opening skit on *Saturday Night Live*. "I'm Gerald Ford and you're not," he told Chevy Chase, then added, "Mr. Chevy Chase, you are a very, very funny suburb." After skits about "Mangled Baby Ducks" as a name for a jam and a douche called "Autumn Fizz," the Patti Smith Group came on. It was past midnight, early Easter morning. Smith stepped up to the microphone and purred, "Jesus died for somebody's sins/but not mine."

A dozen weeks after that sacrilegious moment, Martin Scorsese's *Taxi Driver,* a film that portrayed New York as just another circle in Dante's Hell with a porno theater on every corner, opened. Tina saw the flick and understood why the pimps in Sara Roosevelt Park hassled her. With her Beatle haircut, they assumed she was a child whore like Jodie Foster.

During this time Talking Heads was making enough money from gigs that Chris and David could quit their day jobs (Tina had been laid off several months earlier). The group was scheduled with Blondie, Mink Deville, the Shirts, Tuff Darts, "and others" in a recording session at CBGBs to be included on a forthcoming live compilation album.

After talking among themselves, Talking Heads backed out. They did not want to be permanently identified with the CBGBs scene. For example, the band played two sold-out performances at a SoHo performance space called The Kitchen. The place was founded in the former kitchen of the Broadway Central Hotel circa 1971 as a space for experimental music, dance, theater, video, and other avant-garde performing arts. In 1973 the Broadway Central building collapsed, so The Kitchen relocated to a Civil War–era industrial building in SoHo.

Writer Timothy White was at The Kitchen when Talking Heads performed. He remarked that the audience was as straitlaced as the band, observing, "These onlookers could be refugees from the Young Americans for Freedom or a Midwestern Bible college, so blandly prim are they in appearance and deportment."

One member of the audience was Philip Glass. Tina and David both knew his work. Glass was hard at work finalizing a massive opera with avant-garde Texan performance artist Robert Wilson called *Einstein on the Beach at Wall Street*. It was going to be performed at Lincoln Center that fall. Talking Heads promised they'd come see it.

• • •

Talking Heads headlined CBGBs' bicentennial celebration. John Cale popped by. In particular, he loved David's guitar playing because it was "really spikey. David did the same thing with a Fender guitar that he did with an acoustic. It just contributed to the sound of the band. It had a fragile naïveté about it. There was something risky about that—it could fall apart at any minute."

Later in July, Cale played a few solo gigs around town. These shows were going to be Cale's first attempts at being a solo performer without the baggage of a formal band. He invited David to join him on acoustic rhythm guitar at Mickey Ruskin's new Lower Manhattan Ocean Club. Mick Ronson of Bowie's Spiders from Mars would play lead guitar. Allen Lanier of the Blue Oyster Cult on drums. The group was to be joined onstage by Patti Smith and Cale's old Velvet Underground bandmate Lou Reed on guitar. The band didn't rehearse. Cale liked to keep things off-balance.

Tina and Chris were in the Lower Manhattan Ocean Club audience that night. They saw Cale sit at the piano and play ballads that revealed that he had been Paul McCartney to Lou Reed's John Lennon. Cale, like McCartney, was a master of articulate schmaltz. Then again, a Cale song called "Cable Haogue" started out pretty enough but ended with Cale screaming about his lover opening up her "big fat mouth." When Cale wailed his *Grand Guignol* song "Guts," he unintentionally parodied Lou Reed. But Cale's song "Fear Is a Man's Best Friend" made Reed's existential-supreme album *Berlin,* with its songs about child abuse and suicide, sound like the Carpenters.

Throughout all of the songs played that night, David studiously strummed away on his rhythm guitar, in his dark pants and dark sports shirt with long sleeves to hide his hairy arms. A photograph taken of the concert shows David standing at the end of the stage with his acoustic guitar while Lou Reed faces away from him playing electric. David stares at the back of Reed's skull with Weymouth-like determination. Twenty years later, Tina says that this was the moment that she and Chris had an inkling that David wanted to play with someone else.

There were two musical highlights that evening—a ragged version of the Velvets' "I'm Waiting for the Man," in which Cale sang lead until he was joined by Patti Smith, dressed in jeans and black coat, on the line "Hey white boy whatcha ya doin' uptown?" Smith then folded her hands at her belly and went off on some Rimbaudian rapture made almost unintelligible by her guttural growl. "I'm standing on a highway," she ranted. "I saw shapes comin' in." Pause. "Expectancy waiting for me." Something unintelligible. Then she blurted, "I am going uptown! Black town!" More unintelligible banter until she cried, "Rock 'n' roll niggah . . . !"

The second fireworks moment was Cale's version of Jonathan Richman's classic song "Pablo Picasso." Its lyrics state over and over that when Pablo Picasso tried to pick up girls he "never got called an asshole."

John Cale always tried to pick up girls. The exception was Tina. "I was in love with Tina Weymouth for a while there," he says. He didn't pursue her because her boyfriend was a drummer. "Blondie had the same situation when I approached her when she had a band," Cale remembered at the dawn of the new century. "Her boyfriend was the drummer. And I knew that boyfriend and he was a bruiser. Anybody whose boyfriend was a drummer— you stayed miles away from them. It was just wise to do that."

When Cale's words were repeated to Tina, she found it incredulous that Cale had a crush on her all those years ago. Tina's memories of the night at the Lower Manhattan Ocean Club were limited to images of fifteen-year-old soon-to-be-punk-priestess Lydia Lunch sending mash notes to David onstage—messages that he sensibly ignored.

During late summer, the Republicans nominated Gerald Ford and Bob Dole. The Democratic National Convention took place in town at Madison Square Garden and they nominated Jimmy Carter. On August 23, Tom Wolfe declared that the 1970s would be known as the Me Decade. In September, Jerry Harrison told Tina that he'd come down and jam with the group. He was too broke to take a bus, so he helped fellow Bobbsey twin Ernie Brooks move to New York in his van. There wasn't enough room for Jerry's organ or his electric piano, so he only brought a guitar—he'd only been playing the thing for a few years. Back in 1973, he was literally locked inside a studio with the rest of the Modern Lovers. The producer refused to give any of them water or food until they recorded a presentable take. Jonathan Richman's guitar playing was totally lame that day, so a very thirsty and hungry Jerry picked up the Telecaster for the first time. Three years later, Jerry showed up with a Telecaster at the loft at the "End of the World" on Chrystie Street. "The loft was pretty funky," he would remember. "I came there the first time we rehearsed. I found it frightening. The neighborhood was rough. You took a freight elevator up to a dark hallway. If you had to go to the bathroom you had to go down the hallway in the middle of the night half naked and half asleep. It showed how committed they were."

The four went out for Chinese food and ordered shrimp fried rice—the most food for the least money. They began rehearsing around midnight. Everyone was turned on. When they finally stopped playing at dawn and turned off the amplifiers, everyone agreed they had sounded great with Jerry's extra guitar.

Jerry spent the ride back to Boston seriously considering joining the band. Several weeks later he sat in on a Talking Heads gig at the Lower Manhattan Ocean Club. A giant sax man sat in as well. Jerry would forget his name, only remembering that the guy was so much taller than everyone else. He was wearing stacked heels. It was obvious that Jerry fit in. The honker didn't.

The next day, Jerry and the Heads played a private party in New Jersey. Photographs from the event show the band playing in front of white ruffled curtains at the den window. The carpet is an awful orange. Three ceramic fish hang on the wall behind them. Jerry plays guitar in the far corner of the room, standing behind Chris. Jerry looks like a handsome Satan strumming electric guitar. There's something really incongruous about the whole event, these four peculiar musicians—Satan, Norman Bates, Jean Seberg . . . and the happy-go-lucky Ringo—playing ascetic electric funk with cybernetic lyrics about having "no compassion" on this "happy day" in the heart of suburbia.

On the ride back to the reality of Manhattan, the Heads asked Jerry to join the band. He said, "I can't quit school again. I gotta think about this."

The breakup of the Modern Lovers had really been difficult for Jerry. He had put his own money into the band and never got it back. The sense of missed opportunity was awful. Jerry vowed that he'd never feel that way again. But after all was said and done, he decided to join Talking Heads. "It's probably going to end," he said to himself. "It's probably going to end for reasons I know are a big mistake. I will make sure I can move on." He made the phone call to New York. He told them that he would join if they could hold on until February of next year when he finished the semester at Harvard.

Talking Heads told him, "Sure."

these are the days my friend: summer '76

Tina called Seymour. "We're going to put ourselves back on the market, you know, if you'd like to come see some shows and talk to us, we're up for it."

"Seymour can actually name songs of ours that he's heard," Chris and Tina and David said to each other. "He's not some flunky or A&R guy who could get fired. Better to take it slow and have the support of someone who knows what we're doing."

Seymour Stein remembers dates. "I have no problem remembering the November day that I signed them. That was an eleven-month courtship. When people look back on my career they jump on Madonna. I believe the turning point of Sire records, and hence my greatest moment, was the signing of Talking Heads."

It was after they signed that the Heads told Stein about Jerry. "As unique as Talking Heads are," Stein said, "if they have any roots before them, I would think it would be the Modern Lovers—which is why I thought adding Jerry was such a good idea."

On election night 1976, Gerald Ford was leading in the New York State ballot. Then the vote from New York City was counted. Ford was sunk (what did he expect?). "And at 1:20 A.M.," he wrote in his autobiography, "NBC declared that Carter had won the election."

After Talking Heads signed with Sire, they got an advance check for about $15,000. David took his cut and capped the tooth he had chipped chasing the girl on the boat that brought his family from Scotland to Canada. Then he bought a little color TV set. Now he could watch *Charlie's Angels*—a new show about three models with interesting breasts who fought crime.

TV fare like this was the great American common reality. Young American visual artists were embracing television. Future *Art Forum* critic Thomas Lawson remembered how young painters felt TV presented a "problem and a challenge to visual artists that those post-minimalists were avoiding." In a few years time, any young painter worth his or her boots would be appropriating images from television. Cartoons. Comic books. This wouldn't be any different from what pop artists like Warhol and Lichtenstein had done, but Lawson saw the melancholy in his generation's work. "If pop art represented a kind of optimistic acceptance of mass culture," he said, "ours is a kind of melancholic acceptance."

The new Trinitron didn't make David particularly melancholy. The truth was that he didn't watch it much. "It was more the idea of having a TV," he later said. "Of being a participant in the dominant culture. Of the possibility that through some kind of osmosis I would absorb truths about America by watching TV or maybe just by owning one."

After this purchase, David had enough advance left for key money for a new apartment—a ground-floor railroad on East Fifth Street. His new digs had a stove. A bathroom with a bathtub. A bathroom all to himself.

And then David got a new girlfriend, Mary Clarke of the Tampoons.

She was a petite girl with long dark hair and a pretty face reminiscent of the silent film actress Clara Bow. David had never made much of an impression on her back in Providence. Clarke remembered his public shave, but little else. "I was more in awe—and scared of—Mark Kehoe," Clarke recalled. "I didn't even know Mark's name was Mark Kehoe. I thought his name was Walter Kaputski."

Back in '75, Jamie Dalglish and Susan had been married in Providence. Talking Heads was the wedding band. They played in a carriage house at the bottom of Craft and Benefit Streets as it rained cats and dogs. The groom remembered that Talking Heads played "Psycho Killer." Mary Clarke had been one of the guests. She saw the band and thought, "This is really good. This sounds really different."

On September 20 of the next year, Mary ran into David in New York City at an art opening at the Gotham Book Mart. He gave the girl a nervous smile and told her a story about seeing her inside a subway car, but he couldn't get the door open to say hi to her.

She smiled back.

Clarke was a photographer just like Andrea Kovacs. In fact, Clarke was Kovacs's confidante. Kovacs poured her heart out to Clarke, confessing that she regretted breaking up with David. Regretted being so mean.

Just after the opening at Gotham Book Mart, Clarke got a call from a male writer on whom she had a "huge crush." He wanted her to do the photograph for an article he was writing on David Byrne. She went to David's place on Fifth Street to take the pictures. He was smitten.

Two days later, they got together for dinner and to see the prints. The prominent ones were of David lying in bed, his arms beside his body. "We laughed about them afterward because he kind of looked dead," Clarke remembered.

Clarke overlooked her misgivings and they started dating. She soon learned that her "dead David" photos were an accurate documentation of the way the young man actually slept.

In November David went uptown with Chris and Tina to Lincoln Center to see *Einstein on the Beach* (*at Wall Street* now eliminated from the title). For Manhattan performance culture, this was the artistic equivalent of Nixon visiting China. The first heart transplant. Mary Clarke remembers, "David saw that big Robert Wilson avant-garde-a-ganza at Lincoln Center; Lucinda Childs, Andy DeGroat dancers, et cetera, and I'm sure he was quite taken with it. It lasted for hours, and I remember David saying he had to keep going out in the theater lobby for cigarette breaks, not because he was bored or anything. I think he liked how the flow of it was such that you could do that and not feel as if you were missing anything crucial."

David used the colloquial "I was blown away" to describe his reaction to *Einstein on the Beach*. "I'd previously seen another Wilson piece, *A Letter for Queen Victoria*, at a different theater, so I was familiar with his work, and the same goes for Philip Glass. But to bring them together seemed perfect."

Einstein on the Beach was only peripherally about Albert Einstein. Originally, Glass and Wilson had considered a piece about Charlie Chaplin, Adolf Hitler, even Mahatma Gandhi. They finally settled on Einstein because he was the one historical figure who was the equivalent to a pop star. As the play was conceived, Einstein himself—disheveled, mustached, brainiac—appeared sporadically. Sometimes he played a violin.

The music of the piece is loud, driving, and repetitive. John Rockwell would call the score a combination of "mournful pedal tones" sounding beneath "mad burblings." All its frenetic organ arpeggios are surely played by the Phantom of the Opera as he trips on windowpane cut with too much speed. That chorus frantically singing, "One, two, three, four" over and over are instructors in dance classes in Hell. At other points, the frenzy disappears. The music slows to a kind of cartoon elegance with violins and flutes.

Interspersed throughout the music, monologues were delivered and announcements were made, people danced on the stage around wonderful cartoonish sets that included a steam engine and a brick tower like the Con Ed station at the extreme east end of Fourteenth Street, or up and down a three-tiered tic-tac-toe grid that recalled the abstract geometrics of Busby Berkely crossed with *Hollywood Squares*.

The theater director of the pieces was thirty-five-year-old Robert Wilson. Born in Waco, Texas, the boy had a speech impediment—it took him forever to get words out of his mouth. When Wilson was a teenager, Miss Byrd Hoffman, his seventy-something dance teacher, encouraged the kid to freeform dance to her piano music. This was therapy, Texas-style. Wilson was soon cured. He now spoke like a normal Texan.

From the late fifties through the early sixties, Wilson worked with children with head injuries in Texas. In 1966, during a stay back home in Waco, he suffered a nervous breakdown. He got better. A few years later, Wilson moved to New Jersey, where he adopted an eleven-year-old deafmute black child. In 1973 he began working with an unusual fourteen-year-old named Christopher Knowles. Wilson and Knowles wrote a number of pieces together, including *DiaLog/A Mad Man A Mad Giant A Mad Dog A Mad Urge A Mad Face* (1974) as well as *A Letter for Queen Victoria* the same year.

Christopher Knowles had a mad genius for repetitious Gertrude

Stein musing, punctuated with references to American pop culture. Andy Warhol met Knowles at a party at Leo Castelli's and remarked in his diary that "the Knowles boy . . . sounds so normal when you talk to him, you wouldn't know he's autistic. He answers whatever question you ask, but I guess the problem is he never says anything if you don't ask him."

Knowles's words in *Einstein* are an enchanting ramble. Their distinctive peculiarity gives the piece a narrative cohesion. One of Knowles's particularly beautiful repetitions goes: "All these are the days my friends and these are the days my friend."

In Knowles's jumble of words for *Einstein*, there appear ecstatic references to *Partridge Family* heartthrob David Cassidy as well as "Crazy Eddie's," a now defunct appliance store whose ads were very prevalent in Manhattan consumer culture during the mid-seventies—a pudgy bug-eyed man screamed, "Crazy Eddie! His prices are innnnnn-sane!" Knowles also mentions three of the four Beatles by name, replacing Ringo Starr's name with his own.

Knowles's pop references are too peculiar to be considered camp à la Sontag or cheese. The boy transcended kitsch in a way his elders David Byrne and Mark Kehoe never managed to master.

Picture David Byrne watching all this, getting up and down out of his chair to go smoke in a lobby full of a double mixture of staid Lincoln Center folk and hip downtowners. "*Einstein*'s slowness and the Asian sense of theater as an environment, as something you can enter, leave, and return to, was pretty amazing in a theater context," David remembered. "In music shows it's a pretty common notion. And the cosmic swirl of Phil's music and Bob's stage pictures and Andy De Groat's dervish spinning throughout and Christopher Knowles's texts was just another world entirely."

As exciting as viewing *Einstein on the Beach* was that night, the piece wasn't a complete triumph. As Philip Glass later wrote, "I vividly remember the moment, shortly after the Met adventure [premier of *Einstein*], when a well-dressed woman got into my cab. After noting the name of the driver (New York law requires the name and photograph of cabbies to be clearly visible), she learned forward and said, 'Young man, do you realize you have the same name as a very famous composer?' "

Philip Glass was not given the keys to the city in 1976. He still had to drive a hack. *Einstein on the Beach* lost ten grand a night even though it was a sold-out performance. Robert Wilson paid for a portion of the production by maxing out his credit cards. "Critical thinking about the piece came out slowly over the next few years," Glass says. "It got what you'd call mixed reviews—there were handfuls of terrible reviews. But the piece wasn't mixed. The piece was very clear. The reaction was mixed. A few people booed, but they were drowned out by the cheers."

At the time, Glass and Robert Wilson had no idea of their coming place in the cultural pantheon. "It was too close to the time when we didn't have any place to play. We went from playing in lofts to playing at the Metropolitan Opera House. The transition was too abrupt for us to take it too seriously. I thought and Bob thought it was a tremendous fluke. We didn't realize where *Einstein on the Beach* fit in. We were not steering this ship. *Einstein on the Beach* happened, but it didn't happen because we made it happen. It happened because we made the piece. It was just a tremendous piece of good luck."

In a different context, Seymour Stein said something similar about his own career: "The credit that I get for signing Talking Heads and Madonna is such a joke. It was luck. If someone is great, they're great. I was just ahead of whoever else was there."

As for "punk music." Ugh. Seymour borrowed the term of French film in the 1960s and invented *Nouvelle Vogue*—New Wave music.

Next Seymour convinced Talking Heads to release a single. "With a single ahead of the album," Stein reasoned, "I can get you on a European tour with the Ramones."

The group decided this first single would be the song that Stein had fallen in love with on that warm November night back in '75, "Love→Building on Fire." The B-side would be "New Feeling." The first sessions were produced by T. Erdelyi, aka Tommy Ramone. Linda Stein was present at Sundragon Studios in Chelsea—she provided the hand claps. The real producer of the single, however, was a cat named Tony Bongiovi, a man on the short side with dark hair and mustache. His kid cousin Jon Francis would form the pop group Bon Jovi in 1983.

Back when Bongiovi was eighteen, he engineered sessions with Jimi Hendrix for *Electric Ladyland*. In particular, he was the one who was at the helm when Hendrix ripped through "All Along the Watchtower." Bongiovi and Hendrix were a freaky match. According to Hendrix biographers John McDermott and Eddie Kramer, Bongiovi had never toked dope before, so one night Hendrix held him down in the control room while Hendrix's girl-friend blew marijuana smoke into his face.

A few years later, Tony was elevated to the status of full-fledged producer. He'd just masterminded a hit called "Never Can Say Good-bye" for disco singer Gloria Gaynor. To couple the Heads with Bongiovi was an obviously culturally perverse choice because the downtown aesthetic hated disco. Talking Heads—of the scene, but not of the scene—claimed they embraced the form. Talking Heads rejected cultural elitism. Disco was the music of the people. But this was nonsense. Talking Heads was at heart a dance band. Lenny Kaye once said that Chris and Tina were central to the band. Talking Heads was also a funk band. "That element of blackness shouldn't be underestimated."

And disco wasn't funk. It would take a decade before funkanauts like Nelson George and Rickey Vincent put these sorry days in perspective. They both would write books explaining disco was funk in whiteface. Disco was just going through the motions. Funk was *becoming* the motions. Worse for disco was its racial fakery. It had been created and promoted by white Europeans as a way to exterminate black music. Not only were culture killers like the Bee Gees now broadcast from Harlem, but a soul singer like Millie Jackson had been banished from the airwaves because she sounded *too black*. Ten years before James Brown had sung, "Say it loud, I'm black, and I'm proud." Now the radio bragged that everyone was beige.

Tony Bongiovi was one of the white men responsible for this attempt to dilute black culture. No surprise that he was just a Hollywood type at heart. He told Talking Heads that all he cared about were "bullets on the charts." His pet phrase was "Spin. Crash. And burn . . . Spin. Crash. And burn." Tony B. was a pilot. He lived for flying. "Spin. Crash. And burn."

Chris and Tina and David decided they were fed up with being an art band. They wanted "Love→Building on Fire" to be Staxed up with horn charts. Bongiovi's Tonto was a guitarist named Lance Quinn. He was the one who envisioned the horn charts. "Hey, Dave," Lance would say. "How about they go like *dah dah daaahhh*." David remembers Quinn as sort of heavy. And blond. David remembers that he responded to this suggestion by saying, "*Dah dah daaahhh* sounds good, Lance."

• • •

Being popular was on everyone's mind after they finished the single and piled gear in their station wagon to tour New England and Canada. "I think as we go on we will develop a more commercial product," David told a rock reporter. "I think we can be popular like the Carpenters."

The Heads played New England. They had been driving Chris's father's old station wagon, then a van. Now they'd sprung for a U-Haul truck. They drove to Canada. Someone other than David would drive—"I had a certain reputation of being absentminded or impulsive in my driving."

They drove back down to Boston to pick up Jerry, who'd taken a week off from school so they could rehearse in a cottage that he had purportedly winterized in Ipswich. The first thing he observed was that David had no experience winter driving. Jerry asked to take the wheel. He knew about snow. There was a blizzard, and by the time they skidded into Ipswich, they had to drag their instruments through deep drifts. The cottage wasn't winterized. It was so cold David saw his breath when he sang.

A few days later, the four played The Rat in Kenmore Square. It was clear to the three original Heads that Jerry's Fender Rhodes parts gave a lot of flavor to the old songs. Jerry would help them become a real band instead of a sketch. They hadn't reached the popular heights of "We've Only Just Begun" or "Rainy Days and Mondays," but with Jerry playing 50 percent keyboards and 50 percent guitar ("I would pick which instrument worked best"), the band's sound became more physical, thicker, more sensuous . . . less cerebral. More pop.

During this tour, David had begun feeling good onstage. Less like the existential man. He'd walk around on the street and just couldn't wait to sing their songs. And when they were onstage and the band was playing an instrumental bridge and David didn't have to sing, he would think, "That sounds real nice. I'd like to dance." If people found his dancing odd, well, *Spin. Crash. And burn.* He was dancing as a simple expression of pleasure.

Just like Patti Smith did. She'd really dance in God-drunk joy. She'd do it onstage. Particularly during a song called "Ain't It Strange." She'd start spinning like a dervish—with a difference. The dervishes spin to become one with God. Smith would yell, "C'mon, God, make a move!" before she'd dance. On January 26, the Lord made his move. At the Curtis Hixen Hall in Tampa, Florida, Smith challenged him, did her dance, and stepped smack off the stage. She would later describe the fall like being in

a Road Runner cartoon when Wile E. Coyote runs off a cliff and keeps running until he realizes he's running on air. Of course, Wile E. Coyote was
immortal. Patti Smith wasn't. She fell on concrete, splashing blood everywhere. Everyone assumed she was dead. It turned out that she'd broken her
neck.

CHAPTER 10

3-2-4

In February 1977, the semester was over. Jerry officially joined the band. For the first few gigs, they sounded like a threesome plus one. Jerry thickened the sound, but it was clunky. That feathery-light, just-skipping-around quality was missing. This was not pristine Asian music. This was electric John Philip Sousa. The Heads had lost their clarity without a gain in richness.

Then, over two or three months, it happened. It was fascinating to hear Jerry integrate himself into the band. "If someone writes a book about Talking Heads," John Rockwell recalled, "the interesting thing would be to answer, How did that process happen? Was it totally instinctive and not verbal? Was it consciously directed by David? Jerry is good. I'm sure the writer will get a different story from every person."

Rockwell's challenge is an interesting one. Everyone in the band recalls that Jerry clicked almost immediately. Of course, as the band practiced, Jerry's guitar and organ parts became a better and better fit. But there was something else at work in the acceptance of the new Talking Heads sound.

The audience.

Jerry was aware that a few longtime Talking Heads fans resented his presence. He suggests that the real change that occurred happened inside Rockwell's ears when he finally stopped resisting the fact that his precious trio had turned itself into a quartet.

• • •

Jerry stayed at Chris and Tina's new loft in Yann's building over in Long Island City. "The place is fantastic," he would tell Ernie Brooks. "I have my own room. Tina's brother Yann lives next door. Between the two lofts, they must have 45,000 square feet. They're real urban pioneers in this neighborhood. It's at the edge of the projects. An Italian neighborhood. The whole area is light industry. It's not too dangerous. Nobody has too many problems. Something happens about once a year."

Jerry also read Talking Heads' contract with Seymour. He knew about contracts through the Modern Lovers. This one gave too much money to Sire Records. Jerry would make sure the band negotiated a new one as soon as possible. In the meantime, Jerry made Stein give him a $5,000 advance, then the four Talking Heads set out to record their first album.

At the beginning of March, Sara Dylan divorced Bob. Mayor Abe Beame announced he was running for reelection. The Ramones already had two albums. Blondie, too. Patti Smith's first album had been declared the first CBGBs masterpiece. Her second was the first CBGBs disaster. Television's first album was due out any day now.

Talking Heads needed an album. They had to finish it in a month for release in early summer. Tony Bongiovi would produce. There had been talk of John Cale producing, but Harrison voiced some concerns. He'd worked with Cale on the Modern Lovers. It was great, but now Cale was drinking.

97

The band wasn't entirely pleased with their single "Love→Building on Fire." The horns were an interesting experiment, but Lance's *dah dah daaahhh* sounded more like the brass on the Beatles *Magical Mystery Tour* than Wilson Pickett. But Talking Heads decided Bongiovi's commercial approach lent credibility to the band. What they didn't know was that producers, both commercial and out-there, fall into two categories: engineers who are technically adept at the studio and those who have more of a musician's background. Tony was a technically oriented producer.

Tony B. was a Doctor Kildare with tape. When the session tapes for jazz guitarist John McLaughlin were destroyed, Bongiovi manufactured album cuts from the mangled strands of tape. After Hendrix's death, he carefully stripped a collection of demo tapes of bass and drums so session players could redo the parts. (It didn't matter that the original Experience had included those very instruments.) The resulting record was titled *Crash Landing*.

Lance Quinn and his musical background became indispensable to Talking Heads sessions. The Heads would start playing, and Tony B. would stop them by saying, "You need a guitar part that goes *juh-ja-juh-ja ja-ja*."

What the hell did that mean?

Lance Quinn would walk in and plug in his guitar and demonstrate. Oh. Like that. Suddenly it made sense. Tony B. even tried to get Lance to take over from David and record all the guitar parts, but Lance refused. "Their parts are too strange," he said.

And Talking Heads parts were indeed strange. Generally pop music is anchored on three predictable chords. The chords David came up with were unpredictable, convoluted. Chords are supposed to be in the same key, but David's chords could come from anywhere. By keeping himself deliberately unschooled, he ended up with very sophisticated music.

David preferred Quinn to Tony B., but "the whole politics and diplomacy of having this stranger play on our record was really traumatic." Not that Quinn was an alpha dog. He was gentle, soft-spoken. He revealed that he was a diabetic after he ordered a single piece of cheese for lunch from the deli.

By the end of the month, Talking Heads thought they had an album. Then record company logistics interfered. Sire Records was distributed worldwide by a shoddy outfit called ABC Records. Seymour tells a story about a great executive at ABC who was fired because he had a boss who literally didn't like the clothes he wore. "ABC nose-dived."

Ken Kushnick, another executive at Sire, told a long story involving a drunk scoutmaster accidentally pissing on a Cub Scout's fire as a description of ABC's relationship with Sire. "They couldn't help themselves, so how would they help us?"

Seymour felt ABC had failed miserably in distributing the Ramones. The deal with that company was up for renewal in August of '77. Seymour began to look around for a new distributor. "I did have the support of the ABC promotion manager, who later became the most legendary promotion man of his era, Charlie Minor, who unfortunately got murdered about five years ago by an unhappy woman. Charlie was a real playboy. But he really loved the Ramones. He worked very hard. I played Talking Heads for him. I trusted him enough to tell him, 'This is the most excited I've been since I signed the Dutch group Focus. I'm really more excited. What do you think?' I trusted him. He said, 'If the band will wait, you should wait. The company is on its last legs.' I then went to Warner Bros. ABC was bought up by MCA."

before and after eno

On April 24, Talking Heads flew to Europe to be the opening act for the Ramones. Linda Stein was the Ramones' manager as well as den mother for the trip. "In Europe, the Ramones were pretty disgusting to the Heads," she recalled. "The Heads were polite. The Ramones had no manners. They didn't realize they had no manners. The Heads would be like, 'We're in Belgium, let's have waffles.' The Ramones would complain, 'Where are the fuckin' hamburgers?' If the Heads said, 'White,' the Ramones would say 'Black.' I was like the camp counselor."

Jerry Harrison says, "The Ramones all made a point of saying they loved the Modern Lovers because it was a band more akin to them than Talking Heads."

Johnny Ramone complained to everyone, "The Heads just sat there reading. You couldn't ask Jerry a question, he'd go on reading for an hour."

For Jerry, the most important moment of the tour was when they got to Paris. This was to be the city of his heart. The European promoter was Parisian and showed him around. "I found Latin Europe, particularly France, really different from the U.S.," he later said. Jerry would return again and again to Paris on his own to soak up the culture and the women.

Tina was in her element in Paris, of course. She did most of the interviews because she spoke French. "I liked Tina," Linda said. "I didn't mind Tina. I was married to Seymour. I don't think Tina had any great feelings for me, but she was smart enough to be particularly nice to me."

In between each European town, at each border crossing, the four Talking Heads would discuss and analyze everything. It drove Linda Stein nuts. She described this as "pseudo-academic post-graduate bullshit that was annoying to people who were very cut-to-chase direct."

That was Linda Stein. *Cut-to-chase direct.*

She was born in New York City. She graduated from Columbia Teacher's College. She'd been a teacher. But she had a working-class chip on her shoulder. "Talking Heads had to analyze and reanalyze everything. Whether they're going to do an interview. Every visit to a radio session. And Jerry was more academic than the three of them put together. Jerry went to Hah-vard. He played tennis with his mother."

Actually, Linda Stein had him confused with Ernie Brooks. It was Ernie Brooks, the Bobbsey Twin, who "played tennis with his mother." Jerry had gone to Hah-vard where his undergraduate thesis was a sixty-page essay on the history of the can opener.

When the group got to Zurich, they realized they hated the way the soundman was mixing them. A Scotch roadie named Frank Gallagher said that he would give it a try. Everyone loved the result. Gallagher's mix gave great presence to the bass and drums. Also, Gallagher was a very funny guy, almost as funny as Chris.

Linda found Chris a little silly, giggly, happy-go-lucky. According to Ramones historian Jim Bessman, Chris was the Talking Head who got along best with the Ramones. He'd get stoned with them after the show and bomb around the foreign cities. Chris was quite excited by the girls who were attracted to the Ramones—"Extreme girls, in high heels and usually some kind of bondage dress, with bleached-blond hair done up really big!" Bessman has Chris "admiring" one of the Ramones' girlfriends who wore a "black rubber dress with armpit hair sewn onto it."

Hard to imagine Tina with bleached-blond hair done up really big, let alone a black rubber dress with armpit accouterments. Chris enjoyed intellectually slumming with the Ramones, and Linda Stein watched him work to prove himself in the eternal internal group discussions of Talking Heads. Here, Tina was the boss of *Chris & Tina.*

Tina didn't need big hair.

Linda Stein also felt David was the boss of Talking Heads. "There's a difference between having a leader and saying he's the only one that matters. David was the leader, he was the most musical. Chris and Tina were the rhythm section to David's music." And she loved David's music.

Linda and her charges spent two weeks in London. Everyone crashed at the Stein apartment on Gloucester Place. Linda tried to baby the Heads. She took them to restaurants, made sure they ate. She encouraged them, saying, "Listen, you have got to do a gig on your own, separate from the Ramones."

Somehow they found a tiny place called the Rock Garden, where on May 14 they headlined their first gig. Rock Garden was in Covent Garden. It had a bar and a miniature stage for the band. Performance day started with the Heads meeting Peter Blake, the artist-in-residence at the Royal Academy who had designed the *Sgt. Pepper* cover for the Beatles, and continued with Talking Heads playing their first successful English headline gig. The day ended with everyone meeting Brian Eno.

It was Linda who noticed Eno in the back of the Rock Garden audience with a tape recorder. Linda marched up and took Eno's machine away, then made him sit close to the stage. Brian Peter George St. John le Baptiste de la Salle Eno was born with a freight-train moniker in 1948, in Woodbridge, Suffolk, a small market town near the east coast of England. "My father was a postman and my mother a Belgian immigrant," he wrote in his published diary, *A Year with Swollen Appendices*. He says that he had an uneventful childhood. He and his sister had seen a flying saucer. Eno loved his eccentric grandfather, the old gent who lived in a deconsecrated chapel that was crammed full of stuffed animal heads, African spears, Japanese armor, and dozens of cats. Eno used to hunt for fossils in a nearby woods. By the time he was nine years old, he realized that he wasn't going to ever get a "job." Like Tina, he was raised a Catholic. He went to Ipswich Art School during the mid-1960s.

Brian Peter George St. John le Baptiste de la Salle Eno wasn't a painter, however. In school, he created happenings. Like David, he'd been playing with tape recorders since he was a lad. In art school he'd hang loudspeakers from trees and pipe music into them—a new song for each birch. If Eno decided to create a painting, he'd then throw it into the river as part of the artistic statement. Or he would get bored and stop the painting halfway. Or write instructions for how others could finish the painting. Process was everything. Just like David, he believed that just having an idea about art was enough. Unlike David, Eno had learned this in art school. David invented this philosophy by himself after massive renegade reading.

After the Rock Garden show, there was an exchange of reading lists between the Brit and the Yanks. Phone numbers. In both Eno's version of this meeting as well as from witnesses interviewed for this book, John Cale was present at the Rock Garden. He said something like, "Get out of the way Brian Peter George St. John le Baptiste de la Salle Eno, I want them, you bugger." In John Cale's version of reality, he claims he was not there that night at the Rock Garden.

Either way, the day after the show—a Sunday—Eno met the Heads at the chic English restaurant the Hungry Horse for Sunday lunch. Linda Stein paid. On Monday, there was yet another follow-up lunch at Mr. Chow. Then Chris and Tina went over to Eno's place. He lived in a small house on the outskirts of London. Chris was impressed with its little garden. Eno served them tea. Like Chris and Tina, Eno had made his initial musical contacts in art school. He had gone to an experimental music concert at Reading University where he met the classically trained saxophone player Andy Mackay. They both dug experimental composer John Cage, whose most renowned composition consisted of a pianist sitting at the piano and doing nothing. Even though Eno proudly stated, "I am not a musician," echoing John Cage—who in turn was echoing Erik Satie—Mackay and Eno talked of forming a band called Brian Iron and the Crowbars. Instead, Eno wrote a treatise, *Music for Non-Musicians* in 1968, and Mackay met up with another art student named Bryan Ferry. Those two did in fact start a band. Mackay told Ferry about a crazy kid he knew—Brian Eno. Ferry himself has said that he'll never forget his first sight of Eno—the young man lugging an enormous German industrial tape recorder up a flight of stairs.

Roxy Music, the band the three started, was very much like a cross between the Artistics and the Motels, or rather the Artistics and the Motels were very much like Roxy Music. The members of Roxy Music wore Art Deco costumes along with finned hats and tiger- and leopard-skin fabrics à la Mark Kehoe. Roxy Music's audience would dress likewise, in pillbox hats and veils.

103

In 1973 Eno had quibbled with Ferry about Roxy Music's royalties. Ah, money. The usual item that breaks up rock groups. But groups seldom break up because one of its members wants to record earthworms—Brian Eno actually wanted to add sonic earthworms to a song. He also walked off-stage during a concert in York in July '73. After he gave formal notice to his former blokes back in London, he then ran up King's Road shouting, "God, I'm free. I'm really free." Two days later, Eno wrote a song called "Baby's on Fire" about a baby that is blazing away like the fire-bombing of Tokyo.

Several weeks after Talking Heads were formally introduced to Brian Eno—who was considering producing their next album—the band opened for Bryan Ferry at the Bottom Line on June 23, 1977. This pairing with Bryan Ferry seemed like destiny of sorts. None of Talking Heads would actually approach Ferry and inquire about Eno. That would be like calling up Bob Dylan and asking for romantic advice about his ex-wife, Sara. But if, say, David had the atrocious chutzpah to ask Ferry about Eno, the Brit would have very likely snorted and said, "Well, he's not a *real* musician, you know. You see, Eno is a very clever fellow, but he doesn't know how to play anything. All he can do is manipulate those machines of his. What he does he does very well, but it's necessarily limited music, I think."

Eno, himself, seemed limitless. During those first meetings in England, both Jerry and David went together to Eno's house several times. The three talked up a storm. Looked at books. Played records. They might have even gotten stoned. This joining of David and Jerry and Eno was a new thing, but the pairing of David and Jerry had already monumentally shifted the balance of power in Talking Heads.

In the United States, Mary Clarke explained it this way: "There was this kind of feeling or talk that Chris and Tina were from very wealthy families and David was from more of a middle-class family. It was also like there was a bit of a class conflict kind of thing, which I always thought was bullshit. Chris and Tina weren't the Vanderbilts or anything. They were army brats. When Jerry entered the picture it shifted the balance—to have three people in the band and two of them are a couple, the power base is a little bit stronger."

Eno made the power base stronger still. He and David hit it off over cybernetics. They talked for hours. It turned out Eno had been in New York the summer that David crashed with Dalglish. Eno spent the early summer going to job interviews. Forty-eight of them. Then he tried recording some "desultory" demo tapes for various groups. One of the groups he'd recorded was Television. Eno had not hit it off with Tom Verlaine the way he did with David Byrne.

Eno and Jerry bonded as well. Many years later, Jerry was still impressed with Eno's bookshelves. "You would look at his books and realize that you had half the ones he did, and that you wanted to read the others."

Eno was so hip and cultured, and then there were the Ramones. One day in London, Linda rented a red van to drive both groups to see the Clash play in Brighton. The Heads were intellectually curious about this group. The Ramones were resentful, and saw the Clash as a threat. After the show, Chris and Tina climbed into different seats in the van for the ride back. Johnny Ramone went berserk. "Same seats! Same seats!" he screamed. "We sit in front! We're the opening act!"

talking heads '77

A week after Talking Heads returned from England, David told Mary, "We gotta go pick someone up at the airport." Mary asked, "Who?" David said, "A woman the band met in London." This was Lee Blake. She was the one who had dragged Eno to the Rock Garden. The girl was mad about the Ramones and went to see those louts at every concert they did in Britain. She hadn't been prepared for the opening act. She'd never heard of Talking Heads. But when David did his *tweet tweet tweet*, her reaction was as immediate and strong as Seymour Stein's had been.

"David was just magnificent," Blake remembered. "David was like some mad saint. I fell in love with him right away."

She also thought Tina was brilliant—looking so tiny with that big bass. After the show, Blake introduced herself to Tina and the two palled around London for a few days. Tina said that Lee should become Talking Heads' publicist.

The girl David and Mary picked up at JFK was a little on the heavy side with chic hennaed hair. Mary's folks were away, so everyone crashed at their townhouse on West End Avenue. Lee Blake seemed nice enough, but Mary felt the girl's story didn't hold water. Blake was a journalist. Blake was involved with the British fashion industry. Blake had money, but she didn't seem to *come from* money. Where did her cash come from?

• • •

Mary Clarke had reason to be wary of Lee Blake. The girl was in love with David. Not in any kind of practical way. Lee Blake was also in love with New York City. And Dee Dee Ramone. But David—Blake described him this way, "I'd always had a bit of love for David in my heart. When David was younger, there was this extraordinary fucking Gregory Peck thing about him. He was just very very handsome. Very shy. A little bit gawky, but extremely handsome. He was the combination of the very beautiful man and the boy that everyone wants to mother." She paused and added, "That's very attractive to a woman."

Chris and Tina were to be wed mid-June. As the date was approaching, Mary Clarke bought a Liberty print Cacharel dress at Bloomingdale's to wear to the wedding. She was modeling it for Blake, who had dyed her hair bonewhite in what Clarke assumed was preparation for the wedding. But no. "I'm not going to Kentucky," the Brit chick said. "New York is too great and Kentucky too far away."

Mary made it clear Blake couldn't continue crashing at the townhouse during the wedding. David installed her in Chris and Tina's loft in Long Island City.

Chris and Tina were married in Kentucky on June 18, 1977. The Steins attended. "I had been invited to another wedding the same day in England," Seymour recalled. "A friend of mine who was an A&R man. I had to tell him that I couldn't go. This had come up. This was more than just friendship, it was business and friendship."

Jerry brought his girlfriend, Linda, to Kentucky and David brought Mary Clarke. The consensus among the guests was that David looked like Gregory Peck in his Brooks Brothers seersucker suit.

At the Kentucky wedding, Mary Clarke took a photo of the groom facing the bride. In it, Chris is a good head taller than Tina. She stands straight. He is leaning to his left, his head at one o'clock. Both heads of hair are the same length—page boys. They are obviously in love. A rustic church is in the background. It was hot the day they were married in Kentucky. Tina had *officially* become a married woman in the eyes of God.

The two spent their honeymoon bopping in and out of fifteen-dollar motels on the Georgia coast. A week later they returned to the city where

Tina discovered that she had became a married woman in the eyes of the *Village Voice* as well as God. Mary Clarke's wedding photo appeared on the upper-left-hand corner of the front page of the *Voice Arts* supplement. Most of the cover was taken up by a photograph of a grizzly-looking Baltic man holding a bagpipe. The headline: TRAJCHE RISTOVSKI ON THE GAIDA. The caption under the photo of Chris and Tina read:

Heads Wed

Talking Heads tightened up its rhythm section last
Saturday when bass player Martina Weymouth and drummer Chris Frantz were married in his hometown,
Maryville, Kentucky (population 500). A reception was
held at the Broderick Tavern, which dates from the seven-
teenth century. Music was provided by a stereo.

Tina hit the roof. *Music was provided by a stereo!* It made her wedding sound like some cheap hillbilly hitching. There had been numerous receptions. Formal dinners. Black servants handing out mint juleps. She blamed Mary Clarke for the stereo crack, but Clarke hadn't written the caption. David had seen to it that the photo made the paper. Who knew who wrote the caption. When Mary Clarke was interviewed a few years later and talked about black servants serving mint juleps, Tina became incensed again—now the event seemed like a plantation wedding where crosses were burned. "But there were black servants serving mint juleps," Mary Clarke insisted. "I mean, that's not going to change. I never said it was bad. It wasn't white trash. It was a very Southern, extremely traditional wedding."

Talking Heads played a gig at CBGBs right after Chris and Tina's wedding, and Che Guevara was in the audience. Or at least a guy who thought he looked like Che.

"I had a beard back then and always wore an army jacket," he says. The man was Gary Kurfirst. He was born in Forest Hills, Queens, in 1947. He was a manager.

He began his music career as a promoter in the mid-1960s. Soon he was managing bands. His claim to fame was Mountain when their song

"Mississippi Queen" became a hit in 1969. A friend sent him down to CBGBs to hear Talking Heads. He thought they were great.

Kurfirst had an office in Carnegie Hall. The four came up a day or so later, and he took them out to a Japanese restaurant. Apparently neither Jerry nor David nor Chris nor Tina had been to a Japanese restaurant before. They took their shoes off. The sat on the floor, Kurfirst sitting at the head of the table. He was still wearing an army jacket. He still looked like Che Guevara.

Tina asked him to tell his story.

"I remember struggling with Fidel on our long march in '57 up Sierra Maestra, Batista's men on our asses," Kurfirst said. "No, seriously. In 1966 I started promoting concerts. I was, like, only eighteen years old at the time, and I started promoting concerts out on the Island at the beach clubs. Then I started promoting concerts at the Village Theater in 1967, which went on to become Fillmore East. My first shows were the Doors. Cream. The Yardbirds when Jimmy Page played with them."

Kurfirst stopped talking when the waitress came to the table. She bowed. Not one of the Heads knew how to order. Kurfirst ordered sushi. Then he talked about Jimi Hendrix. He told David and Jerry and Chris and Tina that Jimi had been a "sweetheart." Jimi was "just about the nicest guy in the world." Then Kurfirst talked about how he almost met Otis Redding. "But he died in a plane crash two weeks before he was supposed to play."

Kurfirst also talked about how music had been different in those days. "A different lifestyle. You associated with people because they liked a certain kind of music. If you liked a certain kind of music, you were a certain kind of person. You dressed a certain way. You looked a certain way. You had certain feelings."

Tina argued that things weren't different.

Chris was very impressed that Kurfirst was Peter Tosh's manager. He wanted to hear Peter Tosh stories.

After lunch, Talking Heads met privately and decided that Gary Kurfirst would be their manager. Jerry was the one who worked with Kurfirst on the contract. One of the reasons the Modern Lovers had broken up was because there had been no manager. So Jerry knew they needed a manager, but he also insisted that they put escape hatches in the contract. "Look what's happening to Bruce Springsteen," Jerry said. "He can't record

109

because of litigation with his manager. This absolutely can't happen to Talking Heads."

Jerry wanted a clause that said if Talking Heads income was less than $125,000 the first year and $250,000 the second year, they could cancel the contract. Beyond that, Jerry insisted the contract state that if Talking Heads didn't think the relationship was working, they could bail.

Kurfirst was insulted. "I'm a fair guy. I would let you go."

Jerry held his ground. Everyone signed the contract.

Twenty-five years later, Kurfirst was more amused about exposing the Heads to Japanese food than Jerry's "Springsteenian" escape hatches in the contract. "The Japanese food changed their life. They had never had sushi before. After that meal, I had to put a rider in all their contracts that any club had to provide them with sushi. I remember a time in Phoenix, Arizona. A week before the show the promoter called me and canceled. I said, 'Wait. Why are you canceling?' He said, 'This is Phoenix, Arizona. We don't have sushi in Arizona.' You have to realize this was 1977. Sushi just wasn't that popular outside of Los Angeles and a couple of spots in New York. We were probably the only band in that era that was asking for sushi."

After the wedding and scoring a manager, Talking Heads returned to the studio to face Tony B. again. He had been busy. He added strings to "Psycho Killer." There were now even bird chirps as the song petered away. You could hear them if you maxxed the volume.

The idea of adding strings to "Psycho Killer" sounds more atrocious than it actually was. Bongiovi didn't turn "Psycho Killer" into an Elton John song with lush Paul Buckmaster strings. He'd added psychedelic strings like the Beatles on "I Am the Walrus." The song didn't sound bad. But it sounded like a novelty number. It was understandable that the Heads hit the ceiling when they heard the bird-chirped/symphonied "Psycho Killer."

The group promptly rerecorded the song, but in doing so David changed the second verse. Originally, he sang that he "passed out hours ago." Then he announced that he was "sadder" than we'll ever know. He closed his eyes. Felt the sun on his face. And figured, "Say something once, why say it again?" Now in the revision, David's fruitcake complains about blabbermouths. The original verse was better. There was something more world-weary about it. The killer seemed more poetic. Pseudo-European. Dangerous somehow.

After "Psycho Killer" was in the bag, David began to refuse to sing when Bongiovi was present. "Tony Bongiovi is the one of the biggest assholes I've ever met," he told Mary one night.

If only Brian Eno were producing this album. But the Brit was in Berlin recording *Heroes* with David Bowie. It would be a thick and chunky record. The title track would be the only good song. The chorus, "We can be heroes just for one day," was, as Eno-ologist Eric Tamm observed, a rehashed version of Andy Warhol's "Everyone will be famous for fifteen minutes."

Tony Bongiovi himself didn't know David hated him. From his view, the only strength of the band was in David's strangled singing and peculiar song-writing. The rest of the players were weak. *Tina, queen of the bass players?* Ha! If asked, Bongiovi would say, "Talking Heads, for all intents and purposes, is David Byrne. David Byrne is the writer, the singer, and the stylist. You can take any other musicians from any band and the songs would have come out almost exactly the same."

David eventually got over Tony B. Twenty-two years after recording that first album, David remembered, "We didn't know anything about making records back then. And I'm sure Tony was trying to make our songs a little more accessible. So I figure in retrospect this poor guy took a lot of shit from us that at the time I thought was totally justified." David gave a sad smile. "This poor guy was just trying to help some kids make a record!"

Several events would mark the summer of '77. Con Ed blew. No more electric guitar. About a month after the city blackout, Son of Sam was arrested in Yonkers. Between these two events, Talking Heads cut the rest of their first album and David took to doing a midnight creep with engineer Ed Stasium up to the studio to secretly overdub the vocals.

On many of those nights, while David was recording his secret vocals, Tina Weymouth would pour her heart out for hours to Lee Blake. All she talked about was David. Tina didn't exist in David's eyes. David didn't respect her. Blake mostly listened. The Brit saw Tina as Rochester's wife. The mad one. The one locked upstairs. Tina's panic seemed to grow as the group continued recording and David came more into himself. Tina retaliated by hammering David with a hollow joke, "You'd be a busker in Washington Square if it wasn't for Chris and me."

"Speaking as a woman," Blake says, "Tina must have been in love with David. Because the only time that I've known a woman to be that fixated on a man was because of love. But of course, I couldn't really bring that up then, because she was married to Chris."

And because Blake was a little in love with David herself.

On August 16, Elvis Presley died. The audience at CBGBs was so far removed from American sentimentality that no one cared. Also this month, Tony Bongiovi finished his other record—the "more important one"—a disco version of the theme from *Star Wars*. On September 22, the offices of *Rolling Stone* magazine moved to Manhattan from San Francisco. In retrospect this relocation represents the triumph of the East Coast music establishment over the West. Just a few years back, California rock dominated the nation's musical consciousness. Jackson Browne, Joni Mitchell, and Neil Young were the singer/songwriters of the age. The Eagles were the great American band. Then along came Bruce "Jersey" Springsteen. Even worse, disco. Although the Eagles' *Hotel California* would be released that Christmas and sell a jillion copies, it turned out to be the swan song for Pacific Coast rock. For the next several years, California was as culturally dead as Elvis while *Rolling Stone* surveyed and passed judgment on American rock 'n' roll from high atop Hotel Manhattan. Along with Springsteen and disco was punk, of course. New Wave historians like Clinton Heylin and Legs McNeil have documented that the usual suspects of CBGBs originated every aspect of British punk first. London can be rightfully seen as just another stop on the subway beyond Rockaway Beach.

In this light, *Talking Heads '77*, released in October, was one of the triumphs of the consolidation of Manhattan's musical reign. Remember that vinyl record covers are roughly six times larger than CD covers. Talking Heads' cover seemed bold for its utter simplicity. Its stop-sign red. The words TALKING HEADS '77 appear in green type.

It was designed by David with Jerry's help. "We wanted a Day-Glo cover," he recalled. But Queens Litho, the state-of-the-art album cover firm that Sire used, didn't have Day-Glo. "We got on the phone and found a company that did polka records in the Midwest. They said, 'Day-

Glo? We'd be happy to do that.' When Queens Litho heard that, they said they'd do it."

The back of the album contains an elevated shot of the four Talking Heads. Tina with her Beatle cut looks a little dour. Jerry is lean, in a black shirt. He truly looks a little hungry. David has a five o'clock shadow and looks young. He's not exactly smiling. He seems to be thinking, "Can you believe we're getting away with this?" Chris has a thick head of hair and looks thinner than he will ever be again. The inner-sleeve publicity photo is different. It's the one Sire uses in advertisements. The camera is pulled back. Everyone has shifted positions. Jerry hangs back far to the viewer's left, the old man in the group. Tina stands behind David with her hands folded on his shoulder. He is smiling and looking off to the left. Tina smiles directly into the camera. Beside her stands her husband. Holding his temple, he stares into the camera with a "My God" look.

Where exactly did Chris Frantz fit into the situation between his wife and David? "Chris is a Kentucky gentleman," Lee Blake says. "But he's not stupid, either. I think Chris saw Tina as a convenient wife. They seemed convenient as a couple. You know, the general's son and the admiral's daughter. And don't forget that Chris and Tina and Jerry as well were the sons and daughters of privileged Americans. And they fancied themselves as being kind of quite posh, as we would say in England. And David is from Scotland, which is very austere. And he's been taught some decent principles by his family."

John Rockwell got behind *Talking Heads '77*, this rather strident-sounding recording. He saw it forming a trilogy, along with Patti Smith's *Horses* and Television's *Marquee Moon*, that staked New York seventies underground rock's "claim to greatness." He quoted Chris as saying the music was definitely *white*. Jerry then qualified Chris's statement, "We've absorbed a lot of black influences, but it's still white." Rockwell identifies the music culturally as Asian. "To this ear," he wrote, "there is a persuasive Orientalism to the sound."

Tina asserted that they didn't think of themselves as art rockers. "We're not poseurs." David speculated they would fluctuate between cult status and "fluke mass success." Then Chris, Jerry, and David rapped about singles:

"It would certainly be nice to have singles," Chris mused.

"There's nothing wrong with it," Jerry added.

"But we don't want to try to make hit singles," said David. "We want to make good music in a song format."

"I think we all want to work in a way that allows us to be artists, as opposed to celebrities in a very tacky business," Chris offered.

That must have resonated in David. He had come to realize that he could make the same statements through music that he had made through art. But when Chris used the word *artists,* David saw *conceptual art.* Who knew if Chris saw *painters.*

Real artists.

Rockwell gave Jerry the last word: "If we become successful, it will be because we are an original band and our originality becomes popular."

There is a large difference between rock critics in the seventies and the present. In those days, most of the mainstream publications like *Time* and *Newsweek* didn't have rock critics. These magazines were very insecure about what they should decide would be the next big thing. The *Village Voice* was too scruffy for them. That left the *New York Times,* which had become very important for validating phenomena and acts for the mainstream.

Would a guy like David Byrne ever appear on the cover of *Time* and *Newsweek*? Fat chance. Several months later, *Talking Heads '77* only peaked at just number 97 on the *Billboard* charts. A writer named Gene Di Gregorio speculated that the record's slow sales were due to confusion over the band's alligator-on-the-shirt images versus expectations of the safety-pin-in-the-nose qualities of punk.

During the summer Andy Warhol had begun a new series of paintings. Although these works would be largely forgotten by the time of his death, they are highly representational of the impetus of American art in the seventies and eighties. Warhol and several of his boys would unzip their pants and pee on canvases coated with copper paint. As the piss dried on the paint, it would oxidize. The results were greenish and orange. On June 28 Warhol wrote in his diary:

> I told Tonnie not to pee when he gets up in morning—to
> try to hold it until he gets to the office, because he takes
> lots of vitamin B so the canvas turns a really pretty color
> when it's his piss.

During this time, Tina's ex-sister-in-law Lally Weymouth hosted a dinner party for seventy-four elite Manhattanites. Jackie Onassis and Norman Mailer were guests. Apparently Jackie "turned Mailer on" (or so a witness would later speculate) by asking him about street fighting. Mailer pontificated and demonstrated air punches. Then he strode to another corner of the party where Gore Vidal stood and muttered, "You look like an old Jew." Mailer then punched Vidal. The punchee later testified that Mailer had a "tiny fist."

A cultural trilogy of Warhol's piss paintings and Norman Mailer's "tiny fist" is completed with the fall '77 release of the Sex Pistols' premiere record, *Never Mind the Bollocks Here's the Sex Pistols*. How could so many otherwise brilliant record critics have thought the Pistols' sneering rants were not only brilliant, but holy?

No one at Warner Bros. believed Sex Pistols–style punk would just be a fad. They instructed Sire to promote Talking Heads with three other punkier New Wave bands—the Saints, Dead Boys, and Richard Hell and the Voidoids—with the slogan: "Get Behind It Before It Gets Past You!" Sire's Ken Kushnick would remark, "We spent a campaign's worth of time, money, and effort on those four records, and only one walked away from the rest—the Heads."

As for the music of the Sex Pistols, David connected it to the same prejudice that believed third world music was more spiritual than western rock. The Sex Pistols were as totally bogus a notion. "They're something that was put together by Malcolm McLaren," he would say. "The people fell for it hook, line, and sinker. To me it was like, once again, here comes the rock 'n' roll image of bad boys in black leather. It used to be bad boys in drag, and now it's bad boys in ripped clothing. It's just another romantic notion that Europeans like to go for: The drunk on the corner has more wisdom than the guy in the ivory tower."

The Heads took to the road to support their album. They played Bryn Mawr, Pennsylvania. After the show David Byrne tried to put in words the psychological catharsis he felt while performing. He couldn't. The band played Richmond, Virginia; Pittsburgh, Pennsylvania. David suddenly realized that performing was an exorcism that he performed on himself onstage. They played Rutgers College, New Jersey. David realized he had to "cut this thing out of himself"—self-surgery he could only perform on a stage. Talking Heads played Wilmington, Delaware; Baltimore; the New York Institute of Technology on Long Island; Atlanta and Nashville. David knew he had to get rid of *this thing* every night just to go on living.

Early December, the Heads did a two-week tour of California. Mary Clarke came along. Sometimes Frank Gallagher, the sound mixer, would drive, but unfortunately David often drove. To this day Jerry gets knots in his stomach remembering David barreling the car up to scenic stops. It was a miracle he didn't drive them off the cliffs into the Pacific.

Linda Stein said, "I remember when they played L.A. and Seymour gave them a dinner. And I organized it at Mr. Chow in L.A. It was a really, really, really nice dinner."

Many characters in the Talking Heads story would eat at this restaurant through the years. If the Heads had an official restaurant, it was probably Mr. Chow.

On December 19, 1977, Talking Heads was back in New York. Eno had moved to an apartment on Eighth Street. He wrote a song for his new album, *Before and After Science*, called "King's Lead Hat," an anagram for Talking Heads. He told the band that he would produce their next record. Sire got nervous. The new album Eno had produced for Bowie, *Heroes*, wasn't out yet. The Bowie album before that one, *Low*, had been released earlier in the year, and on it Eno had made the so-called Thin White Duke completely uncommercial. Bowie had recorded that one in a sulk because he had been denied the opportunity to do the soundtrack to the *Man Who Fell to Earth*. Supposedly once the *Low* sessions started, Bowie began having a nervous breakdown. Eno lived on breakfast cereal while the Thin White Duke ate nothing but raw eggs.

That was *Low*. Sire was worried that Eno would "*Low* out" the Heads. "We had to twist Mr. Stein's arm a little to get Eno," Chris later remarked.

The Heads got their way.

On December 27, the Heads played Hilly Kristal's Anderson Theater on Second Avenue across the street from the old Fillmore East. From December 29 to 31, they played Boston and a New Year's party in Philadelphia. Although they were working like crazy to promote *Talking Heads '77*, the album would be better received critically than popularly. At the end of the year, *Talking Heads '77* shared *Rolling Stone*'s Most Promising New Artist award with Peter Gabriel.

Gabriel was as weird as David Byrne. Gabriel had been the lead singer for the group Genesis, but he quit back in 1975. Everyone assumed the group would break up. They didn't. The drummer, Phil Collins, took over the singing. The next year, Genesis would have their first hit. Suddenly, without a weird singer/songwriter, the band was making money.

117

aspects of byrne

Talking Heads discovered that the honey was in Europe. They were bigger on the other side of the big ditch than in the States (Eastern seaboard aside). Sire sent the group on their first headline Euro-tour—twenty-four cities in twenty-seven days: Hamburg. Brussels. Amsterdam. Paris. London. A new group called XTC would open for them on the Continent, with Dire Straits opening in England.

The weather was hideous that winter. The only time the band saw sunlight was when their plane flew above the clouds. But then they only flew once. The four traveled the Continent in a micro-minibus. Everybody had colds. Tina had bronchitis. When the band got where they were going, they would usually find the dressing rooms cold and the beer warm.

"Tina was flipping out on the tour," Jerry remembered. "I had gotten into this paperback series called the Destroyer, about a super martial arts guy. An old friend, a marine, recommended them. You can read them in an hour and a half. We're in this drafty Econoline van. I told Tina, 'Read this book and just escape. It's stupid but just imagine doing the violence.' She was reluctant. But she picked one up and really got into it."

No one in the band had a clue what exactly was tormenting Tina. Lee Blake thought she knew. The girl with the ice cream hair had flown back to England for Christmas and she decided to stay. She and Tina hadn't had a falling-out or a row, but they parted on a sour note. Tina would later call Blake a freeloader. Blake would counter, listing how much work she'd done setting up the band with T-shirt manufacturers, connecting them with British bookings and journalists. Besides, Blake didn't need Tina's bloody handouts. Blake's dad had just passed on and left her something. As for Tina, Blake says, "She just goes off people. Tina digs them, loves them, respects their intelligence, and then she just kind of goes off them. But the truth of the matter is, I left New York City thinking that this woman was so in love with David Byrne that it was going to destroy her. That it was a real wild, unhealthy fixation."

Reports from Europe that the band was miserable filtered back to New York. Gary Kurfirst flew to France to join Talking Heads just before they began the massive British leg of the tour. The manager, bearded, still wearing an old army jacket, arrived in Paris in time to catch the tail end of the farewell party. The next day, the group went to Charles de Gaulle Airport and discovered their London flight was canceled because of snow. Everyone schlepped to the Gare du Nord and hopped a train to Boulogne. The band was packed into their European train seats in little compartments—the train pulling from the station—when Jerry Harrison realized that he had lost his passport. "Shit. I left it at the hotel. . . . Oh, fuck. And our working papers, as well."

The train headed through the black French night with streaks of snow against the window. Everyone fell asleep except Kurfirst and Jerry.

"Gary and I stayed up all night talking," Jerry recalled. "This was when the closeness between us started. Gary understood that I understood what a manager did—the Modern Lovers had been a great education."

Kurfirst understood that Jerry appreciated his manager's wisdom. "Talking Heads should keep our expenses down so we never lose money. Talking Heads should never take so much tour support that the band is heavily in debt." This happened fairly often to new bands. "Talking Heads shouldn't demand roadies and better hotels. Talking Heads should grow into it."

The band followed his advice and became very prideful in their frugality. It was as if Chris and Tina and Jerry were born of Scottish parents like David was.

● ● ●

That night on the French train Kurfirst told Jerry his life story—growing up in Queens, hustling in pool halls, what Mountain was like. Kurfirst later felt that he and Jerry had the most in common. "We were both lovers of sports. And we both loved to drink," he said. A window in time opened for just a moment and Kurfirst caught a glimmer of what would transpire in the music business come the millennium. "God, I miss the late sixties already," Kurfirst told Jerry. "Artists could pretty much do what they wanted. Punk is bullshit compared to then. The more rebellious a group was against society, and against institutions, the more famous and the more popular they were. Jim Morrison will never happen again. I think that it's going to get harder and harder to get famous anymore because they'll shut you down."

They took the ferry to Folkestone in England. The Channel was a tempest and Kurfirst's face turned green. Jerry helped the manager to the tossing deck. "Just stare at the horizon," he advised. "Looking at steady objects cures motion sickness." Jerry was right. Kurfirst survived the voyage. When they reached port, Jerry had to convince British customs he was legit. The officer looked like the English actor who played Dr. Watson to Basil Rathbone's Sherlock Holmes.

"First, I've lost my passport," Jerry told him. "And second, our working papers are at Heathrow."

The officer raised his eyebrow and turned to a coworker. "Did you hear that? This bloke not only lost his passport but his working papers are at Heathrow." He turned back to Jerry. "No one would make up that story. It must be true. You'll have to take care of it tomorrow in London."

Once in London, the band learned that the demon reincarnation of Buddy Holly, Elvis Costello, was about to tour the States and wanted Talking Heads to join him. This would be a great deal for the Americans. Exposure in the Midwest. Talking Heads cut British tour dates. The limey music press began insulting them for these cancellations. So the group added make-up dates.

Tina had the Destroyer to comfort her, but David had nothing. A peculiar thing was going on now that Jerry had become a firm member of the band. David was the front man, but he wasn't the leader. He could never say, "Jerry, this is what we're going to do." He had to be more subtle. More roundabout. With Tina he had to soft-pedal. "I have a song that I wrote and I think maybe the bass part like this would be good. This kind of beat. This kind of feel. . . ." Subtly steering the song where he wanted it to go. This was getting on his nerves.

Then there was this fucking European darkness and all the clouds. David had lost all sense of rhythm on this tour. Daily rhythm. The rhythm of getting up and going to sleep. "When that rhythm gets broken, disjointed, that's what makes people broken, crazy," he said. "Crazy bad. It was a sensory deprivation thing. You break up somebody's rhythm of eating and sleeping, they're going to go nuts."

David went a little nuts.

A rumor circulated that David did something shocking involving a little American flag at the Portobello Hotel in London. Jerry claimed David only pulled a Keith Moon and busted up the room. Whatever the truth, Jerry bunked with David on that European tour. Trashing hotels wasn't usual behavior. What they usually did after a show was go out to a French club or a Dutch bar and drink until their adrenaline came down. "Then you collapsed," Jerry said.

David recalled, "Some bands, if they're driven too hard on tour by management—that can break them up right there. The band ends up hating each other only a year after they make their first record."

It had only been a few months since Talking Heads' first record. Chris and Tina phoned Seymour and convinced him that David had flipped out. The tour was cut short. "I didn't understand myself what was going on," Tina would remember. Seymour was not aware of how fragile David was. Tina tried to tell him that. "But Seymour just didn't understand."

The band returned to New York and "fragile" David Byrne met Mary Clarke at the Algonquin for drinks. For months he had been reading *The New Yorker* cover to cover. He had even gotten into its literary history.

"I read that the Algonquin became famous because the drama critic of *Vanity Fair* [Robert Sherwood] liked to have drinks here," David told her. "He'd have to walk past this freak show that used to be across the street and the midgets there would hassle him because he was so tall. So he asked Dorothy Parker if she'd walk him to the Algonquin to protect him from the midgets. One thing led to another, and Parker made the Algonquin their regular watering hole."

• • •

David Byrne and *The New Yorker*. This was not *Rolling Stone* or *Creem*. Imagine David reading "Talk of the Town." Reading the cartoons and poems. Perhaps David even began to see the mundane aspects of his life morphed into one of those precious *New Yorker* poems:

Aspects of Byrne
(After Weldon Kees)

David eating French fries at the Algonquin; Ghosts
Of midgets huddle outside the door.
Taxis row down West 44th
Nothing here resembles CBGBs and this
Is just fine.

David walking in the Park,
Buying reefer beside the elephant.
David saying, "Hello. Yes, this is David. Sunday
At five? With the Ramones. I'd love to."

David afraid, drunk, maybe sobbing. David
In bed with Mary Clarke. Sleeping like a corpse.
David downtown at Phebes staring at his
French fries. This is breakfast.

David was now spending so much time at Mary Clarke's apartment on the Upper West Side that he decided to move up there himself. This neighborhood has never really had a bohemian history. But the baby boom in the fifties made it trendy because it was the only place in the city where married intellectuals could find big and affordable spaces.

One winter day, Mary phoned David and told him she'd found an apartment down the street from hers on Riverside Drive that was "to kill for." It was between 113th and 114th Streets. It had two bedrooms, living room, dining room, kitchen, and a maid's quarters. David took it. Then he followed his pattern and invited Jerry and his girlfriend, Linda, and Linda's daughter, Natasha, to move in with him.

Natasha was thirteen. She got the maid's room. Everyone got along fine, but Mary detected something troubling beneath Linda's surface. A fragility of some sort. Something dangerous.

Before Talking Heads embarked on the recording of their next album, they gave interviews. Tina mentioned that she dreamed of an "all-girl band." David dreamed of a collaborator.

No one told the two to be careful what you wish for.

I think life is too short to listen to records.

Brian Eno

king's lead hat

BOOK TWO

more songs about buildings and food

In mid-March, Talking Heads left their domiciles on the Upper West Side and in Long Island City and flew to Chris Blackwell's Compass Point Studios down in the Bahamas to make a record with Brian Eno.

The weather there was great. The studio was new and studio time was cheap. Blackwell was the fortyish president of Island Records and was even more of a renegade record company executive than Seymour Stein. He was a Caribbean-born-and-raised white man—the scion of the Crosse & Blackwell fortune (names that still have resonance with the British upper crust).

If Blackwell were a literary character, he'd have come from the pen of a righteous satirist like Martin Amis. As a kid in Nassau, Blackwell palled around with the Hollywood swashbuckler Errol Flynn as well as James Bond's creator, Ian Fleming. Back in 1961, Fleming arranged Blackwell's first job—as Jamaican liaison for the movie *Dr. No*. In 1962 Blackwell scouted locations and earned £2,700. He went to England and started Island Records, which he named after the Alec Waugh novel *Island in the Sun*.

Blackwell's new studio in Nassau housed something Eno had the hots for called an MCI mixer. Eno was a man who appreciated mixers as much as he appreciated women. He believed the mixer was the heart of the recording studio—a large board with as many as nine hundred knobs in neatly arranged rows controlling the twenty-four recorded tracks. It was possible to control the volume as well as the balance between high and low frequencies for each of those tracks. Many producers kept their characteristic mixer settings as trade secrets.

Eno was well steeped in mixer lore. When Talking Heads first set up at Compass Point, he told them, "During the 1950s, producers tended to mix melodic information very loudly, while putting the rhythmic information in the background—frequently the bass line was almost inaudible. As time went on, this spectrum—which was very wide, with vocals way up there and the bass and drums way down there—began to compress, until at the beginning of funk it was very narrow indeed." Eno credited funk groups like Sly and the Family Stone with actually reversing the 1950s concept of sound priorities. "The rhythm instruments, particularly the bass drum and bass, suddenly become the important instruments in the mix."

Eno loved the MCI mixer. But he really did love women more. He lived for sex. In the early 1970s, Brian Eno did a glam number, appearing onstage with Roxy Music wearing lipstick, mascara, feathers, and a Joni Mitchell–style beret. The press assumed he was a poofter, until he started sharing his dalliances with reporters. He boasted that he sometimes slept with six different girls in one day. Or over two days. Or was it eight girls in two days? Or maybe a dozen girls eight days a week. He once rutted so strenuously that he pulled the cartilage in his knee. Another time, hard sex caused one of his lungs to collapse.

Eno fancied that he should be filmed performing intercourse for educational reasons. In 1974 the yet-to-be Pretender Chrissie Hynde interviewed him for the *New Musical Express,* and he revealed to the girl that although he was broke, he was still a sex god surrounded by women. He even asked if Hynde wanted to view his groin. "I've got this new Japanese thing," he explained. "You see, the Japanese don't have much hair on their bodies."

How crestfallen the young Eno would have been back then if he knew that more than twenty years later he'd write: "Do all men leave this life feeling they've seen nowhere near enough nude people, played with far too few private parts, made a pitifully inadequate contribution to the honey-eyed chorus of bottom-slapping, tit-sucking, cock-pumping, belly-bulging lust issuing from the planet, and generally not fulfilled their once extremely promising experimental destiny?"

In the studio, Talking Heads discovered that Eno—along with his

128

Tonto, engineer Rhett Davies—was the antithesis of Crash 'n' Burn Bongiovi. They didn't use headphones. They didn't do retakes.

The band got the basic tracks done within the first five days. Eno recorded Talking Heads more-or-less live, then used his little toys to fiddle with individual instruments on each track. Some of Eno's devices were nothing more than small compressors like the ones found in radios. He would set them all up and link them straight into the deck so he could substantially, yet delicately, alter the sound of the band.

Many of the songs the band recorded were old ones: "Warning Sign." "The Girls Want to Be with the Girls." "Artists Only." Where Bongiovi had tried to weird up Talking Heads by dropping psychedelic strings on "Psycho Killer," Eno worked from the bottom up. On some songs, he added a slight resonance to Tina's bass so it sounded like she was plucking big black snakes. Eno made layers of guitars sound like percussion or twittering insects. Occasionally, he made the sonic space surrounding David's voice buckle and burble as if Byrne were some alien life form broadcasting from a radio in outer space.

Jerry Harrison says, "Eno taught us to use the studio as an instrument. To be fearless. In those days, studio people wore lab coats. It was like getting your blood taken. They're on that side of the glass and you're on this side. Eno broke that down entirely."

Sometimes a friendly disagreement about a bass track or something would come up during the session, and Jerry saw similarities between the arguing styles of Brian Eno and David Byrne and Jonathan Richman—all three, self-educated men. "People who are sort of self-educated and very bright feel emotionally attached to their ideas," Jerry said. "But in college, you're taught to break things down. To give credence to another's argument."

Eno liked monkeying with the intentions of the musicians as much as with the sounds they were creating. He and his painter friend Peter Schmidt created a set of tarot cards called "Oblique Strategies." Each card contained a single instruction. A musician picked one at random, then followed its instruction. For example:

> Go slowly all the way round the outside.
> Don't be afraid of things because they're easy to do.
> Only a part, not the whole.

129

Turn it upside down.

Don't break the silence.

What are you really thinking about just now?

These Oblique Strategy cards have become an indispensable part of Eno lore, although there are few reports of any of the numerous musicians he produced actually using them. Talking Heads never consulted these cards even though one would think David above all would appreciate Eno's "system theory" of playing cards. "I kinda liked the Oblique Strategy cards as this exteriorizing of how the mind actually works," David recalled. "How intuition works. Makes leaps. This was him trying to manifest how this thing works. But if you already do that in your mind, you've got your own interior set of cards. You don't need somebody's else's."

David worked closely with Tina on a new song called "The Good Thing." He wanted to have "Chinese sing-songy" effects on it. He had gotten into Chinese rhetoric, which to him seemed a governmental response to management theory, another concept he had recently become interested in—"Theories about how the structure of a business can be like that of an organism. And how the creative process can be broken down like a flow chart."

These were not the usual concerns of Mao Tse Tung (spelling in 1978) let alone a typical rock 'n' roller. Eno added a massive choir to the piece, made up of the secretaries at Compass Point (one of whom he had a crush on). One could imagine the whole song sung at one of those Red Chinese football-stadium-style group demonstrations, a thousand young women chanting the first lines of David's song, "I will fight, will fight with my heart. I will fight, will fight with understanding."

Never before had there been a rock 'n' roll love song with the singer spouting phrases like "absolute trust" and "try to compare what I am presenting" and "as we economize, efficiency is multiplied." Then come the Chinese girls again, singing, "Cut back the weakness/Reinforce what is strong."

This was not your parents' rock 'n' roll—even if you were born in Red China. David would later call this his "record business" song.

The lyrics of another song, "Stay Hungry," came from a muscle magazine Chris saw on a newsstand. David wrote "Found a Job" after visiting his parents and arguing about what to watch on TV. "Their TV has really bad reception," he told British writer Barry Miles. "My father found it on the street and fixed it up."

The band also decided to cover an Al Green song, "Take Me to the River." Since RISD, David, under Chris's influence, had been an Al Green fan. The Artistics covered Green's "Love and Happiness." "Which was even more ridiculous than me singing 'Take Me to the River,' " David later remarked. Two years before when David wrote "Happy Day," he had envisioned it as an Al Green song. When the song was cut for *Talking Heads '77*, David sang it in self-conscious imitation of Al Green.

"Take Me to the River" went over well when Talking Heads played it at clubs. It was a great world-weary Sinatra-ish kind of song. A man's woman takes his money, his cigarettes. Then she teases him. Squeezes him. And all he wants is to be dunked in a river. David got the song. "It combines teenage lust with baptism. Not equates, you understand, but throws them in the same stew."

"I wrote 'Take Me to the River' in 1973," Al Green recalls. It has been said that Green wrote the song for fellow soul artist Syl Johnson, who recorded it first, but that's not the case. "I didn't really write it for him," Green said. "Me and Teenie Hodges—my guitar player—were at Lake Hamilton in Hot Springs, Arkansas, which is about 180 miles from Memphis. They rent houses and chalets on the lake. At Lake Hamilton you can have a house with a phone. You can have one without a phone. You can have one with or without a TV. Shopping malls are miles and miles away. You're down by the lake. You go and open the sliding door, and there's a screen there, and the lake is out front there, and the whole thing going and going—it's gorgeous.

"We'd stayed out there three days to write songs. That's why we wrote 'Take Me to the River,' because I was down by the river. We wrote it without music really. I was trying to get more stability in my life at the time. I wrote, 'Take me to the river. Wash me down. Cleanse my soul. Put my feet on the ground.' Teenie and I worked out the music when we got back to Memphis."

For the Talking Heads version of this song, Eno suggested that they produce only single notes on the piece. No double notes. The band could just play one *pin* or *bop* or *pang*. The sound was then treated by Eno's synthesizer to give it a delay, an echo. A real "underwater sound" as Tina later put it. The band also wanted the song to appear to get louder and louder without having to begin quietly. To get this effect, Eno pulled a gadget from his bag-of-tricks called a "limiter," a mechanism that "crushed" the sound with more and more severity as the song went on. "It's not actually getting louder," Eno told BBC Radio Two, "but it makes your ears think they're hearing something that is getting louder all the time." He called his version of Al Green's song a "psychological trick."

A great Al Green vibe appeared to be sweeping the planet during this time. Bryan Ferry was cutting the same song for his new album. David thinks this was a coincidence. "Foghat and one of the guys from the Band also recorded versions around that time."

"Take Me to the River" would appear on the second Talking Heads record called, *Tina and the Typing Pool,* which was scheduled to be released in July. The title was David's. After a number of other bad suggestions, Tina lamented, "What are we gonna call an album that's just about buildings and food?"

"That's the title," Jerry said.

The band then began a Northeast tour in May. For David, New England was a piece of cake compared to the last European tour. Jerry swore that there wasn't anyone who understood the road better than Gary Kurfirst. Talking Heads' manager was creating a whole new circuit. Kurfirst would march into a club that previously only billed top-forty bands and say, "I have this act. I know you've never heard of them. Can you give us a guarantee of $200, but I want 50 percent of the door." And they'd do it. "We're awful soft on Tuesdays. What do we have to lose? Two hundred dollars?" Kurfirst was opening up a whole new territory that groups like the Police and Devo would follow.

And onstage in these clubs, David found himself being taken over by the live act even more than he had the year before. "The adrenaline rush for me is complete," he told Barry Miles. "I seem to be running around while everyone else is in slow motion. It's exciting but frightening and wonderful. The only thing that disappoints me is when a crowd shouts out for the better known songs—that's not likely to boost your opinion of an audience."

When playing live, Talking Heads understood the audience could become a mindless beast. You could understand how Bucky Wunderlick's audiences could be driven on a rampage of rape and pillage. But the Heads hated it when the bouncers manhandled the crowd.

On this tour, the band also noticed a peculiar similarity between Jerry and David—both men now shared the common trait of bolting their food. A breakfast of scrambled eggs, potatoes, and toast would be gone in three minutes. A hamburger, forget it.

Then Jerry began throwing up onstage. Not because he ate too fast. Unbeknownst to him, Jerry's body had begun to actually combine buildings and food. Back in New York, he'd spent as much time as possible renovating a loft he'd bought in Tina's building over in Long Island City. This task involved sandblasting the space. Now his lungs and stomach were coated with tiny particles of concrete. Suddenly, without any warning, he'd get sick onstage.

He had become a walking casualty of Manhattan real estate.

Talking Heads returned from the tour a day or two before Philip Glass played a recital at Carnegie Hall on May 28. Glass was now making money. He no longer had to hack. If you asked him about it, he'd tell you that he'd just read one of Mozart's letters describing people singing arias from *The Marriage of Figaro* in every coffeeshop in town. In Mozart's time there wasn't such a distance between a popular audience and a highbrow one. While Glass didn't encounter people whistling *Einstein on the Beach* at Food down in SoHo, he'd finally become popular enough that his pockets were heavy with dough.

He was also aware that he'd influenced rock groups. Friends would play him New Wave records that sounded particularly minimal, or disks by Bowie or Eno or the Cars, and say, "These guys are ripping off *your* ideas." This didn't bother Glass. "People were going to make money off my ideas in a way that I'm not capable of or interested in doing," he told them. "It doesn't bother me. The two kinds of music are just different."

Glass was even hanging around with Brian Eno: "I'd be having French fries and coffee at Phoebe's on the Bowery and Fourth, and Brian would bop by and say, 'Let's go see this new band called the B-52's.' "

Mary and David had been together for nearly two years. Mary believed that with modern relationships two years was the red-flag date. "You're either going to be together or not," she said.

They decided to find a place and move in together. It shouldn't be a big change. They were practically living with each other uptown as it was. It felt comfortable working and relaxing. David had a little typewriter and would type lyrics up in all caps, then just leave what he wrote in the machine knowing that Mary wouldn't read it behind his back. The summer before, Mary's parents went to France, and she and David lived in the Clarkes' row house on Eighty-seventh and East End. The two had lots of privacy. He wrote up a storm.

It wouldn't inconvenience Jerry if David moved out. Jerry was planning to move himself with Linda and Natasha back to Long Island City any day now. It was Jerry who told David about a loft he'd heard about down on East Seventh Street and Avenue A—a six-floor walkup. David and Mary went down to see it. It had light in front and none anywhere else. Across the street was a funeral parlor, but it seemed cheerful as funeral parlors go.

In those days, lofts were not snatched up immediately, so David and Mary decided to think about taking it and make a decision after Talking Heads' next European tour.

The second European tour of 1978 began as poorly as the winter one. The timing stank—it coincided with World Cup soccer championships. The crowds were thin in every country.

At least late spring on the Continent was beautiful. David and Jerry took a week off and motored through the French and Italian settings of *Tender Is the Night* and *Farewell to Arms*. Jerry remembered this trip went great. They had "girls" with them.

Later, David was asked about the dames. "I think we had our girlfriends with us," he said. "They must have flown out to meet us. We went to San Remo. Drove to Portofino. Monte Carlo. We were thrilled to be on the loose."

Mary Clarke said no. She most definitely did not go to Europe.

Jerry Harrison was asked about the "girls" again and looked alarmed. He said that he and David traveled alone. Then he started to say something. Then he went quiet. Then he said, "Until Paris. I had girlfriends in Paris."

In early summer, David returned to Manhattan. Mary said, "I think we should take the loft on East Seventh Street." David answered, "About that loft. I don't think we should move in together." His statement didn't mean he was breaking up with her. In those days, young men and women negotiated all kinds of semi-monogamous confederations. "We would still see each other," Mary said. "Go out to dinner. We were still kind of together. Just not formally. Then it just petered out."

There is something remarkably true yet ordinary about David's romance with Mary. This is not rock 'n' roll. This is not British bobbies bursting into Mick Jagger's home, catching him eating a candy bar between Marianne Faithfull's legs.

More than two decades later, Mary said, "I think breaking up was an honest move on David's part. I also think going on tour—he was *this guy*. Now David is not somebody who would run around on me. But there were all these girls and women throwing themselves at him. Who wouldn't want to take advantage of being young and famous and who wouldn't want to date a lot of women? It's crazy not to be able to partake of that."

After Mary and David had petered out, she kept running into him at downtown clubs. He was always with *a lot* of different women. Others confirm seeing David at clubs with *beautiful* women. In 1978 David Byrne was not yet big enough to be a rock star, but at least he was finally acting like a man about town. Although David admitted nothing about women—beautiful ones or otherwise—he did sum up those days this way: "For awhile I was hanging out and getting high and chatting with people and staying up as late as I could. I didn't have anything else to do except write songs. If I woke up at noon or one in the afternoon and started writing songs, that was okay. But after awhile you can't do it anymore. You have more things to handle in your life besides writing songs."

One of the people David socialized with was Brian Eno. They hung out. They went to clubs. Eno was someone that David felt he could talk to about what was important. They talked about music and ideas. Eno would put on a record—say, Steve Reich's *It's Gonna Rain*. "This is the most important piece of music that I've heard," Eno would insist as he sat back down. The record started and revealed itself to be the repetitious mantra of a black preacher saying, "It's gonna rain."

"Minimal music is like a frog's eye," Eno might say, revealing that he had just read a wonderful essay called "What the Frog's Eye Told the Frog's Brain," by Warren McCulloch. "Frog's eyes don't work like ours. We're always looking about. Blinking. Moving our heads. But frogs fix their eyes on a scene and just stare. A frog soon stops seeing the static parts of the environment. It's invisible. But as soon as something moves, it's seen in very high contrast to the rest of the environment. The frog shoots his tongue out." Eno demonstrated. "And eats it."

It's gonna rain. It's gonna rain. . . .

"The same thing happens with the Reich piece," Eno said.

On June 17, Eno's *Before & After Science* was released. *Crawdaddy* remarked, "Brian Eno is an agent from some other time and some other place who seems to know something that we don't but should." Record review enthusiasm, but was it true that young Eno had been abducted by a UFO? Perhaps Eno was responsible for the colorful art graffiti of dogs barking at flying saucers that had begun appearing in the subways of New York. Perhaps it was even Eno who was behind all SAMO messages that had begun appearing on the streets of NoHo. On Church Street. West Broadway in SoHo.

SAMO as an alternative 2 god.
SAMO as an end to midwah religious, nowhere politicos and
bogus philosophy.
SAMO as an escape clause.
SAMO as an end 2 Vinyl Punkery.
SAMO for the so-called avant-garde.
SAMO as an end 2 confining art terms. Riding around in
Daddy's convertible with trust fund money.
SAMO as an end to this crap . . . SoHo Too! . . .

Then this curious message:

Pay for soup. Build a Fort. Set that on Fire.

Another fortune cookie message began appearing: ENO IS GOD. Those three words appeared everywhere. Bars. Telephone booths. Subway billboards.

When Eno was asked, "Do you think there's a God?" he said, "I don't ever use that word."

While a small number of New Yorkers proclaimed Eno as God, the Lord himself perhaps decided to give Eno a glimpse into divine insight. Eno was out walking the streets of Manhattan when he felt like he'd seen through a crack in reality—his epiphany occurred in Chinatown. This was far from the rarefied air of the Upper West Side, let alone the SAMO territory of SoHo. Eno liked shopping in Chinatown for weird odds and ends. The smell of burned meat was in the air from a shish kebab stand. He passed by windows hung full with dead red ducks. Windows full of water and huge fish with the faces of old men. An Asian dwarf writing calligraphy on the window of a bank. It struck him that New York was like a medieval European city.

New York existed in the Dark Ages.

That was his private vision of New York. Eno's public vision was a compilation album titled *No New York*. It contained music from four New York "No Wave" bands. New noir historian Glenn O'Brien believed that the term "No Wave" came from French New Wave film director Jean-Luc Godard's comment, "There are no new waves, there is only the ocean." The so-called No Wave bands came after the '75/'76 CBGBs era of Talking Heads. The four bands Eno recorded were the Contortions, Mars, D.N.A., and Teenage Jesus and the Jerks. Like Talking Heads, each group contained a female member. A woman played slide guitar for the Contortions. Another woman did organ. Both D.N.A. and Mars had female drummers à la Moe Tucker (Velvet Underground). Someone named China Burg played guitar for Mars, and based on her photo, China was a girl. Teenage Jesus and the Jerks was headed by singer Lydia Lunch, the girl who was sweet on David when he played with John Cale in 1976. These No Wave men and women performed songs with titles like "Puerto Rican Ghost" and "Egomaniac's Kiss" and "Dish it Out." Each of the bands really did dish it out. They blared. All the songs have the same relentless tempo no matter what group is playing them. They all begin at the same dissident space of "Sister Ray."

More than two decades later, *No New York* is quaint but impossible to enjoy. The post–No Wave group Sonic Youth has mined the motherlode of feedback dead dry. One can only guess at its appeal to Eno. This music must have seemed dangerous back then. Dangerous noise. Kids playing with matches downstairs by the furnace.

Tina and David worked together on the cover for *More Songs About Buildings and Food*. They used a Polaroid camera to create a mosaic portrait of the band made up of 529 individual photos.

About this time Tina started to disappear from the public narration of Talking Heads. The record got good reviews, but when *Newsweek,* for instance, did a story on the band, they illustrated it with a dressing room shot that showed Tina sitting behind the guys with her trademark Joan of Arc 'do, but with a troubling dulled look in her eye. Maybe she was frightened. Or in pain. She must have looked that way when she had bronchitis back in Europe. In the body of the article, David, Jerry, and Chris were quoted extensively. Tina was barely mentioned.

The *Washington Post* seemed to think *More Songs About Buildings and Food* was a "punk" album, and after praising Brian Eno's production, said, "None of the musicians . . . seem to have more than an elementary knowledge of their instruments. Chris Frantz's drums and Tina Weymouth's bass never proceed beyond a rudimentary thrashing and any rhythmic nuance is apparently beyond their grasp."

No one in Washington, D.C.—or anywhere else for that matter— was calling Tina the "Queen of the Bass Players" anymore.

It took the *New York Times* almost five months to digest the album. At least reporter Robert Palmer managed to understand the record without slamming Tina. In the fall, Palmer wrote that Talking Heads was a white funk band. He explained that they accomplished this by mastering "grooves." He then defined the term for Caucasians as insinuated rhythms felt in the listener's body. Palmer then correctly pointed out that "essentially all four Talking Heads are rhythm players." He said that the organ and synthesizer "emphasizes the grooves rather than sweetens them." He then praised Eno's wise mixing of David's vocals down below the bass, guitar, and drums. Palmer didn't think "Mr. Byrne [was] a James Brown love machine," but he no longer sounded like an "about-to-be-decapitated chicken." Even the essence of grooves is emphasized by the song placement on side one. Each cut "moves along relentlessly, song to song, groove to groove, with just enough space between selections to signal transitions without losing momentum."

When the summer of '78 was over, so was punk. The Sex Pistols' Sid Vicious had stabbed his girlfriend to death—or perhaps he was successfully framed for her slaying. *(Psycho killer, qu'est-ce que c'est?)* In either case, the murder was the perfect nihilistic end to the punk era. The song that ended the new Talking Heads record was a more devastating attack on suburban America than any of the howling rants on *Never Mind the Bollocks.* It fulfilled the requirements of a punk critique and at the same time was full of eloquence and wit, as well as a catchy melody. The song is called "The Big Country." David got the title from the TV show *The Big Valley.* He wrote the lyrics flying back from Toronto. It begins with the singer flying over the coastline of America. (Jerry plays slide guitar in the background.) David describes what he sees in flat detail like the unreadable French *nouveau roman* author Robbe-Grillet. The singer flies above a baseball diamond. A school. Parking lots. Restaurants. Freeways. Suburbs. He makes assumptions—it's healthy down there. The people enjoy their neighbors. All the kitchens are clean and well stocked with bounty. He can just imagine all those trips to and from the supermarket.

The chorus is very simple. David Byrne sings:

I wouldn't live there if you paid me.
I wouldn't live like that, no siree!

Lester Bangs, the only rock critic of the twentieth century to be canonized by his readers, wrote of this song, "Finally somebody said it: There is nothing beyond Jersey; Jack Kerouac made all that shit up, he was a science-fiction writer."

David would end up feeling sheepish about the song. He'd claim this was not his literal perspective. It was just a song. He added the "I wouldn't live there if you paid me" because he thought, "Wouldn't it be interesting after giving this objective description to just slam it with some biased emotional response to it?"

Imagine young David Byrne of 1972 magically transported to 1978, pedaling his little ice cream cart through rows of neat streets, but not in the suburbs of Baltimore. Imagine him selling Good Humor at Love Canal near Niagara Falls. This is the summer that the citizens have learned that President Carter has declared their town a federal disaster area because of chemical contamination. Children and pregnant women will be evacuated from their suburban homes. Eventually three hundred houses in Love Canal will be buried.

139

On July 10, Andy Warhol cabbed up to Forty-fourth and Sixth Avenue to the studio of Sire Records to do a commercial for the new Talking Heads record.

His only lines were, "Tell 'em Warhol sent ya." For some reason, "Tell 'em Warhol sent ya" got Warhol tongue-tied. "It came out like I was reading it every time," he wrote in his diary.

On July 31, Television disbanded. On August 30, "Take Me to the River" was released as a single. It became Talking Heads' first top-thirty hit. Al Green heard it on the radio. "I think Talking Heads are a super little group," he said. "I thought they were great. I guess the public thought so, too—here and in London. The record sold quite a bit. It's just fantastic."

At the end of the month, Andrea Kovacs wrote David a furious letter complaining that he had ripped off her mosaic photographic style. Mary Clarke remembered that Kovacs's Polaroid work wasn't mosaic so much as continuous action shots like movie frames.

During August and September, Talking Heads toured Boston, Detroit, Chicago, Minneapolis, Vancouver, Seattle, Portland, and San Francisco. Tina remembers, "We were playing in the quad at Berkeley. Just as we started playing 'Psycho Killer,' a guy walked onstage up to Chris and told him Mayor Moscone and city supervisor Harvey Milk had just been gunned down." Talking Heads also played Los Angeles, Tucson, Houston, Austin. The last time the band played Austin, Tina had been the road manager. She'd collect the money at the end of the night and find the club owner sitting with all the cash next to a gun on the table. She remembered all through Texas and Arkansas there were nothing but evangelists on the radio. And they were always talking about the Devil, not one word about God.

By the end of November the band had become the highest-charting New Wave act, as *More Songs About Buildings and Food* hit number 29 in *Billboard.*

How did this happen? There were cuts on *More Songs* that were pretty strange. Take the opening one, "Thank You for Sending Me an Angel," with its galloping beat and David Byrne yellin' out, "Ohhhhhhhhh ho baby you can walk, you can talk just like me." This was a Buck Owens song performed at the metabolic rate of a squirrel.

Maybe David wasn't as odd as he seemed. We can gain insight into his character by examining the movies he watched. "Before we broke up, we went to two or three movies a week," Mary remembered. "I'm sure a lot of people would think we just went to art movies, and it wasn't like that at all. David was definitely checking out mass-market offerings."

The couple passed up intellectual flicks like Lina Wertmuller's *Seven Beauties* or Luis Buñuel's *That Obscure Object of Desire,* and instead ate popcorn at populist middle-brow dramas like *Network* or lowbrow Sylvester Stallone movies. David and Mary saw *Saturday Night Fever* and *Close Encounters of the Third Kind* as well as Brian De Palma's *Carrie.* They went to the now-forgotten futuristic flick *Logan's Run.*

These are simple movies, films not just playing in Manhattan, but in all the cities that Talking Heads had visited.

Other rock groups were also on the road. The Grateful Dead performed in Egypt at the great pyramids. Sid Vicious was out on bail and played Max's Kansas City. Keith Moon couldn't perform anymore. He died that fall. As the air got colder, more SAMO messages appeared on the streets of SoHo and TriBeCa: *SAMO as a result of overexposure.* On Halloween, farther downtown, something called the Mudd Club opened. Located at 77 White Street, it was founded by Steve Maas, ex–University of Iowa writing student. He got money for the club from his family's ambulance and medical-supply business, but a rumor circulated that Brian Eno was part owner—a secret partner. The Mudd Club soon became a hot-spot supreme. David Bowie hung out there. Eno, of course. Iggy Pop. Andy Warhol, who was now doing two piss paintings a day ("I think I may try brushing the piss on the piss paintings now."). And David Byrne when he came back from being on tour. David Byrne with beautiful women.

Another Mudd Club citizen was an African-American seventeen-year-old kid with a blond mohawk and the beautiful name of Jean-Michel Basquiat. He turned out to be SAMO. He and his buddy Al Diaz invented the word when they were stoned. It was pronounced "say mo," as in *same old shit.* SAMO was a play off of that expression and Little Black Sambo, and an Eno-ish anagram of Amos, as in *Amos 'n' Andy.*

At Christmas, Eno flew to Thailand. His first night in Bangkok, he strolled into the red-light district. In the fourth bar he visited he spied the cover of Roxy Music's *For Your Pleasure* pinned to the wall. The German brothel keeper was a fan who sent Eno to his whorehouse up in the mountains. In between bouts in bed, Eno read from a book he brought from New York, *The Class System in India.* He also listened to Beethoven's late string quartets, as well as a BBC recording of spoken English dialects similar to the voice

John Lennon used for "Revolution 9" on the *White Album*. And he enjoyed the girls there for free.

Eno was still a love god.

On December 29, 1978, the Heads played the New Year's Eve party at the Beacon Theater. Talking Heads opened the concert with "The Big Country."

I wouldn't live there if you paid me.

What if you were in an airplane like the narrator of the song and you were flying above New York City? Would you want to live down there? What if you could make out the Mecca of Disco America, Studio 54. In mid-December, some fifty agents of the IRS Criminal Investigation Division backed up by a contingency from the DEA invaded Studio 54—that citadel of everything gaudy and decadent, where only those rich enough or famous enough or gay enough were allowed to shake their booty to hideously vapid disco, that fake music built of the bones of American funk. The officers did not attempt to burst into Studio 54 through the front door. The bouncers would have never let fellows so straight and honest looking through the door. Instead, the police came in through the basement, where they removed a safe with the club's real books. They also found Hefty bags stuffed with cash hidden in the walls. Owner Steve Rubell was later arrested in his Mercedes, with $100,000 in the trunk.

When David sang "Artists Only" on New Year's Eve, the line "I don't have to prove that I'm creative" came out with unusual bitterness. Because David did, in fact. He had to come up with songs for the third Talking Heads album. Their repertoire had dried up. There were no old songs in the can. He didn't want the group to repeat themselves. David believed that the first couple of records are based on your twenty-odd years of experience—however wide or narrow that must be. "The third record is all the experience you've had in between record one and record two. But that experience is basically just touring."

Especially if one's manager was Gary Kurfirst. He would promote concerts himself if a promoter couldn't be found. Jerry would reflect years later that maybe the Heads could have grown more quickly if a different manager had worked that hard to get the record company to spend more money on promotion. Maybe yes. Maybe no. Whatever the answer, David couldn't just write songs about touring. Jackson Browne got away with his oh-the-troubles-of-touring album, *Running on Empty*, but then Jackson Browne was from California.

As the new year began, David wondered if new songs would come more quickly if he wrote them on a keyboard. At least he'd come up with different kinds of melodies. For the first two records, he composed songs by strumming the guitar and using those chords to generate the melodies. His chords sounded strange but they were easy to play on the guitar. It was possible to come up with quirky chords accidentally. An idiot savant with a guitar could produce some interesting stuff.

hoovering

January 26, 1979, was the day that Nelson Rockefeller died in the saddle, "riding," as it were, his young secretary, Megan Marshack, in a love nest across the street from the Museum of Modern Art. Rocky was dead, and it was about this time that Chris and Tina heard Seymour was taking David on a trip to Trinidad.

Chris was hurt. How could Seymour not invite them? Again and again, Chris had told Seymour how much he loved Trinidadian music.

Tina was still steamed about the guitar thing. Three days before their European tour, both David's and Tina's guitars had been stolen from the loft in Long Island City. Jerry had left a door open. Tina was asleep. Chris was over at Yann's. Some guys came in through the front door and grabbed whatever they could—guitars.

While Tina raced all over town trying to replace her guitar in time for the tour, Seymour bought David not one but two guitars. Now Seymour was taking David down to the Caribbean.

David was the golden boy.

Seymour's boy toy.

His pet.

Just like Brian Epstein taking John Lennon on a holiday to Spain.

Linda Stein semi-outed her husband, Seymour, in Legs McNeil's *Please Kill Me: The Uncensored Oral History of Punk*. She babbled that Dee Dee

Ramone once slept with Seymour. "I mean Dee Dee slept with everybody and anybody. And he made you feel good. I mean, he was a professional hooker!"

"Seymour was always active sexually," Chris Frantz said. "In the *gay* way."

"He signed pretty boy bands," Tina added.

"I heard later from people that Seymour Stein was gay," Mary Clarke admitted. "I think there are so many things I was oblivious to and not a part of. I didn't see that in Seymour. I went to his house. He had a wife and kids. Seymour was so nice. Such an interesting person. They had a fabulous apartment at 135 Central Park West. There was a study off the living room filled from floor to ceiling with records—45s. It was the most amazing record collection that I've ever seen."

When David returned it was apparent to Chris and Tina that something had happened down in Trinidad. First, he wouldn't talk about the trip. Second, he wouldn't talk about Seymour except to say, "I hate him."

The week David returned, *SAMO is dead* had began appearing on the walls of SoHo. Basquiat and Diaz had split up. *SAMO is dead* was their epitaph.

On February 2, Sid Vicious was dead, as well. Drug overdose. During this month of death, Eno was in the city helping to mix the new Bowie album, *Lodger*. After bickering at the controls, the two had a falling-out. "I borrow and steal everything that fascinates me," Bowie later said. Mick Jagger once made the comment, "Never wear a new pair of shoes in front of David." By the end of *Lodger*, Eno was apparently sucked dry and discarded.

Later that month, Talking Heads appeared on *Saturday Night Live*. David still wouldn't talk about Seymour or Trinidad. In March, the band appeared on that old warhorse *American Bandstand* to play "Take Me to the River." They didn't exactly *play* it. David sang the song, but Talking Heads pantomimed at their instruments.

Dick Clark more or less invented lip-synching and air guitar (rockers pretending to strum their guitars). *American Bandstand* began in the early 1950s as a bunch of Philadelphia teenagers dancing on a set that was supposed to be a school gym. After the original host of the show was arrested

145

for drunk driving, Dick Clark took over. By 1957 *American Bandstand* was on sixty-seven stations every weekday, and his troupe of professional teen dancers was busy popularizing the Stroll and the Mashed Potato. After the British invasion of 1964, the show seemed out-of-date, but it stayed on the air to serve the social function of reassuring parents that not all kids were hippie drug fiends.

When Talking Heads finished "playing" "Take Me to the River," Dick Clark padded over to chat with David, but the singer went somewhere else inside his head. He froze up.

The show was live. Now Dick Clark could do a back flip and land on his feet. He didn't let David's freeze-up freeze him. Dick Clark passed the microphone over to Tina.

She was shocked. No one ever talked to her. Dick Clark asked, "Tina, is David always this way?" Tina answered immediately. She remembered something Yann's girlfriend, Julie, had said about David—David was "organically shy." So that's what Tina said, "David is organically shy."

That broke the ice.

David later told friends, "Dick Clark looked preserved. He seemed real but in a calculated way." In modern terms, he thought Dick Clark was *virtual real.*

By spring, Talking Heads was ready to record its third album. They went into a New York studio without a producer just to see what would happen, but the result sounded as phony as *American Bandstand*. The band had always rehearsed at Chris and Tina's loft, why not record the basic tracks there with Eno?

So on April 22 and two weeks later on May 6, a Record Plant truck parked outside Chris and Tina's building and ran cables in through the window.

During these two sessions, Talking Heads played some of the most brilliant and obscure songs David had ever written. Tina was on the fence about many of them. But David was great at convincing the band that something crazy would end up brilliant. Take his new song "Paper." It compared a love affair to a simple sheet of paper. Tina didn't like it for a long time. But as they were recording it, everyone's playing got tighter. The song fulfilled her vision of David (as she once told *Creem* magazine), that his songs will "start off a mess but become like a baby koala bear."

David had an even more obscure song called "Air." It was a protest against the atmosphere. "It's not a joke," he insisted. He explained that he wanted to write a song that would be as melancholy and touching as the best songs in *Threepenny Opera*. The song was about a guy who feels so down that *even air feels painful.*

Finally David had written a song about finding a city to live in, a song that only emphasizes how Talking Heads' prejudice has always been for urban homes. If the story of this band were a movie, it would be filmed in Paris. Boston. Providence. Hollywood. Even Milwaukee. But more than any other urban locale, Talking Heads was a story of Manhattan.

At the end of the nineteenth century, kids ran away from home to join the circus. For the last hundred years, kids have run away from home to be writers or artists or rock stars or waitresses. In cities. Maybe Seattle. Maybe L.A. But certainly New York. This town has been the "circus" for how many of the "usual suspects"? Andy Warhol ran away here. So did Jackson Pollock, Patti Smith, Martha Graham, Lou Reed. Even Auden and Trotsky. Where else would David Byrne find a home other than the original Gotham City?

Eno liked what he heard that first day. Two weeks later, on the second day of recording, Tina wasn't feeling so great. Eno found himself at the sink doing the Frantz/Weymouth dishes to help out. As he stood there, he observed David moving around the loft, whistling an idiotic tune as if he were a janitor cleaning up. He told Eno this was music "to do housework by." David Byrne later called this kind of music "Hoovering."

One of David's new songs was *Hoovering supreme*. It was called "Heaven," and its melody was luscious while the lyrics wryly compared paradise to a party where everyone leaves at "exactly the same time." Through the years David has listed the different influences that led to the song: David and Mary went to Bleecker Street Cinema and saw Werner Herzog's *Fata Morgana*, a documentary in which Germans are interviewed about their visions of heaven. David had been listening to Neil Young's *Zuma* and *Tonight's the Night*, and he was trying to write a Werner Herzog/Neil Young song. In addition, the verse was a chord sequence lifted from "The Rose of San Antone." Whatever the influences, the result was a melody that was in theory as pleasant as anything the Carpenters had ever sung. Yet Eno's ear told him the chords in the song's chorus *almost* clashed. The first chord in the chorus was in D major. Eno didn't know that. The next chord was in

B minor. Eno didn't know that either. Although Eno couldn't read music, his ear told him the pairing of those two chords was a very conventional thing to do. But the next chord was A minor. This chord wasn't even in the song's original key. It was a bizarre move. But it worked. It made the song simultaneously incredibly primitive and incredibly sophisticated.

David's new songs were the first that he had written entirely with what he referred to as "the more extensive sound palette that Jerry brought to the band." The melody of "Heaven" was originally in a key that David had trouble singing. Jerry solved the problem by suggesting the whole thing be played in a different key. It worked. Jerry and David found it very exciting to be working this way on new songs.

David always felt that he sang in his natural voice with phrasing similar to speech. Eno encouraged him to push the envelope of his vocal technique. For a peculiar song about an electric guitar getting run over by a car on the highway, David tried to sing as if he was mentally retarded. In the end, he sounded *too* retarded and had to redo the track.

148

He tried to sing "Heaven" like Frank Sinatra. On "Electricity," he ran in place to get a breathy quality into his voice while he sang. On very good speakers you can even hear his keys jingling. On "Memories Can't Wait," Eno used one of his toys to give David's voice a weird reverb, which makes the singer sound less like the usual Swiss mountaineer echoing in the Alps and more like a man being mocked by the voices of devils and demons.

Truth be told, Eno thought singing was mostly inconsequential. He himself liked singing with a nasal voice, singing through his nose as it were. "What I like is when you get a combination of something that's very turned down and dark and sinister, but not dramatic, very underhand and almost inaudible, as opposed to the kind of aggression that people like the [Pink] Floyd use, which is very obvious assault. Iggy Pop does it as well. . . . I like taking something that's played down low-key, contrasting with a voice that's very anguished, making the whole sound grotesque and aggressive in a pathetic and laughable way. 'Baby's on Fire' starts out as though it's going to be very sinister, but has very ordinary words, sung with an incredible amount of passion."

David didn't sing through his nose. He'd secretly grown proud of his voice. Two years before, John Rockwell wrote, "David Byrne's voice has dramatically improved. . . . He started going to a voice teacher because of harshness, and is now working with her to better his vocal quality and control."

David claims that he only took singing lessons for a few weeks, schlepping up to a teacher's apartment on the Upper East Side. The woman made him sing scales. When she wanted him to do Broadway show tunes, he stopped. "I'm not going to sit around my house singing, 'Send in the Clowns.' I'm sorry."

Eno proved he could make Talking Heads commercial with the last year's *More Songs About Buildings and Food*. Now the group wanted him to really weird up the tracks for their third effort—Talking Heads was in a position to make the album that Seymour originally feared they'd make when they let Eno into their cage.

So Eno started to weird the album plenty. No one has ever really understood what *postmodern* is supposed to mean, but by any standards, Eno was turning the Long Island City tapes into a postmodern masterpiece.

On "Electricity," Eno stripped everything from the mix until all that was left is a snare drum and some guitar. To replace the air pockets, Eno and David worked on parts simultaneously without each other's knowledge. For example, Eno would play half a bass part and David would play the other. Then both parts were merged together into one. Later, as Eno was adding a layer of distant bird sounds, he knew that this album was going to be weirder and funkier than any rock 'n' roll record that had come before.

149

CHAPTER 16

fear of music

Before the album's release, David retitled "Electricity." He called it "Drugs." The song begins with Eno's distant birds. Then the percussive sound of metal against metal. Then the drums kick in for real. Something is breathing deeply in the background. Next, a few edgy notes on the guitar. Piano. Then a haunting melody. So haunting it's corny. It sounds like hundreds of mandolins. David starts singing, "All I see is little"—suddenly another voice gives a distorted echo in the background as David finishes his thought—"dots."

What drug is the singer on? He tells us there's too much light. That covers a lot of pharmaceuticals. In the song, David goes into his old girls/ boys stuff of the early days, telling us the boys make a "big mess." The girls are all laughing. The boys are worried, the girls are shocked. And none of these ripped participants knows what they're talking about. What drugs could the boys and girls be on—Bennies? Speed? Meth? Possibly. David felt those drugs were all too *chemical*. They have the spooky edge the song "Drugs" has.

Maybe the song is about harmless marijuana. David claimed that grass made him paranoid. And he did get high a few times when he was performing. "But never so much that I didn't know where I was. And what was going on. A little bit of dope performing felt great, but anything beyond that—James Kirk was no longer in charge of the starship."

Maybe the song is about angel dust. A few years before, David went with Chris, Tina, and Yann to an interior decorator's apartment for dinner. The host offered David a cigarette laced with the stuff. Yikes! A few puffs and David felt scared to death. His legs started to wobble so much he could barely walk.

He had tried heroin only once. It was strong. But in a different way from angel dust. Heroin was the epitome of lethargy. David knew he wasn't going to get any writing done on that baby. He recalled Brian Eno's warning: "If you take drugs your creative threshold drops—simple as that. I've smoked and dropped and what have you, but I don't now. The feeling's always the same: How wonderful everything was, followed by six hours of 'Christ, why did I do this? I wish it would go away.' "

Like many fellow citizens under forty, David felt cocaine was the best drug of its time. "Especially for someone like me who wasn't a very social person. Here was this drug that would make you start chatting up a storm. Everyone was in this room just talking a mile a minute." In the song David tells us he doesn't feel like talking, so he's probably not on coke. "But then cocaine was a paradox. An anti-social drug. Because it was so expensive you didn't want to share. Everyone could end up in little cliques hogging their coke."

Coke needed a booze chaser. Indeed, in the eighties, David would spend a New Year's Eve in Los Angeles with Jean-Michel Basquiat—SAMO himself—doing coke and guzzling champagne. Then they went to the Roxy, where they ran into Madonna, who commented on how drunk they both were. When David bumped into her several days later at the Sire office, she made a sly comment about his previously plastered state. David went beet-red. "The girl knew how to pull a power trip even then," he remembered, then added, "which was pretty easy on me."

Linda Stein says, "Where was I with all these drugs? Legs McNeil made it sound like everybody in the CBGBs crowd was doing hard drugs. I never saw heroin. I never saw acid. There was no cocaine on the road with us. There was no cocaine in the studio. It was not part of the picture. And I'm trying to remember everything that I can. I have nothing to prove. No ax to grind. If there was heroin, there was heroin. It there wasn't, there wasn't. But I'm telling you that was not a part of the scene. I had heard Richard Hell was a junkie, but I never saw anything. I had heard that about Tom Verlaine, but I never saw anything. Everyone said Dee Dee was a junkie, but I never saw it backstage or in a studio, anything that had to do with money. Making a record. Doing an interview. Or playing at a gig. I never saw anything like that."

"Quaaludes were around," she added. "But I don't remember the Heads doing quaaludes."

David Byrne says, "On the road people always had drugs. But if you were home, you had to go out and score them yourself. I wasn't interested. I couldn't do it." Chris and Tina had no trouble copping in Long Island City. Eventually the two had to flee to the suburbs of Connecticut to escape the druggie life. Tina would renounce cocaine—"It made the band paranoid"—and come to believe that the drug caused tinnitus, the secret plight of one hundred rock stars. Tinnitus destroys the upper registers of one's hearing, which is why so many records are mixed too strongly in the lower registers.

When the third Talking Heads album was being mixed, Tina's sisters Laura and Lani came in to do background vocals. On the credits they would be billed as the "Sweetbreaths."

Laura Elizabeth Weymouth had changed her name to Laura Nevada Weymouth. She was the wild sister, the one who couldn't wait to leave home. Lani, on the other hand, was training to be a holistic therapist. Tina noticed the way Eno looked at her. Eno obviously had a terrible crush on Lani. The first chance Tina had, she gave a warning: "He's the kind of guy who just moves through women," she intoned. "Brian doesn't have any regard for women. To Eno, girls are just girl Fridays who bring you your slippers."

David wrote nine of the album's eleven tracks. Two numbers came out of jamming. The first would be called "Life During Wartime." David's lyrics describe a Walker Percy–ish post-apocalyptic landscape where a revolutionary hides out in a deserted cemetery, surviving on peanut butter. "I wrote this in my loft on Seventh and Avenue A," David later said. "I was thinking about Baader-Meinhof. Patty Hearst. Tompkins Square. This is a song about living in Alphabet City."

The second jam had no title, let alone lyrics. David didn't know what to do with it. The piece was a funky-sounding instrumental. He couldn't come up with words.

Then suddenly it was June. Talking Heads had to leave New York to go on their first tour of Asia. The track was left unfinished. But once the band was on the jet winging to Asia, neither David nor Jerry could get that cut out of their heads.

Talking Heads played New Zealand, Australia, and Japan. In Tokyo, the group noticed pairs of Japanese walking around wearing headphones connected to what looked like a single skinny tape recorder. The thing was small and lightweight, but it could only play tapes, not record them. Word was the device was invented so Sony's founder, Akio Morita, could listen to music while he played tennis every Tuesday morning at 7:00 A.M. But Sony product development people feared the average American consumer would find it too antisocial to walk around in public listening to a tape player all by yourself—thus duo headphones. Americans will stroll together two-by-two, sharing the sounds of Supertramp and Village People on their Walkmans.

The name was a problem. Walkman? *Walk like a man*. What about a woman? For America, Sony will call this device the Soundabout. Cargo boats bobbed at the ports of Yokohama ready to float hundreds of thousands of Soundabouts to the Yanks.

Jerry didn't need a Soundabout. He still couldn't get that last instrumental track out of his head. He checked the schedule. There was a two-week break in the tour before it resumed in Europe. Jerry convinced David that they should both fly back to New York and finish the song.

On the thirty-hour return flight to Manhattan, Jerry and David went over the group's new contract with Sire. Jerry decided to help draft it. When they finally landed, he found himself wide awake at 5:00 A.M. (8:00 P.M. in Sydney), sitting at a diner in Long Island City going over legal documents with a highlighting pen.

Jerry proposed that instead of giving Talking Heads an advance and a separate recording fund, Sire give the band a blanket amount of money. The group would use this to record an album and pocket whatever was saved.

Jerry proposed that if Sire raised the price of albums, all Talking Heads advances would go up by the same percentage. And he invented what would be known as the "Inflation Clause." "If the rate of inflation is twelve percent, I want our advance to go up twelve percent, as well."

Jerry's final request concerned gold. The global price of gold was moving very quickly. He wanted the Talking Heads' advances tied to the gold rate.

Sire's lawyer went along with everything but the gold standard.

Jerry met David and Eno and Robert Fripp, guitarist extraodinare, at a studio in the city. Fripp added an ax to the instrumental track. Later two street drummers, credited as "Gene Wilder and Ari," were rounded up from Washington Square Park to beat bongos to the cut as well. The result was a tune that begins with tribal drumming. Had Robert Palmer of the *New York Times* been present in the studio, he would have leapt to his feet and begun pogoing up and down. This was a groove. When the Frippery guitar started, Palmer would have whirled like a dervish.

The song was so infectious Palmer might have found himself making up words for it. Unfortunately, David couldn't. He was too exhausted. And he had writer's block.

Again.

The first time he was stricken was last winter, when he was terrified of writing new songs for Talking Heads' third album. He pecked and pecked at that typewriter, but the words that he typed were tired and lame.

Sire's Ken Kushnick found out about David's dry spell. Kushnick loved David's band so much his unofficial title at Sire was Vice President in Charge of Talking Heads. He'd first seen the Heads open for the Ramones at Max's Kansas City back in the old days. When Chris and Tina and David came onstage, Kushnick had been captivated and amazed. "It was probably one of the greatest things I had thought I'd ever seen."

Kushnick told Seymour that David was in trouble. This was when Seymour took David to Trinidad.

"Kenny told me that David was having trouble writing," Seymour remembered. "The year before [1978], I was in Barbados and I ran into Eric Idle [of Monty Python], who said to me, 'You ought to go to Trinidad.' I did and it was great. The music that I brought back with me was like taking a Q-tip and putting it through my head. It cleaned me up and opened me up. So I wanted to take David down there. I didn't want to go there alone. Kenny Kushnick came. The three of us went down to the Port of Spain together. We went to these tents every night where they had this great calypsoians like the Mighty Sparrow. Souca—soul and calypso, a marriage of R&B and calypso. I'm not trying to take credit, but after that David started writing songs."

Seymour Stein was not Brian Epstein and David Byrne was not John Lennon, and Seymour and David's trip to Trinidad had not been made in the same vein as Brian Epstein and John Lennon's vacation to Spain. Of course, writer's block didn't explain David Byrne's rage at Seymour when they returned from the trip.

Time was running out for the completion of the third Talking Heads album. Jerry tried writing lyrics for the song, but David found the verses too literal. Then Eno suggested David just sing a phonic nonsense poem written in the 1920s by Dadaist Hugo Ball.

Ball was one of the founders of Dada. He was the one who coined the term "Dada" after the French word for hobbyhorse. He helped run the Dada nightclub Cabaret Voltaire in Switzerland. It was the CBGBs of its time. Dada historian Ruth Brandon wrote, "Ball, playing accompaniments, encased in bizarre cardboard costumes, [would] liturgically chant his sound-poems, binding all this anarchy together." The particular nonsense syllables that Eno chose started with "blassa galassasa zimbrabim." Another bit went, "a bim beri glassala glandrid." The words didn't mean anything. They were as impenetrable as the legalese in Jerry's contracts. But when David sings "blassa galassasa zimbrabim," those words cease sounding like nonsense. Instead they mix with the music and it sounds like David is singing in an African tongue.

While Jerry and David labored on "I Zimbra," Chris and Tina vacationed in Hawaii. On principle, Tina didn't like it that David and Jerry were mucking around with *their* album. But Chris was always game for a vacation. Truth be told, so was she.

Tina and Chris had no idea what Jerry, David, and Eno were cooking up in New York. Because the Ball poem sounded vaguely like an African incantation when chanted, Talking Heads would begin an African musical odyssey that would consume them for at least half of the 1980s and almost destroy the group in the process.

David's loft was a few doors down from Tompkins Square, that hellhole of druggy Hieronymus Bosch riffraff. He lived on the sixth floor. He liked to sleep with the window open. He liked to sleep naked. The bed in the loft was sunken. He called it the sleeping pit. "I inherited some goofy design elements, and never saw fit to change them," he recalled. One night David was lying in the pit, on his belly, arms beside his body like a dead man, when what sounded like busy mice woke him up. "God, these mice are noisy," he thought, raising his head. "I peeked over the edge and saw this guy rummaging through my stuff," he said. "I wondered what to do. I was sleeping naked, so my very first thought was, 'I can't jump up and scream at this guy naked, he'll just laugh at me.' So I managed to ever so quietly get my underpants on, with this guy ten feet away. Then I jumped up and yelled at him."

What David yelled was, "Get the hell out." He was channeling Kehoe's old girlfriend, Naomi, complete with Long Island accent. David remembered Naomi telling them how she had been asleep in Providence and awoke to a man trying to climb through her window. She jumped up and screamed, "Get the hell out."

The guy did.

But this was New York City, not Providence. David, a skinny guy covered with hair, jumped up and yelled, "Get the hell out," and the intruder grabbed a letter opener, then held it to the skinny guy's throat. "I know you have money," the robber barked. He didn't know he was threatening the life of David Byrne. He had never heard of David Byrne. The robber was too dim-witted to appreciate the irony of robbing a skinny guy in his underpants who had once sung, "I've got money now/I've got money now."

"He threatened to kill me with my own letter opener," David said. He wondered at the time, "Isn't a letter opener kind of blunt? Would it work? Did I want to find out?"

156

"So I said, 'Go ahead, take the stuff and just get out!' "

After an hour of threats, the guy ripped the phone cord out of the wall and left. David patiently put the phone back together and called the cops.

Then he put some pants on.

While he waited for the cops, he thought about the robber. He thought about Seymour Stein. He thought about being robbed. "When I got back from the Carribean with Seymour," David said, "I found that Seymour's publishing company had a big chunk of the publishing money of our first couple of records. And he basically went and sub-licensed [the rights] to publishing companies in Europe and then didn't cut us in on it. He sold my rights to all these people and just pocketed it all."

David vowed never to speak to Stein again. Seymour Stein was *robbing him blind*. Seymour Stein was a *pig*. Seymour Stein was a *monster*. Although in the end, David had to admit, Seymour Stein was a monster with good ears.

Gary Kurfirst didn't think Stein was a monster. What had happened was very simple: "Stein was changing one set of licensees, and he didn't tell anybody that he was going to make a change, the contract only called for three Talking Heads albums. You don't walk in and say, 'Hey, that's the last record.' Because they won't work it. So Seymour started making some new deals. Word of this leaked out. The companies that had the third Talking Heads album stopped supporting it. I myself was only upset because I hadn't been told. I had been in business long enough that I would have understood what was going on, and I could have maybe set David up to know what was going on, so it wouldn't be a shock. I would tell David that this is a business practice that happens very often."

"Seymour felt David was the genius and all the rest of us were just 'smart,'" Jerry remembers. "I don't think Seymour ever believed me or Chris or Tina were talented totally. Then, everybody knew that Seymour played pretty loose. He was always changing distributors, especially in Europe. And we have been the victim of that a few times. We'll go to Europe and we won't have record company support. We feel burned by him. I am more philosophical about it than anyone else. Seymour is a survivor. I know he's taken advantage of musicians, but he's signed amazing groups. He was a shoot-from-the-hip kinda guy."

157

The day after the robbery, David Byrne had lunch with David Bowie. Bowie had just recorded a song with Eno that he tried to sing like David Byrne. David found this flattering, but when he heard the cut he didn't get the vocal resemblance. Ten years later, David Byrne sang the song, called "D.J.," at a club in Manhattan called Harrah's while Bowie sat in the audience. "It was a lot of fun," Byrne recalled.

The four Talking Heads reconvened in England. They played some television shows. They also had to quickly name the new record. Tina told *Creem* magazine that Jerry had suggested *Fear of Music* as a title for their second album, *More Songs About Buildings and Food*. The title didn't fit those songs. But it did fit the new songs.

Another story has it that David Byrne was reading a book called

Music and the Brain, about a woman who had seizures while listening to Tchaikovsky's *Valse des Fleurs* and that the title came from this.

In either case, Tina pointed out that the record industry was in recession, so everyone had *fear of music.* She was right. In 1979 the bottom fell out of the pop market. Revenues plunged more than 10 percent. This would be pegged as the "disco disaster." Things would get worse over the next few years. During this time some executives thought that the evil was home taping. One kid on the block would buy a record, then tape it for all his pals. Then they'd all listen to Donna Summer's *Bad Girls* and the Doobie Brothers and *Barbra Streisand's Greatest Hits, Vol. 2* on this devil tape player from Japan, now called the Walkman.

David wasn't sure about his take on fear. Some said it was the only logical emotion for sentient Americans. A near meltdown had occurred at Three Mile Island in Harrisburg, Pennsylvania. A female San Diego teen shot down some elementary school children because, as she said, "I don't like Mondays." John Wayne would never again save the wagon train because he finally died of cancer. Strange Islamic turmoil had allowed a bedeviled bearded Ayatollah to take over Iran. Thousands of Vietnamese boat people were drowning in the South China Sea. Finally, any day now, Skylab, a seventy-seven-ton orbiting space station, would enter the atmosphere and hurl to Earth, a man-made meteorite.

David wasn't particularly fearful—not even when the guy held a letter opener to his throat. If pressed, he would say, "I don't know about this fear business, but I do love Charlie Manson's quote about paranoia being the highest form of awareness."

Jerry wanted to design the cover for *Fear of Music.* He had it in his head that the cover of the third album should light up, but that proved to be too expensive. Then he had noticed the textured rubber flooring of Yann's kitchen and bathroom. He wanted that to be the cover.

Jerry called the president of the company that designed the flooring. *Could they get a million square feet?* Yes. *Could they thin the covering down?* Yes.

But the money. The money the money the money. It cost too much. Then Queens Litho said they could do it in cardboard.

After the album was released on August 3, John Rockwell reviewed it. He didn't mention the textured cover covered with all those rows of little X's.

"Once again, a word of caution of the sort that seems necessary whenever another of these products of the New York sensibility is released," Rockwell warned. "This is not a pop-rock record in the conventional sense, and pop fans may not warm to it at first, or ever."

Out of many reviews—including Rockwell's—only Lester Bangs's *Village Voice* review captured in words the monstrous intensity of *Fear of Music:* "In the Middle Ages, the population of Europe felt so haunted and tainted by the Devil, so hopelessly damned, that they developed a predilection, as manifested in the paintings of Bosch, for taking all this damnation and redemption stuff as a kind of huge joke, with God, Satan and the demons as cartoon characters. . . . David Byrne seems to be a kind of dowser's wand to neuroses and trauma [as] he strolls . . . placid, bemused, humming little tunes to himself. Sometimes I think *Fear of Music* is one of the best comedy albums I've ever heard."

The single for the record, "Life During Wartime," peaked at number 80. The lyrics in the refrain, "This ain't the Mudd Club," put the the nightspot on the cultural map forever.

Originally owner Steve Maas was going to call his joint the Molotov Cocktail Lounge. But he had started a film company with Amos Poe called Mud Films (because a critic once complained that the latter's films looked like "mud"). Maas decided to call his club Mudd with two D's after Samuel Alex Mudd, the doctor who treated John Wilkes Booth after he shot Lincoln.

On August 16, the Heads played the Dr Pepper Festival in Central Park with a group of girls in beehive hairdos called the B-52's. John Rockwell was on the lawn. After all this time, he found himself warming up to David. The guy's singing was still grating, but the critic observed that the singer's stage presence was commanding. This was no longer a man who looked like a deer caught in the headlights. Chris and Tina were superb as usual—Tina wearing a magenta dress over pumpkin-colored jeans. She still got him hot.

When Rockwell left the park, he figured he'd go home and write that Talking Heads was the harbinger of the forthcoming 1980s. But by the time he got downtown, he backed off. Forecasting is dangerous, critically speaking. Instead, he'd write something a little more watered down, like

"Talking Heads are clearly the most characteristic and talented band to emerge from the New York underground rock scene in the late 1970s."

In honor of *Fear of Music*, Fiorucci, the hip clothing and geegaw store, did a window display celebrating industrial surfaces. The dock-plate-pattern vinyl floor covering sold for $9.75 a square yard.

Sometime in August, Talking Heads played CBGBs with Patti Smith. No one suspected that in just a few months Patti Smith would renounce rock 'n' roll and exile herself in Detroit. As for the Heads, the sheer volume of the live performance made the new *Fear of Music* songs entertaining, if not good. Bootlegs reveal the band tried to duplicate the incredible neo-psychedelic tone Eno had created. When David sang "Air," he even squawked out a cartoon voice in an attempt to duplicate what Eno had done to his voice on the record. Talking Heads ended up in Emerson, Lake and Palmer's boat—the album was too complex to be played by just the four of them. It never occurred to the group that the only way the four could play the new *Fear of Music* songs was to reduce the songs' arrangements, perhaps duplicating the original haiku sound they had achieved when they were starting out as a trio. Jerry could have played guitar while David just sang.

On August 4 and 16, as well as September 4, Eno invited a group of musicians, including David and Chris, to jam at RPM Studio in Manhattan. On September 13, 1979, producer Sylvia Robinson—the Mother Teresa of hip hop—released the first rap record, Sugar Hill Gang's "Rapper's Delight." On September 20, Bob Dylan performed "Gotta Serve Somebody" on *Saturday Night Live*. Dylan had been born again. During the fall, Tina told a reporter that Talking Heads "offers an alternative to disco, rather than approaching it from what seems like the tail end of the dog. We just wrote songs that we liked ourselves."

Further into the autumn, Talking Heads played Peoria, Illinois. The town was plastered with posters that said *Fear of Peoria*. Adrian Belew, David Bowie's Kentucky-born guitarist, went to see them. Belew had just moved to Springfield, Illinois—drifted really. He had been living in Nashville and needed a change. And he had some friends who had built a music studio in the town where Abraham Lincoln once practiced law.

Belew had seen Talking Heads once before in Nashville. They played at a place called the Exit Inn. "I actually didn't like them very much," Belew recalled. "I didn't think they were very accomplished yet."

Then he started getting their records. He dug them. Somehow Jerry Harrison recognized Belew in the lobby of the theater in Peoria—*Bowie's guitarist*.

"Will you come onstage and play on the encore?" Jerry asked him.

"What song?"

" 'Psycho Killer.' "

"I don't know it."

"All you have to do is just sort of play some freaked-out guitar stuff at the end, like a long jam, you know."

So at the encore, Belew did just that. He had learned how to replicate sound effects on his guitar. Belew's guitar could honk like a car horn. It could squall like a seagull. As a matter of fact, he could get a complete menagerie out of his Fender Strat—elephant bellows, lion roars, goofy seal yelps. Belew played animal guitar up in Chicago. Down in Nashville. Then the disco era killed his circus. Live music was out. He took shelter, playing at Holiday Inns. Playing drums, not guitar, because he absolutely hated the songs he had to play, like "Tie a Yellow Ribbon 'Round the Old Oak Tree." He found a gig in a Nashville bar where he could play Steely Dan, so he left the drums and took up guitar again. Frank Zappa was in the bar that night. He invited Belew to come to Los Angeles and audition for his band.

But Belew didn't have to audition for "Psycho Killer" in Peoria. He went crazy at the end. He played for five glorious minutes. He left the stage to thunderous applause.

Belew's playing made a big impression on David. He would call his own guitar sound "thin, clean, and clanky" as opposed to being "chunky, distorted, and macho." He believed in what Dylan famously called (in a slightly different context) a "thin Mercury sound." David saw the guitar as the first scientific musical instrument. But Belew had discovered the mammal, yes, the mammal lurking in the guitar. After Peoria, David changed his style on "Psycho Killer." He tried playing it over the top like Belew. Tina said rather wistfully, "Even though I loved Adrian and he was fabulous, I loved what David had been playing. But David gave up all his stuff and tried to do simulations that weren't as good as what Adrian does and weren't as good as what David had been doing. I was sorry about that."

In the fall, the British rock magazine *Trouser Press* published an extensive interview with the four Talking Heads that revealed much about the relationship between David and Tina at the close of the 1970s. The interview recited numerous tidbits about *Fear of Music*, of course. We learned that originally "Electric Guitar" ended with sounds of thunder, rain, car horns, but the band deleted the sound effects because, as Tina said, "People would hear it every single time they played the song and get tired of it." David talked about "Animals" and its rejection of the concept that chimpanzees and rhino and water buffalo are noble savages living in harmony with their environment: "Animals are obstinate beings with lots of problems of their own."

Tina was also asked if the band ever had problems telling David what to do. "Well, we tell him what works and what doesn't," Tina answered. Chris piped up and said that David appreciates criticism as long as it's "clear and constructive."

"There is a streak of defiance in David," Tina said. She said he hated anything clichéd. She said he allows himself to be nervous because nervousness is not a cliché. "When he sits down in a chair he'll try to sit down in an unusual way just because he wants to be an individual." According to Tina, David didn't take advice very well because everyone was always giving him advice. Tina talked about how important it was for David to have his name on songs.

Asked if she worked *with* David or *for* him, Tina replied, "I don't feel in David's shadow at all."

Then Chris commented that interviewers tended to talk to David instead of the other band members because it is easier to interview one person than four. Tina added, "Well, it's natural. They relate to other writers and they probably figure that if they were writing songs in a band they could find anybody to back them."

Tina assured the magazine that David knew that if he got a different bass player, "he'd have a hell of a time," because Chris and Tina are "completely supportive" of David. Because Chris and Tina purposely diminished their image. They did this not to their detriment, but in order not to distract from David's performance. That was why Tina still looked at David while she played her bass. It was imperative that she pay attention to David's vocals so she knew how to play. "David can't see us as much as we see him, so it's important to give as much support was we can."

David was carrying the double burden of playing and singing. "We held David's hand for a period of time," Tina said. "Now David's very confident." Tina said they held David's hand because he wasn't a born leader.

"Initially, you wanted him to be a leader more than he wanted to be one?" the magazine asked.

"No," Tina answered. "Talking Heads never really had a leader."

On November 29, they were back in Europe at the Edinburgh Festival. David Byrne and his leaderless band performed in his homeland with the Chieftains and Van Morrison. At year's end, Talking Heads was in Germany. A Czech reporter who'd slipped out of the Soviet bloc arranged for an interview. He talked to Chris and Tina separately from David, but Chris and Tina in turn first quizzed him, "Tell us about the Plastic People." When the fellow finally began to question them, he asked: "How do you feel now about the fact that David is leaving the group?"

At first Tina thought she had misheard. It was the man's stumbling English. But then he repeated himself. "No. I'm sure David Byrne is not going to work with you again."

Chris and Tina were shocked. David had said nothing about this. He had been more private and distant than usual, but that was David. Neither Chris nor Tina was able to directly confront him about the I'm-going-to-quit-the-band statement he'd made to the Czech reporter. Once everyone returned to the States, David disappeared. No one knew where he'd gone.

remain in light

Manhattan in December of 1979 was Joseph Beuys's town—the German artist was enjoying a monster retrospective at the Guggenheim. He was inescapable. Every hip Manhattanite now understood why Beuys had become obsessed with constructing sculpture of animal fat and felt. The catalog to his show explained that during the war, Beuys crashed his warplane in the Crimea. A few days later, some Tartars found his frozen body and revived the German pilot by wrapping him in fat and strips of felt.

Just as rock history is riddled with myth, the story behind Beuys's "crash" is likely a fabrication. In an *Art Forum* article, Benjamin Buchloh convincingly argued that the only evidence of the crash was a photo of Beuys standing beside his downed plane. "Who would, or could, pose for photographs after a plane crash, when severely injured?" Buchloh inquired. "And who took the photographs? The Tartars with their fat-and-felt camera?"

Whatever the truth behind Beuys's plane wreck, Tina, queen of the bass players, decided that she and Chris should quit the crash that Talking Heads had become.

"I've had it with David's head games! David is like a bad guru! A bad karate teacher! A Rasputin! A guy who develops the will, but not the heart chakra!" Tina Weymouth no longer thought of herself as a "good Catholic girl," but she digressed into the Catholic divine: "That was the whole point about God giving us free will. Free will is what love is. David is just into control."

Chris agreed with her on that point.

"I can't stand it anymore," Tina raged. "Let's leave him! Let's do our own thing! We should have kicked him out of the band! We never needed him! We've never needed him as much as he needs us!"

Chris was the easygoing one in the group, but he was no passive goof like Ringo, and he certainly wasn't under Tina's thumb. Talking Heads was the greatest thing in his life. It was inconceivable to him to split up the band. He wouldn't budge. Things soon escalated to the point that the Frantz and Weymouth union seemed more perilous than that of Talking Heads. The two took a long vacation to save their marriage, and thus save the band.

Jerry Harrison came back from the *Fear of Music* tour and went straight to work producing records. He worked with a group called the Escalators in New York. He went up to Canada to work with a French band that wrote songs about fucking in elevators. He produced a record by a New Wave soul singer named Nona Hendryx, recording down in Philadelphia at the old Sigma Sound studio. Jerry wanted to hippify the Philly Sound, that combination of strings and funk of the O'Jays, Teddy Pendergrass, the theme from *Soul Train.*

"We had fun," Hendryx said about working with Jerry. "I was an experiment for him. His specialty was the music side of it. Singing-wise, I knew how to sing and what to sing."

"We had fun," she said again. "The record sounded nothing like *Soul Train.*"

165

Chris and Tina saved their marriage by exploring voodoo (*vodun* or *voudoun* to those in the know) rituals in Haiti. The two hung out with the renowned reggae rhythm section Sly Dunbar and Robbie Shakespeare in Jamaica. They beat Haitian drums together every chance they got.

They also decided to get an apartment in Nassau in a building right above Compass Point Studios, where the black typist who Eno had the hots for worked.

Chris and Tina came to Compass Point first. When David showed up, he didn't say where he'd been. He told Tina, "You know, I had this really bad dream again." He didn't look at her as he spoke. Tina asked David what he dreamed. "I dreamed that my head was cut off and none of you noticed."

"Ho ho," Tina said. "That sounds pretty heavy-duty. How did this happen?"

"Well, actually my head was still attached," he said. "But it was as if it had been cut off and put back on."

David showed up at Compass Point with a secret. He had just cut a record with Brian Eno.

The project began after Eno introduced David to a wild trumpeter named Jon Hassell. Hassell had a slender frame and hollow cheeks, a medieval pilgrim lost in TriBeCa where he lived in a loft with walls of white enameled bricks. Cushions on the floor. He fed his puppy raw carrots.

His trumpet playing was close to electric Miles Davis. Hassell blew it through a device that delayed the sound while altering the pitch. His trumpet was spooky. Like a Dr. Seuss bird. Hassell told ambientologist David Toop, "Basically, I play the mouthpiece, not the trumpet. I blow it like a conch shell."

Hassell was a student of Stockhausen. He recorded with minimalist masters like Terry Riley and La Monte Young. Eno got his vision of "fourth world music" from Hassell. Hassell spoke of "coffee-colored" classical music of the future. He believed half the planet lived in the fifteenth century while the other half was pure *Blade Runner*. The music of the fourth world would adopt new modes of structural organization from both. It would be a combination of Indian ragas and Gil Evans juxtaposed with the sound of Malaysians beating the rivers with dishes and taking their tribal baths.

Hassell stated at the time that "David and Brian came up with this idea that we should go off into the desert someplace with an eight-track recorder and make an album that, at the time, we were thinking would be somewhat like the Residents' *Eskimo*—that was a *faux* tribe, invented, that doesn't exist. . . . So we conspired to do this together. They were going off to L.A. to look for a place."

All winter, Eno and David drove through the Mojave but could not find a suitable location for their desert tribe. They ended up recording inside studios in Los Angeles. A month or so later, they mailed Hassell a cassette. It was an early version of a song called "A Secret Life."

It was very eerie. Mid-tempo beats. Indiscernible things. Maybe alive. Maybe not. There was an Arabic melody. Thumpings. Clicking in the background. A detached car muffler or maybe an amplified guitar case—

various "percussion" instruments that Eno had brought with him from New York junk hunting. Then Arabic voices begin singing, their voices treated through a synthesizer and sounding like Hassell's trumpet.

For unknown reasons, "A Secret Life" didn't impress Hassell and he declined the invitation to join Eno and David in California. Twenty years later, David would forget why Hassell didn't come out to California. Hassell couldn't have been all that bugged—he showed up later at Sigma Sound to blow on the new Talking Heads album. "Maybe he had a hot date?" David joked dryly. "He's a ladies' man—or was at the time. Maybe he had something special going on that I didn't know about. Or maybe it was financial—Eno and I financed the *Ghost* sessions ourselves."

In Japanese filmmaker Akira Kurosawa's 1950 masterpiece, *Rashomon,* the same story is told from four points of view: a thief, a woodcutter, a samurai's wife, and her dead husband. Although the tangled narration of Talking Heads and Eno and the album they would create next isn't as melodramatic as Kurosawa's tale of rape and murder and the talking dead, a conflicting narration is the only clue available to us to figure out how much the creation of a great work of art is an accident, happy or otherwise.

Talking Heads met at Compass Point Studios in the spring of 1980.

It had been agreed that rather than David presenting lyrics and melodies, they would jam together. Songs would come from riffs. "I Zimbra" was used as a starting point. Three weeks later, Brian Eno showed up. At the beginning he seemed reluctant to record with the band again, but after he heard tapes of what they'd done, he said, "I absolutely love the direction you're going in. If this is the way you want to continue, I'll produce the record." He brought in his engineer, Rhett Davies.

The Bahamas made David feel like a Graham Greene character. He couldn't understand why Chris and Tina got an apartment there. Nassau was a horrible place. A stack of poor villages on one side of the island. Big hotels on the other. Whites-only residential communities. He never understood why Chris Blackwell ran a studio in this tax-haven town. *Let's do some quasi-legal offshore banking. Let's launder cocaine money.*

The only thing Nassau had going for it was pretty nice snorkeling.

David Byrne also remembered that Talking Heads and Eno all

arrived at the same time and began recording from scratch: "Eno convinced us to bring along his engineer, Rhett Davies, a nice guy who freaked out once there, partly due to not knowing what we were trying to do, and partly, I suspect, because Eno would ask him to record without giving him time to get a sound. So Rhett left after a few days. And Dave Jerden, who Brian and I had worked with, was called in." Jerden complained under his breath about having too record too quickly, but handled it.

Tina told these stories: Eno and David had some kind of falling-out over the two's "secret" record. Then Rhett Davies bailed. No one remembers exactly why. Tina remembers him saying, "Every time you play something really great, Eno goes and erases it. And I'm sick and tired of it. I can't stand it. I can't stand the way he's honing in on you."

When exactly Dave Jerden arrived is unclear. The stopgap engineer was a kid named Stephen Stanley. A few years back when he was seventeen he'd engineered a session for Bob Marley. According to Tina, every morning Stanley would take her aside and tell her how Eno and David had rerecorded her bass tracks. "Look. This is really bothering me. These guys keep missing beats." Tina would hoist up her bass and replay what had been rerecorded.

Jerry Harrison is a discreet man. He doesn't tell stories. He keeps any axes he has to grind hidden from reporters and stool pigeons: "The recording started out and everything went incredibly smooth. Rhett was trying to break away from Eno. He was developing his own career. He didn't want to be under Eno. So he backed out. Then Eno tried engineering for awhile. Then he called up Dave Jerden. We just knew we'd made this amazing music."

To cap off the *Rashomon* aspects of the recording, in the fall, David would tell the *Daily News* that this record "wasn't intended to be a Talking Heads LP at all, but after we put some tracks down, some of the sounds started taking shape and became songs. I was very unsure of it, but toward the end of the rehearsals I was really pleased with the progress, and I thought to myself, anybody who doesn't like this is nuts."

The basic tracks Talking Heads laid down were rhythmical, pulsing, and minimal—they were all in one chord. Each part was recorded as a long loop of song. Compositions were created by switching different loops on and off. Or merging them together. David explained it like this: "Any part you play is going to fit with any other part. So you can close your eyes and switch a bunch of them in and out and you'll get this dramatic change of texture, but everything will still at least melodically work together."

What would become the album's most striking song began as a strange David Byrne guitar riff. He listened to it, then added a second riff. He liked that one better, and boosted it so it became the dominant sound. Then Eno alternated eight bars of the second guitar riff with eight bars of the first. At this point, the track was nothing more than the "Weird Guitar Riff Song."

Eno and Talking Heads discovered that they could layer tracks like sonic lasagna. Half a dozen bass tracks were meshed together. David believed that this was the first time a pop record had been composed this way in a studio. The experimental German rock group Can had once made a record this way, but *Melody Attack* was going to be a pop album. *Melody Attack* was what they'd begun calling the album. It was taken from the title of a Japanese game show.

Jerry was in dreamtime in the studio down there. He knew they were capturing music that was astonishing. They'd successfully turned the studio into a musical instrument. A tribal instrument. Most of the tracks felt like jungle songs. Layered percussion. Spidery riffs.

But no melodies or lyrics. These songs were making David rethink his vocal style. In the past, his vocal melody could be limited, because the chord changes were complex. The tension in a song was caused by the music, not the singing. He tried singing words to "Weird Guitar Riff Song," but they sounded stilted. Then Eno tried singing some nonsense syllables over the cut. David said he'd listen to the tape and see if Eno's nonsense could inspire him.

Then the group took a break. Everyone would rendezvous in New York in three weeks' time and finish the record.

Big mistake. David had writer's block again. Just like after *More Songs About Buildings and Food*. No words. No melodies.

It was very hot and muggy in New York that summer. It felt like a short-order cook was flipping burgers on your face.

Jerry booked the Heads into New York's Sigma Sound on Fifty-third and Broadway where he'd cut the group a good deal. Sigma had established itself as an R&B studio. Jerry convinced them that by letting Talking Heads work there they could get a whole new clientele. But with David's block, there was nothing to do. In frustration, he would pick up a bass guitar and add a new line. Jerry and Eno started tinkering with the music. Chris and Tina stopped coming to the studio on a daily basis. When they did show, Tina complained about the tracks being changed. Everyone was on edge.

Eno and David and Jerry began to doubt the music they'd recorded. Maybe it was too monotonous. Maybe it was the musical equivalent of felt and fat. Someone discovered that guitarist Adrian Belew was playing at Irving Plaza. Eno and David and Jerry went to the show.

Belew looked more like a high school science teacher than a guitar god. Backed by a small band, he stood onstage letting his guitar warble and bellow, until it sounded more reptile than mammalian, like a Japanese monster movie. Godzilla rising from the water. Belew wrestled up these sounds using fingers and technology—both his Fender Strat and Jaguar were connected to a Roland guitar synthesizer. After the show, David and Eno and Jerry cornered him in a stairwell.

"Hey, look, we're doing this record. Could you stick around for a day and play on it?" Jerry asked.

Belew had planned to drive back to the Land of Lincoln the next day. "Well," he said, "I think I can."

He brought his guitars and synthesizer to the studio the next day. His Roland worked just like a keyboard synthesizer—it took the basic sound from the electric guitar and toyed with it. Was this kind of aural adornment necessary? Jimi Hendrix didn't need such a thing. Belew always justified his technology with this analogy: "Writing a song on your acoustic guitar is like drawing with a pencil. Or an artist could do 3-D animation with a computer, which is similar to what I do with the synthesizer." He had other devices. "They're all just tools to me. Just colors on my palette." Belew himself had no technical finesse. Most days he felt like he could barely plug his equipment in. He just saw the synthesizer as expanding his vocabulary.

Eno and David played Belew some cuts from Compass Point. It was great watching his face. The guitarist obviously loved what he heard. There was something *infectious* about Talking Heads' new music. Belew didn't say this to anybody, but he figured it was Eno's doing. He had worked with Eno when Eno had produced David Bowie. Eno had a unique ethereal approach. An abstract approach. Belew's enthusiasm fired up both Eno and David; they became believers again. *Melody Attack* was no white elephant. Eno put on a cut that would eventually be called "The Great Curve" and said, "Well, look, David is just going to sing in this song later." Eno pronounced the word *sing* as though singing lacked particular significance. "Just play something where you think you should play it."

Belew complied. He listened for about two minutes. Then he stuck in a guitar solo that was so steely his notes were like the beams of a skyscraper. An Empire State Building of wires screaming from their tremendous weight.

Then Belew stopped. The song kept going. David would have to just sing around the playing.

How hard is rock verse anyway? David discarded rock lyrics when he was growing up. "The words were, for the most part, pretty stupid," he said. Now he looked to Africa. When Africans forget the words to a song, they just make something up. David had all the tracks they'd recorded, including the "Weird Guitar Riff Song," on a cassette. He was trying to figure out words by making up onomatopoeia Eno-style melodies to the tracks.

That was how Eno worked. He sang nonsense. He'd lean into a portable tape recorder and scat-sing something like "ba-do-de-be-de-n-do-day" (an example he gave when Chrissie Hynde interviewed him). Then he would listen to it again and again until he didn't hear it as nonsense anymore. He heard words. "Then I write them out and they become the words to the song." Eno knew many people believed that the meaning of a song was vested in the lyrics. To Eno, that has never been the case. "There are very few songs that I can think of where I even remember the words," he liked to say, "let alone think that those are the center of the meaning."

As far as Eno was concerned, you could stick a Hugo Ball sound poem made up of nonsense words in every damn song they'd cut. Paul McCartney had often begun his Beatles songs with nonsense lyrics. He replaced them later. One song that began as an ode to scrambled eggs became "Yesterday." "It's Only Love" began as "That's a Nice Hat."

David, however, was having difficulties coming up with even scrambled eggs. It was difficult to hear a melody in the tapes. There were different notes, harmonics, and aspects of the chord that changed so it sounded as if there were chord changes, but in reality it was the same root pattern repeating over and over.

Writing lyrics for *Melody Attack* songs was murder. For a song called "Born Under Punches," David implored, "Look at the hands of a government man," rewriting "Don't Worry About the Government"—while Eno added a verse for the chorus that he took from a summer headline in the *New York Post:* "And the heat goes on." This was a nice image on paper, but a poor choice to sing. Say the word *heat.* Now sing it. The word begins with a soft vowel. At first "And the heat goes on . . ." sounds like the chorus to the Sonny and Cher song about the beat going on.

For the next song, David loosened up and didn't repeat himself. He'd been influenced by this new thing called rap. Chris brought in Kurtis Blow's new rap track *The Breaks.* David found himself doing a rhythmical rant on . . . facts. "Facts are simple," he said, "and facts are straight. Facts are lazy and facts are late. . . ."

Lyrics, then melodies, were coming quicker now. Another set of words came from the books he was reading. He'd get the best line on the album after reading a text about the Great Mother—"the world moves on a woman's hips."

172

Hula dancers. Belly dancers. Women with Hula-Hoops. Women with the world orbiting her ass and pelvis. "Many of the lines in the album were inspired by having read Robert Farris Thompson's *African Art in Motion,*" David said.

Then he put down his books and turned to straight speech for influence. He started listening like crazy to a variety of different things. He listened to a recording of John Dean's Watergate testimony. He found a record of ex-slaves telling stories. He listened to motivational speakers—their musical cadences and occasional non sequiturs were mind-blowing. Then radio preachers. Television preachers. Weird, weird Protestant orators. The airwaves in 1980 were filled with people ranting about all kinds of out-there stuff—their baby got the stigma. Their mama spoke in tongues. The politics of rapture. David found passion in their diatribes, a passion bordering on the ecstatic. These American words transcended the nonsense stew from where they came. David wanted to achieve this kind of rapture in his lyrics. He was playing "Weird Guitar Riff Song" on his little tape player when he found himself shouting: "You may find yourself behind the wheel of a large automobile."

He was a radio minister filled with the Holy Ghost. David shouted, "And you may find yourself in a beautiful house." Pause. "With a beautiful wife." Pause. "And you may ask yourself, 'Well . . . how did I get here?' "

David, himself, had never considered turning to Jesus like Bob Dylan. (In an interview, David referred to that conversion as "Bob Dylan found Jesus and went soft. . . .") David grew up white-bread. Presbyterian and Methodist churches. He was not, as the media reported, raised a Quaker. His mother converted when he was in college. Presbyterian and Methodist churches were safe churches. Parishioners prayed and sinned and were in danger of going to hell, but the ministers didn't usually talk about it. The ministers certainly never spoke in tongues like in the Bible Belt. In the days of David's childhood, most Americans didn't have a clue that thousands of Southerners picked up rattlesnakes with their bare hands because Jesus had told them to "lift up serpents."

Anyway, David did not believe in any bearded old man up there. He saw God as a force that guided and united our finest actions and sensibilities. A force that couldn't be explained. Because the force doesn't fit causal rationality, we all call it God. David believed, "There are things that are difficult to measure with scientific instruments." God—and music—were two of them.

Then David's lyrics for the "Weird Guitar Riff Song" took a curious waver. He began ranting about water. The water was "dissolving." The water was "removing." There was "water at the bottom of the ocean." He urged listeners to "carry the water at the bottom of the ocean." Then to "remove the water at the bottom of the ocean." This curious watery bit is likely the result of a book David had been reading since he'd come back from Europe, *African Rhythm and African Sensibility* by John Miller Chernoff. The author was a white professor who'd gone to Ghana to study drumming in 1970, the year David graduated from high school. Chernoff spent more than eight years writing and revising his book, an explanation of how African drummers have conversations with each other, the lexicon of their thumping as complicated as speech. One of the conversations they might have had concerned water: "If your head is hot, water will cool it/If your child is growing, the water he will use/If water kills your child, use the water/There is nothing without water/Water is not the enemy. . . ." Those are a nondialectic portion of the lengthy lyrics to "Water No Get Enemy" quoted in the book. They were written by the African musician Fela, and likely influenced David's water trip.

David took a break from writing to go to a design firm with Eno to hear pitches about the cover for their album. It was going to be called *My Life in the Bush of Ghosts*, based on an African novel of the same title by Amos Tutuola. David hadn't read the book. He and Eno just dug the words in the title.

M&Co. was pitching the *My Life in the Bush of Ghosts* cover. The design company was headed by a bespectacled thirty-one-year-old named Tibor Kalman. The *New York Times* would one day call Kalman "the self-styled bad boy of the graphic design profession." He was a harsh critic of formalistic, or what he pejoratively termed "professional," design. The "corporate-sounding cadence" of M&Co. was "meant to give an aura of mystery and to confuse his more straitlaced clientele, who always wanted to know what the M was."

Tibor—who looked like an owled up David Letterman—found David Byrne "a curious, bobbing, restless, young skinny kid." He found Eno a "real arrogant fuck who never looked you in the eye."

Kalman was a foreigner like Eno, born in Budapest. He had escaped with his family when he was seven.

Eno stalked out of the meeting, mumbling that he'd just as soon do the fucking cover himself. But he would soon discover there was no hurry. He and David were in danger of being sued.

David hadn't written any lyrics for *My Life in the Bush of Ghosts.* Instead he and Eno added *found* dialogue and singing to the tracks. They captured some amazing stuff. A radio exorcist. An Egyptian singer. One of the cuts included portions of a talk by the late Los Angeles evangelist Kathryn Kuhlman. Her voice and manner of speaking had been hypnotic. She preached as if your personal salvation would soon become money in her bank account. On the Byrne/Eno track called "Into the Spirit Womb" her voice is heard cooing, "Sit down by my side. Tell me all about those wonderful experiences when you were . . . able to see into the spirit world." She ends her dialogue by suggesting, "seeing angels are just as real in your life—and my life—as they were in the life of Lot. . . ." At the last minute, Kuhlman's estate prohibited the use of her Lot observation for secular ends. Apparently, Oral Roberts was behind this move. David was told that just before she had died, Oral had flown from his beardless city of Tulsa to her L.A. deathbed and convinced the dying medium to sign over the rights to all of her rants to him.

Now not only did Eno and David have to finish the new Talking Heads record, they would have to redo a cut on a *My Life in the Bush of Ghosts* song.

This secretly pleased Eno.

Tina was right when she thought she detected tension between Eno and David earlier that summer. Eno wasn't completely satisfied with the tracks they had cut. He believed they should hold off the release of the album while David was determined to press ahead. Ha! This Kuhlman problem made Eno recall a pair of Oblique Strategies: *Retrace your steps. Is it finished?* Once he and David started monkeying with one track, there would be no reason to stop.

In the meantime, Jerry had Nona Hendryx come in to sing background vocals on *Melody Attack*. She lived on the Upper West Side. She'd come down to the studio around six or seven. Sing past midnight. Then go home.

David and Jerry and Tina were sticklers about the way they wanted Hendryx to sing. "Black singers sing very differently," Hendryx explained. "Enunciation. David had a very specific way he wanted the rhythm of a chorus to fall. It might not seem right to us when they were singing it. But he had a specific rhythm in mind."

For many songs, Hendryx sang as a trio with Eno and David. Jerry described the first time he heard Eno singing with Hendryx like this, "I heard a voice in Brian that I had never heard before. Eno is very English on his solo records. But he was excited about African music. With Hendryx he was able to be careless—carefree with a passion that would have been wonderful for him to explore." Jerry thought it'd be great if Talking Heads went down to Compass Point and served as his back-up band. As it turned out, this would never happen. And Eno got deeper into ambient music. "It was equally interesting," Jerry said. "But it was safe for him."

Nona Hendryx says Eno galvanized the Talking Heads' talents. "Eno just gets on with his music and life and doesn't try to follow the music business and success. He's an artist."

Eno was also a reserved Englishman. Something he didn't share with anyone was that he was in mourning for the death of his dear friend Peter Schmidt, who had died earlier that year. Schmidt was the man with whom Eno had developed his Oblique Strategies. "My friend Peter Schmidt used to talk about 'not doing the things that nobody had ever thought of not doing,'" Eno would write. "Which was an inverse process—when you leave out the assumption that everybody had always made and see what happens . . . you discover that the absence of something was the revelation of something else. Buñuel, the filmmaker, said, 'Every object conceals another,' a message that I often relay to the studio when overdubbing starts."

The magic of *Melody Attack* was delicate and frail before the overdubs. But now it was strong. Jon Hassell came in to overdub "Houses in Motion."

Jerry's cover for *Fear of Music* was nominated for a Grammy, but it lost to the tepid wonder *Against the Wind,* by Bob Seger & the Silver Bullet Band. This cover of *Melody Attack* would be Chris and Tina's shot for a Grammy. As with every Talking Heads album design, the process was torturous and involved. Tina decided that she and her husband would create one of the first computer-generated album covers. The two drove up to MIT in Cambridge, Massachusetts, and worked with their chief hacker, Walter Bender.

176

These were still the steam days in terms of computer technology. Bill Gates had not yet become Daddy Warbucks. There were no PowerBooks. In fact, computers were as lumberous as hippopotami. The mainframe at MIT took up several rooms. Tina was told the thing was attached to the Defense Department, so they could use it only "unofficially" when the students were gone.

The cover was to be a series of warplanes flying over the Himalayas. This was the "melody attack." The back cover would be a group portrait. Chris and Tina and a programmer named Scott Fisher loaded four photos of Talking Heads online.

Just four heads. Eno's face wasn't included. An album producer wasn't usually portrayed with the band, but at the finish of *Melody Attack* Eno wanted the record to be credited to both Talking Heads *and* him. The Heads held firm. *No way.* Jerry said, "If Eno had said, 'I want to do a solo record—would you be the band,' we would have jumped at the chance." Neither Jerry nor David remembered David's comment to the press that originally *Melody Attack* wasn't meant to be a Talking Heads album.

Next came the issue of songwriting. Normally, the writer or writers who come up with the melody and lyrics are considered the songwriters. But that did not apply to the expansive music Talking Heads and Eno had just created. Sometimes a bass line or guitar rhythm defined a song's direction. Eno was determined to get what was his—credit and money. A few years earlier when he worked with Bowie on *Low,* he got screwed out of credit. That wouldn't happen again. For Talking Heads, Eno devised a mathematical formula to assess royalties based on each band member's memory of their specific contributions to each song. To do this, everyone wrote down the percentages that other people had contributed to each cut, excluding themselves. Jerry tallied the sheets. They were, of course, all vastly different. In the end, it was decided the credit would read, "All Songs by David Byrne, Brian Eno, Chris Frantz, Jerry Harrison, and Tina Weymouth"—the names arranged in alphabetical order.

The programmer, Scott Fisher, and Tina shared a passion for masks. They decided to put a mask on each face in the group portrait.

If Tina had exercised her wicked sense of humor, she would have had David, Chris, Jerry, and herself wearing Eno masks. Instead, she used the cursor to blot out the band's faces with blocks of color.

David's chin looks like his mouth until you know better. The only thing recognizably David left on his face is his peering right eye.

Jerry's Pan-like face was almost completely obliterated by the computer squash. Chris made himself look almost noble inside his mask. He turned his wife into a party girl with her lips painted. Talking Heads will never become rock stars hiding their faces this way—which, in a way, was the point.

Back in New York, Tina showed David what they had created at MIT. He told her the work was fine, but M&Co. was going to do the cover.

Tina said, "David, we've always done our own artwork. Why do we need some graphics department to do that for us? We have an in-house at Warner Bros. We're doing our own artwork. We don't need this. We don't need Tibor."

"He's ah—" David said. "He's doing it for free."

After Eno sulked out of the meeting with Tibor Kalman, the older man peered at David Byrne—*the curious, bobbing, restless, young skinny kid*—and considered. Tibor had heard of the problems the Heads had had with the textured *Fear of Music* cover and had proposed to do this cover for free—for the publicity. David explained to Tina that M&Co. was suggesting all sorts of textured covers made of sandpaper, velour, and sinister goo. But Tina held firm to the computer art she and her husband had just completed. David backed down. M&Co. would do the typography and the rest of the album design.

"Typical David," Tina remembers. "Penny-wise, pound-foolish."

Melody Attack was a very cool, very Japanese title, but the four Heads decided it was too flippant for the music they had just recorded. As David later said, "Besides not being all that melodic, the music had something to say that at the time seemed new, transcendent, and maybe even revolutionary, at least for funk rock songs."

With *Melody Attack* gone, the warplanes were relegated to the back. The four "masked" Heads became the cover. Apparently it registered with no one that the warplanes make no sense. What did they have to do with Talking Heads or the new title, *Remain in Light*? Tina didn't worry about this at the time. Kalman later remarked, "It was the same period as the Iranian hostage crisis, so the planes seemed appropriate."

Tina's input didn't stop with the cover. She told Kalman that she wanted simple type for the title. All caps. Bold. Sans serif. "It doesn't matter if it's Bristol or Helvetica. I'll leave that up to you." Kalman's people followed her instructions, and also came up with a brilliant typographical idea on their own. They inverted the A's in T∀LKING HE∀DS.

Walter and Scott and the others at MIT used initials and code names in the credits because this certainly hadn't been an official MIT project. Chris and Tina decided their joint credit would just be C/T.

178

By early summer, Talking Heads had a record cover. Everyone finally agreed on the album's song order. There would be three long cuts on Side One—swirling songs containing long instrumental passages. Side Two would lead with David's preacher song. Then a track similar to Side One but shorter. Then a cut that was a David-ian narration. Then an Arabic song. The album would end with a glorious tune that didn't really belong on *Remain in Light*. It was more a throwback to *Fear of Music*. But the song was too good to leave out. Jerry had been the chief architect of the piece. It was called "The Overload."

David's contributions to this song were said to be influenced by things he had read about a British group called Joy Division. He had never actually heard their albums, but he had read about them. The band played sublime dirges with a tribal-cum-industrial beat. Joy Division made schizophrenic trance drones. Soundtracks for nonexistent sci-fi movies. Ceremonial music for deep-tech fascist gatherings. The band's singer was Jim Morrison without the fire. Iggy Pop eating glass instead of cutting up his chest. David worked on the mock–Joy Division song without listening to any of their albums. When he finally heard Joy Division, he was disappointed. They sounded closer to a conventional rock group than he'd thought. David had been fooled by the music critics. As for "The Overload," it ended up sounding more like post-*Animals* Pink Floyd.

It was mid-summer and still the album had to be mixed. Sire was now barking at the band. They were way behind schedule. Jerry stayed with Eno in New York to mix half the record with John Potoker while David went to L.A. with David Jerden to mix the other half at Eldorado Studios.

If David Byrne were to write one of those "Idiot's Guides to . . ." books, his *Idiot's Guide to Mixing* would begin like this, "The definition of mixing varies, but in a typical case imagine that each instrument that plays on a piece of music, and even subtypes of those instruments (a drummers' bass drum, for example), is on a separate track, and therefore can be manipulated separately from all the others. It can be made louder, eq'd (made bassier or more trebly), and affected in numerous ways—twisted, echoed, repeated, whatever. It can also be, in many cases, silenced. This allowed us, on records like *Remain in Light*, to orchestrate and arrange songs by pushing buttons. In one section certain groups of instruments could be heard, and in another section they would be replaced by others—with some carrythrough, in most cases. This is mixing the tracks. . . ."

As the album was being mixed, another turbulent consideration came up. How on earth could Talking Heads play this new music live? The band had just landed two important gigs, the Heatwave Festival in Toronto, Canada, and Wollman Rink in Central Park. The money was too good to pass up. The group could run through the *Fear of Music* tour playlist, but wouldn't it be wonderful to perform some of the new songs? Eno warned everyone that a four-piece band wouldn't do. "The music was too dense. You need at least nine more musicians."

Not that Brian Eno was going to join Talking Heads onstage. Rumor had it he had stage fright. David says, "I believed Brian when he said he had stage fright. But it might also have been that he's not much of a musician in the playing-an-instrument sense. Naturally, he felt he did his best work behind the scenes, as many contemporary DJ's and remixers should probably learn. Eno is actually a better soloist, guitarist, et cetera, than he lets on, but he must know that if he keeps the mystery intact he will always have more power than if he shows his hand. He did plenty of speaking tours, which to most of us musicians is a vastly more nerve-wracking prospect than grooving and singing."

179

• • •

Expanding the band became a foregone conclusion. While David was mixing in Eldorado out west, Jerry began rounding up the extra "heads."

"The band was the result of the work I did with other people," Jerry said. "I had bass man Busta Jones who called me up to play with the Escalators. Then we went down to Philadelphia and I produced some demos for Nona Hendryx. I met Bernie Worrell—keyboard man—through Busta. Dolette MacDonald had sung on the Escalators album." They found percussionist Steve Scales, of funk duo Ashford & Simpson, through Bernie. And finally, Adrian Belew was added on guitar.

The Expanded Heads played together for the first time at Chris and Tina's loft. Although Jerry served as the band leader, Bernie Worrell had the most to do with crafting the sound. He was a musical prodigy who studied at the New England Conservatory of Music in Boston, as well as at Juilliard in the city. When he funkicised himself with Funkadelic, the combination of his Euro culture and Afro background was—as funkologist Rickey Vincent suggested—as if Shakespeare and Stagger Lee were dropping acid together in *da 'hood*. Everybody's ear in the Expanded Heads shifted to Worrell. Once he established the rhythm, everything fell into place. Everyone knew Bernie was the funkmaster.

On August 19, four days before Toronto, the Expanded Talking Heads met David (back from L.A.) for the first time. Some of the new players were wondering who this skinny white dude was. "David didn't even know how to talk to these black people," Tina would later say. "He didn't even understand what they were saying half of the time."

She liked the additional players. They made David seem less the leader of the band.

The group put together a forty-five-minute set, then flew up to the Heatwave Festival in Toronto. The Pretenders and B-52's were on the bill—both Gary Kurfirst bands. Elvis Costello would perform as well. Elvis was not Che's client, but then Che was no longer Che—Kurfirst still wore army jackets, but he'd shaved his beard.

The crowd would be 70,000 strong. Kurfirst and Jerry Harrison had planned what can only be called a "lunatic entrance" for the group. There was to be a full moon the night of the concert. Jerry and Gary flew to Toronto to scope out the outdoor stage at Mosport Park. Sure enough, the moon would rise just above the stage. Talking Heads were scheduled to play at dusk.

As the afternoon of the show progressed, Jerry realized the moonrise was in jeopardy. Every act had rushed their set. The show was going faster than planned. He looked for ways to stall. He used the bathroom a lot. He lost equipment and papers. When the show finally started, the moon rose in the sky.

"Lunatic and funk!" Worrell thought from the wings.

Only five Heads were onstage to play "Psycho Killer": David, Chris, Tina, Jerry, and Adrian Belew. For the next number, "Warning Sign," Steve Scales scampered out. Busta and Bernie joined the group for "Stay Hungry." Finally, singer Dolette MacDonald slinked onstage for "Cities" (at the last minute, Nona Hendryx couldn't make the show). With the complete Expanded Heads now onstage, David announced, "We're not the same as we used to be." David Byrne told the audience the next song was "I Zimbra." Then new stuff.

"Once in a Lifetime."

"Born Under Punches."

"Crosseyed and Painless."

The nine-member Talking Heads closed with "Life During Wartime" and "Take Me to the River."

The band was so jazzed they ended up playing their forty-five-minute set in just half an hour. Belew remembers trying to duplicate Robert Fripp's guitar solo in "I Zimbra" and becoming an action-painting blur. He played like Jackson Pollock painted—in quick drips and swirls.

181

Frank Gallagher, the soundman, sweat Scottish bullets as he tried to keep track of all the new Heads.

The suits in the audience nearly wept.

Seymour felt like he was watching Carlos Gardel, the great Argentinean tango artist.

The show was repeated four days later on August 27 when the group played Wollman Rink. After an opening set by the Japanese techo-pop group the Plastics, the ten Expanded Heads (including Nona Hendryx) were introduced to 125,000 New Yorkers.

This time they played a seventy-five-minute set. John Rockwell was there. He was exhilarated. He hadn't expected the group's music to expand in quite this way. A rowdy group of kids suddenly transformed into a Marine Corps battalion. Welcome to polyrhythms.

Most Western music has a singular beat—this is why a marching band playing "Stars and Stripes Forever" can march together down Main Street without the rows of musicians running into each other. African music is polymetric—containing two or more independent rhythms that weave together and systematically sync up. Different meters doesn't mean an African marching band would just be a chaotic jumble of rushing bodies on Main Street. Rather, perhaps every other row of musicians would be marching at a different rhythm than their neighbors, the entire band synching up at each stoplight with a grace that would put John Philip Sousa to shame.

Whether Talking Heads was playing Africanized techno funk or rococo rock 'n' roll, Sire and Warner Bros. was thrilled with the sound of the Expanded Heads. Only a few New Yorkers on the Great Lawn at Central Park were unhappy with the Heads' new sound and players. All they heard was Talking Heads playing *dance* music.

"Death to disco!" they shouted.

David was too pumped up to let catcalls get under his skin. Later, it pissed him off that any kind of funking danceable music would be lumped together with disco. In political terms David saw it this way: "Disco was black. Disco was gay. The 'disco sucks' movement was actually a veiled way of saying, 'Blacks and gays suck.' "

David didn't like lame rock journalists. White people understood reggae now because the Police had fooled around with rasta rhythms, but no one had heard rhythmic music like *Remain in Light* since 1975. That was the summer when Talking Heads first played at CBGBs. It was also the summer that Joni Mitchell, surely the whitest of white women, released her amazing *Hissing of Summer Lawns,* a record that is both true to Mitchell's North American vision while simultaneously borrowing unself-consciously from African instrumentation and polymeter. Although the record went gold, *Rolling Stone* dared to proclaim it the "Worst Album of the Year."

Rock journalists were meatheads.

David decided to include a bibliography with the *Remain in Light* press kit along with a statement explaining how the album was inspired by African mythologies and rhythms. It would stress how he himself had been influenced by John Miller Chernoff's *African Rhythm and African Sensibility.*

When Chris saw this press release and bibliography, he went red.

Two college artists, David Byrne and Mark Kehoe, Providence, Rhode Island, circa 1973.

(Courtesy of Mark Kehoe)

(Courtesy of Mark Kehoe)

This must be the place: David Byrne turned into a living map of the United States, circa 1973.

(© Stephanie Chernikowski)

Tina Weymouth at a party
at CBGB, mid-seventies.

(© Stephanie Chernikowski)

David Byrne's
Baltimore girl,
Joan Lobell, dressed
as Orson Welles.

(Courtesy of Mark Kehoe)

Chris Frantz at
the same party.

To Marc
Best Wishes
Orson

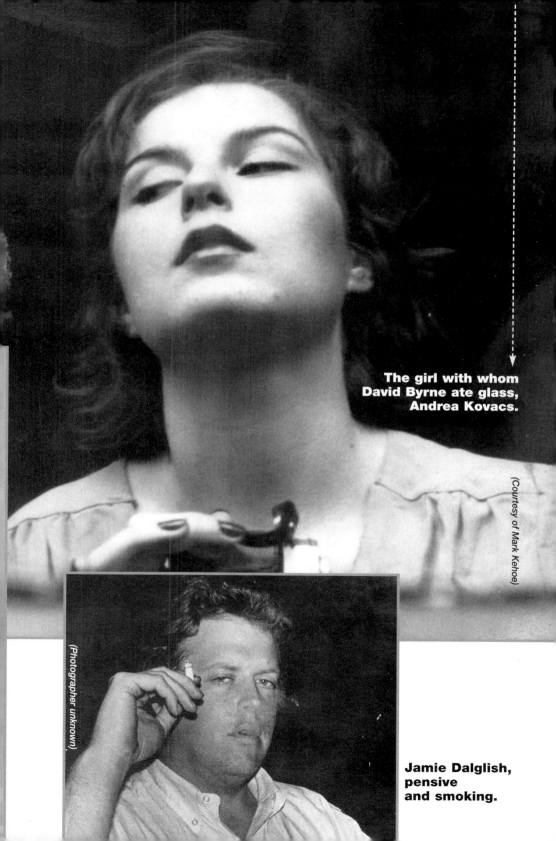

The girl with whom
David Byrne ate glass,
Andrea Kovacs.

(Courtesy of Mark Kehoe)

(Photographer unknown).

Jamie Dalglish,
pensive
and smoking.

Hilly Kristal hoisting himself aloft in front of CBGB.

Seymour Stein with his two favorite artists, Madonna and David Byrne.

(Courtesy of Mary Clarke)

Mary Clarke: The girl with whom David Byrne went to the Algonquin.

Tina Weymouth and Chris Frantz's wedding in *The Village Voice*.

MARY CLARK

HEADS WED

Talking Heads tightened up its rhythm section last Saturday when bass player Martina Weymouth and drummer Chris Frantz were married in his home town, Maysville, Kentucky (population 500). A reception was held at the Broderick Tavern, which dates from the 17th century. Music was provided by a stereo.

VOICE **ARTS**

(© Mary Clarke)

© Stephanie Chernikowski

Jerry Harrison and David Byrne playing electric guitars.

Talking Heads in the drink, Part One.

Talking Heads in the drink, Part Two.

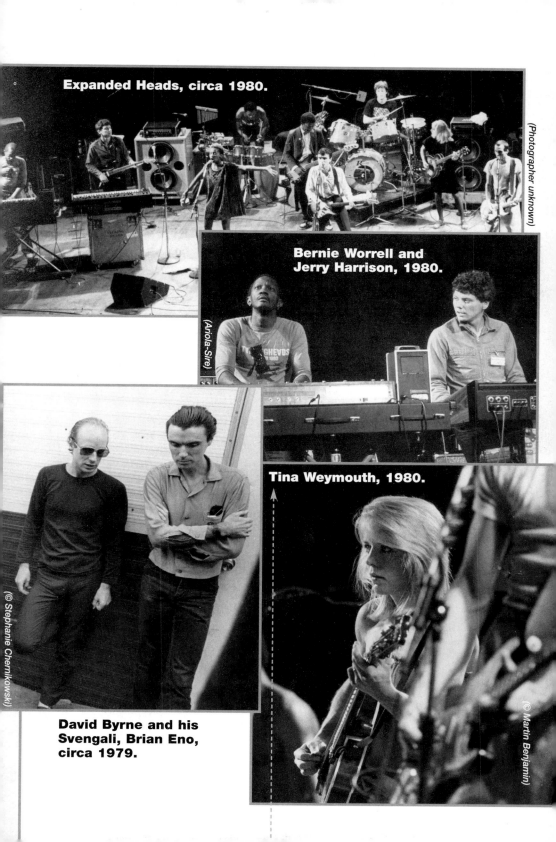

Expanded Heads, circa 1980.

Bernie Worrell and
Jerry Harrison, 1980.

Tina Weymouth, 1980.

David Byrne and his
Svengali, Brian Eno,
circa 1979.

Tina Weymouth covered in chocolate, circa 1980.

The Big Suit.

The Big Suit again.

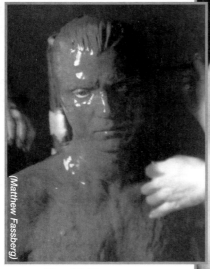

David Byrne covered in chocolate as well.

"I've never hit an African drum in my life," he yelled to Tina. What was all this African crap? James Brown, after all, turned his entire band into a drum kit, using polymeter. Since Little Richard's day, New Orleans drumming emphasized polymeter. As Rickey Vincent wrote, "Down there subtle counter rhythms were maintained simultaneously with the primary beat."

The psychedelic funk record *Remain in Light* was released during the first week of October. When Tina saw the back of the album, it was her turn to flip.

Below the four flying warplanes were the titles of the eight songs on the album. Below that, songwriting credits did not appear listing the names David Byrne, Brian Eno, Chris Frantz, Jerry Harrison, and Tina Weymouth in alphabetical order. Instead, these words appeared:

ALL SONGS BY DAVID BYRNE, BRIAN ENO, TALKING HEADS

Everyone's name appeared on the cluttered inner sleeve credits, but the typography and layout were so confusing that all it really did was reflect the level of picayune anality the band had gotten into bickering over credits and royalties. For example, under the instrumentation for the bass player ("basses"), Jerry Harrison appears first. Then Tina Weymouth. Then David Byrne. Finally, Brian Eno. For keyboard, Tina Weymouth came first. Followed by David Byrne, Brian Eno, Chris Frantz. Last on the list is Jerry Harrison. The session players are also mentioned, but no one is designated as a Talking Head.

Just who are these Talking Heads? No way to tell from the cover, everyone's face is covered with big red blotches.

Tina believed Tibor monkeyed with the credits on the back of the album. David told him to. Eno planted the idea in David's head.

Worse, M&Co. began getting credit for the computer graphics, the ones created by HCL, JPT, DDD, WALTER GP, PAUL, C/T. On May 5, 1999, Tibor Kalman's obituary in the *New York Times*—surely our society's most concise summing-up of an individual's career—stated that Kalman's "metamorphosis into a progressive design impresario came when M&Co. designed a Talking Heads album that featured four digitally manipulated photographs of the group members (before personal computer software made this a common graphic conceit) and a title with upside-down letters. From then on, M&Co. received attention in the design trade press for pushing beyond the conventions of design and typography."

Tina was even more burned when Tibor commented about the four airplanes, referring to the Iran hostage crisis. Those airplanes were Grumman Avengers. Tina's father used to fly those planes—those four red airplanes flying over the Himalayas were meant to honor Dad!

"Tibor made a whole career out of that album cover," Tina remarked.

Chernoff's book *African Rhythm and African Sensibility* examined the musical enhancement of life in African rural communities. In Chernoff's view, African rural communities do everything from paddling canoes to beating yams rhythmically. Right about now the fragile community of Talking Heads appeared to be breaking up.

Tina began bad-mouthing David and Eno in the press. Her most repeated bit of venom went something like this: "By the time Brian and David finished working together for three months, they were dressing like one another. . . . I can see them when they're eighty years old and all alone. There'll be David Bowie, David Byrne, and Brian Eno, and they'll just talk to each other."

In his book, Chernoff writes of a fat woman dancing with a short thin man and "everything the man did emphasized the woman's mass and grace as well as his own energy and skill." Remember Tina staring at the back of David's head on the stage of CBGBs? Everything the girl did emphasized the man's theatrical nervousness as well as his energy. His skill.

Back then, Talking Heads had heart. Where was the heart in this portion of the band's history? An amazing passage in Chernoff's book is this quote from a drummer named Alhaji Ibrahim Abdulai:

Whenever they slaughter a cow for you to pick the important meat, you must pick: heart and tongue. These two
meats, they are the right meat, they are the important
meat, and they are the bad meat. Why is that I say so?
Without the tongue, you can't speak; without the heart
you can't think or make a decision."

Where was Tina's heart in her tirades against David and Eno? Where was David's heart when he doctored the album credits? Where was Eno's heart when he predicted to the press that Talking Heads would soon disband?

John Rockwell always saw the conflict in Talking Heads as simple jealousy. "Tina and Chris were jealous of the fact that David was more interested in what Brian had to say than what they had to say," Rockwell claimed. "Eno was a fascinating character. The fact that David would be seduced by him—and I don't mean they went to bed together or I don't mean they didn't go to bed together—I haven't a clue, but what I am saying is that on a psychological level Brian is very seductive. As *extraordinarily charming* as Eno was, he could switch it off. You can be working with him and wanting to wear each other's clothes, and then, *flick!* Brian is gone."

This squabbling is a distraction from *Remain in Light*'s transformative beauty. Writer James Kaplan's life was changed after hearing a cut from the album on the radio. He was driving east on Route 24 near Short Hills, New Jersey, when David's preacher song, "Once in a Lifetime," came on the radio. "The context was rock 'n' roll yet this isn't rock 'n' roll," he wrote. "Not in any familiar sense. The voices were not white voices trying to sound black; the subject was not love or the singer himself or rock 'n' roll itself; the melodic structure was not yet another variant of the twelve-bar, three-chord blues. The song sounded as much like an American Indian rain dance or a Buddhist chant as it sounded like rock. . . . What I was hearing seemed at once removed and intimate, visionary, funny, ecstatic, optimistic and pessimistic. It somehow linked the abiding earth to the sense that we live, nowadays, in a TV set whose channel was constantly being changed."

When John Rockwell wrote about *Remain in Light* he finally got the Talking-Heads-are-Asian idea out of his head: "Black music had always lain at the roots of the supposedly hyper-intellectual Talking Heads style. The Talking Heads retain hints of song structure by shading the choral overlay more carefully than most African and funk groups do. In graduating to funk, Mr. Byrne merely proves he was willing to evolve along with black music—unlike so many white lovers of 1960s rhythm and blues who had never been able to accept the '70s in black music."

expanded heads

Much to Talking Heads' surprise, Warner Bros. was so impressed with the Expanded Heads that they ponied up money for a national tour. The company had just gobbled up Sire and made them a wholly owned subsidiary. In the fall of 1980, this seemed like a good thing. Seymour Stein was made vice president of Warner Bros. Records, as well as the head of the Sire logo. The deal freed up a lot more publicity money.

The national tour of the Expanded Talking Heads began on Columbus Day in Los Angeles and then headed back east. Nona Hendryx saw the group's dynamics as dominated by the socialization power of black music. "There's a vibe that a lot of black people bring with them," Nona remembered. "You do music and you do it in a fun way. And you get silly. You get funky and you make music. There was a lot of laughter."

Of the expanded group, John Rockwell speculated, "One does wonder if the other three Heads—Miss Weymouth and Mr. Frantz in particular—are quite so sanguine about merging their identifies into a ten-member band as Mr. Byrne appears to be."

Nona Hendryx went back and forth on the tour (the other backing singer was Dolette MacDonald), but she was there enough of the time to decide there were no conflicts. "I was there when everyone was still having fun with one another." Hendryx saw the band behaving like a rhythm-and-blues band. A band of gypsies. A throwback to the Rolling Stones—and Nona had toured with the Stones as a backup singer, so she knew what she was talking about.

Here was the group: Bernie Worrell. He was a philosopher. He could always hit his point in a couple of words. Then there was Busta Jones, the second bass player. Everyone called him wild and crazy and coarse and rough. The other percussionist, Steve Scales, was what Nona Hendryx called "one of the silliest people on the planet." Scales was the one who lit up a room when he entered. Everyone called him the Sergeant. He had been in the military. He liked to showboat, talk in a loud voice. He'd keep things together when people's egos got out of hand. Finally, there was Adrian Belew. Onstage, he played zoo guitar. Offstage, he was a quiet and good-natured lama.

The Expanded Heads ventured into wild virgin territory. The stage show consisted of the band standing in a long line onstage—no risers—with Chris's drum kit in the center as the anchor, or as the axis of a propeller.

On one end of the propeller was Bernie. Ricky Vincent called his mastery of the walking bass line on his keyboard a "Thumpasaurus gribble grind that forever hanged the bottom groove in popular music." When Worrell played with Talking Heads, he left spaces for the others to play in.

Jerry was stuck over at extreme stage right. He realized that having the musicians position themselves in a row made the music wildly unwieldy at times. Some nights the two halves of the band would begin playing different music. Often it was a glorious chaos that worked even though it shouldn't have.

Sometimes there were bad nights when the equipment wouldn't work. The mix wasn't right. An amp crapped out. Drums fell apart. Microphones gave feedback. *Uh oh, here comes Steve*. Steve Scales would lighten people's spirits with his clowning around. On the other hand, if somebody was rushing the tempo, he'd set them straight.

Then there was Adrian Belew. He *belew* everyone away with his rhino guitar. Belew had just moved from the school of Frank Zappa, where the music was very complicated and demanding, to the school of David Bowie, where he was given a certain amount of freedom. With the Expanded Heads, he had *total* freedom. His role was to fill in all the things that had been done in the studios—solos and colors and things that no one else could do. Talking Heads' music was a lot of fun. He thought, "They're on their way *up*."

Belew appears to be the only member of the band who didn't partake of what Chris called "the Funkadelic lifestyle."

"I think I was seen as probably being a little naive and square because I really wasn't interested in those things," Belew confessed. "Those things" mean drugs and party favors.

For awhile Belew was given the unlikely roommate of Busta Jones. Busta the wild man. It was obvious to Belew that Busta was on a self-destruct mission. One night in Paris, Belew was shaken awake at five in the morning. Busta, along with James Honeyman-Scott from the Pretenders, wobbled into the room high on coke. Belew looked up into their faces and saw them as dead men.

And that's how they ended up—men who died of drugs on the road.

Adrian did most of his hanging during the tour with Chris and Tina. As Chris was drawn deeper in the Funkadelics, it was just Adrian and Tina.

The woman was always on edge. Belew figured it was two things. Whatever her thing was about David. And her problems with Busta, the twin bass player.

Nona Hendryx thought, "Busta helped Tina lock down the bottom for the group. He really brought the funk element."

It never dawned on Hendryx that Busta was one man who wasn't about to stare at the back of David Byrne's head as he played his bass. The simple fact of it was Busta had better and bigger chops than Tina. Bernie Worrell believed that Busta didn't have the patience to let up and show Tina how to play. Worrell had to have a private moment with her before a show to demonstrate alternate fingerings that would work. In the end, Worrell thought Tina held her own—for a *female* bass player. "She's cute with the big bass."

Jerry saw the problem more clinically. The music required inter-locking bass parts. That meant Busta had to play one line while Tina played another. But Busta didn't have enough discipline to just play his part. He kept funking into Tina lines. For some numbers, Tina wouldn't even play bass. She'd play a rinky keyboard part or just sing.

David loved the Expanded Heads. He found himself locking into all the musicians around him. When the group was in sync, they became what David described to himself as a "multi-cellular organism." He lost some of his identity. This was new for him. He felt a confused joy. Publicly, David claimed to journalists that Talking Heads weren't playing rock 'n' roll. Rock was Daddy Warbucks. Talking Heads had gone African. Talking Heads had embraced communal tribalism. "In the African tradition, we had to learn when *not* to play, and that goes against a rock musician's capitalistic way of thinking, which was to get as much as you can for yourself. In scarifying our egos for mutual cooperation we got something—dare I say it?—spiritual."

In addition to his spirit, Dolette and Nona (when she was on the tour) tried to teach him dance moves. Nona talked a lot about funk with David. She thought he had a spacey tautness to him. She didn't think he was the band's leader. There was no musical director. The group was organic.

As for David himself, he felt like a dancing fool who experienced a state of ecstasy after each show. He no longer felt like he'd had to cut something out of himself. He wanted to whoop and holler. He wanted to shake everyone's hand and say, "That was great. That was great."

It wouldn't be until well into the tour that Tina realized a truth that made her want to eat her own liver: To the audience, having eight or nine musicians standing in a row behind David made him stand out even more. The additional musicians solidified David's status as the leader of Talking Heads.

Bernie Worrell always knew that David was the band's Big Cheese. Everyone could have input, but David had the final say. David liked Worrell's suggestions. Worrell wanted to write songs with David, but he didn't push it. He arranged musical parts. Taught the man funk. The one thing that made Worrell edgy was David's secretiveness. His being into himself. Maybe this was protective. You don't want to broadcast your ideas or someone will steal them.

189

The band played Boston and Worrell took David "across the railroad tracks" from the Conservatory of Music to a soul food restaurant Worrell had loved as a student. He was only partially surprised to learn that David had never had chitlins before.

"Well, you just gotta try it," the keyboardist insisted.

David ordered a side plate.

He ate the whole thing.

He ordered another dish.

"David Byrne can eat." Worrell chuckled. "I can tell you that."

Just a few days before Ronald Reagan won the presidential election, the *Remain in Light Tour* played Radio City Music Hall. A few days after

Ronald Reagan won the election, they played in Jersey. Sometime between these two concerts Tina made a startling suggestion to Belew: "Think about joining Talking Heads as a fifth member. I haven't mentioned this to anyone else. But think about it."

In late fall of 1980, the original "fifth" Head, Brian Eno, had *Rolling Stone*'s Kurt Loder over for tea. They met at the domed one's loft (Eno had a receding hairline; "domed one" was his new moniker). It was the eve of Eno's first trip to Africa at the invitation of Ghana's minister of culture. Loder carefully noted the stack of records in the loft, *Les Liturgies de l'Orient, Music of Bulgaria, Actual Voices of Ex-Slaves,* and Parliament's *The Clones of Dr. Funkenstein.*

Eno told the reporter that after he and David had completed their album, he wanted to go off and work on his own. Then he had been convinced to journey to Compass Point Studios not as a producer, but as another musician.

Eno didn't use the words "session musician." Session musicians don't usually have any say on the music being recorded. But Eno didn't use the words "fifth Talking Head" either. Obviously his position was ambiguous. "Things got pretty difficult at various times; there were all sorts of levels of angst going on. Some of them were for personality reasons, and others were for accentual reasons. But the group has been together six or seven years, and one of the things that affected *Remain in Light* a lot was this history of friction within the group." He then said, "They weren't particularly things that I wanted to deal with. But I had to."

Belew thought becoming the new fifth Talking Head was tempting, but whatever those "things" were that Eno didn't want to deal with, Belew didn't either.

A month before Ronald Reagan was actually crowned head of state at the inauguration, the Expanded Talking Heads toured England. U2 opened. The Heads got a few catcalls from the audience about the blacks in the band. It was rare to see a band this integrated. David Byrne just shrugged this off. He realized he was going to have to actually dance onstage. Previously, he had just twitched.

On December 8, 1980, John Lennon was shot and killed in New York City. The Heads were somewhere in Europe and were only told of the murder as they left the plane. In New York City, Lennon's death was a public event. People gathered outside the Dakota and in Central Park. The radios played the man's music all day. In Europe, the killing was just news. Just more American gunplay. Eno was in Ghana. He spent his nights with a stereo mike and headphones, sitting outside for hours listening to the amplified environment. It is unknown what Eno did when he learned about Lennon's death, but he should have gone out and listened to the amplified bugs. (He might have even heard *beetles*.) It is known that Eno brooded heavily about America during this time: "What I dislike most about America is its lack of a sense of honor. Americans are more willing than anyone else to bare their hearts to you, as if you want that, as if that's a good thing. The whole idea of New York was people walking around exposing their neuroses to you on the assumption that this so-called honesty is good for everyone. One of the aspects of a sense of honor was withholding, keeping certain things as your own secret, part of your identity."

When the Expanded Talking Heads played London, Belew got a call from Robert Fripp asking him to join a new incarnation of King Crimson with Fripp and Bill Bruford. Belew said, "Of course. Let's talk about it."

King Crimson or Talking Heads?

Later in France, Belew talked with Jerry about joining Talking Heads. Tina was championing him. Jerry told Belew he loved his playing. "But we're going to move real slow about you joining the band." Jerry didn't seem as enthusiastic as Tina. "What does David think?" Belew asked. The answer was that no one had talked to David. Yet.

Belew liked David.

David was a quiet guy. He was pretty much the way he seemed in videos. He wasn't a Bahwana for the group. He was more of an abstract thinker. Actually, David was a strange guy who was hard to figure out. Belew thought he had a screw loose in a good way. He had a great laugh.

Belew could imagine being a fifth Head. Or rather the sixth Head; Gary Kurfirst was the true fifth Head. Belew had very mixed feelings about Kurfirst. Belew couldn't tell how honest and straightforward Kurfirst was as a manager. The two never really hit it off.

But then there was Robert Fripp. Belew knew Fripp a bit. Fripp was a complex guy. Fripp was a human being. People tend to make him out to be some kind of strange deity, but he wasn't. Belew thought it was a misconception to assume star musicians are something other than people. David Bowie and Frank Zappa were not gods.

Belew remembered Zappa flying him out to Los Angeles to audition. It was the first time he'd ever flown across the Mississippi. A limo picked him up at the airport and whisked him away to Zappa's mansion in the Hollywood Hills. There was nothing but chaos inside. People moving equipment while Belew stood in the middle of the room trying to sing and play Frank Zappa material. Zappa himself was sitting behind a twenty-four-track console smoking a cigarette, saying, "Okay, try this . . ." And then, "Okay, that's enough of that. Now try this . . ."

Belew got the feeling in his gut that he was blowing the audition. When Zappa told him to unplug, Belew loitered around. He watched keyboard players and percussionists audition. At the end of the day, he had a quiet moment with Frank and said, "Hey, Frank. You know, I don't feel like I did well enough. I'd like to show you. You know, I thought we'd sit somewhere quietly and I could show you that I play these songs and sing them."

Zappa said, "Fine, let's go upstairs."

They went up into his living room and sat down on a purple couch. Belew put his little Pignose amplifier beside him, facedown on the purple couch like he'd practiced at home. He did the audition a second time.

Zappa reached out his hand and said, "You got the job."

Part of Tina's anti–David Byrne campaign was airing her re-audition horror story to the press. She claimed that she had to re-audition for Talking Heads after they signed with Sire in 1976. "It had nothing to do with Seymour," she said. "It had to do with David's paranoia. David made me re-audition time and time again. Anytime David felt insecure I was his whipping boy. Every time he couldn't come up with something he'd beat me up about it. I had to go through the motions of an audition but it was a complete joke. The whole time it was so painful for me. It was like a mock trial. I had to do it over and over again."

David says, "Tina had to re-audition? I don't remember that. That sounds like a Tina story to me—what a horrible tyrant I was. At some point I was a tyrant but I don't think I did that. I may have asked, 'Are you sure you want to do this? We're going down a road here and it looks like it's going to go for a ways. Are you sure you want to do it?' Reconsider things."

• • •

On a night in Italy, Tina told Adrian that she didn't just want the guitarist to become a member of Talking Heads. *No? What else?* She wanted him to replace David.

"I don't think that would work out," Belew said very carefully. "David Byrne is very important to the band. I wouldn't even want to try and do that."

That was the stuff of madness!

twyla tharp

Backtrack a month or two. It's still a toss-up whether Reagan or Carter will win the November election. Carter may still achieve an October Surprise— the freeing of hostages in Tehran. During this time, thirty-nine-year-old dancer Twyla Tharp was sailing over the Golden Gate Bridge in a silver Jaguar driven by her forty-something lover, Bill Graham. Both Tharp and Graham were famous. Tharp was a modern Martha Graham. Bill Graham (no relation to Martha) was the proprietor of the Fillmore West in San Francisco and the Fillmore East in New York, and had been the 1960's version of P. T. Barnum. Tharp told him that she saw no reason why dance couldn't be as big as rock. She'd performed dances to the Beach Boys. Bruce Springsteen. Worked with Paul Simon. The *Washington Post* didn't call Tharp the "hip darling of the ballet set" for nothing. Now she wanted to do something bigger. "Why can't dance be as popular as rock 'n' roll?" she asked Graham. She wanted what was called a "mega hit" in those days. Perhaps an upcoming rock band would work best. She asked the Jaguar's driver to suggest a group. He said, "Talking Heads."

Graham and Tharp's affair was short and sweet and ended amicably. Tharp returned to her apartment in New York and picked up a copy of *Remain in Light*. She didn't love it, but it had what she would later call "a lot of physical drive to it." She could imagine women and men moving their bodies to the beat.

She called David. She caught him at home during a brief lull in the

Expanded Heads' tour. David almost burst out laughing when she said who she was. He knew her name but not her work. Her knew she was a big-deal dancer. And his life was being consumed by dance. He was learning to dance onstage. He was about to do some video work with an L.A. choreographer named Toni Basil, who worked with the kids who invented break dancing. The kids danced up the face of walls, thrusting their arms in and out in some sort of martial arts. Other aggressive steps had names like vogue, punking, boogaloo, and popping. David had been so inspired—Eno, too—that for awhile they imagined that the *Bush of Ghosts* record was being made for breakdancing.

David wondered what Tharp's work was like. He agreed to meet her in TriBeCa at Magoo's.

As early as 1980, SoHo's game was gone. The real artists had split. TriBeCa (Triangle Below Canal Street) was the last stand for cheap artists' housing. Magoo's was the "Alamo," the last *real* artists bar left. Burgers. Shell steaks. *You want Euro-trash nouvelle cuisine, go up to SoHo.* Magoo's was owned by a character named Tom Chaipis. He was a legend. He sometimes accepted art to settle tabs.

Twyla Tharp was one of the authentic regulars. She arrived in TriBeCa in the summer of 1963.

David Byrne was eleven years old.

During those TriBeCa days, Magoo's clientele were mostly blue-collar workers from the nearby American Thread Company. Tharp lived in a $75-a-month loft on Franklin Street with her then-husband. It was almost as raw as the Chrystie Street loft—exposed wooden beams, brick walls, wood floors. Tharp's space had a toilet. She called the neighborhood a "residential desert." SoHo was two blocks away, but of course there were no Laundromats or grocery stores in SoHo in the early 1960s. She had to trudge all the way up to Bleecker Street in the Village to buy food or clean her clothes in the same Laundromat as Bob Dylan and Suze Rotolo.

Down in TriBeCa, Tharp was forced to live secretly. Her building was zoned for business, not living. She had to hide the mattress. Cook on hot plates. Tear up envelopes so no one could figure out where she lived. Take her garbage out at night, and drop it in different garbage cans so she wouldn't draw the attention of some building Gestapo to her dwelling place.

In 1980 the real estate war was over. Tharp supposed the good guys had won. She arrived at Magoo's a little early and waited for David Byrne.

If you passed by Tharp's table and glanced at her, you'd see an odd duck. She was a little moon-faced. To an unschooled eye, the woman's short hairdo was a cross between a Louise Brooks bob and a Beatles mop top—thick bangs flopped from her brow to her cheekbone, revealing an earlobe. In coiffure lingo, her 'do was a "wedge." It was a big deal back in 1976. Both *Time* and the *New York Times* singled out Tharp as an aesthete wearing the cut popularized by ice-skating star Dorothy Hamill. The wedge was first cut by a Japanese hairdresser at Bergdorf Goodman who was inspired by the contrast between the modesty of a woman in a kimono and eroticism of her revealed neck.

Tharp was thirty-nine years old. Her neck was still smooth. When David Byrne finally showed, the woman's first thought was "What a kid."

And so preppy. His hair was slicked back. He had a book bag. She noted his tight jeans. Twyla Tharp was a woman who admired men's bodies. She looked at his jeans again. As trim as he was, David was no Elvis.

The rock star ordered tea. Twyla had a shot and a beer. She and David were both unfamiliar with the range of each other's work. Twyla was under the impression that David represented Talking Heads. He was the songwriter so it made sense she should meet him first. They had no idea what the collaboration would be. Twyla suggested David come see her troupe dance. He agreed.

David went home and watched some videos of recent Tharp dances. Twyla had made her first dance as a little girl when she killed a rattlesnake with a hoe. Conceptually, her work hadn't really changed. Observers wrote that her dances were about speed and balance. Shuffles, slouches. Fluid shrugs. Fast shrugs. Faster splits. Slaps. Slinky shifts. Dirty looks. Innovative pastiches of ballet. Jazz/anti-jazz. Martian athletics. An apology for the human body. A mockery of human fragility. Her dance could be tacky, flippant. It was composed of gestures derived from American social life. *Village Voice* dance critic Deborah Jowitt wrote that Tharp's dancers retained "the spontaneous edge, the casualness, the occasional inelegance of people dancing for pleasure." Prominent *New York Times* dance critic Clive Barnes saw her as the choreographic equivalent of Dorothy Parker.

She was no stranger to pop music. Besides the Boss, she had previously choreographed to Randy Newman, Frank Sinatra, and Chuck Berry. In

1973 she even made the Joffrey Ballet dance to the Beach Boys. Tharp's mocking flippancy had irked the classical dancers. After three weeks of work, she stood up and said, "Look, those of you in this room who do not want to do this work and do not like what I'm doing, I really want you to leave. And I don't want you to ever come back."

Three-quarters of the Joffrey left the room. The piece, *Deuce Coupe*, premiered in February in Chicago. "The ballet steps are like a primitive's-eye view of classical style," the *Times* said, "fascinating in their plainness and angularity, and the social dances are rich with crazy, campily corny suggestion." *Deuce Coupe* was a hit.

While David was digesting Twyla Tharp's videos, Toni Basil and her dance troupe performed at the Kitchen in Manhattan. Her punking, boogalooing, and popping street boys were joined by some classical ballet dancers to do a routine to *Swan Lake*. David was impressed. He was looking forward to going out to L.A. to work with her next month.

David and Kurfirst had been thinking about video clips. This was a new and inexpensive way to promote a band. John Rockwell had just declared that the entire record industry was "teetering on the edge of the video disk era." He identified the pioneers of video music as Bob Dylan *(Renaldo and Clara)*, Todd Rundgren, and . . . Dolly Parton. Rockwell didn't think that Dylan and Rundgren and Parton would save music, "but the potential for the creation of something really new is palpable and surely somebody soon will realize that potential." That writer should have consulted a Ouija board before he wrote this piece. The pointer would have surely spelled out three letters—MTV.

After seeing Basil at the Kitchen, David went down to TriBeCa to watch Tharp and her troupe dance to cuts from *Remain in Light*. He liked what he saw. He offered to make her a demo tape of dance music.

"I know you can do it," she said. "You don't have to make a demo."

"Okay. I'll start." Video was one thing. This was performance art.

In her autobiography, Tharp wrote that her agent said she was crazy not to wait for contracts to be signed. But Twyla didn't want to wait to work with David. There was chemistry there.

This is how they'd work. David would submit a rudimentary track, usually a groove and some sketchy chords. Twyla would listen. If she liked it, she'd play it for her troupe and see what happened. "I could make it

197

appear that the two entities, the dance and music, were created or emerged simultaneously," David said later. He didn't want to follow the storyline too closely.

Dance is narrative and Twyla and David decided this dance would be about a dysfunctional family. How would the story unfold? David revealed himself to be a magic realist. Or, at least, living in a cartoon. Twyla thought David "substituted ambiguity for artistry." He found a base in the absurd. She did not. Twyla remembered her Grandmother Croa's admonishment, "Don't story me." Twyla believed *that fiction was synonymous with lying, that fiction took you straight to hell.*

At least they agreed on this starting point: A horror story about the American family. Wait. There would be a black French maid in it. Everyone in the family would be scrambling for a . . . pineapple.

Although both David and Twyla had grown up strange and crazy, neither had had a childhood encounter with a French maid or a pineapple. It would be a stretch to say that the noisy music David was creating was representational of the way his own Scottish parents would rise each morning by turning on the radio, television, and alarm clocks all at once. Although the main action of the dance would take place inside a suburban house, the place would not be demolished like David's two childhood Baltimore homes had to make room for a highway and parking lot.

Twyla Tharp's childhood was just as crazy. She was born to a stage-struck mother named Lecile, who named her first child after a champion pig at the Indiana State Fair. The pig's name was "Twila Thornburg." Lecile substituted a "y" for an "i" because she thought it would look better on a marquee. She was adamant that her daughter would "grow up to be famous."

Twyla had three siblings. Twin brothers. Another sister named Twanette. No way to tell what livestock (if any) that child's name reflects.

Tharp's family uprooted itself from Indiana and moved to the California desert town of Rialto when Twyla was ten. Her parents built a drive-in—the Foothill Drive-In Theater. The girl spent her childhood working the concession stand. Her parents showed B-films, as well as Doris Day and Rock Hudson comedies. Unlike David, who had thrived as a movie usher, Twyla wrote that she never saw a Hollywood film she liked. But she found the drive-in a fantastic incubator of sex. The young girl would prowl the cars peeking in windows to see couples necking and petting.

The dysfunctional family in Tharp's dance would not feature the

Tharp twins, who were both named Stan (for Stanley and Stanford). Born to Lecile in 1942, the twins would only speak to each other in a language of their own invention. Twyla never said if they ever learned to speak English. In her autobiography, Twyla tells us how Stan and Stan killed mice. Flushed $3,000 down a toilet. Wore their diapers like turbans on their heads.

The Dysfunctional Family Dance would be tacky, perhaps reflecting Twyla's upbringing in California desert culture. She had an eclectic and chaotic education in square dancing, tap dancing, hula dancing, and making rope twirl and dance. Young Twyla also spun batons. Played the piano. The viola, too. She could even beat a drum kit. She was never asked whether or not she enjoyed all these tasks. She was just a kid—and you know what that means: "You either do it or you run away."

CHAPTER 20

cheaper than
dancing lessons

David went out to L.A. on his own in January to work with Toni Basil. She was a cute woman with one of those wonderful cartoon mouths. Her childhood had been as western as Twyla's. Like Twyla, she had been born somewhere else. After her family moved west, her father fronted the house orchestra at the Sahara Club in Las Vegas. Her mother was a dancer. Basil graduated from Las Vegas Senior High School in 1961.

David Byrne was nine years old.

Basil drifted to Los Angeles to become a dental technician, but ended up getting work as a dancer with Elvis and Ann-Margret in *Viva Las Vegas*. Later she choreographed the Monkees in the movie *Head*. She also got minor roles as a space cadet in *Easy Rider* and *Five Easy Pieces*. In the early seventies, she formed a dance troupe with seven men who called themselves the Lockers. David knew the Lockers—"They'd dance on *Soul Train* wearing big hats that looked like pizza pies." Now Basil was working with a new group of dancers, a bunch of street kids called the Electric Boogaloos.

David asked Basil if she could do a cheap video for the *Remain in Light* track "Crosseyed and Painless" using the Electric Boogaloos. He gave her somewhere between ten and fifteen thousand dollars out of his own pocket.

If the video worked out, he'd go to the record company and ask for his money back. Kind of lease it to them. That seemed fair.

What Basil came back with was an African-American video ballet. It begins when a jiving innocent is offered a wad of cash from a slickster in a pink suit. A tough then menaces the innocent with a shiv, a liberal interpretation of the line, "Sharp as a knife/Facts cut a hole in us." A lovely Hispanic babe rolls around displaying plenty of cleavage. Then all the dancers make moves on a blank stage and the empty streets of L.A. There are some cheap-looking special effects, dancers become animated silhouettes. In the last shot of the video, the innocent walks up to a tacky L.A. bungalow where a car covered with a white sheet is parked on the front lawn.

The video would not age well. None of the dancers—Poppin' Peter, Robot Dane, Skeeter Rabbit, McTwig, Scally, and Ana Marie—can act. The more abstract movements are quite beautiful, but the melodramatic pantomime is pure cheese now. What dates the video the most is that it all looks like rehashed Michael Jackson. But the opposite is true. Michael Jackson copped his moonwalk from the Electric Boogaloos.

All this is hindsight. Back in 1981, David loved what Basil did. He said, "Let's do another one together."

David had acted in a rock video once before, back at RISD. Chris shot it for his video class. He had David and a few other kids lip-synch to "Mustang Sally." Basil was more ambitious than Chris Frantz, of course. She had David lip-synch his song "Once in a Lifetime" while making extremely stylized gestures.

Most of their work consisted of Basil helping David's gestural grammar. He'd perform different dance steps while being videotaped. Basil would then watch the footage—she never watched him in person—and tell him how to refine the moves: "If you're going to do that thing with your hands, make it a little more rectangular. Don't be sloppy. Make it look good for the camera."

The foundation of all David's moves was a smacking-the-forehead stagger of a flamboyantly toupéed TV preacher of the times, Ernest Angley. Byrnologist John Howell called Angley "the Liberace of televangelists." The video for "Once in a Lifetime" begins with the image of David's head dunking in and out of the screen. There is a blue background. Then a white one. David appears in a black suit, white shirt, bow tie, and glasses. He begins making rigid preacher gestures. Burt Lancaster in *Elmer Gantry*. Close up,

201

David's face is covered with sweat. When he sings the line "You may find yourself in another part of the world," a B&W film of a circle of African natives dancing on their knees is behind him.

For the first chorus a full-bodied David Byrne does an animated monkey dance with four smaller David Byrnes. For another chorus, suddenly the screen is full of the blue backdrop again as David floats above it singing about water. The blue resembles a child's plastic swimming pool more than it actually resembles water. David does his spastic preacher thing in the foreground while four smaller David Byrnes do different synchronized gestures. Near the end of the video, there is a quick shot of David backlit before a black-blue smoky background—an image that is reminiscent of *Alien* or maybe an Arnold Schwarzenegger movie. Then a final shot appears of David from the shoulders up, wearing his white shirt. He's not sweaty. He's not looking deranged. He's not asking, "How did I get here?" He looks quite Gregory Peck–ish, reminding the viewer that David Byrne is not a geek, but actually a handsome man. The camera can love him if he lets it.

The video for "Once in a Lifetime" was astonishing at the time. Here in the oversaturated second-generation MTV era, its power is only slightly lessened. David's shtick hovers somewhere between the quaked obnoxiousness of Moe Howard of the Three Stooges and the eternal comic grace of Buster Keaton.

While David was making the video with Toni Basil, they also had a brief—what do you call it?—fling. Back in New York, Twyla Tharp, who liked younger good-looking men, became David's lover as well when he returned from L.A. Later that year, after Seymour Stein saw how loose David was getting onstage, he joked, "Boy, it's a lot cheaper than taking dancing lessons."

my life in the
bush of ghosts

My Life in the Bush of Ghosts was released in the winter of 1981. It proved to be an aural psychedelic *National Geographic* of percussion and melody and voices that had the power to drive a listener to the very borders of schizophrenic vision. To describe this music dryly and without metaphor is impossible. Do you really want to know that someone plays something called a bodhran on cut two? David van Tieghem adds scrapped percussive instrumentation on cut three. Might as well say the unsung hero of this recording is engineer Dave Jerden, the primary sonic architect of *Remain in Light*. He not only captures the incredible diversity of synthesizers and electric guitars, but also the cardboard boxes and ashtrays and lamp shades Eno and David beat as percussion instruments. Jerden could make an ashtray sound as rich as a drum kit.

The music on *Bush of Ghosts* is not quite beyond descriptive language. But almost. None of the music is pleasant. The tunes are toxic. Scary. There is singing on this record, but the prevalent voices are men and women talking. *Bush of Ghosts* begins with a buggy synthesized beat. Then a whitebread male voice announces: "America is waiting for a message." These are the first words spoken. They will be repeated. "America is waiting for a message." The rest of the record will be the message America is waiting for.

In the course of *Bush of Ghosts*, a man will say, "I'm sorry. I committed a sin." An African-American preacher will rail, "Help me somebody." Another evangelist will invite listeners to "come with us," his voice sounding as sinister as Satan's as we hear the man perform a literal exorcism. He asks, "Do you hear voices? You do? So you are possessed."

These cuts can only be called post-Christian. They trace the root of America's Jesus much deeper than Billy Graham. The counterpoint to the Christian vibe on the album is a Muslim one—a third of the songs contain sampled Arabic singing and melodies. The Arabic cuts' relation to the Christian cuts is beyond language. Christianity seems blunt and stupid while Islam is elegant. "America is waiting for a message."

The Islamic political subtext on the record has nothing to do with elegance. The message is straight from 1980: "America has suffered great humiliation from us. First we drove up the price of gasoline. Then we let the Ayatollah kick your butt."

David and Eno's combination of music and "borrowed" speech was very culturally influential. More than one writer has credited *Bush of Ghosts* as the influence for industrial, house, even rap and hip-hop. *Bush of Ghosts'* pairing of space funk with Arabic overtones has some historical justification. Rickey Vincent quoted James Jamerson, Stevie Wonder's influential bass player: "My feel was always an Eastern feel. A spiritual thing. Take 'Standing in the Shadows of Love' [the Four Tops song]. The bass line has an Arabic feel. I've been around a whole lot of people from the East, from China and Japan. Then I studied the African, Cuban, and Indian scales. I brought all that with me to Motown."

The music is funk and Arabic and good old-fashioned space music. The final cut on the album would sound at home integrated into Side Two of Pink Floyd's *Meddle*, the wigged-out section where something is howling among the crows in a desolate cornfield. The spatial qualities of *Bush of Ghosts'* last song, "Mountain of Needles," brings water to mind. Water, not mountains.

Brian Eno was likely the only man in the world disappointed in *Remain in Light*. "God, it could have gone further," he said at the time. "If I had carte blanche to write whatever I wanted, I would have taken it over the top." But *My Life in the Bush of Ghosts* is as over-the-top as a record can be. Eno has attempted to top himself since, but so far he hasn't.

• • •

In midwinter 1981, Eno and David got together to do publicity for *Bush of Ghosts*. They met with reporters in Eno's SoHo loft. A sublet. Lots of windows facing north and south. Lower Manhattan buildings outside. A few pieces of furniture in the space—one white sofa. A captain's bed used as a catchall. A bass guitar on the bed. Under the windows, a divan. A record collection against the wall: Motown. Miles Davis. Robert Wyatt. Olatunji. Arabic drones. A long table in the corner.

During one interview, Eno finished an omelet and shared lemon-scented tea with David, who lit a Triumph cigarette and seemed shorter than he really was. David was fidgeting and looking nervously out the window. He spoke of the different spirituality found in Africa. Spirituality is not dogma. Protestant. Dour. Spirituality is fun. Africans have fun being spiritual. Africans can be spiritual and smoke a cigarette, zen-like. Africans can be spiritual and have a stiff drink. David denied he was culturally poaching the music. "I don't think it's like putting on a new set of clothes and 'Here we are, it's all new.' It's saying, 'This might be a clear version of what we've been trying to do anyway'—or a more refined version. . . . Besides, I saw more and more similarities between African music and black American music."

Eno then told the reporter that loss of the Kathryn Kuhlman sample was a blessing in disguise (he would have to work that term into the Oblique Strategies). "We just had to rework that track. This came up after we'd done *Remain in Light* and doing that record gave us quite a lot of new ideas about how we could approach our record as well." Eno believed the two records helped each other. The reporter believed that Eno and David were getting along so splendidly that "future collaborations seem a certainty."

In late winter, Talking Heads got together for what they called a "money" meeting. They didn't have as much dough as they thought they should have. David would later report that the group wondered "where all the money went."

To keep solvent, they played Japan. There the band discovered the audience wasn't allowed to dance. If a Japanese kid stood up, a guard shoved him back down. This wasn't exactly Hell's Angels stabbing Meredith Hunter at Altamont, but it pissed David off. He went to the microphone and told the guards to stop. He told them in English. No one translated his words for them. The kids stayed seated.

• • •

On Valentine's Day, a show called *New York/New Wave* opened at PS1 down the street from the Talking Heads' loft in Long Island City. Lines of people snaked around the four-story Victorian building. Inside hung photographs by Blondie's Chris Stein and Suicide's Alan Vega, as well as photographs taken by David Byrne. He liked shooting hallway lights and making montages of them. He'd also fallen in love with a particular yellow-brown chair at the Sunset Marquis Hotel in L.A. and had photographed it a number of times lying on its side, its back, and upside-down. David had a love affair with inanimate objects. "The highest love is the stupidest love," he later wrote. "The sublime is in the banal."

The sensation of the show was the ex-SAMO work of Jean-Michel Basquiat, which included a white-on-black painting of a car with the caption, PLUSH SAFE, HE THINK.

Nine months earlier Basquiat had become a star at what was called the Times Square Show. People were still talking about how he had shown up at that opening wearing dreadlocks and a T-shirt that said GUMBY WAS BAD! David had gone to the show. He didn't know what to make of some of his new friend's paintings. "I found the SAMO writing and the script was completely different from Basquiat's new stuff on the wall. The SAMO was very clever and provocative and intellectual. The writing was based on the kind of prose printing style of capital letters the way architects do. Architects all adopt the same style of writing when they write on blueprints. It was strange to see Basquiat go from formality to being willfully primitive. I found that confusing—his adopting the pseudo-primitive typography. The images and text and appropriation was beautiful, but the 'I'm gonna make it look sort of African' I didn't quite get."

Around the time of the PS1 show in '81, one of Andy Warhol's friends, Glenn O'Brien, decided to make a film called *New York Beat,* about the downtown art world. He gave Basquiat the lead. He'd play a starving artist evicted from his apartment. Deborah Harry would play the angel who delivers him. Downtowner John Lurie was supposed to be in the movie, but turned down a part after O'Brien asked Lurie's black girlfriend to make them some pancakes.

The East Village was replacing SoHo as the nexus of New York's art world. That weird/sloppy graffiti art scene has been celebrated in *Art in America* as "Slouching Toward Avenue D." Storefront galleries like Fun and Gracie

Mansion began opening. Good restaurants began popping up in Alphabet City. Ironically, this was when David left the East Village and bought a loft for $130,000 in SoHo.

David knew some of his new neighbors. John Rockwell had just moved from his loft in Little Italy to one in SoHo. He now had a wife and child. Rockwell called the artists in his building "pretend." Chris and Tina would eventually get a SoHo loft, but then, as Tina said, "We couldn't bear the financial strains. Nor the neighbors who were *petit bourgeois*."

The Lower East Side of Manhattan, which David had abandoned, bears some responsibility for the bullet pumped into President Ronald Reagan at the end of March. In the New York apocalypse movie *Taxi Driver*, Robert De Niro's downtown cabby (the evil twin of Philip Glass?) tries to kill a presidential candidate on the streets of Manhattan to get the admiration of Cybill Shepherd. After De Niro fails, he blows away Harvey Keitel, the Lower East Side pimp of child-whore Jodie Foster.

John W. Hinckley, Jr., a twenty-five-year-old drifter, was in love with the actress Jodie Foster. On March 30, combining the Lower East Side logic of De Niro with his own psychotic reasoning, Hinckley shot Ronald Reagan to win Foster's heart. He failed to kill the president. He failed to win the young girl's heart. When David heard the news, his first thought was that he was "pissed that 'they' didn't get Reagan."

During this time, Jerry's mother was sick, so he began commuting between Milwaukee and New York. In Manhattan, he rented a top floor apartment on Twelfth Street and Washington. These were the early days of the yuppification of the West Village. In just a year or so, a trendy restaurant, Tortilla Flats, would open downstairs. But in 1981 the area was still a vacant neighborhood of warehouses and artist housing. A good neighborhood to get some thinking done.

In Milwaukee, Jerry reflected on how cosmopolitan his life had become back in Manhattan. Milwaukee pace was so contained and . . . human. He had grown up in a suburb here. He had loved being a kid in the suburbs. Jerry used to ride his bike with his friends to the bluffs by Lake Michigan, where they slid down hills of mud. They rode west to the river and messed around on the railroad tracks. When he was in high school, his first garage band was on TV. *The Doctor Bop Show*. It had been broadcast from the top of the Shrader Hotel building in downtown Milwaukee. Jerry remembered riding up the elevator twenty floors and then walking up two flights of stairs. The studio was a tiny ten-by-ten room, and the camera was behind a glass wall.

Doctor Hep, the host, wore a white smock with a stethoscope around his neck and a reflector on his forehead. He was pushing thirty. He stood in front of Jerry and talked to the boys and girls in the audience about how Doctor Hep was a teenager just like them.

Jerry's head was just visible over Doctor Hep's shoulder on camera, which caught the kid grimacing and rolling his eyes.

Most Talking Heads fans had no idea what Jerry did in the group. The guitar parts they assumed were played by David, and the keyboards by Eno. Of course, if they read the absurd credits on *Remain in Light* they might think Jerry was the bass player.

Jerry's main task was straightening out the contrapuntal and harmonic relationships of the music for the band. What he wanted to do now was his own solo record and worry about his own contrapuntal and harmonic relationships. He wanted to explore time signatures other than 4/4. For example, in a new song called "Things Fall Apart," Jerry experimented with superimposing 7/4 against 3/4 against tired old 4/4. One could certainly still dance to this song, but it required more complex motions than just doing the twist or simple pogo.

Jerry would record these new songs in a little studio he found that was built in the basement of a childhood friend's home. The studio had been an old Eisenhower-era bomb shelter and it rented for $1,000 a week. That was cheap compared to New York prices.

The guy Jerry rented this bomb shelter/studio from recorded commercials there during the day. Jerry worked at night. Bernie Worrell, Steve Scales, Adrian Belew, Dolette MacDonald, and Nona Hendryx all either flew out to record there or overdubbed tracks back in Manhattan.

Nona was impressed with how assured Jerry seemed on his own. "Jerry was more confident out from under Tina and David. Talking Heads primarily centered around David. Now it was Jerry developing his own voice."

dysfunctional
family dance

In March, John Chernoff read some interviews in which David Byrne and Eno praised his book. The author wrote both of the musicians letters suggesting they hook up. At the same time David got Chernoff's address from fellow enthusiast Peter Gabriel. David wrote a letter by hand to Chernoff saying he found his book inspiring. Their mutual fan letters crossed in the mail.

The two met in New York in the late spring. They hit it off. David had asked Jon Hassell to join him at sessions to create music for *The Dysfunctional Family Dance* he was creating with Twyla Tharp. Hassell begged off. When David asked John Chernoff, he said sure. He was thrilled. He camped out at David's loft and the two went into Celestial Sound at Second Avenue and Forty-ninth Street every day for several weeks.

Julie Last engineered most of the sessions. Ms. Last, the one-time assistant on the mixing of *Fear of Music* at the Record Planet, was one of the few successful woman producer/engineers in the city. Twyla Tharp would later write: "David chose the collaborators at these sessions carefully. He had particular theories about engineers and often chose women, believing that females feel lower vibrations with greater sensitivity than men because of the structure of their guts."

Years later, David Byrne was asked if Twyla's comment was true. He shrugged. "The bass/guts theory might be accurate. I dunno."

Jerry flew in from Milwaukee for most of these sessions that were watched over by the loving grace of Julie Last's sensitive female abdomen. Chernoff found Jerry very bright. A good sense of humor. Chernoff was a stranger to all these guys. They were very helpful and patient in terms of explaining what they wanted. "David had ideas that were sort of interesting," Chernoff recalled. "I had brought a bunch of different instruments. I would make some demonstrations, and David would say he liked this, or that. Then I would play out a number of tracks, and he'd say a particular idiom, and add different rhythms, different parts, and then he would also suggest ways of altering the instrumentation. He didn't want everything on the same one drum particularly. He might say, 'Okay, can you play it on these two notes or three notes?' There were, say, three tones in the rhythm, or two tones in the rhythm—I'd play part of it while he'd play part of it on a piano."

Chernoff never had the sense that David was in a hurry to get what he wanted. Most of the time Chernoff felt like they were winging it. Chernoff fought off worries of feeling like an amateur in the studio. Or worse, an impostor. He knew there were a lot of African drummers around New York. "Why me?" he often wondered. "I can drum fine. I'm not unhappy with my music. But why bring me all the way to New York where there's drummers galore?"

Jerry thought Chernoff was a better writer than a drummer. But David felt he had found a companion mind in Chernoff. Later Chernoff realized that he hadn't walked into the studio as a guy who was a product of a tradition or an idiom. He walked in as a fellow citizen of the world.

Chernoff was no purist. "I had no problem with David manipulating the sound of my traditional drums with electronics. On one track, I played the inside of a piano like a percussion instrument. On another, David played the electric guitar with pencil erasers."

To Chernoff, a rookie to the big business of pop music, it didn't seem like much had been at stake at these sessions. They seemed so relaxed. Chernoff and David sat down and decided that the assigned percentages of credit for compositions would be based on the number of tracks Chernoff worked on. The credits would state he played on eleven of the twenty-three cuts that made up Twyla Tharp's *Dysfunctional Family*

Dance. He shared writing credits on four songs, including "Big Business," the one to which he contributed "galloping guitars." He didn't think he was being taken to the cleaners. He figured this was the way it was done all the time.

Twyla Tharp showed up once or twice at the studio. To Chernoff, she seemed happy with the music. One day when they were all listening to a rhythm track—"The whole place was jumping. They had these big speakers. And everybody was dancing. Dancing. All but her. Twyla Tharp was leaning against the wall, you know, watching. Now, I don't know what she was thinking about, but she was definitely . . . I don't know what to say, I don't want to characterize her, it might sound like she didn't care or was negative, because she was certainly enjoying the scene, but it was as if she was restraining herself from trying out movements, if you know what I mean. I mean, that would be a nice interpretation."

David's other collaborator, Brian Eno, showed up at the studio a few times. Eno was friendly enough, but as remote as Tharp. This was his self-absorbed state. Chernoff found himself regretting that he hadn't been part of *My Life in the Bush of Ghosts*. What a record that could have been.

Jerry was really the coproducer of this album. He and David soon moved the production to a better studio called Blank Tape on Twenty-eighth Street between Fifth and Sixth where Jerry introduced David to engineer Butch Jones and Yogi Horton. "Yogi was an amazing drummer," Jerry would remember. "He eventually jumped out of a window. Or was pushed. He'd gone to one of the Southern schools where they have marching bands and make them run on one time and play at another."

211

Jerry's influence—as well as that of additional players Bernie Worrell and Adrian Belew, the latter playing mini-Moog as well as guitar, "steel drum" guitar, and "floating" guitar—make the cuts sound almost like Talking Heads. Unfortunately, most of the pieces are instrumentals. They're all curious and interesting, but none of them is as spectacular as the cuts with vocals. If David had added more lyrics, *The Dysfunctional Family Dance* could have been the greatest music that he and Jerry had produced so far.

Of the five—possibly six—vocal cuts recorded during these sessions, there is a great dance song about a bride and groom, their heads filled with poison. This could be a Talking Heads song. The subject is echoed in another song about poison—a weird burbling percussion number that sounds a bit like *My Life in the Bush of Ghosts*.

Ever since *Fear of Music*, David had been threatening to write a song about economics. "Big Business" isn't quite it. The song's "galloping guitars" sound a bit like the beginning of the theme from *Bonanza*. Then David sings that he's had enough of "big business." An uptown strut called "Big Hands" disclaims responsibility for things that go wrong. The singer keeps his *big hands* to himself.

The cut "Eggs in a Briar Patch" sounds like an outtake from *My Life in the Bush of Ghosts*. The spoken voice of a preacher calls out, "Lord! I've been a bad boy." He then blames dope and liquor for his soul's avoidance of deliverance.

"Big Blue Plymouth (Eyes Wide Open)" is one of the best songs that David has ever written. You can listen to it a million times and not realize it's the first car song ever written about *not* driving. David is sitting in a parked car with the doors and trunk open and a naked girl beside him with her "eyes rolled back in her head."

After working in the studio, David and Twyla would go home and read *The Golden Bough* together. David, in particular, loved James George Frazer's collection of global myths and folk beliefs and examination of magic, with chapters that include "The Burden of Royalty" and "The Seclusion of Girls at Puberty," as well as "The Omnipresence of Demons."

Although Frazer didn't write a chapter called "Big Blue Plymouth," if he had known about David and Talking Heads, he would have.

Twyla believed David wanted to find the residue of ancient thoughts in the most up-to-date aspect of society. She was after the principles that created universality in art. What attracted her to David the most was the way he managed his intense innocence. "He would never let himself be intimidated by his own innocence," she wrote.

David the innocent was planning a trip to Bali to listen to gamelan music and record the croaks of frogs.

Around Twyla's apartment, David would play his ukulele. She believed the great tension in the tiny instrument was well suited to her lover's energy. She learned that his normal rhythm was quadruple time and the ukulele worked well in that small bright range. "Part of David's desire to make music comes from his own wiry body's need to bob around," she wrote. "His angular, jerky style was already heavily influenced by early East L.A. break dance."

The two seldom danced together—although once at a studio he got her to help him create a track by banging on pots and pans.

Twyla Tharp had an eleven-year-old-son, Jesse Alexander Huot, whose father, Robert Huot, had been an artist/teacher at Hunter College in the early 1960s. He had designed costumes for Twyla. When she was pregnant in the 1970s, they made Dalglish-ish videotapes documenting Jesse Alexander's progress. They split up after his birth. Jesse grew up into a precocious New York kid. Once, when one of his mother's lovers called up, the kid asked him if he'd been to a certain party the night before. The suitor had not. "Oh, well, it was a very small party," said Jesse.

Jesse liked David, but didn't see him as a substitute father. David tended to haunt the house, listening to music. Once when Jesse and his mother were arguing over what television station to watch, unintentionally re-creating the drama of David's old song "Found a Job," David responded by threatening to throw the TV out the window.

the genius of tina

Tina Weymouth says, "You writers don't know anything. Nobody knows anything. David takes credit for things. Twyla Tharp had been using a Tom Tom Club album to warm up her dancers. She loved it. She was told, 'Those people are the founders of Talking Heads.' One of her dancers told her that. 'Well, you got to get in touch with them to see if they can make some music.' Somebody gave her David's number and he said, 'Well, the Tom Tom Club isn't available. So I'll do it.' So he cut us out just then and there until it was fait accompli."

According to Tina, "poor" Jerry Harrison even showed up at the studio and thought that he was working on the *next* Talking Heads album.

Memories are strange animals. Memories can't wait. The Tom Tom Club didn't exist when David Byrne met Twyla Tharp. Four, five months later, Tina was going nuts. David was working on yet another non-Heads project. Jerry was off in Wisconsin making a record. The last thing he had said to Tina before he'd left was, "Just go make a solo record yourself." He reminded her how popular she was in France—she had a built-in audience. Tina followed Jerry's advice and went into a New York studio and tried laying down some tracks.

Apparently the process was a disaster. She went back down to the Bahamas, where she lamented to Gary Kurfirst about the experience.

"Tina was feeling very insecure, very depressed about it," Kurfirst recalled. "I did what a manager is supposed to do. I told her how great I thought she was, that she shouldn't let anything get her down. And she should go make a record."

Gary went to Chris Blackwell and got studio time for Tina at Compass Point. Her husband, Mr. Frantz, worshiped Blackwell. This was the white man most responsible for taking reggae global. In 1964 Millie Small's ska song "My Boy Lollipop" had become Island Records' first six-million-selling hit. But the world really changed in 1972, when Bob Marley was stranded broke in England with Bunny Wailer and Peter Tosh. Blackwell gave them £4,000 to go back to Jamaica and make a record. If and when they returned, they'd get £4,000 more. The lads didn't take off with the money. Bob Marley and the Wailers cut the album *Catch a Fire*. Rasta would soon take over the world the punks had tried to conquer in the late 1970s.

Tina and Chris invited Adrian Belew to join them in the studio. They offered to fly him and his wife to the island and put them up. Belew said sure.

He was surprised to learn how many pop stars lived in Nassau—Peter Frampton, Robert Palmer, even Emerson and Palmer (minus Lake). Gary Kurfirst had a house there as well.

Chris and Tina lived on the top floor of an apartment building that housed most of the musicians who worked at Compass Point. The building stood at the top of the hill with Compass Point below. It was a quick walk. The three rehearsed in a building called the Tom Tom Club; it was given that quaint name because, as Tina reported, there were no numbered addresses in that part of town. Then the three went into the studio with Steve Stanley and recorded three tracks: "Wordy Rappinghood," "Lorelei," and "Genius of Love."

Of the three, "Genius of Love" is a tremendous piece of music. It has an infectious, unforgettable hook. Chris Frantz and Adrian Belew came up with the song's beginning after Chris copped a beat from Zapp's "More Bounce to the Ounce." Belew added a rhythm guitar part. Stephen Stanley then came up with the keyboard melody. Tina later wrote the words. "What ya gonna do when you get out of jail? I'm gonna have me some fun. . . ."

When Blackwell heard "Genius of Love," he was floored. Tina cooing, "I'm in heaven with my boyfriend." The song was a Valentine to Bootsy Collins and Smokey Robinson and Bohannon. (Did Blackwell hear right?

Did some girl really purr in the background, "We went insane when we took cocaine"?)

Blackwell said, "These guys are fuckin' good." Chris and Tina got the go-ahead to do an album. They made a verbal agreement with Adrian not to sign any contracts or get any suits involved. They would just make a record and work out the details themselves.

"What I remember is that they invited me to come to the Bahamas," Belew says, "and stay in their place and work on songs. The idea was originally we'll just do one or two songs, maybe three or four and when we get enough songs, then maybe we'll put together a record. So it was really done in a very casual manner. It wasn't planned out, we are doing a record and here are the parameters on it. None of the business was worked out on anything, so I went and spent the amount of time that I had there and I can't remember what the next thing was. Frankly, I wrote quite a lot of the record. In fact, there were several tracks where I played everything. All the instruments. The one that's called 'L'Éléphant.' I did play quite a lot on 'As Above, So Below.' "

Everyone was happy making this record. Then Fripp phoned Belew again to bug him about King Crimson. Chris and Tina still wanted Belew to join Talking Heads. But David was incommunicado in Bali. King Crimson was the proverbial bird in hand. Belew really wanted to join Talking Heads because he loved their music so much. But he also, of course, really wanted to join with Robert Fripp and Bill Bruford. He couldn't afford to wait for David to return from Bali—Fripp needed an immediate answer. Belew chose King Crimson.

He had to tell Tina of his decision. Before he had the chance, Chris Blackwell invited him over for an afternoon at his Ian Fleming house. At one point in the conversation, Blackwell said, "Well, you're doing a lot of things, playing with all the great bands and stuff. Is there anything else you want to do?"

Belew didn't have to think before he answered. He had been sending demos to every record label in the country and none of them were responding. "I really would like to do my own record," he said.

Blackwell replied, "Well, great, well, would you like to be on Island?"

"But you haven't heard any of the music or anything."

"That's okay," Blackwell answered.

Adrian Belew had a record deal.

• • •

Belew's whole career was ruled by grace and dumb luck. He remembered playing with Frank Zappa. Each night, everyone except the bass player and drummer and Frank would leave the stage and Frank would take an extended guitar solo. At one show in Berlin, Belew saw David Bowie and Iggy Pop standing by the monitor mixer. The guitarist walked over and said to Bowie, "David, I just want to say thank you for all your music that you've done over the years."

Bowie said, "Great, how'd you like to be in my band?"

The Zappa tour ended two weeks before Bowie's began. Belew went to Zappa, who had already said that he intended to take three months off to edit his movie *Baby Snakes*, and said, "Rather than doing nothing for three months and taking your money, Frank, I'll go play with David for four months and come back."

Frank said sure. Only it didn't work out that way. Zappa decided to fire his whole band and start over.

Belew told Tina of his plans to join King Crimson. They had tapes and tapes of his guitar work. They told him they would wait for three months and then finish the record when he returned to Compass Point to record his solo album. He left and recorded *Discipline* with King Crimson. He played on David's *Catherine Wheel*. He played on Jerry's solo record. Chris and Tina did not wait. Tina called up her sisters Lani and Laura and said, "Come on, let's make a record."

In June, David was back from Bali and traveled with Twyla to London. She decided she needed a bigger conclusion for *The Dysfunctional Family Dance*. She wanted about fifteen minutes of more high-energy pieces for the end. This section became known as the Golden Section. It was incredibly physical and demanding of the dancers, pushing them to their physical limits.

David pumped up and recut "Big Blue Plymouth," and he wrote a new song, "What a Day That Was." God, the song was driving. It had hooks. It sounded like the best thing he'd ever written.

Maybe it would even be a hit.

In July, Adrian Belew returned to Nassau just an hour after Chris and Tina had left. A copy of the finished tape *Tom Tom Club* was waiting. At the first listen, he discovered that many of his electric guitar solos—a few that were the best ever—had been erased. He also discovered that some of his licks had been turned into melodies. He was perturbed.

Chris Blackwell had rights to the European release of *Tom Tom Club*, while Warner Bros. kept American rights. But Warner Bros. didn't hear a hit on the record. So after the typewriter rap song "Wordy Rappinghood" became a semi-hit in Britain, and "Genius of Love" even bigger, Blackwell arranged for a *Tom Tom Club* EP to sneak into America as an import. First, 40,000 copies were imported. Then 75,000 copies. "Do you still believe it's not a hit?" Blackwell taunted Warner Bros.

The label decided to release *Tom Tom Club* in the fall.

Belew, meanwhile, learned he had not been given any song credit for "Genius of Love." He wasn't given songwriting credits at all, not even for "L'Éléphant," which was 100 percent his. He phoned Chris and Tina—"I think we need to talk about the business deal."

They stopped returning his calls.

He backed off. This record was a goof. It wasn't like *Tom Tom Club* was going to go off the charts.

pagan TV babies

During those Tom Tom Club days, MTV was launched. For twenty years we've been MTV-ed to death, so it's easy to forget the concept was not a sure thing in the beginning. MTV was the child of thirty-four-year-old John Lack. His right-hand man was Robert Pittman, the twenty-seven-year-old son of a Methodist minister from Mississippi. Pittman was the future husband of Sandy Pittman, the most hated woman who ever climbed the Himalayas.

Robert Pittman is the one to pay attention to now. Although he did not create MTV, his was the vision behind its triumph. *Esquire*'s Joseph Dalton once wrote that this transplanted Southerner had one of those faces that "might get old in a hurry, but not for about thirty years." Pittman was the numbers cruncher with "the face of a choirboy." He was the "fellow you watched in a poker game." His eyes seemed a little strange. As a kid he had been thrown from a horse and lost an eye.

Coworkers at MTV who liked Pittman called the one-eyed man a quick study. His detractors said he had a brief attention span. When the ten-year anniversary of MTV was celebrated on August 5, 1991, at Robert De Niro's restaurant TriBeCa Grill, Pittman bounced up to Robert Morton, producer of the *David Letterman Show*, and said, "We're gonna break some glasses tonight!" The two men then proceeded to hurl glasses and sugar bowls against the wall until De Niro's waitresses threw the entire group out.

This is an image to keep of Pittman—furiously flinging sugar bowls at the wall. He wasn't breaking any sugar bowls a decade earlier when MTV launched on August 1, 1981. Pittman had figured music TV would snag teenagers, kids who were ritually dismissed by the TV industry as *low users.* But teenagers bought gum. Stuff to stop pimples. Soda pop. A music station was the vehicle to reach them. MTV went on the air at 12:01 A.M., broadcasting from facilities in Fort Lee, the Jersey town where the George Washington Bridge begins or ends.

Bad ju ju was in the air. Astronaut Neil Armstrong refused to allow his voice to intone "One small step for man, one giant leap for mankind" to an animation of the MTV logo being planted on the moon. The first video played was a song few remember today, by the Buggles, a British group even fewer remember. The chorus went, "Video killed the radio star."

There were only 125 video clips (including two from Talking Heads) available from American record companies at the time, versus more than triple that amount from England. This discrepancy between American and British video-clip vision allowed an inordinate number of silly English groups like Duran Duran to became vastly more popular than they deserved.

The launch went more or less smoothly despite the absence of Neil Armstrong. Pittman did throw a fit because the sequences were all screwed up and veejays announced the wrong songs. When David Bramson, president of Backstreet Records, left the premiere, he commented, "I hope MTV shows us some of the best of black music, as well as rock."

Of course, MTV wasn't interested in running the African-American ballet, "Crosseyed and Painless," but David Byrne remembers MTV running "Once in a Lifetime" pretty soon after they started broadcasting. "They didn't have much 'content,' as they call it now, so they accepted a wider range of stuff," David said. "Eventually they played the song on radio, too. But not at first. At first it seemed too funky—black—in an odd way."

By summer's end, Twyla Tharp had titled her *Dysfunctional Family* piece *The Catherine Wheel,* after the name of a twirling fireworks display. The Catherine Wheel is also the name of a medieval torture device. Three centuries after Christ's birth, Catherine of Alexandra refused to give up her Christian faith and marry Emperor Maxentiues. That pagan ordered her to be broken on a stone wheel. As his flunkies were beating the poor woman's bones, the wheel broke. So they chopped off her head.

Catherine was made a saint.

In the month before the premiere of *The Catherine Wheel*, David dragged Twyla to a late-bird appointment with Jean-Pierre Lentinat, a French reporter. The two showed up at Lentinat's sublet at 10:00 P.M. The place was a mess of open suitcases and filled ashtrays. David stood frowning at the clutter. Lentinat was ashamed. Then he thought, "Shit. Fuck you, big American rock 'n' roller." He smiled at David Byrne and said, "Think of your pad before you became a rock 'n' roll star."

David gave a small and very dry laugh. He was thinking no doubt about 195 Chrystie Street with the toilet down the hall. Lentinat saw Twyla as a small ferrety woman in a black tailored suit, both withdrawn and slightly cantankerous. The Frenchman thought her name was Twyla *Harp*. "Don't worry, we're not remaining here," David said to Twyla. "We're dining with friends in a large loft with white bricks."

The three moved on to Jon Hassell's loft. David mentioned that he regretted not getting to Africa. He told how he *funkicized* the B-52's when he produced their album that summer. He then played a tape of Balinese frogs croaking. The Frenchman would later write, "At the end of a few minutes, these small beasts seem to play a repetitive, unforeseeable, and hypnotic music."

221

Hassell observed all this, but didn't say much. He felt like he was the real composer. He was happy to work occasionally with David and Eno, but on the whole didn't want to have anything to do with rock 'n' roll. "I do not want to be considered for life as the Talking Heads' studio musician," he would tell people.

Jon Hassell thought of himself as a traditional composer. His work had a methodical approach. A system to create a new language.

"Avant-garde composers are satisfied to import and to tie up in new packaging," he would tell you. "And the pop musicians just pin tourist memories on their walls."

• • •

On September 22, *The Catherine Wheel* premiered along with new Tharp dances called *Short Stories* and *Uncle Edgar Dyed His Hair Red*, and the older work *Deuce Coupe*. *The Catherine Wheel* was presented with the "support and encouragement" of Emanuel Azenberg, as well as the Shubert Organization and "Mr. Fillmore" himself, Bill Graham.

The *Times* daily reviewer believed the dance was about *layers:* "The dancers wear layers of clothes, there are layers of curtains and scrims. The shadows reproduce live movement." The *Wall Street Journal* saw the household as stylized "*Clockwork Orange* cruelty occasionally punctuated with black humor . . . so overburdened with symbols as to render itself meaningless." Critic Anna Kisselgoff tried to explain the narration of the dance in the *Sunday Times*. A man comes on the stage in a top hat. There's a woman in a bridal veil. The squabbling family. A black maid. Different groups of disco dancing and what she calls "pineapple snatching." The pineapple is a fruit. It's a bomb. Then people are crushed by the Catherine Wheel itself. Then a man and woman have a shoving match. A man tears a pineapple apart. The black maid grimaces. Stuff is thrown around. Then there is a "brilliant pure-dance section in which Miss Tharp has expanded her vocabulary as never before." There are kicks. Stamps. Rolls. Leaps. The music, which Kisselgoff doesn't comment on, now "becomes more exciting."

Kisselgoff pronounced the piece two-thirds bad and one-third terrific. Clive Barnes, an old Tharp nemesis, said something similar in the *Post*. Her piece was simultaneously "very good" and "very bad." Even "very boring." The first part of the dance was so dull "it would hardly have caused a stir in a disco." He liked the end very much. He said it was "parasitic Bolshoi." But Clive Barnes seemed tired of Twyla. Seven years before in 1976, he wrote perhaps the most energetically deranged dance criticism of the seventies when he pronounced that Tharp's work displayed the emasculation of men with "a certain charm, wit and even good nature." He went on: "This particular approach to dance masculinity—I think it could be called something classy like 'castration'—finds a parallel in the ambiguity with which Tharp views classic dances, as opposed to modern-dance and baton-twirling." He then revealed that when she was younger she confessed to him that she wanted to be the next Martha Graham. "But now she probably wants Martha to be the first Twyla Tharp."

To celebrate the opening of *The Catherine Wheel*, Twyla took her sister, Twanette, to Studio 54. It was so noisy inside, Twanette had to shout to her big sister to be heard. Twanette was excited. She was designing Jacqueline Onassis's new house on Martha's Vineyard, and she told Twyla that as Jackie O. was exploring the half-finished house, a former Hell's Angel/now carpenter had carried the woman up to the Widow's Walk. Twanette's story was overheard by many and would later show up in a *New York Times* "Notes on People."

Two weeks after *The Catherine Wheel* opened, a screaming woman tried to stab a Winter Garden ticket taker with a fork, then jumped up on stage, wielding her fork like a switchblade. The dancers scattered. Twyla and the house manger rushed onstage. The woman lowered her fork, jumped offstage, and escaped from the theater.

What did John Miller Chernoff think of *The Catherine Wheel*? When friends asked him, he looked to the floor for a moment, then said, "Personally, well, I, of course, wanted to see or hear a little more of myself in the mix." He laughed. "I hadn't been aware of how much more David Byrne was going to add in terms of the songs. It came out a little more rock oriented. I'm on the African side. But that's just the way things always work, right?"

It was during this time that *Tom Tom Club* was officially released. It sounded like harmless kid's pop with hints of Africanism. It peaked in *Billboard* at number 23. (*Remain in Light* peaked at number 19.) The Weymouth/Frantz album had two hit singles: "Genius of Love" and "Wordy Rappinghood." Jerry Harrison's *The Red and the Black* was also released by Sire. The music was plainly derivative of Talking Heads' material without David's wit or strident voice. Finally, David Byrne's *The Catherine Wheel* was released on November 18, 1981. When Robert Palmer of the *Times* pointed out the irony of using polymeter to describe a dysfunctional family, David admitted that there was a contradiction. "I've noticed that even when I write songs about horrible things, the act of performing them with a group of people can be enjoyable." Twyla, who was present at the interview, stressed that the dancers all come together in the end as a family.

In public, Talking Heads seemed more committed to their union. They still appeared more Addams family than Brady Bunch, but they no longer seemed to be embittered. Everyone had released an album. David maintained his credentials as the brains of the group because *The Catherine Wheel* contained songs as glorious as anything Talking Heads had recorded. Tina and Chris had more oats because their record was making money.

As for Jerry, well, no one was rushing the record aisle to grab *The Red and the Black*. But he had relevance. He got individual publicity. He could complain to the newspapers that he had had these songs for awhile, but neither David nor Tina or Chris had been interested. So he did them himself.

Next, Talking Heads went public to announce they were *not* breaking up. This was a little like married friends calling you up to say, "Guess what? We're not getting a divorce." David would tell the newspapers that Talking Heads was having a good time. Chris would tell the newspapers that the four were socializing together. They laughed at each other's jokes. "And let me tell you," Chris said. "It's welcome relief."

Even Tina was happy in her caustic way. *Tom Tom Club* was all over the radio. It was in the clubs. It was a hit. Tina used interviews as an opportunity to take snipes at Tom Tom Club detractors. She mused that Tom Tom Club was somehow too "authentic" for regular Heads fans.

Wrong. Tom Tom Club was, in fact, a celebration of frivolity. Frivolity has its place in American popular culture. Bugs Bunny is frivolous. Slinkies are frivolous. Bubble bath is frivolous. Frivolity is fun. But Talking Heads had never been frivolous or corny. Never cheesy. If you followed Talking Heads in 1981 and you bought their records, went to their shows, *cared* about the directions they were taking in music, the Tom Tom Club record—with its almost Basquiatian album cover of elaborate felt-pen doodle drawings of three rather ugly girls singing alongside tiny men playing guitars and congas and palm trees and other nonsense—might seem so frivolous you wanted nothing to do with the music inside.

Tina bragged that *Tom Tom Club* was getting legitimate feedback "from above 110th Street." And it was. *Tom Tom Club* was popular because "Wordy Rappinghood" was clever, the melody to "Genius of Love" was really sweet and catchy, and the Weymouth sisters were so obviously white girls.

In fact, the girls were as white as white girls get. On "Wordy Rappinghood," they actually sang a string of nonsense words that sound something like:

> *Rum some-some ah! Rum some-some.*
> *Koonie koonie koonie koonie um some-some.*
> *Ay kay ay yippie ay kay ae!*
> *Ah-who-ah! Ah-who-ah, knee-key-chee.*

In the history of recorded music, there is not a more gaudy, ridiculous, and brilliant chorus than this. Only Bucky Wunderlick's chant of "The beast is loose / Least is best / pee-pee-maw-maw" from Don DeLillo's *Great Jones Street* comes close.

The passage of time makes us more detached from a work of art. Listening to "Ay kay ay yippie ay kay ae! Ah-who-ah! Ah-who-ah, knee-key-chee" decades later is amazing. The easy thing would be to say the Tom Tom Club is so bad it's good. But that's not quite right. The Shaggs—that trio of sisters who sang about the glory of their parents in 1969—produced a record that is so bad that it is good. The Shaggs sisters couldn't sing, but they also couldn't play their guitars and drums.

Tom Tom Club is different. *Rum some-some ah!* The drums and keyboards and guitars are top-notch. *Rum some-some.* The music is only banal the way most dance music from disco to techno is banal if you're not actually dancing. *Koonie koonie koonie koonie um some-some.*

But what makes the Shaggs and Weymouth girls eternal sisters are their voices. *Ay kay ay yippie ay kay ae!* None of them can sing. Now, that never stopped No Wave singers from belting out a song. But the Shaggs and Tom Tom Club are good white girls with meager voices. *Ah-who-ah!* The Weymouth sisters pumped themselves up with enthusiasm and it emphasized the Caucasianality of their voices. *Ah-who-ah, knee-key-chee.*

The distance of time can also make the banal seem fantastic. Two decades later, the Tom Tom Club's dance vibe seems as quaint as 1930s Hawaiian music. At the same time, the oddity that is the voices of the Weymouth sisters sounds wonderfully out of whack. *Tom Tom Club* no longer sounds frivolous. It is filled with the kind of grotesque beauty whose only parallels are the goofy little cartoonlike demons in Hieronymus Bosch paintings. The difference is that one work of art is about people in hell and the other is about people who are in hell but don't know it.

The newly happy Talking Heads began choosing tracks for a live album. David listened to the tapes, then digitally corrected some sour notes in his singing. Those who heard about the record figured Sire was cynically assembling a live album because Talking Heads was breaking up. This wasn't the case. Talking Heads felt a live album was a way to acknowledge the tremendous transformation they'd made from a four-piece group to the expanded multiracial Heads.

This racial aspect went against the times in a way. Although integrated bands weren't new—the list could include the Jimi Hendrix Experience, the Allman Brothers, Sly and the Family Stone—multiracial bands were down normal. The first video David Byrne and Toni Basil had made, "Crosseyed and Painless," would never be played on MTV. Their videos were "narrow cast," an Iron Curtain marketing term that set limits on the scope of the prospective audience. Robert Pittman was into something called psychographics—a practice of categorizing viewers by stated attitudes, observable social behavior or lifestyle, and psychological traits. Pittman targeted an audience of twelve- to thirty-year-old Caucasians who were into "music culture." Music "serves as something beyond entertainment" for these white folks. Music to them represents their "values." Their "culture." He was hunting "a culture of TV babies" who can "watch, do their homework, and listen to music at the same time." These kids didn't need linear thought processes according to Pittman. "My parents can't have two people talking to them at the same time. They can't understand what's going on. My parents can read *The New Yorker*. I can't. I get bored because it goes too much from point A to point B to point C."

Apparently none of these nonlinear TV babies were into black music. At the *Billboard* Video Music Conference earlier that year, a bigwig from A&M said, "God forbid people should be exposed to blacks on cable."

Rick James, the thirty-three-year-old Motown artist, began a public anti-MTV campaign, claiming that MTV was "setting black people back four hundred years. . . ."

You know, money talks but it don't sing.

Sherrie Levine

the big suit

BOOK THREE

speaking in tongues

Sometime during the winter of 1982, Tina and Chris strode into Danceteria in Chelsea, the happenin' place midway between the downscale downtown hipness of the Mudd Club and the uptown Bianca-Jagger-on-a-white-horse Studio 54. The two were there for a show by Busta Jones. Jerry was backing him on keyboard. Tina watched the show with Chris from the bar. She studied Busta, cool, all pumped up, strutting the stage, dangerous. She was not jealous of this man. She was sure of that. She'd just given an interview in which she owned up to that dark emotion. "I am like a jealous lover if I hear someone playing *my* bass," she said. It was as if that other person were making love to Chris. How *dare* they? She heard the voice of her bass calling and she had to run across the room and start stroking it. That's what she told *Bass Magazine*. "I have to go stroke it and play it again."

She loved her bass guitar. She looked at Jones clutching his— thrusting it through the air. Just like a man. She decided that she would never share a stage with this jerk again for the rest of her life. Of course, she'd be onstage holding her bass while he'd be the one at the bar (or since Busta was Busta, *under* it). Her thoughts broke abruptly when Busta made an announcement, his arm outstretched in welcome.

David Byrne jumped up onstage.

At that moment, Jerry and the band started playing. David was suddenly singing, "Heard of a van that is loaded with weapons . . ." They ripped through "Life During Wartime."

Tina said that at that moment she felt sick to her stomach. She and Chris sat at the bar, banished from their own band.

On February 14, Tina made love with her husband. Chris Franz was not a bass guitar, and Tina got pregnant. This was the intention of the congress. It was a good thing.

Several months later, the double live album *The Name of This Band Is Talking Heads* was released. Until the early eighties, live albums were mostly musical fodder, a way to fulfill contractual obligations until a *real* record could be released. Most live shows, and thus albums, were just a note-by-note duplication of the prerecorded music. No improvisation. No unexpected covers.

A few musicians, however, really changed their tunes around in performance. Bob Dylan, for one. The late 1960s cottage industry of poor quality bootleg recordings of legendary Dylan performances hinted at how exciting live recording could be. They might even reach the level of art. Dylan didn't release an official live record until 1974. But he made up for lost time by whipping out two more live albums between '74 and '82.

The Name of This Band Is Talking Heads was somewhere between *Bob Dylan at the Budokan* and *Before the Flood* in terms of justifying its own existence. Album One, Side One was recorded live in a studio in Maynard, Massachusetts, in the fall of '77. Side Two was recorded in the Capitol Theater in Passaic, New Jersey. Both sides of Album Two were recorded in Emerald City and Cherry Hill, New Jersey, as well as Central Park and at the Sun Plaza Concert hall in Tokyo—all shows during '80 and '81.

The package contains no recordings from '75 and '76, when the band was a trio and sounded wonderfully primitive (half a dozen bootlegs attest to this). The difference between pre- and post-Harrison was like the division between the Old Testament and the New. This change should have been documented—although to include early CBGBs-era Talking Heads music would require a triple album. Who shelled out for those?

The second record of *The Name of This Band Is Talking Heads* preserved the excitement of the expanded group. A song like "Houses in Motion" is positively transformed from the album version. On the live track, Dolette MacDonald's voice sours behind David's in a way Eno's nasal squawk on the album never did.

The only failure on the Expanded Heads cuts is "Take Me to the River," although it fails in an interesting fashion. When Talking Heads played the song as a four-piece, the contrast between the soulful lyrics and David Byrne's edginess made the piece his, especially when he was lamenting that his girl took his cigarettes. The Expanded Heads play the song sounding like a good *Soul Train*–style bar band. The song returns to Al Green's soulful domain, and is now found a little wanting.

Live albums were one thing, but one almost never saw live video footage on MTV. Apparently Robert Pittman's Coca-Cola babies preferred lip-synching and pantomime rock bands—a viewer could play air guitar and know that Billy Idol's guitarist James Stephenson wasn't really strumming his guitar either. Not that there were many Coke babies watching MTV in 1982. The music channel had severe geographic limitations: It wasn't on cable in Los Angeles or in Manhattan. It wasn't catching on in the regions where it was available. Pittman wanted to come up with a slogan to transcend the channel's dismal state. Adman George Lois remembered the famous tagline he worked on in the early 1960s, "I want my Mayyyy-po!" He came up with a six-syllable poem of perfection for Pittman that went, "I want my MTV."

The Expanded Talking Heads took to the road that spring to promote—ironically—a "live" album. There were several casualties and some additions to the band. Nona Hendryx was absent from this tour. But not Dolette MacDonald. Guitarist Alex Weir of Brothers Johnson replaced Adrian Belew. Bernie Worrell described Weir as, "Energy to the max! Stage showman! He contributed different dance steps to the show which David took up." Weir was more a rhythmic guitarist than a lead player. Gone forever would be the Noah's Ark of animal sounds on Belew's electric guitar.

Busta was gone. Tina could hold her own now. She was pregnant and doing double performance duty—the Tom Tom Club opened for Talking Heads. Tina's sisters were on the tour. The Tom Tom Club's keyboard player was Bob Marley's Tyrone Downie—a man who did not get along with that *other* band, Talking Heads. Downie kept things on edge. He fought with the black Expanded Heads. He didn't share his drugs. He dragged his wife with him on tour. He'd menace the woman when she talked to Jerry Harrison.

Tina felt she had to defend Downie because he was her keyboard player. But she also found his hostility somehow refreshing. Let Downie be the disgruntled one. She was surrounded by her sisters and a baby growing in her womb and a lot of money rolling in from her hit record.

When Talking Heads played Yugoslavia, a "reporter" as well as "news" photographer trailed the band around Belgrade trying to take photos documenting "decadent America rock and roll lifestyle." The photographer asked Jerry and Downie to pose beside unmade beds. Step into elevators with budding teenage girls.

Downie freaked because it was impossible to score coke in Belgrade. His wife couldn't take it anymore. She lied and said that her mother was sick back in Jamaica. She left him and flew out of the country.

When the Iron Curtain tour was about to leave the country, there was a hitch with the passports at the airport. It was then Downie had his biggest freak out of all. He leapt on a chair and started screaming at Chris and Tina, who by now were his last defenders.

Jerry stood with his hand to his forehead, sure they were all going to be arrested. Fortunately, they had a government handler who was sympathetic to decadent Americans. Downie was escorted to the first plane that was leaving the country and put aboard to fend for himself.

Back in Illinois, Adrian Belew was putting the experience of working with Tina out of his mind. She wasn't answering his phone calls. She wasn't sending him any money. Through intermediaries, he learned that she considered him just an arranger, not a writer. Adrian Belew recalled, "But back then, I just didn't want to go to court and do all that stuff. I just was at a point in my career where I felt like, 'Gee, I've got so much other stuff going on, I don't want to do this ugly stuff. It just doesn't look good.' Later, after the Tom Tom Club sold a million copies, I learned that Chris and Tina bought a house in Connecticut. I think I got about $8,000 for the record."

Bernie and Jerry spent a lot of time together this tour. They often sat in the hotel saunas together. There in the steam and sweat, Bernie found Jerry a beautiful loving spirit. Very intelligent. Very talented. Good family man.

Tina loved to think of Jerry as a ladies' man. Today Jerry smiles about that. Back in those days, he'd been restless. Linda had some problems. Whenever Jerry went on tour, his heart got suckered. He'd come home with this hopeful feeling that maybe things would change. But things hadn't.

234

"Perhaps if Linda and I had been in the same city the relationship would have ended earlier."

He felt obligated to stay with Linda because of Natasha. He'd stick around until she was old enough to be on her own. This devotion didn't mean he was going to be monogamous.

The Expanded Heads was playing Tokyo in late April/early May 1982, when Jerry ran into a fashion model he'd met a few months before at a Philip Glass concert at Danceteria. This second meeting in Tokyo occurred in a restaurant where the entire Expanded Talking Heads was gathered.

The woman's name was Adelle "Bonnie" Lutz. She was in her early thirties and a knockout. The girl was of Japanese and German-American descent. Her father, Walter Lutz, had been a Lutheran minister sent to Japan during the war, where he fell in love with bamboo (first), and then Adelle's mother (her Anglo name was "Mona"). The couple married and lived in Kobe until the late 1940s when General Douglas MacArthur declared that war brides must return to America to retain U.S. citizenship. The Lutzs went to Cleveland where Walter opened a bamboo museum. Although the enterprise was a bust, the couple soon had two daughters, Adelle and her sister, Tina (who would later marry Michael Chow, celebrity restaurateur).

In 1966 the Lutzes returned to Tokyo where Adelle became the head model for the Shiseido cosmetic company. "I was cute by comparison," Tina Chow said. "But Adelle was beautiful."

235

Adelle was presently in Tokyo to study ceramics and lacquer. She arrived at the restaurant that night with a complete entourage.

Jerry felt particularly charming that night. Everyone stood talking. Jerry began shooting Adelle his love vibe. She told him that David had invited her to the restaurant. Jerry didn't think about David. He just kept shooting her his ray.

Adelle had actually already met David and Twyla Tharp when they were hanging around backstage at the Chinese Opera at Lincoln Center. Adelle's family had produced the show. She felt David and Twyla were there to do what Adelle called "infusing"—soaking up influences for what would become *The Catherine Wheel*.

Gary Kurfirst was at the restaurant. He sidled up to Tina and whispered, "Jerry is putting the make on Adelle. But David is interested. Sit next to Jerry at the table and keep him away from her."

Tina maneuvered the chair-play at the table and successfully boxed Jerry in a corner away from Adelle. He was forced to turn off his love ray. His petal wilted.

What restaurant? No one remembers. David chose the place, so it might have been an Italian one. Or French. David liked these kinds of restaurants in Tokyo as a joke. The food was good, but there was always something a little bizarre about them. They never got the native aspect of the culinary process they were duplicating quite right. For example, Japanese Italian restaurants put fish eggs on the pasta.

David wanted to flirt with this woman but he didn't know how. He kept looking at her and looking away. She'd never met anyone who was this shy. This was worse than going to the dentist. Luckily, one of the friends she'd brought with her was an artist from New York who couldn't stop talking. Then there was German fashion designer Jurgen Lehl. He had been quite nervous at the prospect of meeting David. Adelle wrote, "When Jurgen is around people that he is in awe of, he tends to attack them. This did not help to put DB at ease."

It was a painful meal. But when Adelle told David that she'd never seen him onstage, he invited her with Jurgen to the Talking Heads show in Tokyo.

As everyone was leaving that restaurant in Tokyo, David cornered Jerry in the men's room. "I'm really interested in this girl, do you mind not competing?" he said.

Jerry just gave his sly smile and said, "Sure."

A true ladies' man could always back down from his junior. Offstage, David was too shy to even be more than a third-rate pick-up artist let alone a full-fledged ladies' man. Standing there in the restroom, Jerry realized that Tina was right. He was a ladies' man. Not only that, he was the samurai of ladies' men. If this were a David Cronenberg film, Jerry would have stood before the mirror and flicked his love vibe to and fro out of his forehead. Or maybe he would have simply given a brilliant soliloquy. As the water ran in the sink, Jerry Harrison would say, "A man never grows up until his father dies. I think there is truth to that. I'm so youthful looking. I always thought I had plenty of time to do things. But then a few years back, my mother got cancer. Then my father went into the hospital to have a pace-

236

maker put in, but during the operation his kidneys shut down. He was rushed to intensive care, but he died."

Jerry would stop talking and turn the faucet off. He'd look at himself for the first time in the mirror. "Suddenly my mortality became incredibly apparent," he'd say. "That's when I decided to become a true ladies' man."

The Talking Heads' Japanese tour was over. There was a few weeks' layover before the group continued on the American leg. Everyone agreed to meet in the Bahamas to do some recording. They were going to make a record without "an Eno." Without any producer. A record on their own. David could write the lyrics, but the music would be written and credited to David, Chris, Jerry, and Tina.

But David didn't show. Tina worried that something bad had happened. She called Twyla Tharp. "Do you know where David is?"

"No," Tharp answered. "Isn't he with you?"

David was courting Adelle in Japan. He'd won her when she saw him perform.

"I was amazed at his onstage transformation and control of the stage with transcendent abandon," Adelle accounted. "Offstage, DB was the deer caught in the headlights. Onstage, DB was completely comfortable wearing his stage personas. Or rather, revealing himself layer by psychic layer."

David has said that he never saw Twyla Tharp again after meeting Adelle. Twyla Tharp wrote of the end to her relationship with David in her autobiography, *Push Comes to Shove:*

237

> Soon after [*The Catherine Wheel* tour] closed, David and I
> agreed to split up. Talking Heads had just returned from
> Japan, my company from Mexico, but it was our temperaments, not our travel schedules, that did us in. The truth
> was we only loved being close to the mystical and the out-of-control; deep down, each of us felt a need to be in
> charge—a conflict that became clear over *The Catherine
> Wheel* video. I raised the money for the project and I was
> going to direct. David felt differently, and after a brief
> meeting in my kitchen, we parted.

That spring, Basquiat threw a big party at his SoHo loft on Crosby Street to celebrate his opening in a group show at the Marlborough Gallery. David was back in town and he showed up. David Hockney, the photographer/painter was there, and David Byrne accosted him. "I started doing these photo montages a few years ago and I think it was before you were doing them."

David Byrne was claiming David Hockney ripped him off much the same way Andrea Kovacs had accused the first David of the same thing years before over his mosaic-Polaroid cover of *More Songs About Buildings and Food.*

David Byrne was pretty high at that party.

Hockney ignored the kid.

David thought Hockney was wearing a hearing aid, or maybe listening to opera. In any case, the party ended early when the upstairs neighbors called the fire department.

Also in spring, Brian Eno confessed to the *Chicago Tribune* that he was infected with high finance like everyone else in these Ronald Reagan days. His interest blossomed shortly after he moved to a loft only a short yuppie's stride from Wall Street. Every morning when Eno went down to the newsstand to get his *Times*, he'd find himself paging through all the financial journals and tip sheets. He began learning all about Standard and Poors. Junk bonds. To this musician, it was like listening in to somebody else's phone calls. Eno began investing in high-tech companies. "I don't expect to make any money in the stock market," he said. "But I'd like to understand how that world works. My philosophical inclinations are toward anarchism, but I often find that most people who call themselves anarchists don't have the faintest notion of how capitalism works."

On May 26, Tina, Chris, David, and Gary Kurfirst were going uptown in a checker cab. "Oh, guess what," Gary said. "I just heard the Tom Tom Club record went gold."

Silence. There was a palpable silence that became a presence in the taxi. The traffic outside the cab didn't get louder, the absence of speech created a vacuum. An avant-garde playwright like Robert Wilson could have created a performance piece of this event. On the stage, the pedestrians surrounding the cab would walk to and fro in exaggerated steps, giving voice to the horrible sucking silence inside the taxicab.

Finally, Tina spoke. "This is wonderful news," she said. "But it would have been better if it had been Talking Heads first."

David said nothing.

Finally Kurfirst said, "Now we've got to see some Talking Heads records to compete with Chris and Tina."

Seymour Stein said, "I always wanted David to have success outside of Talking Heads because I never wanted the Tom Tom Club to be something that bothered him or something held over his head."

Jerry believed, "The success of the Tom Tom Club reignited the competitive spirit of Talking Heads. We stayed together longer."

"I've had some second thoughts about what I should and shouldn't say about the Tom Tom Club," Adrian Belew remembered. "First of all, I'm not a person who holds a grudge about anything. Even though my experience with the Tom Tom Club at the time was not good for me, I don't really care. It's twenty years ago. Who cares? If I ran into Chris and Tina tomorrow I'd be as friendly as I always am. For, you know, there's no reason not to be."

On July 30, 1982, the Tom Tom Club mini-album *Under the Boardwalk* was released. It was harmless pop, but those white voices of the three Weymouth girls were now a thin joke.

From July through September, the Expanded Talking Heads toured Europe again. David was now dancing regularly onstage each night. His self-generated choreography would one day be cataloged by Byrnologist John Howell as spastic duck, knock-knee, Indian-snake, guitar, possession, vibration, jogging, leaning back, and wiggle.

David saw that the confluence of African rhythms, funk, gospel, and rock 'n' roll had become a spiritual release for him. "This is a church," he thought. He saw that the funkier it got, the more ecstatic it got. In funk, as in a lot of African music, there was more than one rhythm happening at the same time. As David felt the different rhythms moving through his body he was transported. "It takes you out of your mundane time into another time. Music establishes another clock outside of your wristwatch. Beats and pulses and melodic phases become another reality. Anybody can jump into it. It's a not too dangerous trip you can take for a short period and then you can come back to your everyday life."

David always believed that God revealed himself in an instant. In epiphany. Music was it for David. God revealed and was revealed in David's spastic duck. His knock-knee. His Indian-snake, guitar, possession, vibration, jogging, leaning back, and, yes, his wiggle.

At different times during the year, Talking Heads had flown to the Bahamas to work on a new album. The new songs were more developed than those on *Remain in Light*. What was the band playing now? Pop/funk? Art/pop? Funk/art?

They took guidance from a Caribbean keyboard player named Wally Badarou. David felt Badarou "cemented" several important songs.

Badarou was a twenty-eight-year-old classically trained pianist. He had written and performed on Grace Jones's *Warm Leatherette*. Written the soundtrack for *Kiss of the Spider Woman*. And had a dance hit called "Chief Inspector." Thus, his nickname was the Chief Inspector.

Chris and Tina dug him because of a common background. The father of the Chief Inspector was a West African diplomat, and Badarou had grown up in London, Madrid, and Paris. He then served in the army. He played in bar bands. Out of the army, he decided to make his parents happy and get a law degree. But law school made him miserable. He gave up his bourgeois comforts to become a musician. He eventually connected with Chris Blackwell, who was looking for a keyboard player for his Amazonian singer Grace Jones.

David dug the Chief Inspector because, like David himself, when Badarou was a kid he wanted to be a scientist. Badarou had wanted to be an aeronautical engineer.

The band would record a bit, then David would return to Manhattan and begin pacing his SoHo loft singing gibberish into his little tape recorder. Gibberish in the meter of the songs. All day and night the melody that came up would keep playing in his mind. But he paced his loft mostly in the middle of the night. Searching for words. Typing them down. He would end up typing pages and pages. David was typing in tongues. It wasn't like using a Ouija board. Or maybe it was, but imagine using your tongue to slide the little glass pointer around. David ended up saying *something*. The things he wrote felt right. The words weren't just random. David was actually saying something, it just wasn't in a linear fashion.

He wrote a verse about "making flippy floppy." David had no idea what "flippy floppy" was. "The words just sounded kinda funky," he said. "Kinda nasty. But kinda fun." Then he wrote some words about moon rocks. The astronauts had been able to bring back 842 pounds of them. David remembered when the rocks had gone on tour in the seventies. He remembered that Neil Armstrong came along before MTV. He remembered it was once significant to drink Tang. It was a way to drink what a moon man drank. Then David wrote another song, one that began with perhaps the truest words he'd ever written: "Who took the money? Who took the money away?"

David also wrote a song called "Addiction." It was about the devil. Not the real Devil with a capital "D." He wasn't about to sing about Satan. David didn't even believe in Lucifer. The Devil was just people listening to themselves. David was writing about a theatrical devil. He'd just seen Mabou Mines do a production called *Dead End Kids,* comparing the guys who developed the atom bomb at Los Alamos with Dr. Faustus. That devil was an old blues singer.

Finally David wrote the lyrics to what would be Talking Heads' most poignant song. "Home is where I want to be . . ." the lyrics begin. The song, "This Must Be the Place," is an extension of the homesickness of "The Big Country" and "Cities." In fact, this song is perhaps the most whole-hearted tune about home since Stephen Foster's "Old Folks at . . ." without being sentimental or mawkish. David confesses, "I'm just an animal looking for a home."

A den. A nest. A hole.

A home must have love. David wants the listener to "love me till I'm dead." The singer also commands, "Hit me on the head!" Ignatius Mouse braining Krazy Kat with a brick. Singer Shawn Colvin, who covered "This Must Be the Place," loves the line "You have a face with a view." "I feel good every time I get to sing that line," she wrote on the liner notes to *Cover Girl* (1994). David wanted that line to evoke a nineteenth-century British poet describing his beloved's face as if it were an English landscape. A Scottish landscape.

During the time David was writing about home, Seymour had just signed a new female singer from his room in a New York hospital. He wasn't in for anything serious, but he actually ended up handing the girl her contract as he lay in bed wearing boxer shorts, a drip feed stuck in his arm. This girl made him nervous. He talked a mile a minute while her demo tape blasted from a boom box. The girl thought he was nuts, but he was the president of Sire Records. "He likes my music—I'm not going to complain," she thought. This was a girl named Madonna.

Seymour didn't want Madonna to think she was signing with a guy halfway in the grave. "The first week I'm out I want to take you out to dinner," he told her. "I want you to see me when I'm well."

He was obsessed with this. "I want you to see me when I'm well."

As soon as his doctors sprang him, Seymour phoned Madonna. He told her he'd take her to dinner. He knew she was poor. She looked forward more to a meal than to socializing with him. He remembered how when he first started taking David out to restaurants, the kid would stuff biscuits and food from discarded plates into his pockets as if this were his last chance to ever eat again.

"I'm free every day this week except I have to go see Talking Heads playing at Forest Hills," Seymour said to Madonna on the phone.

She gave a squeal. "I'd love to go see them."

Seymour took her to Forest Hills. A number of interesting people were sitting in the audience, including Susan Sontag. Sontag, intellectual prima donna of Manhattan, actually used to hang out at CBGBs, but this was the first time she'd ever seen Talking Heads live. She was there with a guest. Just as David Byrne once sat in the audience of *Einstein on the Beach* and watched Robert Wilson's stage design, Robert Wilson sat beside Sontag in the audience watching David Byrne. This was the first time he'd ever seen Talking Heads.

Robert Palmer of the *New York Times* was in the audience and he would later remark that the band seemed thoroughly integrated—not only in the racial sense. The year before, the Expanded Heads had sounded like a quartet with guest musicians. Now the Expanded Heads was a tight eight-piece band.

Tina especially seemed tight. Robert didn't miss Busta. He knew what he would write for the paper: "On Saturday, her playing was wonderfully deft and solid, and it meshed seamlessly with Mr. Frantz's authoritative drumming."

242

After the show, Seymour brought Madonna backstage and introduced her to David (her encounter with a ripped David and Basquiat would happen later). They chatted. Madonna looked like a lynx and David just stood there like a happy dog. Later, as Seymour was leaving with Madonna, David caught the record mogul's eye and gave a flamboyant thumbs-up. Seymour was pleasantly startled.

Next Susan Sontag came to meet David and introduce him to Robert Wilson. The theater director had never met anyone as instantly compatible as David.

On October 14 and 15, Twyla Tharp premiered her first post-Byrne piece, *Nine Sinatra Songs*. These were eloquent descriptions of class. The second piece was called *Bad Smells*. In it seven dancers act out the fiction of a cataclysm that has reduced them to tribal brutes. As her dancers danced, a video monitor projected live images of the action on a screen above the stage. It was as if MTV was metaphorically looming above us all. Two months before, Manhattan Cable had begun broadcasting MTV in New York City. The country was going crazy for MTV.

Video was still young enough that it could be considered art, not cliché. Back on August 1, the Museum of Modern Art selected some video clips for their archives. They chose a promo from *Lick My Decals Off* by Captain Beefheart. Laurie Anderson's "O Superman." And Talking Heads' "Once in a Lifetime."

Almost twenty years later, David remarked, "It was a nice thing to put in press releases, but really, so what?"

In the fall of '82, MTV was less concerned with art. They were still battling charges of racism. Of fifty video clips they rotated, only one video highlighted a black group. Yet seven of the thirty-five best-selling albums in the nation were by black performers. Do the math.

Robert Pittman disagreed, of course. "You can't be all things to all people," he said. "We don't play Barbra Streisand either and she's big."

David visited Adelle again in Japan. She noted that DB (as she would refer to him in letters) was shy in life but not in Japan. He was very much at ease moving through all things Japanese. DB had a way of sitting or squatting as he read a book or waited for a train that was peculiarly Eastern. She decided that if there is such a thing as reincarnation, DB must have been Japanese in a past life. "And a farmer at that."

On November 4, on another island, in another part of the world,

Talking Heads worked on their album in the Bahamas. Tina was already in labor as the group was laying down the last lines on the last track. Bernie Worrell showed up with Funkadelic's brainchild, George Clinton. Clinton walked up and put his hand on Tina's stomach. The next day Robin Weymouth Frantz was born three weeks early.

Later, George Clinton told her, "I scared that child out of you."

Several days later on December 1, a different black man released a record called *Thriller*. No one could have foreseen how dramatically it would change the music industry.

Throughout the winter of '82–'83, Basquiat was in Los Angeles. So was David Byrne. So was Madonna. Basquiat was a Talking Heads fan. He and David spent time at Mr. Chow. So did Basquiat and Madonna. Basquiat gave paintings to Michael and Tina Chow in return for food and drink. A witness of that time (interviewed by Basquiat biographer Phoebe Hoban) remembered Christmas Day as being particularly hot. "We were out at this beach house, and Madonna had the Yellow Pages in her lap and she was feverishly looking for a pharmacy that would deliver condoms to Malibu on Christmas Day."

Shortly after Karen Carpenter died on February 4, 1983, David flew to England to produce a record by an obscure group called Fun Boy 3. Their music is not important, but one of the songwriters had written a song about being molested by his teacher on a trip to France. It was a true story. It started David thinking about how much he avoided autobiography in songs.

"Velvets. Frank Zappa. Most music and musicians' inspiration seemed to come out of other music," he realized. One of the things that made the songs he wrote for Talking Heads so unique was that the inspiration was coming from other sources like books and movies. He felt his songs ended up telling him what he was going to be doing a year from now. The best way to explain it was, "The song tells me what I'm feeling in a kind of coded message, and a year later I realize, 'That's why I just got myself into this jam.' "

The new Talking Heads album cover would be created by Robert Rauschenberg. He was a quirky enough American. Had he been born a contemporary of David Byrne's, Rauschenberg might have very well fronted a rock band himself instead of becoming a visual artist. But he was twenty-seven years David's senior, born in Texas. During the war, Rauschenberg served as a kind of a semi-shrink for shell-shocked soldiers in an asylum north of San Diego. He then went to Paris on the GI Bill and painted studies of naked women. Unfortunately, after he shipped the work home to Texas for safe-keeping, Mom painted bras and panties on the nudes.

Art critics agree that Rauschenberg's first seminal work was *Erased de Kooning Drawing*, which is exactly was what its title says. Two years later, Rauschenberg painted his quilt and called the work *Bed*. He later attached stuffed fowls and poultry to silk-screened collages and called the work "combines." This form climaxed with the late 1950s title *Monogram*, which consisted of a stuffed paint-smeared Angora goat with a car tire wrapped around its belly.

For the Talking Heads cover, Rauschenberg designed a complex assemblage of clear and variously tinted parts made of moving plastic. It would be murder to assemble. Jerry began calling manufacturers to come up with a way to make a record that was a work of art in packaging as well as music. He would be on the telephone off and on for months trying to get everything in sync. It would prove to be such a grind that Jerry was prevented from doing a second solo record. His ear stayed glued to the horn for hours, discovering that no one knew how to mass produce Rauschenberg's vision. Finally, a company who printed on bread bags figured out a way to construct what the artist wanted. High school students—kids who made Oscar Meyer wiener packages—would assemble the things in Prince's hometown of Minneapolis.

At the end of February, one particular song was playing every minute on at least one radio station from California to Maine—Michael Jackson's "Billie Jean," a poignant plea against a paternity accusation. There was a video of Michael doing the moonwalk he stole from Toni Basil and the Electric Boogaloos.

MTV barely played it.

Robert Pittman was drawing a line in the sand. Michael Jackson did not fit MTV's format. MTV's "twenty-three-year-old viewer with an income of $30,000" did not care about Michael Jackson's paternity angst.

Supposedly CBS's Walter Yetnikoff became so enraged at Pittman that CBS threatened to hold back all promotional videos unless MTV relented and played Jackson. That meant no more Pink Floyd. No more Billy Joel.

So MTV played "Billie Jean."

Later, both Pittman and Yetnikoff denied that MTV had been muscled into running the clip. But with MTV airing "Billie Jean" night and day, the great emancipation act of the recording industry had begun. Soon MTV was even playing Jackson's new video, "Beat It," a work MTV historian R. Serge Denisoff called "the 'Stairway to Heaven' of rock videos."

Thriller sales of 80,000 units per month trickled down to an increase in sales for other artists. A kid would buy *Thriller*. Take it home. Like it. Like even more the feeling of purchasing something that made him feel good. Then go back to the record store and buy an album by Prince. Or Tina Turner.

Or Talking Heads.

Tina's baby was four months old. The new mother found herself getting up in the middle of the night and writing songs for the Tom Tom Club the day before they were to be recorded.

This record was going to be a bigger hit than the first record. The Tom Tom Club was going to be as big as the Carpenters.

Tina wanted the glory, and Tina needed the money.

That winter, David Byrne called a meeting of the band to show them drawings that resembled a set by Robert Wilson.

"This is what I want to do for the next tour," David said.

Tina looked and thought, "Oh, shit."

"Are you sure, David?" she said. Tina was not troubled by David's artistic intent, but because what he was proposing—sets, props, audiovisual materials—looked expensive.

An-arm-and-a-leg expensive.

Tina didn't like to complain about money, but she didn't feel anyone was making any but David. Gary Kurfirst was in the process of renegotiating the contract, but who knows how long that would take.

"You know, David Bowie did a tour like this," Tina said. "We've heard nightmare stories about that. This is going to cost a lot of money. It's going to be very difficult to take on the road. It will have to travel, David. Robert Wilson stays in the same place. It is a beautiful idea, but it's going to be very hard on the road crew. They're going to have twenty-one hour days."

David could not be dissuaded. Next David wanted a big suit.

Much had been going on since he'd been to Japan the previous fall.

First, Adelle Lutz got David involved on a Robert Wilson project she was working on called *CIVIL warS*.

Adelle was in awe of Wilson. "He has such a huge vision," she told David. "It's an opera built in five different continents telling different parts of the story of Robert E. Lee and Lincoln." They would all come together next year at an art festival held during the Olympics in Los Angeles. She laughed. Anybody who would undertake such a Melvillian thing must be "slightly potty."

"I will say this about Bob," Adelle said. "He's *big* in every way. He wasn't born in Texas for nothing. And no one paints the stage with light the way he does. His technical rehearsals are as much about lighting as they are about staging and blocking."

Robert Wilson himself said, "The big expanse in all my pieces is me trying to duplicate the Texas skyline." Soon David was thinking big like Robert Wilson.

The inspiration for what will become known as the Big Suit came at another dinner in another restaurant in Tokyo. Adelle and David were there with Jurgen Lehl. David was drawing a figure on a napkin. He said, "The next time I tour, I should have a costume."

The German made a pronouncement: "Well, David, in the theater everything is bigger than real life."

David thought about the Kabuki theater pieces that he and Adelle had been overloading on in preparation for working on the Wilson piece. All the Kabuki costumes were very rectangular. He drew a picture of someone wearing a Kabuki costume on his napkin. The person's head looked like a very small ball.

247

"I thought, 'What if you take that kind of silhouette but put it in a Western business suit?' " David said. "I've become fascinated with the idea of taking things that look very everyday or commonplace and stretching that somewhat rather than making something totally fantastic and imaginary. I like to restrict myself. Take a business suit—a business suit has to look like a suit, even if it's made of pink fur. It makes reference to the businessman. It had some kind of psychological meaning besides being a costume. It's a businessman in prison buying a suit or lost in his suit or his suit was swallowing him. It implies all these other things that a wild costume that didn't have those references wouldn't say."

• • •

David Byrne thought about business suits when he went to a Sumo match with Adelle. Again, he heard Jurgen's rather pompous pronouncement, "Well, David, in the theater everything must be bigger than real life."

David imagined Sumo wrestlers in suits.

Big suits.

The Rauschenberg cover was still a bitch. It wasn't ready. Andy Warhol had once designed a complicated cover for a Rolling Stones record—trousers that unzipped revealing a male pelvis in white underpants. The zipper was real. Apparently there were problems in constructing the package so the zipper wouldn't scratch the vinyl album inside. That was nothing compared to the logistical problems of Rauschenberg's plastic impossibility. The only good thing about the delay was that it gave Jerry and David time to fiddle with the remixing. The devil song "Addiction" had been used on Robbie Robertson's soundtrack for *The King of Comedy*. It was as close to a blues song as Talking Heads had ever done. Robertson said he liked a rougher mix better. It sounded more "swampy." David changed the title to "Swamp." Then he and Jerry went back into the studio and swamped up other cuts as well.

The record absolutely had to be out on June 1 and the Rauschenberg cover couldn't be finished in time. Warner Bros. then decided that the special sleeve would raise the price of the album too much. It would be released later as a special edition. For now, David created a quickie cover. He took the four photographs of a chair he'd tipped over in the Sunset Marquis Hotel in Los Angeles and placed them on each corner of a square bordering a large blue swirl. M&Co. designed interesting typography by changing the spacing of the letters:

TA LKI N GHE ADS
SP EAK IN GI N
TO NGU ES

The new Talking Heads album was released on June 1, 1983.

The songs were funky. They were also synthesizer-based. Many years later, it's apparent that the Heads were recording prog funk.

The first song was also the first single, "Burning Down the House."

The song cooked. Tina's bass line was from a Black Uhuru song in which Robbie Shakespeare played this *dum-diddit-dum*. Everyone in the band decided that the Chief Inspector was responsible for making this song sizzle so much. They decided that Wally Badarou would produce the next record they did.

The most beautiful bit of music on the record is the keyboard on the last song on the album, "This Must Be the Place (Naive Melody)." The parenthetical phrase in the song, "Naive Melody," comes from the fact that everyone played instruments at which they weren't technically proficient. Tina played guitar while Jerry played bass. David VanTieghem, a percussionist performance artist, played bottles and other objects. Both David and Badarou played keyboards. David played the solo in the piece. How can you describe a melody in words? The song's notes move around in a way that is familiar and different. The notes wrap themselves up in each line like a perfect piece of sushi. The notes are like new shoes that don't need breaking in. The notes are like taking a different freeway home and enjoying the view so much you don't care whether the trip was longer or shorter than your regular route.

This album, which begins with a song about a house burning down, ends with a homesickness song that's sweet, not schmaltzy.

After *Speaking in Tongues* came out, Talking Heads was respectable enough to be reviewed in the *Wall Street Journal*. " 'Speaking in Tongues' brings the band back to 1977 when as students fresh from the Rhode Island School of Design, they found themselves gaining critical acclaim and loyal following with their charming and precise minimalist rock and their odd simple lyrics delivered by David Byrne's bleat of a voice." The reviewer goes on to suggest one can hear the "renewed joy" that David, Weymouth, Frantz, and Harrison get from playing with each other.

It makes sense that the *Wall Street Journal* reviewed the record. *Speaking in Tongues* would be the first Heads album to sell a million copies. The largest percentage of the title was sold as prerecorded cassettes. Maybe the Walkman wasn't so evil after all. For the first time, American kids were buying more tapes than records. To beat the Japanese at their own game, American record companies had been making prerecorded tapes more exciting. *Let's include longer remixes. Extra stuff.* Five songs on the cassette of *Speaking in*

Tongues were longer than on the LP. "Moon Rocks" was only thirty-eight seconds longer, but "Making Flippy Floppy," "Girlfriend Is Better," and "Wild Gravity" had extended instrumental passages that lengthened each cut by more than a minute. Finally, "Slippery People" clocked two minutes, thirteen seconds longer than its poorer cousin on vinyl. What a paradox. The longevity of a vinyl was more than one hundred years while prerecorded cassettes were lucky if they lasted a decade. The extra beef on these cuts would be lost forever—or lost until another form of prerecorded music came along.

What a peculiar environment in which to release an album with a cover meant to be taken as a serious work of art. On June 29, the Robert Rauschenberg package was finally on store shelves. On July 11, Andy Warhol walked around the Village and stopped at Tower Records on Broadway and Fourth Street to buy the Rauschenberg version of *Speaking in Tongues*.

He remembered he was once walking down Fifth Avenue and popped into a record store where the song "Heroin" was playing over the sound system. It was so strange to hear Lou singing those songs. The music still sounded so good to him. It brought him back to those wild Factory Days.

If only it were really true that people would be famous for fifteen minutes and not a minute longer. . . .

The clerks recognized Andy and asked him to sign the album jacket. It was the original cover he had designed, the one with the banana that you could peel the skin off of.

"Does MGM keep reissuing this?" he thought. Then frowned. "I never got any money at all from this record."

Warhol brought *Speaking in Tongues* home. Sire had manufactured 50,000 copies. The cover is an offset lithograph on what's called "vacuum-formed plastic." The plastic is thick and malleable. The back side of the album cover is a reddish spinning disk. There are images in it that are hard to distinguish. A bedside lamp and a bed with rope on it. Or is it a garden hose? There is a ruler. A motorcycle or bicycle. The grill of an automobile. If you turn the album over, the images are clearer. They appear in black and blue. The prominent twelve o'clock image is the motel bed with a hose. Then there is a cow. The profile of a man who looks uncomfortable, as if he is passed out facedown on a bar. There is a car. A ruler. A bicycle. A white slip hanging on a windshield. The title and songs appear on the square that has the motel bed. This design is a simplification of Rauschenberg's

Revolver, a 1967 acrylic on Plexiglas piece that likely now sits in a museum somewhere. *Revolver* is huge and composed of silkscreen images that revolve separately by motor. The viewer can control the rotating disks with switches. Supposedly the varied combination of designs is *endless*.

The box Rauschenberg designed for *Speaking in Tongues* is vaguely interesting, but not endlessly. It's no *Mona Lisa*. It's not even a good Bob Seger cover. It would, however, win a 1984 Grammy for "Best Album Package."

Warhol played with the cover a bit, then put it away. That night he recounted in his diary how Rauschenberg had bitched to him that he only got $2,000 for *Speaking in Tongues*.

"And I told him he was right," Andy Warhol wrote in his diary. "He should've gotten $25,000."

A month earlier in May, a dinner plate crusted with paint had sold to a private collector in Maryland for $93,500. The object was called *Notre Dame* and was "painted" by a young artist named Julian Schnabel. This heavy sugar price was seen as a sign that the art racket had bounced back from the recession of the 1970s.

The city estimated there were somewhere between forty and ninety thousand artists living in Ed Koch's New York. This included Jamie Dalglish and Mark Kehoe, and someone named Robert Longo.

Longo was a twenty-six-year-old fellow who was starting to be recognized in a way Dalglish and Kehoe were not (and would never be). He was raised a dyslexic Long Island kid who intended to be a football player, but after he screwed up his knee, he went to North Texas State University because he wanted to live near the locale where *Easy Rider* was filmed. He eventually ended up at art school in Buffalo where he became boyfriend to a chick named Cindy Sherman. He was the one who encouraged her to start taking photographs of herself. The couple moved to New York City in 1977. Sherman got instantly famous. Longo took a little longer.

Back in 1980, he had his first New York gallery exhibition at the influential Metro Pictures. The show was called *Men in the Cities*. It contained huge black-and-white charcoal and graphite portraits of men in business suits recoiling from gunshots. Longo did studies for the images by taking friends up to the roof of his loft on the South Street Seaport and photographing them being struck by tennis balls.

In June '82, Longo met David Byrne at the Mudd Club. He would mention this meeting in any official biography published in conjunction with his work.

In July 1983, Talking Heads rehearsed for six weeks on a New York City dock. The show was complicated. David would enter the stage first with a boom box, which would play a beat, and then he would sing "Psycho Killer" on his acoustic guitar. After that, each member of the band would be added one by one along with the risers and platforms on which they performed. Each song would then be like a little play, with lighting changes. And props—David wanted to dance with a hat stand like Gene Kelly. The climax of the show would be Tina and her sisters taking the stage to sing "Genius of Love," followed by David entering again in costume. He'd wear the Big Suit he'd had manufactured for him and sing, "Who took the money? Who took the money away?"

That is, he'd come out and question the money if nothing screwed up backstage. Props were late. Cues were missed. David Byrne was observed screaming, "Holy shit, what the fuck's going on?" over and over. He was observed freaking out in public. Freaking out in front of his parents who had shown up for the rehearsal, driving from Baltimore in their Honda Civic plastered with politically correct United Farm Workers bumper stickers.

David had never been good about losing his temper. Years ago when he lived on Chrystie Street, he had a fit and wanted to smash something, so he chose a clock radio because it was already broken.

Once the tour got on the road for real, there was a new crisis every day. At a midsummer concert in Montreal, Talking Heads opened for the Police, and David had a brief psycho supreme moment onstage.

The Police were the ones who chose this venue, but the band had only sold 4,000 tickets. The promoter begged Kurfirst to let Talking Heads join the bill. They did. The show sold out—35,000 people. David knew that above a hundred people, a show was never going to be intimate. But people could catch glimpses of what he was doing. As the audience got bigger so would his gestures.

He saw the crowd as an organism. When it grew to certain size, the organism heard and reacted differently to things. An audience would become a different social body. A different kind of thing would move them.

Jerry had a little different view of a big crowd. The worst thing about big ones was that the closest person could be twenty feet away. Jerry liked to look down from the stage and see someone's face and play to them. Get a dialogue going.

Twenty feet away was a problem. Jerry was a little nearsighted.

The chief way to reach so many people was the big cabinet speakers called the bass bins. Bass bins pushed the air forward so people farther than ten feet in front of the stage could hear the band.

253

But the Heads couldn't use the bass bins. That equipment was segregated only for the Police. This was standard stadium policy in the 1980s. The opening act would never upstage the main show if they were denied the use of the bass bins.

The Police/Talking Heads show also had video screen setup—a novelty in those days. The crowd, all 35,000 of them, would be able to see closeups of band. They would be able to see what Sting looked while he was singing. Tina had once seen Sting stand on a stage stuffing his face with cheese and bread while he sang. With the video camera, even the audience in the nosebleed seats ten miles back would be able to see every detail.

If David tried to eat cheese in his Big Suit while he sang, only those in the front twenty feet away would know it. The video camera was also off-limits to Talking Heads.

Talking Heads began their show, and suddenly a Police flunky was standing on the stage with a video camera propped on his shoulder. He began wandering the stage as if Talking Heads wasn't performing until David walked up to him as far as his mike cable would go and gave him a shove.

This is one of those moments about which all the participants tell a different story. The way Tina saw it, David shoved the camera out of the Police technician's hand and it broke. Another version of the story has David reaching out and simply unscrewing the lens cap, burning up the sensitive photocells on the interior.

This is the better story. Let's declare it is the truth.

David continued with the show. Because the crowd was so large, no one really knew what was going on. And the audience didn't know that the Heads didn't have bass bins. "The music was too good," Worrell recalled. "We kicked the Police's butt that night. I was so pissed I could have done it by myself."

Worrell didn't view the Talking Heads show as a Robert Wilson piece. He did see a comparison between the Heads and the theatricality of a P-funk show. Both George Clinton and David Byrne were concept people. Stage props. Stage presence, similar in that way. "And in the lyric context, the way George put messages to the masses. If it's political he'll color it with humor. I think David is clever that way also."

David was not an unreasonable man. But his show seemed to be getting out of control. They burned through production managers like marines in Beirut. It took two semis to transport the sets. Three busloads of people. For the sound check, the roadies had to roll all the sets and risers onto the stage to make sure everything worked, then roll them off again. Tina joked about changing their touring corporate name to Headache Tours.

Then in Lexington, Kentucky—very close to Chris's hometown—David got a death threat. A note was passed backstage that said: "I'm going to take out the psycho killer."

The band pleaded with the security people to put metal detectors at the door, but they refused. David was a trooper. He did the stage show—he just moved around a little more than usual.

Finally, David gave Adelle an SOS phone call, and she flew from Japan. After that, he lightened up. Told jokes. Didn't break as many clock radios when things fucked up onstage.

On August 21, John Rockwell saw Talking Heads perform at Forest Hills Tennis Stadium. He noted how white the audience was. "Preppy funk triumphant," he thought. He felt some of the Robert Wilson–ish big show stuff impeded rather than augmented the performance. Finally, he felt like the show was imitating video, which was the tail wagging the dog.

As the tour progressed, David Byrne saw that people were going nuts for "Burning Down the House." This was the first single off the album. And the first video.

By the summer of 1983, MTV was huge. Television culture guru John Fiske ranted, "MTV is an orgasm. . . . No ideology, no social control can organize an orgasm. Only freedom can. All orgasms are democratic: all ideology is autocratic. This is the politics of pleasure." MTV sold advertising time to 140 companies. It seemed like most of the products were blue jeans.

The video for "Burning Down the House" was prime MTV material. The film begins with the sun setting on a suburban house similar to the ones

David grew up in—the ones destroyed to make way for freeways and parking lots.

The video then alternated among several motifs: The band, all dressed in white, "play" their instruments in a kind of suburban art nouveau gymnasium stage. David and others have their stark faces projected on the side of the suburban house (it's night). David and Chris and Tina and Jerry are replaced by a child, a fat man, an old woman, and a tall wholesome-looking fellow. Shots of David from the rear as he performs before a B&W projection of a crowd.

It's amazing that a form so young—"music videos"—already had rituals and clichés by 1983. But they did. And the former art students that made up Talking Heads couldn't resist mocking these conventions. Since the on-camera band isn't actually playing instruments, why not substitute a child or an old lady pantomiming playing? The absurdity of music videos is mocked even more when the boy climbs onto David's back so he can reach down and be the one strumming the guitar. The camera pulls back to reveal the other impostors—fat man, old woman, and wholesome fellow—reaching around the other band members and playing their instruments as well.

This is a nice idea, but it gets sillier with repetition. Two years before, Brian Eno identified and dismissed this aspect of music videos: "Nobody has ever yet been faced with the task of making a film you can watch as many times as you can listen to a record. So far, videos have been either psychedelic, which doesn't sustain itself over a lot of watching, or else they have been . . . the singer mimed to the song, and there were some clever light effects and that sort of thing." Eno experimented with filming video images and discovered that the slower and more static an image is, the more like a painting, the better the thing bears up to repeated viewings.

A more satisfying image Eno-style in the video for "Burning Down the House" is one of David's back as he is playing before the projection of an audience. Variations of this image would be intriguing to watch for the length of the entire video. The image inadvertently serves as a cultural prediction—although David's ass was perhaps not as masculine as Bruce Springsteen's, it forecast the blue-jeaned backside of the Boss's *Born in the USA* album cover that would dominate national consciousness during the next year.

Finally, the image of David's face projected on the side of the house is intriguing. The last image of the video is of David's moonlike face racing along a highway.

The video helped "Burning Down the House" become a hit, but more important was radio play. The song even aired on black radio. As the tour wore on, when the band started the song, the crowd would let out a roar and start screaming. Really screaming hard.

David was ecstatic. He'd look down at the crowd and think: "Look! Look! People are really excited. They really like this song. They know it. They've heard it. They've listened to the record. Hey, we've reached a larger public. We're doing all we set out to do!"

This was an unqualified moment of triumph for David. He felt the band was doing interesting music that was still within the framework of pop. He realized that there were like minds out there in shopping-mall America. The band was tapping into a common feeling.

Tina could tell David was feeling really happy imparting a Bucky Wunderlick "erotic terror to the dreams of the republic." David would do his dance to "What a Day That Was" (from *The Catherine Wheel*), and he'd hold a flashlight under his chin and look exactly like Edvard Munch's *The Scream*. Of course, the flashlight-under-the-chin trick was old hat. But it always worked. She loved watching David with his mouth open like a big hole. And now when he sang that song, he'd turn his face between each phrase and look directly at Tina and laugh his head off—a private laugh that only she could see. Then he'd turn back to the audience and the camera and be back to that stone-faced hole-in-the-head look. Tina found it wonderfully terrifying!

In September 1983, the second Tom Tom Club album, *Close to the Bone*, was rushed out to capitalize on "Burning Down the House." This Tom Tom Club effort was created by the usual suspects (minus Belew), including Wally Badarou, Tyrone Downie, Steve Scales, Steven Stanley, Alex Weir, and the wild Weymouth sisters. The new Tom Tom Club is another fun-time album like the first, containing perfectly competent pop songs like "Pleasure of Love" and "The Man with the 4-Way Hips." Each song is mixed state-of-the-art circa 1983 with tight drums and robe synthesizer. And while Tina and her sisters still sing in their deranged weak white voices, they never cry out anything as over the top as "Koonie koonie koonie koonie um some-some."

All those nights that Tina was up scribbling down songs, she did good work, but compare her album to Madonna's maiden self-titled album released at the same time. If you could switch the vocals, Madonna's voice would have made *Close to the Bone* her first hit, while Tina and her sisters singing "Lucky Star" and "Borderline" would have generated zero radio play.

Gary Kurfirst loved the Big Suit tour, but got a little melancholy remembering when it was just the five of them. They'd go out for dinner. Go to a movie. Go to a bar. That wasn't to say that he didn't like everyone in the new group. He did. He had to shake his head. They were all screwballs. Strange individuals. Everyone had their own way of doing things. But now, as the group got bigger, everyone was splitting off into groups of two and three.

Bernie Worrell would one day reveal the deepest secret of the Big Suit tour. When the band had downtime, the "girls" would split off and go to the mall. Malls were the place to get beauty products and the girls had to stay beautiful. The girls and Bernie. He'd go with them. "I'm not into malls except for girl watching," he claimed.

But he went to get his son wooden toys. He'd have them shipped back home to Plainfield, New Jersey, where he had a house on a dead-end street. The park was just around the corner. That's where he lived with his wife and his son who had been born with epilepsy and cerebral palsy. Bernie bought the boy wooden toys with rounded edges so that if he had a seizure he wouldn't hurt himself.

Somewhere in the middle of shopping-mall America, David Byrne got the disillusionment of his life. This man who had recorded half a dozen records, signed numerous contracts, been on every show from *American Bandstand* to *Saturday Night Live*, learned from a chance comment from Kurfirst that "Burning Down the House" had become a hit due to money passing hands. Years later this still upsets David. "Although payola was not supposed to happen, it does."

But of course, payola happened. And would always happen. Alan Freed knew that. The man who invented the term "rock 'n' roll" was also indicted in 1960 for accepting payola to play certain songs on the radio. This charge wrecked his life and he died of drink. His peer, Dick Clark, had interests in numerous companies that benefited directly from the songs he promoted on *Bandstand*. But unlike Alan Freed in 1983, Dick Clark was alive and wealthy and still appearing on television.

David wasn't a complete greenhorn. He knew there were many ways a greased wheel guaranteed a hit. For instance, MTV would play certain clips from a label in return for exclusive play of other clips. This was not illegal because the Communication Act's Section 508—the law that busted Alan Freed—did not apply to cable.

No one went on record to state exactly who got paid what. Gary Kurfirst told that he "had a meeting with Warner Bros. one time, and went in there asking for something for the band. And they said no. And I said, 'What do you mean? Look how much airplay we got.' Warner Bros. turned around and said, 'Yes, do you know how much we paid for that airplay?' "

258

Seymour Stein said years later, "There isn't a hit that isn't bought. There are no natural hits. It's the nature of the beast. I'm surprised that David was upset about it because in reality, with all the money in the world, you can't make a hit out of a bad song." He was quiet for a moment. "And Warner Bros.—especially in that period—they played by the rules more than their competitors." He paused. "Sometimes to my frustration."

David said, "I don't know who was involved or what happened, I know a fair amount of money was spent to break that song. It wasn't that the song didn't have merits or we didn't connect. But that connection can't happen without other stuff thrown in. A little extra help. . . . A lot of little extra help. . . . Money. Maybe that's the way things work. But it was disillusioning at the time."

In fact, now when the band played "Burning Down the House," David found himself looking at the audience and thinking, "Oh, what a bunch of sheep. You've all just been bought by hearing one song on the radio that's been bought." He was losing his faith in the audience, for the people he was singing for.

"I don't think I ever got it all back," he said decades later. "Ever since then it's been very easy for me to see the public, the critics, myself included, go for somethin' that's been orchestrated. Sometimes that orchestration has been done well, and if the thing that's being pushed actually does have some merit or tap into something, well, then it works. We all hear it. And we all think, 'Hey, I like that song.' Or, 'I like that movie.' Or whatever. We all think it was our own."

At a stadium show at Red Rock in Denver, as the band played "Life During Wartime," David ran through the bleachers and the spotlight stopped on a couple that was rutting like sheep in their seats. The spotlight focused on those two for the entire song. David was pissed, but now he knew how Jerry and Bernie Worrell felt. The lights weren't often on them. In fact, there were times when both keyboardists would be playing away in the pitch dark chatting with each other. Bernie would yell, "See the cute girl out there in the third row?" Or Jerry would laugh. "Look how funny David looks from the back."

Jerry felt that there had been much more equality when Talking Heads was a four-piece band. The lights shone on everyone then. There was no question that David was the lead singer, but the fans related to the group. In the Big Suit tour, the singers were the stars. Jerry felt in the background.

The video of "This Must Be the Place" depicts the Expanded Heads as one big family. The first shots are of David munching on something. Jerry swigs a beer. Tina turns off the light. Home movie footage begins running. Singers Lynn Mabry and Ednah Holt are kids dancing before a log cabin and in front of a houseboat. Then Chris and Tina are wearing silver space suits and twirling their son, Robin (also wearing a silver space suit).

Next, home movie footage of Steve Scales walking by a car wearing a tux as if he's about to go to the prom. Or maybe just an important date. A young Jerry in combat fatigues and a hunting cap doing military drills with a small rifle. Then home movie footage of Alex Weir riding a horse. Bernie Worrell dressed like an Indian by a teepee while playing a little electric hand keyboard. Then a quick old image, taken from above, of a very little David in a cowboy hat.

Steve Scales takes the screen down and the entire band stands, then descends into a basement. It's cramped, but well-lit; there are no shadows. Just a moderate amount of basement chowder like bottles and a refrigerator. The band now pantomimes playing their instruments while David lip-synchs. The black musicians and Jerry are all expressive, having fun. Tina is stiff. She doesn't film very well. David's face is quite striking. He has modified his weird look somewhat. He does a dipping thing with his head. He closes his eyes in concentration. He looks like a man who has never seen *A Hard Day's Night* and is making up this lip-synching-rock-singer thing as he goes along. The last image is of David's mother—plump and matronly—coming into the basement with refreshments.

This video is very dated, but not camp. Certainly, the idea of the

Heads getting together and watching home videos then going down into the basement to rock out is corny. But the issue of racial harmony in the film—Caucasian and African-American home movies side-by-side—is too poignant a fantasy to sink the thing into the realm of cheese.

During the fall of 1983, Robert Pittman was still defending himself against those who claimed MTV practiced segregation. "I don't know who the fuck *these people* are to tell people what they should like," he said. "They sound like little Hitlers or people from Eastern-bloc communist countries. The good thing about America is that people rule. That's the essence of America!"

Ronald Reagan's America was introduced to a new kind of black man in the fall of 1983. This fellow was big. He was muscular. He had a beard and a mohawk. This black man was about as complex as a DC Comics superhero. His name had the simplicity of Dr. Seuss. He was an ex-professional wrestler named Mr. T. He was starring on a television show called *The A-Team*. It displayed forty-six acts of violence per hour.

Jonathan Demme was a filmmaker, and the way he saw it, David Byrne was Buster Keaton reincarnate.

Demme was a thirty-eight-year-old native of Baldwin, New York. He was known for his trademark saddle shoes and his soup commercials. In the mid-seventies, Roger Corman, legendary producer of cheap exploitation flicks for American International Pictures, lifted Demme aboard the great Hollywood gunboat just as he had done for Peter Bogdanovich, Francis Ford Coppola, and Martin Scorsese. Demme made two schlocky films, *Caged Heat* and *Crazy Mama*, back-to-back in 1975, and then he got to do his own thing. He made quirky little pictures, including *Melvin and Howard*, a charming shaggy-dog story about the owner of a gas station who picks up Howard Hughes in the Las Vegas desert.

Demme started to smell money, and in 1983, like a fly drawn to some carnivorous plant, he found himself signing on to *Swing Shift*, a big budget flick with a big star, Goldie Hawn. God, he hated this picture. While he was finishing it, he decided to make a small film about a big suit.

He'd seen the Expanded Talking Heads on tour earlier in the year at the Greek Theater in Hollywood and loved it. He understood David's cinematic staging. That show would make a perfect movie. Demme's people contacted David's people. David had loved *Melvin and Howard*. David got into Demme's car and a deal was made. The two raised $800,000 to make what would become *Stop Making Sense*.

Up until now, "rock concert" flicks more or less stank. Back in the 1960s, D. A. Pennebaker had filmed a Dylan tour in hip black and white, but Demme believed Martin Scorsese's *The Last Waltz* and Neil Young's *Rust Never Sleeps* were the only recent rock films that were any good. He was determined to make a perfect one. The most important thing about the film would be what it wouldn't contain. There would be no backstage interviews that pulled a viewer out of the concert experience.

He would film just the show. Nothing more and nothing less.

Demme talked to each of the original Heads to ask, "How do you see me doing this movie?"

Tina was flattered that Demme came to her. She felt like nobody bothered with her or Chris anymore. In theory, Tina disagreed with the way the show started—David walking onstage to play "Psycho Killer." As Tina had always seen it, the narration of the Big Suit tour was an erroneous version of Talking Heads history—the band started with just David. No way. "It's a false narrative but it made a good show," she thought. The next number made no sense to Tina—Lynn Mabry singing harmony offstage with David on "Heaven" while Tina played bass. "What did that represent in Talking Heads history?"

Demme couldn't tell her. But the number was staying. He also told her that a single Tom Tom Club number would appear in the film—"Genius of Love." It would be used as the intro to David's big entrance wearing the Big Suit.

" 'Genius of Love' is a slow funk hip-hop tune like nothing else Talking Heads did," she told Demme. "I only agreed to do it for the tour. Talking Heads is our neurotic little child. Tom Tom Club is our party girl. I don't want to get those wires crossed."

Tina's husband took her aside and told her that he really wanted her to sing the song. The band needed to do a number so David could get into his Big Suit.

Oh, what nonsense. Tina felt the band could do an instrumental jam while David got into his goddamn Big Suit. Besides—as Tina told the story—the break was more an excuse for David to take a coke break. As he always said, "I've gotta got put on my Big Suit and take a toot!" But Chris was firm. He convinced Tina to sing "Genius of Love."

"I'll do it for the show," she said. "But only for the show."

Demme assured her that although the song would be part of the concert, it would be cut from the film. But then he told Tina that she'd sing it with the Talking Heads' backup singers, Lynn and Ednah.

That was too much. Her sisters should join her. Laura and Lani were going to be in L.A. during the concert to do an appearance with Tina to promote *Close to the Bone* on *Soul Train*. Demme explained that the concert would be filmed in Hollywood at the Pantages Theater, which seated more than 2,500 people. Because of the way the Pantages speakers were set up, a singer couldn't hear herself from the stage. Laura and Lani were not trained for this kind of situation. They would sing out of tune.

Jordan Cronenweth would be the film's cinematographer. Not only had he been the man behind the camera for the Beatles films *A Hard Day's Night* and *Help!*, he'd also shot *Blade Runner*. David was awestruck at the prospect of working with Cronenweth. Never mind the Beatles, *Blade Runner* was such a great film—Philip K. Dick's futuristic acid world had been made so vivid in wet weather and blue light. David sat down with Cronenweth to work up some post-expressionist lighting effects. This would be one psychedelic Philip K. Dick rock flick.

As for the film's mise en scène, Demme made an artistic decision that was practically Eno-esque. The movie would not be montages of strumming guitars and beating drums. The shots of the musicians would be long, almost leisurely takes. You would get to know each musician as he played his instrument as if he or she were a character in a film. Demme saw the Big Suit show as a complete narration, not a symbolic reenactment of the history of Talking Heads, as Tina believed. The Big Suit show was a three-act play documenting the spiritual journey of a hapless white guy who was trying to "get down." At the end of show, the hapless white guy finds his mojo.

Just as the Big Suit number always started with David singing, "Who took the money away," money almost quashed the film.

"We had a little trouble there," Bernie Worrell recalled. "Because Gary Kurfirst didn't want to 'do the right thing' as far as money goes."

262

Bernie and the other Expanded Heads members were getting a flat fee for doing the film. Bernie wanted a royalty. He started negotiations with Kurfirst, but when things came to a standstill just before the concert, Bernie refused to appear unless he got his cut.

"Kurfirst was on the stingy side," Worrell said, but then reflected, "Well, who isn't on that side of the business? It's hard separating money from the music—get it straightened out in the beginning. 'Cause in the beginning it soured us. Everyone was really up for doing the film, but then they discovered the financial information and that brought a damper on it. Then the infighting between managers and what not. . . . Then the other side gave in a little. It was a shame to waste that energy because of something like that."

With only one more day to go before the show, Ednah showed up with a new 'do—a brutally short-cropped cut. An L.A. cut. Almost everyone made polite noises, but David spit out the coffee he was drinking and looked at her in horror. All during the show Ednah and Lynn would shake their heads and their long hair and they always looked terrific.

What a little head Ednah had now!

Ednah spent the next twelve hours getting a hair weave so she'd have hair to shake.

There were once three Pantages theaters in Los Angeles. They were built by and named after vaudeville producer Alexander Pantages. Only two stand today. A lesser Pantages is on 532–536 South Broadway in downtown L.A. It is a somewhat seedy office building with a movie theater entrance beneath a seven-story Renaissance revival facade.

The second Pantages Theater on 6233 Hollywood Boulevard is a glorious building down the street from Philip Marlowe's office. This Pantages first opened in 1929 and seated 2,812 people. The theater's architect, B. Marcus Priteca, was a maestro of Art Deco constructions. The Hollywood Pantages is a combination of Zigzag Moderne and Mayan temple with towers embossed with Indian maidens.

According to L.A. architectural anthropologist Charles Moore, the theater's most "mind-boggling exaggeration of an already extravagant style" occurs in the women's powder room, where actresses like Katharine Hepburn and Bette Davis once powdered their noses while the Oscar presentations occurred on the Pantages stage.

It was Christmastime 1983 in Hollywood the night of the first Talking Heads show. A Santa stood near the Pantages on that warm night, ringing his sad little bell. Demme decided that for the first concert, he'd shoot all the crowd shots. He lit up the 2,812 seats with hot arc lights. The crowd came in and sat. Then the band came out and played through the glare. The audience squinted and shielded their eyes and went collectively limp. They felt like 2,812 lab mice. The nine members of the band got uptight. The show got worse and worse, and then just sank. They almost didn't do an encore. Why bother?

The next morning, while Demme was editing *Swing Shift*, he realized this catastrophe was in fact a gift from the gods of rock movies. "I don't have to show an audience at all," he thought. He could dispense with cross-cutting between the audience in their seats and the band onstage. Audience shots were the cinematic equivalent of canned laughter. When Martin Scorsese filmed the audience in *The Last Waltz*, he seemed to be saying, "Hey, these people are having a good time; you should be, too."

That night, the cameras rolled only on the band. Each band member but David was given an X on the stage to stand on and wasn't allowed to leave that mark. This was for the lighting. But staying in one spot was hard. This music made you want to move. To dance. "Takin' it to church," as Mabry and Holt said. But woe to the girl who danced off her X.

On the second or third night, Tina's sisters were in the audience. She hadn't had a chance to warn them about "Genius of Love." When Tina took the stage without them, the two Weymouth girls were enraged. This caused a family riff among the Weymouth girls that made the discord among the bloody Lear sisters—that's *King Lear*—look like something out of *The Family Circus* comic strip.

stop making sense

After shooting the film, David went to Japan. His reincarnated Japanese farmer's body may have felt great comfort doing a perfect Nipponese squat there at the station as the bullet train approached, but his mind was still that of an American. He thought American thoughts. He made American observations. Take his view of Japan. To David, Japan was like a Superman comic "Bizarro" world. Everything in Japan looked the same, but everyone was talking backward.

In Japan no could mean yes.

Japan was a mirror in which David could get a fresh view of America. He could see New York City. Baltimore. Providence.

"The Japanese have the trappings of American mass culture," David thought, "but they've all been skewed and they have a slightly different meaning. Their reference points are different. Semantically the signs don't function as the same thing over there that they do over here. It's just different. It's like here you might affect a certain look and it implies rebelliousness, but in Japan the same look implies belonging to a group. So instead of being exclusionary you're being inclusionary."

The year before, he had made a trip to Japan to work with Adelle on Robert Wilson's *CIVIL warS*. David would write the music for the portion of the event called the "knee plays." These were the "joints," or short routines between larger acts. One of the functions of a knee play is to mask the sound of hammering as the next set is assembled. David figured that he'd use Japanese percussion.

Not that he knew how that would fit with what happened onstage, because no script had been written in the traditional sense. Wilson just showed him some drawings. But Wilson had rounded up some incredible and bizarre Japanese performers. There was a nutty troupe called Butoh who insisted on covering themselves with white dust whenever they performed, walking around wearing clear swim masks over their crotches, squishing their genitals.

Wilson even got Tamsaburo Bando, the most famous Kabuki actor of the time, to work with him. He was a wisp of a man who played ingenues onstage.

Adelle Lutz and DB went to some Tokyo Kabuki dance pieces and a lightbulb went on in DB's head.

A Japanese lightbulb.

Kabuki movement would be perfect for his knee plays. Kabuki movement might seem very contemporary if you used different costumes and makeup. David found himself doing the equivalent of puttin' fish eggs on spaghetti—he was going to mirror Japan.

He arranged for some recording sessions with traditional Kabuki musicians/percussionists in Tokyo. The results were awful. David went into a full Japanese squat in the middle of the studio and said, "This just sounds like fake Japanese music."

Robert Wilson wasn't worried about the music. He trusted David. He felt compatible with David. Fifteen years later, he describes their relationship like this: "David Byrne is fascinating because in some ways we're a lot alike. He is very visual. We could codesign something and talk about the look of something. His manner of dress, whatever, is closer to mine than someone like Tom Waits. David's nature is cooler. The humor is kind of distant. Tom is a romantic. I make different decisions working with Tom than I do with David."

Both Wilson and David Byrne had all-encompassing aesthetics. Wilson studied architecture and painting, and David studied cybernetics and conceptual art; the theater and music were just extensions of that work to both of them. Wilson put it this way: "We don't see a difference between living and working. It's not like we get up in the morning and go to an office and come home."

In Japan, after David heard a recording of a funky New Orleans

266

brass band called the Dirty Dozen, he gave up the idea of traditional Japanese instruments. The Dirty Dozen was for him. In early winter of 1984, David flew to New Orleans. The city was awful. The delta was freezing. David went into the studio with the Dirty Dozen, but nothing clicked. He realized that the Dirty Dozen's own arrangements came out of jams, live shows, improvisations, and the general vibes of place. The band didn't know how to impart that feel to previously written parts.

He squatted down in the control room to think.

"Geez, that guy looks Japanese," thought one of the Dirty Dozen.

The Expanded Talking Heads regrouped in March and kangarooed to Australia for some gigs. Ednah wasn't available, so Elton John's backup singer, Stephanie Spool, joined the band. The girl learned the parts right away.

Australian winter is the reverse of ours. It was late summer in Sydney, where Talking Heads played. They also played a festival outside of Melbourne. These shows reverted to pre–Big Suit format. They didn't use the risers and the whole Robert Wilson setup.

David's heart wasn't in this tour. It felt like the Big Suit show had pushed the envelope of the live stage show as far as it could stretch. Each night in Australia, he worked on his score for the knee plays. He composed on an Emulator, a digitized synthesizer that was able to counterfeit the tone and timbre of any other instrument. Night after night, he sat in his Aussie hotel room with synthetic trombones and trumpets and French horns squawking.

Talking Heads went to New Zealand to play at a week-long festival. The audience had camped out the night before in the rain. By dawn, the crowd looked like New Guinea mudmen. Melvillean cannibals. Woodstock after the rain.

The band took the stage in the afternoon. David opened the show by bringing on some Maori girls, the indigenous Polynesian inhabitants of New Zealand. After the girls took to the mike and begin talking about Maori rights, they were booed off the stage by the mudmen.

So the band started the show, but David stomped off the stage himself after two or three songs. Chris, the official peacekeeper, hopped off his drum kit and convinced David to return. A few songs later, David split again. Chris hauled him back. Finally, by the third or fourth time David disappeared, the band kept on jamming.

267

Later, Tina asked David what went wrong.

"I don't believe in playing for people in the mud," David answered.

At the end of the month, David found out that Robert Wilson's nine-hour theatrical extravaganza, *CIVIL warS*, that insane vision of American history involving Abraham Lincoln and polar bears and Hercules, which had been performed in fragments all over the globe, would not have its world premiere in Los Angeles for the Summer Olympics in June of 1984 because the funding fell through.

David's *Knee Plays* was still intact and scheduled to be premiered at the Walker Art Center in Prince's hometown, Minneapolis, on April 25. An earlier version of the work had gone through dress rehearsals with Tamsaburo Bando in Tokyo. But in Minnesota, Adelle was now working with Hanayagi Suzushi, another Kabuki dancer. "We had a great amount of time to do Kabuki movement drills over and over, day after day," she remembered. "When DB and Bob finally arrived and we presented them with a company of dancers moving as one unit through the exercises, DB and Bob liked it so much that many of the movements in *Knee Plays* are indeed traditional Hanayagi School movements."

John Rockwell flew out to Minneapolis for the premiere. He would report to his readers in New York City that the plot of *Knee Plays* traced the transformation of a tree into a boat into a book and into a tree again. The eighth scene particularly pleased him when nine dancers did a dance wearing doctor's smocks. He also liked a dance in the twelfth scene when a performer danced with a giant baby Buddha head on his shoulders. He didn't have much to say about David's music, which was played by local musicians.

Knee Plays was quite pleasant theater music, but too derivative of New Orleans funeral music and nightclub striptease music and *Threepenny Opera* (without banjo) to be an artistic triumph in its own right. At the same time, David had not written ambient Muzak—that form of elevator music that Eno had been indulging himself in since last working with Talking Heads.

Rockwell had little to say about the narration that occurred roughly after every other number. David's flat but friendly prerecorded voice would be heard giving a recitation over the brass music. First, he told of a woman getting dressed. Next he described businessmen driving down the freeway. Then he discussed what happened to sound inside a movie theater when the audience goes out to the lobby. In talk number four, David confessed that he wanted to walk off with someone else's grocery cart at the supermarket. For number five, David recited a list of objects. Then he made predications about the future for number six.

Rockwell's review ended with a lament that the entire *CIVIL warS* would not take place that summer in L.A. He quoted Wilson saying with bitterness, "I thought this would be the thing that brought my work back to America."

On April 24, *Stop Making Sense* premiered at the twenty-seventh San Francisco International Film Festival. The film begins with stylish credits created by Pablo Ferro. While *Stop Making Sense* had been being mixed in Los Angeles, David went around Hollywood taking Polaroids of the signs on Pentecostal churches and tire repair shops to show to Ferro—"This is the kind of lettering I'm talking about." Pablo then showed David the hand-lettered credits he'd done for *Dr. Strangelove*. David loved them. "Let's go with this," he said. "Do the same thing."

After the credits—the shoes. White shoes. Walking. These feet belong to David. We soon see that he's wearing a cream-colored suit without a tie. He sets down a boom box that bangs out a percussive beat and then David starts strumming "Psycho Killer" on his acoustic guitar.

For viewers who had never seen David Byrne perform live, the effect was spooky. It's those eyes. They're simultaneously innocent and malevolent. Put David in a stare-down with Charlie Manson, who do you think would win? It's no wonder David was compared so often to Norman Bates in those long-ago CBGBs days. What would John Douglas, the FBI profiler quoted earlier in this book, think of David if that "mindhunter" could see David playing guitar and doing his version of the funky chicken with his neck?

Near the end of "Psycho Killer," David does a very long dance, strumming his guitar. As the camera follows him we see that the stage is nothing but a debris of boxes and ropes. We see roadies dressed in black setting something up. Kabuki roadies. If the audience members think like the Japanese, they will just not "see" the workers dressed in black. Neil Young used a similar technique when he dressed his roadies up like hooded Jawas.

As for David's dance, it looks like an elaborate stumble. It's as if he's about to lose his balance, but then he lurches into a simple dance step. According to Tina, David was incorporating Fred Astaire's moves

269

from the number called "I Left My Hair in Haiti" from the movie *Royal Wedding*.

Next Tina comes onstage. Her blond hair is long. Her big bass is colored blue. David and Tina play "Heaven."

"You know how something really weird happens in cinema," she says. "When you're filming a man running from a car, the car might be two hundred feet behind him, but on film it looks like it's just inches—it looks enormous? That's what was happening to me. I looked huge. I always stood right in front of my amps, right there. And looked huge."

She looks huge because she is wearing a clown costume. It's only when the camera finally changes angles that you can see that she is wearing a baggy pants suit. She looks like she's been fitted in service-station couture.

The Kabuki roadies now wheel in a drum set and Chris climbs into the driver's seat and begins the galloping beat of "Thank You for Sending Me an Angel." This is the one song that duplicates what Talking Heads sounded like as a trio. It's a spare muscular sound.

Here comes Lucifer with a guitar slung around his neck. It's Jerry wearing pink shoes. The band plays the song about fighting over what show to watch on TV, "Found a Job." Jerry is the only Talking Head who looks like a rock 'n' roller. He does a Rudolph Valentino seductive thing with his neck as he plays. Jerry remains the samurai of ladies' men.

Next, Steve Scales, Lynn Mabry, and Ednah Holt walk out as Jerry hops up on a riser to play keyboards. A black scrim lowers, hiding the backstage wreckage. The women are wearing matching gray shorts/baggy tops outfits. Scales, bearded and skinny, crouches over his bongos as the band plays "Slippery People." Lynn and Ednah do a get-down dance. When the song is over, Steve Scales jumps up and thrusts his fist at the audience, yelling, "Oh, yeah."

It's as if he's saying, "Now the show is really going to begin." And he's right.

Alex Weir and Bernie Worrell come out and the band plays "Burning Down the House." The camera lingers a bit on Worrell. He has a mustache. He seems the oldest one onstage. He raises his arms above his head. The funk patriarch.

When the camera shows Alex Weir, he seems young. His hair is a little out-of-date. It's almost a 1960s afro. He is playing an electric guitar. David is playing an acoustic one. Weir does this running in place thing with his legs.

What happens now that the entire band is onstage has a fascinating, and largely unspoken, racial subtext. The additional musicians are all African Americans and they dominate the stage with exuberant joy and unwieldiness. At this point, in this song, even David looks like he should leave and let the real musicians do their work.

Chris remembered: "We thought we knew how to rock and then these people came onboard. Just look. It's fantastic."

If you were watching this movie at the San Francisco Film Festival, you'd see that many people had left their seats and were dancing in front of the movie screen. The theater was literally shaking. You wouldn't know this, but the theater manager was up in the projection room freaking out. He wanted to stop the movie and make everyone sit down. Someone, perhaps Demme himself, calmed him down.

Back on the screen, David has taken off his coat for "Life During Wartime." When did he do that? Jerry is playing guitar again and dancing with the women. These last three songs have been so tight and exuberant. The movie is a good document of a good rock show. But these numbers also lull us into thinking that *Stop Making Sense* is just a regular rock show.

Almost.

David is doing a feminine New Delhi cum Berlin nightclub dance where he sways his hips and raises his right arm and lowers his left, then reverses the movement. You could imagine Marlene Dietrich doing this dance. Maybe Cyndi "Girls Just Want to Have Fun" Lauper. No need to consult Susan Sontag for this one—this is pure camping-out gay style.

Suddenly, David giving aerobic semaphore. Jogging in place. Then racing in circles around the band. He crams as much energy into three minutes' worth of gesture as you could find in a forty-five-minute Vegas act.

Now we see David from the back, his white shirt drenched with sweat. "Thank you," he is saying. "Does anyone have any questions?"

There is an abrupt cut. The words DOLL FACE and PUBLIC LIBRARY appear in huge white letters on a red backdrop. Then the word ONION.

This starts the Robert Wilson portion of the show.

Does anyone have any questions? At the Pantages, this began the intermission. In the movie, the cut between "Life During Wartime" and the new song "Making Flippy Floppy" is the first sloppy moment in a film almost devoid of sloppy moments. In only a few shots so far did we see any cameramen creeping around. This is because on the second show, the cameras shot the band from the left side of the theater. On the third show everyone shot from the right.

Back on the screen groups of three words appear in billboard-size letters behind the performers:

**AIR CONDITIONED
UNDER THE BED
DRUGS**

David had decided these are words that seem funny when you see them by themselves.

**VIDEO GAME
SANDWICH
DIAMONDS**

David would later claim to have been influenced by the work of L.A. painter Edward Ruscha.

**PIG
FACELIFT
STAR WARS**

Tina would later claim that David was giving Ruscha credit for retro-influence because David didn't know Ruscha from Russia in 1984.

**GRITS
DOG
TIME CLOCK**

Thank God, Tina has taken off that awful jumpsuit. She's wearing a white tunic.

**DIGITAL
BABIES
DUST BALL**

Before the song is over, new sets of three-word phrases appear.

BEFORE   DINNER   TIME

BEFORE   YOU'RE   AWAKE

LATE   AT   NIGHT

Then a red light floods the stage and David does his Satan number, "Swamp." David doesn't look psychotic, but he does look evil. He makes all these tight fascist gestures. Hand signals from a hanging judge. Then he moves around with a dead leg like a skinny Charles Laughton from *The Hunchback of Notre Dame*. David's energy now equals or surpasses his African-American bandmates. But he is too damn weird to be anyone's bwana.

Then the band plays "What a Day That Was" from *The Catherine Wheel*. The only source of light appears to be coming up from the floor. It creates a mask of shadow on everyone's faces. Tina saw it as Edvard Munch's *The Scream*. Jerry thought everyone looked wonderfully ghoulish like the old Vincent Price movie *The Abominable Dr. Phibes*. But this is a *Blade Runner* moment. Cinematographer Jordan Cronenweth created this effect—the band never looked this outlandish live. Cronenweth loved light as much as Robert Wilson. Perhaps more than Wilson. Cronenweth thought of light as something that was as intangible as spirit while being as physical as flesh.

The band plays "This Must Be the Place" while slides appear of a woman's arms and belly and bare butt. Those body parts belong to Adelle Lutz. There is a single slide of one of David's limbs. No wonder Dalglish called David naked the "hairy skinny thing."

273

Now David dances with the lamp. It's a modified Woolworth's floor lamp. Regular Woolworth's lamps only came up to David's cheek. He had to add an attachment to make it as tall as a tall woman. Many nights the three lightbulbs explode as he does this dance. For the filmed sequence, the three balls of light stay intact, even as David tosses the lamp from side-to-side, catching it with an incredible look of joy on his face. He looks like he could do this for hours if someone would let him. Then he is going, "Ah-rrooo," sounding exactly like Warren Zevon singing "Werewolves of London." The number is over.

David now puts on a pair of glasses. He does the mad evangelist dance of "Once in a Lifetime." The camera rarely leaves him. With the glasses on, he looks more like a poindexter than a preacher. Apparently some of the gestures are not preacher moves but movements he borrowed from dancers he saw breakdancing Japanese-style in Goyen Park in Tokyo.

Then Tina sings "Genius of Love."

Demme lied. The song was left in the film. When Tina first saw it, she sat in her seat, aghast. After the screening, she railed at Gary Kurfirst. She hunted down Demme and showed him her fury. He was sorry. "Genius of Love" was staying in the film.

274

David now makes his entrance wearing the Big Suit. The Big Suit appears to have a life of its own as David dances to "Girlfriend Is Better." David found that the suit amplified each of his gestures. David isn't working as hard as it looks like he is.

Many years later it must be said that the Big Suit doesn't really look all that big. One can imagine someone wearing it to Limelight and not getting a second glance. Perhaps back in '84, David could have even worn it to Danceteria without seeming out of the ordinary.

David leaves on the Big Suit as he sings the next song, "Take Me to the River." Musically the song does not transcend its soul roots, but the Expanded Talking Heads are so tight and good—and David sings as if he truly understands about the Bible and underage sex—that the Expanded Heads have become peers of Al Green.

Well. Almost. David takes his Big Suit Coat off and does the song in his Big Pants. David claimed the padding was in the hips, not in his butt—"I am a wide man not a fat man." Technically he may be right, but in those Big Pants, he looks like a cross between Gumby and Ralph Kramden.

As the song ends, David is suddenly wearing a red baseball cap. Everyone is screaming—including Jonathan Demme. Apparently he added his vocals during the mix. Then David introduces the band.

Then the band does "Crosseyed and Painless." David has untucked his shirt from his pants and is doing that funky chicken thing with his neck again while he plays guitar. The camera tends to film him from the waist up just like Elvis on *Ed Sullivan*. Of course, in Elvis's case, it was to hide his eternal pelvis from the eyes of virginal teenage girls. In David's case, it's to hide those absurd Gumby pants.

David was once asked, "Did you ever want to be Mick Jagger?" He responded with the confession, "I might have tried it once or twice onstage. Sometimes it worked. You'd get a reaction. The audience would like it. I'd go, 'Come on. That's too easy.' It doesn't take you or the audience anywhere they haven't been." In an outtake from *Stop Making Sense*, David did an imitation Chuck Berry duck walk in the middle of "Cities."

David looks so happy.

He looks like he's the one who has just invented the duck walk.

we begin bombing in five minutes

Theater. Records. Movies. *Boston Globe* television critic Ed Siegel made this observation: "Just as every clown wants to play Hamlet, it seems that every rock musician wants to be a filmmaker."

David was no different. First he became bicoastal. He and Adelle rented a house in Laurel Canyon. The place's owner had AIDS and had fallen on hard times. David let the guy live out the rest of his life in the "guest garage."

Next David approached the screenwriter Stephen Tobolowsky—a friend of Demme's—to write a script. David showed Tobolowsky some photographs. One was of a little girl standing in the road. Another was a fat guy holding a sign that said LOOKING FOR A WIFE. It was Tobolowsky's job to figure out how to put the pictures into a story.

"How about a celebration of a town?" Tobolowsky said.

David dug that. They wrote the first draft of a script in three weeks. Things got a little abstract during this time. David decided he wanted to have a dinner scene in which the food is rearranged into a geometric/abstract arrangement on the table. You'd just see the hands of the cook. He had sketches of hands that he showed Tobolowsky, drawings of Richard Nixon's hands that David had sketched from a book of newspaper photos.

This is not how a script usually got written.

Tobolowsky lined the walls of David's house with storyboards. The plot concerning a number of characters in a small town was almost jelling, but it needed a hook. David said the characters and situations would all be based on stories he'd read in the tabloids during the Big Suit tour.

In this early storyboard there was no David. He wasn't going to be in the movie at all. He was hoping to cast the weatherman from TV, Willard Scott, as the lead—as the narrator. Or maybe that radio-talk guy Paul "and now for the *rest* of the story" Harvey. But neither Willard nor Harvey responded to David's overtures.

"Well, their loss," David later said. "They coulda been on *Roseanne*."

Now that David had a script he liked, he went out to hunt down some money. He'd never made a movie before and he hadn't been to film school, but he was a known figure. Prince's *Purple Rain* had just opened that July. Rock auteurs could make successful movies. David was smarter than Prince. David was probably a better actor than Prince as well—David had been cast in a PBS show Jonathan Demme was directing to play a nerd with a cigar fixation. (The script was written by Tobolowsky's girlfriend, Pulitzer Prize–winning playwright Beth Henley—who would later be recruited to work on David's script along with her beau.)

277

David had no trouble getting meetings with Hollywood tycoons and riffraff. But getting money out of them was another story. He was even granted entrance to the Beverly Hills mansion of Julia *You'll-Never-Eat-Lunch-in-This-Town-Again* Philips. He found her in her office inexplicably hunched over Bunsen burners and test tubes among discarded scripts looking like some female Dr. Jekyll. David knew this wasn't going to be a typical schmooze session.

It wasn't. But it ended the same as the others, *nowhere.*

At least Warner Bros. Records gave David a little basement office to work out of. He found that he didn't miss New York as much as he enjoyed his new Hollywood life. The L.A. kitsch, the L.A. ephemerality of everything. The very American-ness of it all was energizing. He woke up each morning (or noon) to birds chirping. He had his coffee in the sun. He even experienced earthquakes. Little ones. They were weird and fun.

On October 1, the live album *Stop Making Sense* was released. It was unusual to release two live albums so close together, let alone the soundtrack before the movie, but the record company suits made a wise judgment. The film warranted a soundtrack album. In the end, this would turn out to be Talking Heads' bestselling album.

It only contained nine of the sixteen songs from the movie:

The Movie	The Album
Psycho Killer	Psycho Killer
Heaven	
Thank You for Sending Me an Angel	
Found a Job	
Slippery People	Slippery People
Burning Down the House	Burning Down the House
Life During Wartime	Life During Wartime
Making Flippy Floppy	
Swamp	Swamp
What a Day That Was	What a Day That Was
This Must Be the Place (Naive Melody)	
Once in a Lifetime	Once in a Lifetime
Genius of Love	
Girlfriend Is Better	Girlfriend Is Better
Take Me to the River	Take Me to the River
Crosseyed and Painless	

A month earlier, a limited edition LP of the *Stop Making Sense* soundtrack was released, containing a twenty-page book with text by David Byrne, production storyboards, and Byrne-ian tidbits from *Knee Plays* outtakes, such as: "People will do odd things if you give them money. If you keep your money in your shoe, then people will know which bills are yours. If you crumble your money into little balls, it will never stick together. The best way to touch money is by the edges. U.S. money is the worst-looking money in the world."

David didn't get any money together, crumpled in someone's shoe or not, to make his movie that fall. During this time, it seemed like music videos might replace cinema. MTV was so hot and big that Pittman's empire was charged twice with violating the Sherman and Clayton Antitrust Acts. Record companies had budgeted $100 million to film around 2,000 video clips.

Back in New York there were big bucks in the art world as well. A

Newsweek article revealed that Robert Longo now commanded $40,000 for a single work. The article was illustrated with a photograph of the artist looking up under from a mop of hair as he lit a cigarette beneath his drawing of David in the Big Suit.

On October 19, *Stop Making Sense* opened in New York. The movie got such great press that all Americans, or at least all New Yorkers, knew about David Byrne's Big Suit. One month later Rich Hall appeared on *Saturday Night Live* wearing a replica of the Big Suit in a mock fashion report. David saw the parody later on videotape. He was flattered, but didn't see what was so damn funny about it.

David was out in Hollywood when it aired. He had connected with an independent producer named Ed Pressman. In Peter Biskind's seminal book about seventies filmmaking, *Easy Riders, Raging Bulls*, Pressman is described as a mama's boy with a rich mama. Their money came from a family toy business. Pressman produced Terrence Malich's *Badlands*, the fictionalized 1958 road trip adventure of psycho killer Charlie Starkweather. The movie starred Sissy Spacek and Martin Sheen. It was a masterpiece.

Pressman was an independent producer who had an office at the Warner Bros. studio in Burbank. David drove up for a meeting. He found the office was near a rear entrance, right by the little guard booth. Pressman's setup itself wasn't shabby, but it wasn't plush. Ed Pressman was a bald short man. His second-in-command, Neal Wiseman, looked like a Jewish Bruce Willis.

David brought a copy of his script. "A long script," Wiseman remembered. "It had all these great David Byrne stick drawings. It was the densest thing I'd ever seen. It took me multiple readings just to get a sense of what it was about."

David intrigued Pressman. He recommended paying for development of the film themselves. Projects get lost when they go through the studios. They finished only one out of every hundred projects they start. "We financed the film ourselves," Pressman recalled. "Then we met with Mo Ostin and Warner Records came in. Ultimately, Warner Pictures came in and gave us three million dollars."

The November showdown between Reagan and Walter Mondale was only a month away when a curious 45 was released by a little label called

Sleeping Bag Records. The disk began with the voice of Ronald Reagan intoning, "My fellow Americans, I'm pleased to tell you today that I've signed legislation that will outlaw Russia forever. We begin bombing in five minutes."

This was no Ronald Reagan impersonator. The president of the United States had said those words as he was testing a microphone. They were meant as a joke.

Jerry first heard of Reagan's gaffe on public radio and felt that it summed up everything that was ridiculous about the Reagan presidency. "Everyone has the right to kid around," Jerry felt. "But that was too public." He went on, "I hated Reagan's gutting of people's civil rights. I thought everything he stood for was awful. They say what a great job he did with the economy. He drove us into debt. Sure, he bankrupted the Soviet Union, but he almost bankrupted us as well."

Everyone heard *about* the Reagan "joke," but almost no one had actually *heard* it. Jerry decided to change that. He tracked down a copy of the tape through a college radio station. Just as Eno and David had lifted the voices of Dunya Yusin and Reverend Paul Morton from the airwaves, Jerry snatched up the Gipper's.

"My fellow Americans, I'm pleased to tell you today that I've signed legislation that will outlaw Russia forever. We begin bombing in five minutes." Reagan says that on the record, then drums and funky synthesizers start, and the voice of Ronald Reagan is screwed with. The words "I'm pleased" are repeated over and over. Other words are scrambled— "outlaw Russia forever/forever/forever." His words "five minutes" echo hundreds of times in one moment and they create a whole mountain of language.

The word *hip-hop* was still an underground term, but Jerry had used all the common hip-hop tools of the time to do *Twilight Zone* tricks to Ronald Reagan's already *Twilight Zone* voice.

He then worked with coproducer Daniel Lazerus and funk bassist Bootsy Collins in the bomb shelter to create funk à la Reagan Apocalypse. "If the song is a hit," Jerry quipped, "I'll be willing to share royalties with 'lyricist' Ronald Reagan."

When the song was finished, Jerry couldn't find a major label who could guarantee the record would be out in time for the election, so he had the thing rushed out on a micro-label, Sleeping Bag Records.

• • •

Jerry's disk *Bonzo Goes to Washington* lacks the electric brittleness and invocation of *My Life in the Bush of Ghosts*. But its political message must be considered in terms of the times. In the autumn of 1984, Greil Marcus wrote in the *Village Voice,* "Reagan starts out slowly, but then his voice changes, blurs a little. He rushes the ending. He rushes it because while this really is a joke—you can hear people laughing in the background—it is also unmistakably sexual. The lust in the passage is what makes it so terrifying. It's anything but unknown for soldiers to fuck the corpses of women killed in search-and-destroy missions; they're turned on by death. That, that exactly, is what you hear. Over and over, shifted, speeded up, slowed down. It's *viva la muerte* turned into *la muerte, l'amor*. It's sickening."

Jerry's 45 had no effect on the race, of course. Reagan annihilated Mondale. A landslide. Everyone knew Reaganomics and Reagan's contras and ketchup-as-a-vegetable were destined to dominate the rest of the decade.

Right after the slaughter, *Einstein on the Beach* was revived at the Brooklyn Academy of Music. On opening night, Philip Glass turned to Robert Wilson and said, *"Einstein on the Beach* is more avant-garde and revolutionary today than it was when we created it nine years ago."

Wilson knew what he meant. He agreed. Back before Reagan there had been so much happening in the art world, a burst of energy that was like a bulldozer. "Think of all those different dancers and theater artists working in their lofts," he said. "Trisha Brown and Meredith Monk."

"And Richard Foreman," Glass added.

"Back then we didn't need theaters. People came to see our work in our lofts and workshops."

The two men went quiet. *And now?*

The whole country was becoming homogenous with *Miami Vice* cocaine money and Mr. T. posing with Nancy at the White House. If things kept going to hell, in another ten years *Einstein on the Beach* would probably seem radical enough to get Glass and Wilson locked up.

281

After the holidays, David met with Chris and Tina and Jerry in New York to play them some new songs for his Hollywood movie about tabloid stories. All the songs were little vignettes. The lyrics had come before the melodies. This is how David had written songs before Eno.

He sat before the band and played choppy chords on his piano with what was later described as an electronic "rhythm thing" keeping the beat. The songs for the movie sounded country and New Orleans. Genre songs. He had some other new songs that sounded like fun pop. Like songs from the old days.

Later that day, David was asked in an interview, "You're now in a position where you could just put out David Byrne albums, or call any groups of musicians you hired Talking Heads. Why maintain a band at all?"

David answered, "That's a good question. At the moment, anyway, it seems like everybody contributes something. Sometimes it's pretty intangible. Sometimes it's just advice or a point of view or a comment." David reported that the Heads could say things to each other "without risking offense." He then mentions, "Other times it's specific things, like a great bass part Tina comes up with." He speaks historically of the Heads, looking back to living together in the loft at 195 Chrystie Street, "There might be a chance bands like ourselves . . . could compete with the big boys. We could never compete in terms of musicianship—you could always find a better guitar player. But it would be difficult to put together a group of people and have the same kind of thing result." He then shrugged. "At least, that's been the working assumption."

In January 1985, David put on a performance piece, *The Tourist Way of Knowledge*, for a benefit for Mabou Mines at the Public Theater in New York. A witness reported that David wore a cardigan sweater right out of *Father Knows Best* and narrated a slide show depicting a cross-county vacation with a deadpan reading drawn, in part, from a diary he had written as a ten-year-old.

Tom Tom Club played with the B-52's in the Rock in Rio festival down in Brazil. When they came back David realized he had no idea when his movie would get made, let alone be released. Talking Heads needed to release an album this year. So the band holed up in a studio for a month and learned David's new pop songs until they could play them one after the other like a bar band.

Then the four Talking Heads ducked into Sigma Studios for February and March and cut a quick album. The whole group seemed psychically guided by one of Eno's least followed Oblique Strategies, "Think of the radio." They were recording a nice little pop album without sturm und drang. Part of it was lack of focus. David was more wrapped up in his movie than the record. He didn't feel this record was going to be a major artistic statement.

Recording songs this way was a gas for Chris. This was good-time rock 'n' roll. On one song, he got to tap something called a ride cymbal for the first time. On another, he played a march beat all through a song. Things were so relaxed and quick for the group that as the new album—tentatively titled *Wild Infancy*—was being mixed, the band rehearsed songs for David's movie. When the mixing was finished, the band went back into Sigma and recorded the basic *True Stories* instrumental tracks.

These weren't band songs. They were film songs. The difference between the next Talking Heads album, now titled *In Defense of Television* instead of *Wild Infancy*, and the film tracks made David muse about the *notion* of a band. Take the Beatles. It was assumed that the band members were all more or less equal, wrote and performed their own songs, had a certain amount of self-determination. It became an important item—the band as a whole *stood* for something, everybody more or less said the same thing, as if the group were on a mission. "Bands happen," he thought. "But gosh, they don't last forever."

That winter Robert Longo exhibited a silhouette-sculpture of David Byrne titled "Heads Will Roll" at the Brooklyn Museum. The *New York Times* described the work like this: "[Longo] combined elements projecting a '50s (the decade of Mr. Longo's birth) nostalgia; a kitsch plastic and metal sculpture taking off on Sputnik and AT&T's logo; a cut-out silhouette of the [sic] '50s clad rock star, David, and a relief drip-and-splatter painting that not only summons up the power of Jackson Pollock's work but also makes a cliché of him."

More art *New York Times* style: On February 10, Basquiat made the cover story of the *New York Times Magazine*. The next month, Basquiat had his second one-man show at Mary Boone. In the catalog Robert Farris Thompson wrote, "Afro-Atlanticist extraordinaire, he colors the energy of modern art (itself in debt to Africa) with his own transmutations of sub-Saharan plus Creole black impress and figuration. He chants print. He chants body. He chants them in splendid repetitions. . . ."

David showed up at a party catered by Adelle's brother-in-law for Basquiat at the Great Jones loft where Basquiat was now living. This was Andy Warhol's loft. The same building where he and Dalglish had stood out front and leafed through Warhol's old copies of *Life* magazine.

283

• • •

Richard Longo seldom crossed paths with Basquiat, but continued to mention David's name whenever possible. "I became an artist while someone like David Byrne became a musician," he said in interviews. He would then mumble about the intellectual requirements to create art. "I watch movies, I watch TV, I know about Michelangelo, I'm into dance. All of a sudden I go back to a tradition—making art objects or like making record albums. Surrender is about the pressure of being an artist. It is as if the artist really becomes essentially the worm in the bottom of the bottle of culture. You absorb all of the poisons." In another interview, he said, "My art evolves out of a monstrous ego. I basically created a religion—which is me—and I worship it every day."

284

Basquiat's new paintings had titles like *Irony of Black Policeman, Jim Crow, History of Black People, Origin of Cotton, Famous Negro Athletes,* and *Oreo.*

At the end of the winter of '85, Philip Glass had asked David for song lyrics for a kind of pop album. Glass had also gotten lyrics from Paul Simon, Laurie Anderson, and a neo-folksinger named Suzanne Vega.

Everyone gave Glass typed sheets of lyrics except David. He came up with something as elaborate as the film script he had shown Pressman. He handed Glass several unnumbered pages covered with clumps of stanzas, each printed in a different colored ink.

Glass was supposed to put it together.

Later, Glass presented a tape of two songs, "Liquid Days" and "Open the Kingdom," based on Byrne's lyrics to the lyricist himself. After David listened, he smiled and said, "That's just how I thought they would work."

Writer Jerome Davis uncovered the story that one day in the winter of 1985, David was signing publicity posters in the Village Tower Records on Broadway when he looked up to see his old lover Andrea Kovacs in the crowd. He hadn't seen her since she walked out on him leaving behind a single Polaroid so many years ago. At Tower Records, she slipped him a note that read, "Would you like to come to a Buddhist meeting around the corner tonight?"

David shook his head. "I'm sorry," he answered. "Not tonight."

Then he returned to signing posters.

Back in 1976, David Byrne and Andrea Kovacs and Jamie

Dalglish and Mark Kehoe had started out at roughly the same level of social status—David's chances for fame seemed the dimmest of the four. But now David had surpassed his peers. Dalglish would hear of the money that Julian Schnabel's paint-encrusted plates got and wail, "Why aren't I famous?"

Mark Kehoe did art and movies and he wasn't famous, but he wasn't as bitter as Dalglish. Kehoe still palled around with David every now and then. One night David brought Kehoe to a special screening of the new David Lynch movie, *Wild at Heart*. As they rode up an escalator toward a crowd of reporters, David warned, "They'll be yellin' and wantin' my picture. Just act naturally."

Suddenly, a woman at the front of the swarm recognized Kehoe and started jumping up and down excitedly, screaming, "Mark Kehoe! Mark Kehoe!"

This cracked David up.

A little after the film viewing, Kehoe finally broke up with Naomi and entered a *Lost Weekend* phase. He showed up one night at David and Adelle's SoHo loft extremely lubricated and asked to use the bathroom. When he came out he slurred out an unfortunate comment about the room's Asian decor, "It's sort of like a Shirley MacLaine movie in that bathroom."

He didn't expect anyone to get his cultural crack. But Adelle got it. Shirley MacLaine taped her eyes back to play an Asian in the 1962 movie *My Geisha*. Adelle narrowed her own eyes at Kehoe and said, "Was that a racist statement?"

A wise man would have apologized when he'd sobered up. Kehoe didn't. He never socialized with David again.

David kept in touch with Jamie Dalglish. One day in the mid-eighties, he went over to Dalglish's new studio on Eighth Street to look at recent paintings. David had to use the john, where he found a mock *New York Times* cover Kehoe had created and given to Dalglish for his birthday mounted on the wall. It was full of satirical articles, one of them ridiculing David. He quickly left the studio without saying a word to Dalglish.

In New York City it is hard when fame visits your friends and passes you by. (It's unlikely they handle it any better in Nebraska.) Depending on one's neighborhood in Manhattan, the *Sunday New York Times* is available as early as seven on Saturday night. By midnight, you can buy it anywhere. The May 5, 1985, issue of the *New York Times Magazine*—the jewel of the Sunday paper—had David's face on the cover with the caption: "David Byrne: Thinking Man's Rock Star." A man has to have arrived at some pinnacle of power to be designated a highbrow pop artist by the *New York Times*. To a citizen of New York, this is a big deal.

Chris knew about the cover. The band had spent hours with the writer, Ken Emerson. The four of them went together to a photo shoot. On May 5, Chris rushed to the newsstand to get the *Sunday Times*, expecting to find his and Tina's and Jerry's photographs all on the cover with David's.

Forget the cover for a moment. Chris was interviewed for the *Times Magazine* story. He was portrayed as the happy-go-lucky Head. The one who was just thrilled to be there. The Talking Head who read comic books. It was easy to overlook the fact that he was a college-educated artist married to a college-educated woman (who pointed out to the *Times Magazine* that the first audiences at CBGBs were composed of "painters . . . almost exclusively").

Now Chris was portrayed as a jocular force, perched on his drum kit, puncturing bad jokes with drum rolls. The magazine also rewrote band history to Chris's benefit—David returned to RISD in the early seventies to visit "his friend" Chris Frantz. There was no mention of Mark Kehoe. Chris got to show off his fluency with black music by saying one of David's licks was more or less straight DeBarge. Chris also got in one of the last words of the piece when he spoke of how sweetly Tina and Jerry would sing harmony behind David, who was now actually "crooning."

Chris's wife mentioned David in his Big Suit. "He takes the most obvious thing, and people all go, 'Genius! Genius!' " Tina ended the article by saying Talking Heads would transcend the sleaziness of rock 'n' roll.

The article wasn't bad. But David was on the cover, not the whole band. This was dirty pool. Chris would later tell a *Rolling Stone* writer that he was so enraged that he practically beat David up.

Earlier in the spring of 1985, "Tipper" Gore, wife of Senator Al Gore, walked by her eleven-year-old daughter's room just in time to hear Prince singing about masturbation on "Darling Nikki," the song that closed Side One of *Purple Rain*. Tipper was shocked. Shortly after the Heads' *Times Magazine* article was printed, Tipper issued a public statement accusing the record industry not only of encouraging children to masturbate, but rebelling against their parents as well as "killing babies." Five senatorial and cabinet wives then formed the Parents Music Research Center.

Who knows how American history might have changed if Tipper had happened to walk by her daughter's room and the girl was listening not to Prince, but to a deranged high-pitched man squealing something about "Old Mother Reagan."

In this quick twenty-nine-second song, Old Mother Reagan is revealed to be dumb and dangerous and surely won't get into heaven. This was the first song on the record *The Blind Leading the Naked* that Jerry Harrison was producing in Milwaukee for the Violent Femmes. This Badger State group was the musical equivalent of the *Wisconsin Death Trip*, that coffee-table picture book of turn-of-the-century rural murder and suicide. Jerry also produced a record by Elliot Murphy up there. Murphy was so taken by Jerry's town, he titled the record *Milwaukee*.

Meanwhile, back in New York: Chris and Tina were talking to a friend of theirs, Donald Monroe, about doing a video for the new album. Monroe was a friend of Andy Warhol. "Why don't we have lunch?" Monroe offered. "Andy would love to see you guys. It's been years."

David was in town and Tina invited him. He said sure. On Wednesday, May 15, Chris and Tina showed up at Warhol's new studio. Andy was late. David was late. David popped in thirty minutes late. Still no Andy. David hung around for about fifteen minutes. He didn't talk. He just wolfed the food. He left.

Meanwhile, Andy Warhol was having an awful day. His dog, Amos—named after the chocolate chip cookie—was sick and at the vet. He called his office. His flacks told him Talking Heads was waiting. Damn. The pop artist rushed downtown (his cab cost $6). In his diary, he wrote: "The lead one had left. They're friends of Don's and he and Vincent were trying to get them to do video work. But I always felt I've known them for so long. They went to the Rhode Island School of Design." Later that day "someone" called Warhol and said, "Jackie Curtis OD'ed. He's gone." Warhol wrote, "And that wasn't something I wanted to hear."

Commuting between New York and Hollywood that spring, David ran into the Viking editor Nan Graham. "How is the book coming?" she asked.

287

Book? What book? David was startled for a moment. Then he remembered that he had first run into her at the airport last January. Nan Graham was a diehard Talking Heads fan. She had approached David about doing a book. David was intrigued. He pitched his idea of a published screenplay with film stills from an *imaginary* movie—like Cindy Sherman with text. Making the new record had interfered with creating that work. He told her about the movie he was making for real. His screenplay was influenced by Robert Wilson and weird stories from the *Weekly World News* tabloid. People who read the script said it was like Thornton Wilder's *Our Town*.

David had read *Our Town* himself. He liked it, but found it too sentimental.

Nan wanted David to make a book about the movie he was about to make. But the book should be more than just a screenplay. Kind of an annotation to the film. She paid David $200,000 for it.

little creatures

The album *In Defense of Television* was released on June 10, 1985, under a new title, *Little Creatures*. The cover was as great and complicated as the one that graced *Sgt. Pepper*. It had been painted by "outsider" artist Reverend Howard Finster of Summerville, Georgia, a southerner who received visions from God and then rendered these holy hallucinations in tractor enamel. David came upon Finster's stuff in a New York gallery. In a Sire press release, Chris said, "It should be pointed out that Finster's work is represented in some of the most chi-chi galleries from New York to San Francisco. Like the new record, his stuff is hip."

Howard Finster himself said, "The one that sings for them, he sent me a note and told me he wanted me to do a painting for their album cover. He sent me the dimensions of it, and he sent me a picture o' him and the other ones in the group, and he wanted me to draw him holdin' up the world. . . ."

On the cover, in the middle of a painted landscape of blue sky, black piles of rock and several towers that look like wedding cakes, David crouches wearing only shoes and underpants, holding the world on his back. Chris is beside David, peering over a small church. Above Chris, Jerry is peeking around one of those curious piles of rock. Tina is parallel to Jerry on the other side of David. There are hundreds of little animals and people and combinations of both. Women in red dresses ride the backs of giant leopards. A red snake curls around a pile of stone with I AM NOT OF THE

WORLD I AM A RED LIGHT FROM GOD written on it in white paint. The cover is loaded with text. Warnings about Satan. Other messages are like: STRANGERS OF OTHER WORLDS LISTENING IN ON TALKING HEADS.

Tina said at the time, "Finster does work that is supposed to be impossible to make, such as his spiral tower that he is building onto his church which follows no blueprint. I like to hope that we made *Little Creatures* in the same spirit that he painted our album cover."

"Talkin' Heads' publisher sent me $2,100 dollars just for the copyright," Finster said. "Some o' my fans don't even know the Talkin' Heads. They're not interested in rock 'n' roll, but thousands of 'em bought that album because my cover's on there. So the Talkin' Heads gained some new fans."

Little Creatures was more than a record cover. Finster said this of the music inside, "Rock 'n' roll's not even my kinda music, but some of it's pretty good. I like Elvis and R.E.M. What I've heard of R.E.M. sounds pretty good to me. And Talkin' Heads, too, but I haven't heard all theirs. I haven't even met these."

Had Finster been more rock literate he'd have heard this record as one made by Prince if he possessed the vocabulary of John Lennon. The songs have a slapdash ease about them equal to Prince's best work, but the simple lyrics aren't idiotic. As John Rockwell wrote, "This is the simplest, happiest, most tuneful—and most potentially commercial—album this archetypal New York art-rock band has made yet."

Tina sardonically joked that *Little Creatures* was their *White Album*. White as in Caucasian. Jerry felt *Little Creatures* was the *least* challenging of their records. David, on the other hand, was very pleased with the album. It wasn't a safe record. It was a new kind of experience. It was new to David to write pop songs. "It was a pop record," he says. "But that's okay. For me that was okay. This is part of what I like. I'm not going to deny it. I like a nice pop song, too."

Besides, he realized, pop songs are the folk music of high-tech countries.

Little Creatures was a terrific pop album that was accessible at the time, but not *of* the time. It's worth considering song by song.

And She Was The song starts with David yelling, "Hay!" Drums begin pounding. Then a steady but subdued Roy Orbison–style rhythm guitar starts chugging. David then sings about a woman lying on her suburban lawn who begins floating up into the sky. She is soon flying over the same suburban landscape that the narrator of "The Big Country" flew above, but she makes no judgments. She is at home everywhere on the ground, just as she is at home flying in the air. She takes off her dress and floats out of this world naked.

In a way this is David Byrne's *Born in the USA*. It has the same kind of down-to-earth authenticity of Bruce Springsteen's tales of disillusioned Vietnam vets and abandoned brides. Of course, "And She Was" is about a woman floating in the sky—not exactly territory the Boss covered. The song is rooted in fact, however. David used to know a girl he would later call a "blissed-out hippie chick" when he lived with Kehoe in Baltimore. The girl used to drop acid and lie down in a field and then levitate over the Yoo-Hoo chocolate factory. "It seemed like such a tacky kind of transcendence," David later wrote. "But it was real. A new kind of religion being born out of heaps of rusted cars and fast food joints. And the girl was flying above it all."

Give Me Back My Name This is an edgy somber song with as many quirky chords as anything from *Talking Heads '77*. Tina sings with David on this cut. In an interview disk that Sire created to promote the record, Tina said she possessed a "very, very small voice. And, by the way, so does Liza Minnelli. So does Barbra Streisand."

Creatures of Love This is a cheerful country and western tune. David and Tina sing in touching harmony, "I've seen sex and I think it's okay."

The title *Little Creatures* comes from this song. The year before, David told Tina, "I had a dream that there were all these little creatures."

"What do you mean?" Tina asked. "Little crabs?"

"No," David answered. "Creatures of love."

"The song doesn't mean anything," Tina claimed. "But we are so amazing because we put meaning to it. We listen to these songs and we think they mean something. Someone was having a conversation and it meant something to the person having the conversation and that impacted on David. But David never knew what anything meant anyway. David just takes persona and people and uses them as his own. It's art. Trickery. It's all trickery. It's his idea of art."

The Lady Don't Mind This melody was originally written for *Speaking in Tongues*. It's the only song whose music is credited to David Byrne, Chris Frantz, Jerry Harrison, and Tina Weymouth. It has an infectious Ricky Ricardo rhythm and horn chart. It's a reminder that Talking Heads have always felt rhythm. Certainly Chris was the original funkster and reggae-holic back in college. And David's sense of rhythm can't be overlooked. "If you wanted to really give David a great gift," says Lee Blake, "you'd give him some mad obscure record that you'd found with the greatest rhythms." Then she added, "He's a brilliant rhythm guitarist, you know, David. Not many people pick him out for his rhythm guitar playing. He likes people who feel rhythm in their pelvis. I said to him last week, 'You've got to promise me that you're going to teach my baby how to play rhythm guitar.' "

Perfect World David and Tina sing about the "perfect world" with the continued rhythmic joy of the last cut. The chords and melody are a reworking of "The Good Thing." The lyrics themselves go back even further. David had been paging through some discarded lyrics and found some couplets that Chris had written in 1974 along these lines *This is a perfect world because you're a perfect girl*. David liked them and paired the lines up with some of his own. He even sings perfect falsetto on this cut.

Stay Up Late This is a wonderfully dangerous song in which David flies against Dr. Spock etiquette and mischievously suggests that we keep a baby up past bedtime. After all, a baby is just a plaything. As David sings this, he even gives a nasal snort after the refrain, a good-natured but evil sound that takes Eno's "nasal" singing to the wall.

"Stay Up Late" was an anthem for mid-eighties parents—at least in New York where there was a mini–baby boom going on. Yuppie parents had to deal with nannies and day care. In some circles, having a child was like getting an Akita. Designer dogs. Designer babies. Why not make the baby stay up all night long?

When *Little Creatures* was about to be released, David complained to Tibor Kalman's wife, Maira, "Everyone is having kids—Mother Goose just won't cut it." Maira decided to turn the lyrics of "Stay Up Late" into a children's book.

Maira (the mysterious M in M&Co.) was a painter and doodler, and if we believe the biographical material she provides, she was "born in Morocco to the Prince and Princess of Constantinople" and lived in New York City where she ate "bonbons by the barrel." The Kalmans would eventually have two children, a girl named LuLu Bondoni and a boy named Onomatopeia.

Kalman's illustrations for the book *Stay Up Late* are wonderfully long-limbed caricatures of Manhattanites throwing a helpless baby around like a beach ball, all painted in wonderful Matisse greens and yellows.

Walk It Down This electric strut starts with post-Eno treatments going on in the percussion so it sounds like a monstrous *Star Wars* reptile rhythmically jiggling the flaps around its neck in time to the music. This song contains the album's only line about money: "I took my money, I bet my life." Considering David's other financial lyrics, it's a modest mention. In the Sire press packet, however, the four Talking Heads talked plenty about money. These were the Reagan years. Money was everything.

Of money, David said, "We proved that it's possible to do something without compromise and sell it in the marketplace with everything else . . . and make a living at it. That's an inspiration to many people."

Tina said, "Now that we are getting bigger and making more money, it's complicated the situation while we try to adjust. But we still try to use our wealth and influence to bring other artists to the public." Later Tina explained to a reporter how they make their money from royalties: "We break it down into thirds. Rather than fifty percent for the top line melody, fifty percent for the lyrics, we do one-third for the musical arrangements, one-third for the top line melody, one-third for the lyric. We each get one-fourth of one-third. I'm very happy to have eight percent of a song."

Television Man This long song has the kind of global beat that would make it a fit on either of the last two Talking Heads albums, but it's not as Eno-fied with weirdness or prog keyboards. It also ends with David leading a chorus in a lengthy recitation of "nah nah nah." He must have died laughing in the studio.

Road to Nowhere On this Arcadian marching tune, Tina said she used the same bass rhythm from "Burning Down the House." A choir was tacked on at the beginning because David was embarrassed by the simplicity of the song. But he shouldn't have been. This deceptively cheerful song achieves a resigned but joyous look at forthcoming doom. Is it global? You know, asteroids striking the Earth, Ebola in the water system, old-fashioned H-bomb dropping. Or just our own certain forthcoming deaths? David doesn't say.

This may be Talking Heads' most infectious song to date. What a hoot it is to close this album.

When *Abbey Road*—another pure pop album—came out, critics had a field day analyzing the body language of the four Beatles strolling across a St. John's Wood zebra crossing: George in flared blue jeans, Paul barefoot holding a cigarette, Ringo with his hand in the same swaying position of George and Paul, and finally John in white with his hands sunk in his pockets. What did it mean? According to Beatles biographer Philip Norman, it represented Paul's funeral procession. "John, in his white suit, as the minister; Ringo, dark-suited, was the undertaker; and George, in his shabby denims, the gravedigger." Paul, meanwhile, walked with bare feet, an arcane symbol of death.

On the back of the *Little Creatures* sleeve, the four Talking Heads are photographed standing side-by-side wearing multicolored psychedelic peasant costumes. They are not crossing the street. Jerry, once a newcomer to the trio Talking Heads, is positioned first, followed by Chris, who stands next to David, who stands next to Tina. David and Tina are wearing crowns. Jerry and Chris are bare-headed. A wedding picture?

M&Co. is the brain behind the costumes and the staging. The costume designer and photographer's intention was to make it look as if the band had just stepped out of the Finster painting. When the print came back, the multicolored clothes made the band look fat, so the photo of the band was slightly elongated like an image on Silly Putty.

What we see are four people who know this photograph is a really dumb idea.

The Sire press release for the album dared to ask, "Is Talking Heads going to break up?"

"It's a question that's been on everyone's lips since David got his own apartment and Chris and I got a loft in 1977," Tina said. "It's become tedious because obviously we will break up eventually just to mutate into something better. Just now I feel good about the band because *Little Creatures* was my favorite album since the first Tom Tom Club LP. Let's put this old question to rest once and for all, please."

Later, to a reporter, Tina says, "The band is, for all intents and purposes, David's anchor, in reality. It's his family, whether he hates it or loves it; it's what he keeps coming back to. It's where he feels comfortable." Then she grew tired of talking about David. What about Tina? What if Tina left the band—what then? No! She'd never do it. Tina said she still had a lot to "resolve" with Talking Heads. If Tina Weymouth were to leave this band now—"forget all the other implications, like being a jerk to all our fans, et cetera"—it's probable that she would be left with the same unresolved problems. "I have to resolve these things with this band before I can grow to do something different."

She never says exactly what those "things" are.

Jerry was a distracted ladies' man in Milwaukee. He met a woman named Carol. They started dating. A month later, he looked up at Carol as she was walking across the bedroom and he realized that he had slept with her the previous year.

"Yeah," she said. "We've met before."

Wow. He was still a ladies' man. But Jerry also felt like Carol's soul mate. She felt that way about him as well, only she was engaged to another man. This was getting messy. But it was also very very good.

Jerry rendezvoused with David down in Texas to help scout locations. He still thought that the four Talking Heads would be in the movie.

David does not remember the story going this way, that Chris and Tina and Jerry were to be costars in the movie. But maybe he's forgotten, because all three eventually bombed out of the picture. Tina and Jerry both say that the three other Heads were supposed to play different townspeople in the film while David would run the town's radio station—his character was trying to find himself a woman.

Chris and Tina felt the story was a good idea, but then they read the script and hated it. It was flat and dysfunctional. Tina thought it made fun of Texas. Not to mention family life.

Anyway, their two characters were portrayed as buffoons. Chris and Tina decided to bail out gracefully. Maybe things would get better down the road. They decided to let the movie become David's baby.

As for Jerry, he didn't think the band could survive being *directed* by David in his first movie. He left the project as well.

true stories from the mid-eighties

It was a wise time for David Byrne to be making a movie. MTV's initial heyday was surely over. *Rolling Stone* claimed that MTV had lost 25 percent of its viewers. Bob Pittman refuted the magazine. He tossed out some numbers that were supposed to be contradictory, but they weren't. He claimed by "creating misinformation" *Rolling Stone* was fucking with the musicians and their own "loyal readers."

Promotional videos were still needed for *Little Creatures*. David didn't have time to star in one, let alone direct it. He was down in Texas scouting locations . . . by himself.

Warner Bros. wanted the first single to be "And She Was." A Portland filmmaker named Jim Blashfield pitched a video animation using color Xeroxes. This was perfect. There was no way to get all four Talking Heads together, so they would create a band by Xerox.

When Blashfield heard he got the gig he called up his buddy, Gus Van Sant, saying, "This is the big time! I'm making a Warner Bros. video."

"Who's the rock group?" Van Sant asked.

"Talking Heads."

"Hey, I went to art school with those guys."

Blashfield ended up hiring Van Sant for $100 a day to fly to the Bahamas and shoot photographs of Tina and Chris. Van Sant was grateful for the money, any money. He was really struggling during this time, and took whatever work he could get to finance the editing of his first feature, *Mala Noche*.

"I had dinner at Chris and Tina's apartment in Nassau," Van Sant recalled. "It was kind of wild. I remember next door was a loud party and Chris said that it was 'a rock cocaine party.' I had never heard of the stuff. What I remember most about the trip was that Nassau seemed like a cocaine boomtown."

The resulting video for "And She Was" is quite replayable as far as animation goes. A woman we never fully see floats her legs above suburbia. Occasionally, badminton birdies fly past her legs. Suburban seraphim. Head shots of Chris and Tina appear drinking coffee in time to the music. These are beautiful images for feeling at home while floating above American culture.

David scouted Texan locations in the ninety-five-degree summer heat. Sometimes he'd wear a Charlie Chan hat and little round sunglasses. An observer wryly commented that David "resembled a 1930s tourist in some hot colonial outpost."

He thought about the Lone Star vision of America as he visited shopping centers and tract houses. Observed cows munching grass. Lord, was Texas an existential landscape. "Stick some people out there, they're all on their own," David thought.

By planning to film in longhorn country, David was intentionally or unintentionally appropriating Robert Wilson's vision—the flat horizon line that Wilson had spent his theatrical career trying to duplicate.

David's film would concern itself with the town of Virgil, Texas, a town preparing to celebrate its 150th birthday by putting on a "Celebration of Specialness." David himself would star as a sort of guiding narrator, cruising through Virgil in a red convertible and "a greenish cowboy suit the color of electrified lichen" (as film critic Janet Maslin would put it later in the *New York Times*).

The movie would be a series of episodic tales inspired from the *Weekly World News*. One story would concern the laziest woman in the world, who never leaves her bedroom. Another character would be a woman deeply obsessed about "cute" things. Then there would be the couple who had not spoken for thirty-five years.

By August 1985 David was camped out in Dallas, inside a small house-turned-office. He had a fifteen-member production staff. The office was on a back street in what was politely called a "marginal neighborhood." The one-story beige brick structure had once been a hospice for people with terminal diseases.

In Dallas, David held a seven-hour audition at the Arcadia Theater and saw some 130 acts. There was a man who set his foot on fire. Another guy with dancing goldfish. David filmed a street parade in McKiney, a Dallas suburb. A hurricane named Juan screwed up filming a bit.

To unwind one night, David went dancing at some joint called Club Lingerie. Adelle loved to dance, but David felt too self-conscious to dance in L.A. Texas was different. A man could shake himself in public here. Another night, David went to a blues club and college kids came up to ask, "Hey, man. Are you David Byrne?"

"Yes, I am."

"Prove it, man. Show us your driver's license."

David flipped out his wallet as assuredly as Sergeant Joe Friday would show his badge.

David was now a rock star, and he understood it was a necessary thing, this mythologizing of rock stars. He saw it as part of an entertainer's function to live out the myth. He would deny in interviews that there ever was a moment that he thought, "I'm a rock star and goddamn it's good!"

"I've always been embarrassed," he answered. "Because I never bought into the rock star mythology. To be somewhat primitive and prone to fits of violent rage or other kinds of passion. To me, the rock star is some kind of primitive. An idiot savant who can't really function in the world and would rather get onstage and do something wonderful and entertain people."

Jerry had always been amused that in the video for "And She Was," his head appeared floating across the screen during the line about "joining the world of missing persons."

He told Warner Bros., "I think it's a mistake to only have David direct videos. All of us have talents." He didn't tell them that he believed most rock stars made ridiculous videos because of their lack of education. He kept that to himself. Instead Jerry said, "We have to make four videos, one directed by each of us."

Warner Bros. would only agree to do three. Everyone in the band did storyboards and then voted on which they liked best. The first was for "Lady Don't Mind." The concept was from both Jerry and Tina. Jim Jarmusch, eternal hip citizen of downtown Manhattan and the director of *Stranger Than Paradise*, would film it.

In the end, the video Jarmusch shot is pretty to look at but fairly ridiculous. The visual motif, which Jerry devised, was the transformation of black-and-white images into color. There are nice shots of the roof lines of the Lower East Side—including some buildings that look identical to the ones on Great Jones Street.

Unfortunately, the urban landscape is cut with silly shots of the band pantomiming their instruments while sitting in a room. In a particularly ridiculous maneuver, David gestures on a ladder while Chris and Tina and Jerry spin in fast motion.

The other recurring image is of Tina from behind wearing a long kimono that looks like a cross between a sleeping bag and a nun's habit. She stands listlessly in a Lower East Side apartment. She is illustrating the lyric of the woman who jumps out of a window, prejump. She never faces the camera. There are several shots of Tina from the back opening her kimono away from us, as if she is flashing the blank wall in front of her. These images were Tina's creation.

Down in Texas, David's crew found him extremely shy. Intense. Given to staring at the ground. Talking in near whispers. He was also spontaneous. He'd see a strange dog and incorporate the pooch into the script.

"There was a great spirit on the film," Pressman recalled. "I think *Badlands*—working with Terry Malick—was like *True Stories*. There was a feeling that this was something special. It was never a problem getting people to work for below-scale salaries just to be involved with David." Pressman thought a moment and said, "What makes a good director is the ability to inspire people. Some directors have dominating personalities like Oliver Stone or Brian De Palma. And some directors like David or Terry Malick have a very quiet demeanor, but still command the right amount of respect and charge. Their films somehow reflect their personalities."

All actors in the film stayed at the same hotel. Texan artist Jo Harvey Allen played a character called the Lying Woman.

In the movie, the Lying Woman knows the real Rambo because she was a nurse in Vietnam. The Lying Woman wrote most of Elvis's songs and

"Billie Jean" for Michael Jackson. It was love for the Lying Woman that got John F. Kennedy shot.

At the end of the day the cast would ritualistically go to the rushes. Jo Harvey Allen felt like they were all kids rushing out into a Texas morning to find condensation on the milk bottles and "Mom coming out and pointing out the thundercloud."

She wasn't in character when she said that. She thought David's movie "had a wonderful innocence to it. He's like some kind of spaced-out Mr. Rogers. There's no time that I worked with David that I didn't fall into one of those magical moments that took me into another realm."

Spalding Gray, an actor who started with the Performing Garage in SoHo, portrayed Earl Culver, a man who has not spoken to his wife, Kay, for years. (She was played by Pressman's wife, Annie McEnroe.) Kay likewise refuses to talk to her husband. They communicate through their children.

Gray felt David was the most perversely wholesome person he'd ever met. "David's core of innocence is still intact," Gray said at the time. "I don't mean this in a bad way—but in another lifetime he might be hospitalized. Luckily, he found his life raft in art."

David took time off from the movie to codirect, with Stephen R. Johnson, the video for "Road to Nowhere." It ended up winning the Video Vanguard Award at the second annual MTV Video Music Awards. The work was as crammed with eye stuff as a painting by Dalí. Prominent images are a series of a black-and-white David running in place in a gesture copped from Robert Wilson, as well as a hodgepodge of circular imagery, including a basketball, a birthday cake, blood pouring over a globe, and water spiraling down a drain.

Band members also appear in the film. Chris and Tina reenact the finish of the John Boorman film *Zardoz*, in which a husband and wife experience marriage, giving birth, and their own death in twenty seconds. After a pair of leather-masked professional wrestlers dressed as businessmen slam briefcases at each other, Chris and Tina appear slow dancing. There is also a prominent image of Jerry's hunky naked torso covered with white color.

301

The video ends with an image of David himself sitting on a throne, perhaps the throne in his mind, while hundreds of little animated things hop

---

and spin and gallop around him as his hair blows in stop-motion animation, and he literally becomes a Reverend Howard Finster painting.

In his book *Hiding in the Light*, Dick Hebdige gives a close "reading" of "Road to Nowhere." After making references to Stalin, Michael Jackson, Nazi death camps, the A-bomb, Jean-Luc Godard, feminism, and the poetic but meaningless proclamation that "philosophy is homesickness" (that sounds like a lyric from "This Must Be the Place"), Hebdige declares that all of us are on a road to nowhere, and David's response to mankind's condition is to just laugh. Hebdige unintentionally zeroed in on David's biggest personality trait—he's really just a big kid who loves to laugh.

"People meet David," Lee Blake said, "and they just want to sort of stare at him, and they think he's going to start talking about all kinds of art things all day long, but he's got an incredibly great sense of humor. I mean, he cracks me up. I've always made David laugh. And if you made David laugh, he absolutely loves you because he loves to laugh. He loves the joy of things."

Ann Keating, a private investigator who knew David through her ex-father-in-law, author Robert Farris Thompson, described him this way: "He always looked like he was secretly smiling more than he felt comfortable letting on. Not that he was swallowing the smile, more like he was saving it for later—to grin widely while he padded around in the safety of his own apartment."

The MTV Awards were given on September 13, 1985, at Radio City. Jean-Michel Basquiat, Keith Haring, and Andy Warhol all went. "Jean-Michel arrived in a limo," Warhol wrote in his diary. "He said he didn't want to go with Keith because Keith was too pushy. And it did get sick later on—Keith just wanted to be photographed so badly. And he wanted to go with me so he'd be sure to be photographed."

David wasn't there in person, but appeared in a video that showed him walking in a Texas Laundromat wearing a garish madras jacket and madras pants. He moved down an aisle and found his award inside a washing machine.

Chris was the one who developed the concept for the video to "Stay Up Late." It was the most satisfying Talking Heads video yet. Its premise is very simple—each of the Heads is wearing a white jumpsuit and is connected to a hoist, which dangles them before a white background. As the hoist raises and lowers Talking Heads, David lip-synchs about making somebody's baby stay up late.

There is an intuitive, yet completely illogical, connection to baby-hood—these adults dangling at the mercy of the whims of whoever is controlling the winches.

Later in September, *Music for Knee Plays* was released, the brass parts played by moonlighting *Tonight Show* band members. In November, CBS threw a party for Bob Dylan at the Whitney. Lou Reed and John Cale were present. It appears Chris and Tina were there as well. Meanwhile, Basquiat was fading from the scene. On December 22, he celebrated his twenty-fifth birthday at Mortimers. Phoebe Hoban wrote that the birthday boy's drug habit was so extreme that rumors were circulating he had AIDS. He had lost a front tooth. His face was covered with blotchy sores. Andy Warhol showed up. So did Tina Chow, Adelle's sister. Someone gave Basquiat a custom-made Stetson hat. Now he could be just like a Texan in *True Stories*.

The New Year—1986—began with a bang as the space shuttle *Challenger* exploded live on network TV on January 28. When David saw the *Challenger* blow and leave that immortal Y-shaped smoke trail, he didn't have much of an emotional reaction except, "Wow. Look how big that explosion is."

That may have been Ronald Reagan's reaction as well. He fully intended to give his scheduled State of the Union speech that night until his wife talked some sense into him.

The *Challenger* disaster had implications for MTV—they killed their moon landing logo.

In February, David was finishing up production on the movie. A decision was made to release Talking Heads' version of the *True Stories* songs. Overdubs and vocals had to be added. David was harried, but really excited. *True Stories*, the movie, was surely going to take the band over the top. He was so sure. He even vetoed a chance that Talking Heads would be part of the Live Aid benefit. "That would have catapulted us the way it did Peter Gabriel and U2," Jerry says today with regret. "We would have been one of the top bands in the world. The opportunity was ours to take. Because David was so obsessed by this movie, we didn't go."

What did happen was that everyone moved to L.A. to be near David. Chris and Tina rented a place in Santa Monica. Jerry and Carol lived on the canals of Venice beach. It was a miserable winter in L.A.—it rained all the time. Chris was homesick and cold. Tina was homesick, cold, and pregnant again.

Jerry, on the other hand, was having a great time. He was snuggled in with Carol. And he really loved Venice. It was his favorite place. He had hung there when he was in L.A. with the Modern Lovers. In those days, Venice was full of retirees. Walking on the beach had been surreal. Those were the days of Charlie Manson. You could really feel Manson energy in the air. Phil Kaufman, who'd cremated his friend Gram Parsons's body in the desert, had once produced a record for Manson. Phil told Jerry a story about dozens of Mansonites coming over the wall that surrounded his house one night. He turned his big movie spotlights on them and captured them all frozen on the lawn with knives in their teeth like pirates. One of Phil's guys came up from the back of the house and fired a shotgun in the air. Everyone scattered, yelling, "Charlie told us to get the music. Charlie told us to get the music."

To this day, when Jerry drove 405 through that cut in the Santa Monica mountains, he got the chills. There was just something about the feeling along Mullholland. On the other hand, the architect in him thought it was brilliant of Manson to map all those cement rivers they have all over the valley. Manson could go from Death Valley all the way to L.A. in a dune buggy without ever being spotted by the cops.

In America, when you are a real rock star, you must do publicity for your new record. When you are a movie director you must do publicity for your forthcoming film. David was both. He spent more time with reporters from *Esquire, Ms.,* and countless newspapers than he did with Adelle. What David said about this time fifteen years later is: "I got a little carried away with the press when the movie came out. I thought, 'Well, this is great. All this cover stuff. This is going to promote the band and the movie.' " Then he gave a sheepish smile and admitted, "There might have been too much time doing self-promotion."

Of the dozens of interviews with David Byrne that were written in 1986, most of them were done at lunch. One reporter met him at his favorite North Beach bar and grill, but they found the joint was mobbed with tourists, so David suggested they stroll to Chinatown where they would have lunch in a restaurant with a glass tank full of live frogs in the window.

If David didn't actually meet a reporter in a restaurant, some nourishment was always consumed during the interview. The result of all this journalistic noshing and yacking was tremendous data about what David Byrne likes to eat. One of the lines that he himself intoned in *Knee Plays* is, "I thought that if I ate the food of the area I was visiting, that I might assimilate the point of view of the people there." We might in turn ask, "If journalists were to eat the food of David Byrne, might they assimilate his perspective?"

Start with David at breakfast. He has been reported to have cottage cheese on toast with Mexican seasonings on top. "I also like peanut butter on crackers in the morning," he said. In one interview, David declared the best breakfast is leftover pizza.

David has been recorded eating in a peculiar fashion. As it has been stated time and again, David eats quickly, but never mushrooms. Mushrooms he just picks at.

He once carefully lined up a row of almonds along the spine of a leaf of lettuce before eating them.

At other interviews, David only admired the food instead of actually eating it. He looked at a display of fish cakes and cucumbers and chocolate and said, "It's so challenging to find food that doesn't wilt under heavy lighting and that looks edible." He once became so excited about the way the food looked in a San Francisco cafeteria that he jumped on a chair and shouted, "Nobody eat it yet!"

In August, Robert Pittman announced he intended to resign from MTV. The year before, he tried a leveraged buyout of the company and failed. He'd had enough. He'd clear out his desk by the end of the year. He'd walk away with $2.3 million in MTV options.

Talking Heads had two videos planned that commented on the art of MTV Videoland America.

"Wild Wild Life" mocks lip-synching by portraying a lounge in middle America where everyday people get up and lip-synch/pantomime-play to the Talking Heads song. Some of the cast of *True Stories*, notably John Goodman, appear. Jerry does four different bits disguised as Billy Idol and Bruce Lee and Prince and a Latin ladies' man. Chris appears as an awkward kind of tubby guy. The only memorable performances are from Tina, who whips off a blond wig to reveal a bald head, and this mousy-looking skinny guy who does a great imitation of David Byrne's body language. "Wild Wild Life" was meant to be a parody of MTV videos, and it would win an MTV award itself the following year. David laughed and thought, "I guess it was so close that it was assumed to be the real thing."

The second video was "Love for Sale"—a montage of real and fake television commercials. It was a brave move making this video, considering how much trouble Neil Young had getting "This Note's for You," his anti-commercialization of rock video, aired. Because of Young's tribulations, David made sure every product to be included in the video was approved by MTV beforehand. David even designed the storyboards around the merchandise, which included Pan-Am, Polaroid, Colgate, Isuzu Cars, Canyfields Ale, NutraSweet, Ben-Gay, V-8 Juice, Right Guard, Purolator, Close Up, Oreo, York Biscuits, Mr. and Mrs. Butterworth Light, Old Spice, Country Rock Mastercard, Aim toothpaste, Heinz, and Motorcraft Oil.

The only memorable image in the finished video is Tina Weymouth being drenched in milk chocolate and turned into a candy bar.

"I remember 'Love for Sale' costing eighty thousand dollars to produce," David recalled. "Which was staggering to me at the time."

In August, Tina gave birth to a second son.

By late September, David was up in Cambridge, Massachusetts, where *Knee Plays* was in previews at the Loeb Drama Center. David was asked by the *Daily News Magazine* if he was rich now. "I'm doing okay. But I didn't have enough to finance this movie. Or retire."

Three years earlier, in 1983, David had told the *New York Times*, "Sooner or later we're bound to fail. . . . It's just inevitable that we'll put out a disappointing album sooner or later, isn't it?"

Here it was, the ninth Talking Heads' album, *True Stories*.

As good as David was singing voodoo-style on "Papa Legba," the *True Stories* songs were sung better by the actors in the film. The tunes are as catchy as the ones on *Little Creatures*, but the new songs sound too generic both lyrically and musically. Jackson Browne or Don Henley could have sung "City of Dreams." Picture Cyndi Lauper singing "Radio Head" from a wrestling arena. And finally, a big "We Are the World" sing-along for "People Like Us." That last title is another David Byrne homesickness song that declares people like you and me can feel at home anyway, even in an America without truth or justice, as long as we have "someone to love."

Even David regretted the album's release in the end. He believed

Sire should have put out a legitimate soundtrack recording with Pops Stables singing "Papa Legba."

"Those songs weren't for me to sing," David said later. "I got talked into releasing that by friends." Is this true? Jerry would believe David intended the record to be released from day one, and now he was backpedaling.

A record David should have *really* regretted releasing was the mostly jokey instrumental *Sound from True Stories*, a one-disk collection of miscellaneous background music that ranges from cocktail lounge shtick to generic-sounding minimalism to a steel guitar instrumental of "City of Dreams." None of the fourteen cuts ("Cocktail Desperado," "Brownie's Theme," "Dinner Music," "I ♥ Metal Buildings") was worthy of being preserved on vinyl.

On October 4, *True Stories* premiered at the New York Film Festival. One film critic suggested it was easily the year's most original movie, a cross between *Paris, Texas* and *Badlands*. Another writer saw the film as *Nashville* without the plot. A particularly high-brow critic claimed the movie was a variation on the tenets put forth by the School of Spielberg and its branch campus, MTV. David's film was a combination of Spielberg's belief that suburbia had a subconscious and MTV's belief that within every yuppie there lurks a Little Richard. Finally, Ed Lachman's camera work was singled out and praised for its off-center American quality, as if he were Norman Rockwell's punk son.

All those interviews, then the ultimate magazine experience. *Time* magazine had seen its heyday by 1986, but the magazine still possessed a somewhat muscular media power. *Time* contributor Jay Cocks proposed a fall cover story on David Byrne. Once it was written, *Time* asked David to design the cover. This was a privilege. The only other subject who got to create his own cover had been Robert Rauschenberg back in '76.

Tina made a paranoid claim that *Time* magazine had intended to feature the entire band, but David sneaked into the offices and substituted a shot of the band with a picture of himself.

The truth is, David was very nervous the cover wasn't going to come off at all. Ronald Reagan had just brought the Evil Empire to its knees at the Iceland summit. Historians would later claim that it was Reagan's Star Wars bluff that ensured the end of the Soviet Union.

There was also domestic and international brouhaha over a downed contra cargo plane. On the national front, David was competing with evangelicals in Alabama who claimed textbooks were full of illegal "secular humanism."

In the end, neither Iceland nor the evangelists beat David. ROCK'S RENAISSANCE MAN said *Time*'s headline on October 27, 1986. David was declared Singer, Composer, Lyricist, Guitarist, Film Director, Writer, Actor, Video Artist, Designer, and Photographer.

David had submitted three possible covers to the *Time* editor. The one that ran was a cubist self-portrait of the artist. His face is broken into two rows of four colored photos—eight squares total. Top row to bottom row, left to right, the squares are blue, yellow, magenta, green, yellow, purple, green, and blue. David has a green and blue chin. Yellow and green forehead. The collage is in the tradition of the Polaroid mosaic he and Tina took for the cover of *More Songs About Buildings and Food*. As well as in the tradition of Andrea Kovacs and David Hockney.

The article begins with David hunting African fire ants in the middle of the night in the Texas panhandle. It goes on for more than 1,500 words about David as a Gregory Peck dosed out on lithium before it mentions Tina or Chris or Jerry. It goes on for another 1,500 words, including "David Byrne and the Heads were one of the few New-Wave bands to groove on black music and learn from it" before Tina is even quoted.

What she says is that she remembers David was always doing conceptual art in school. "David has never been one for draftsmanship," she said. "David would do anything to get attention. He'd do anything on a dare. He'd go to a party wearing a red taffeta dress."

The article is illustrated with eight photographs of David. There is a profile shot of him with Adelle Lutz—the couple looks stage right, Adelle with her hair pulled back, looking quite lovely although the lighting is too bleached. There is a photograph of David in the Big Suit along with an insert shot of him wearing cowboy leggings and a cowboy hat, fingering the gun in his holster. This David is three years old.

The article contains two band shots. In one they are dressed up like a sophisticated Holiday Inn lounge band. In the other they are wearing costumes from the video for "Wild Wild Life": David and Jerry as Latin lovers with black mustaches, Chris in a black cowboy costume, and Tina with fake leopard skin and a bald head.

The article ends with Spalding Gray saying that David doesn't like to say good-bye. Gray doesn't mention that David will sometimes just leave a restaurant or party or hitch-hiking ride on the Maryland highway without saying anything. The interview is followed by a show business article that claims Manhattan's avant-garde, such as Philip Glass, Laurie Anderson, Robert Wilson, and Twyla Tharp, are "conquering" the county.

Time magazine founder, Henry Robinson Luce (1898–1967), believed that at heart Americans are pilgrims, and that the twentieth century was America's continued pilgrimage into greatness. He wrote, "In years to come, there will be an American poet who will write not only of the love of the American land and not only of the making of a nation; that future poet will write of a people who love beauty and surround themselves with it and live in it."

What would Henry Luce have made of Renaissance Man David Byrne and his vision of America in *True Stories*? Luce wouldn't have cared that Ed Lachman's photography is stunning. It's unlikely Luce would see the similarities between the film's first shot of a road to nowhere and the photograph of U.S. 285 in New Mexico taken by American chronologist Robert Frank. Luce might recognize a like mind when David begins the gentle voice-over and alerts us that everything we're seeing used to be underwater. Dinosaurs used to lumber here. And on this spot, "the Spaniards fought the Mexicans. The Mexicans fought the Americans. The Americans fought the Wichitas. The Wichitas fought the Tunkowas. The Tunkowas fought the Comanches. The Comanches fought everybody."

As this curious film continues, it is unlikely that Luce would see it as a pilgrimage into greatness. He wouldn't be amused at the lip-synching contest at a cocktail lounge. Nor by the parade down Main Street the next day with its dozen Shriners in red fezzes driving miniature red Ford Mustangs. Nor a scene shot in an evangelical church. Nor by the fashion freak show. And certainly not by the Friday Night Talent Show that consists of ventriloquists, yodlers, and yo-yo virtuosos.

Luce would see the Americans who inhabit Vigil as exalting no one. The Lazy Woman is not on an American pilgrimage. Neither is the Lying Woman. Not even the Cute Woman and her little rabbit slippers. David's movie neither mocks nor celebrates these characters. Luce would have probably agreed with Jerry that if it hadn't been for the tremendously empathetic performance of John Goodman—the ladies' man without a lady, a man who so desperately wants a wife he advertises himself on TV and puts a sign

WIFE WANTED on his lawn—the movie would have been nothing more than an American freak show.

But after making that judgment, Luce might reconsider. It's easy to overlook the star of the film, the narrator, David, that pleasant young man in a black cowboy hat (gently mocking the tradition of the bad guy wearing such a color). With his strange Americanized Scotch accent and earnest, nonjudgmental observations, David is a compelling screen presence. And he does love, or thinks he loves, this Coca-Cola land. He probably even *believes* the things the Lying Woman says. He secretly wants to wear the Cute Woman's bunny slippers. He yearns to slip into bed with the Lazy Woman.

Near the beginning of the film, David describes the automotive choreography of cars passing his red convertible as it drives down the Texas road to nowhere. There is the "adventurer." The "marshmallow." The "nomad" and the "weaver." "It's fancy driving," he says. "Things that never had names before now are easily described. It makes conversation easy."

During this time, Tina had a dream about the Renaissance Man. In her dream, Tina has missed all the rehearsals for the next Talking Heads tour because David advertised them in a newspaper, and Tina—as David well knew—doesn't read newspapers. The band takes the stage but they don't play a single note. The audience gets up and leaves. The next day, the newspapers that Tina claims to never read give the concert rave reviews. "Even in my dreams, the Renaissance Man can do no wrong," she lamented.

Time magazine printed five letters in response to the Renaissance Man story. Four of the letters agreed that David was a genius. The fifth was from one F. Everset Gilbert of Dansville, New York. He pointed out that "singer, composer, lyricist, and guitarist" are part of one field and "film director, writer, actor, video artist, designer, and photographer" are part of another. If David Byrne were a true Renaissance Man he would also master statecraft, metaphysics, tragedy, comedy, history, and "maybe the sonnet to boot."

When asked about the stories in the *Times Magazine* and *Time*, David says, "I felt like I deserved this attention. I thought some of the hyperbole was a little over the top. But I felt *Stop Making Sense* was a great film. *True Stories* worked out pretty good. I was very proud of the stuff. It was thrilling to get the recognition. My willingness to receive that recognition was getting a little out of hand. The press was only too willing to give it to me to the extent that all I had to do was volunteer. I was getting a little carried away with it. A lot of the things they were saying were exaggerating it. It appeared to people that I was saying that stuff. That I was making those claims. I wasn't."

A true Renaissance Man must have a book. And David's first one, *True Stories*, was published along with the movie. It was a handsome oversize paperback of 190 pages that contained the screenplay, along with color photographs of Texas road culture by William Eggleston and David's own Polaroids of curious Texan debris, such as metal buildings ("the dream that modern architects had at the beginning of the century come true," David wrote). Of course there are movie stills, too—David in his black cowboy hat smiling over a luminous green cocktail with a pink umbrella poking out of the ice cubes. The book also contains entertaining supplemental texts such as a *Wall Street Journal* article entitled "Why Do Hot Dogs Come in Packs of 10 and Buns in 8s and 12s?"

David's book begins with the oft-repeated claim that *True Stories* began as true stories found in the *Weekly World News*. But the book ends with this disclaimer: "Although the name of the movie is *True Stories*, I am saddened and disappointed to have to admit that a lot of the stories are made up." But then, David explains, a lot of the stories in the tabloids he used for inspiration were made up. "To tell you the truth," he wrote, "I don't even really care."

The band was now gnashing its teeth because David would not tour. Publicly, David would say that he loved performing in front of people. But *Stop Making Sense* took the Wilsonesque stage show as far as he could take it. "The music concert is a boring anachronism," he said. "I'd rather go to Vegas."

David remembered, "I wanted the band to play the *True Stories* songs in concerts at drive-in movie theaters. There were so many of them out of commission. These just kind of empty spaces. It would be fun to play there and have people drive in. Wind down their windows. Sit on the hood of their car or whatever, sit on their lawn chairs and see a show."

The year before, at the 1985 Florence Film Festival, the great Italian director Bernardo Bertolucci went to a screening of *Stop Making Sense* and witnessed audience members leaping out of their seats and dancing in the aisles. He said, "This is my fantasy! This is my dream! To have the audience dance in front of my movie!"

Bertolucci never forgot the experience. A year or so later he phoned David to tell him about *The Last Emperor*, a film he was completing about the last official emperor of China. Two other composers, Ryuichi Sakamoto and Gong Su, were working on parts of the score. Bertolucci wanted David to provide the opening theme, as well as other incidental music. "But I don't want *chinoiserie*—fake Chinese music," Bertolucci said. "No *dink-dink-dink-dink-dink* . . ."

David agreed to this restriction. He studied Chinese music and wrote the score. In November, he premiered the music on a New York radio show. Then he took calls from listeners. The first caller said, "In the beginning, the music sounded like bad germs in your body starting up a cold." Another caller said the music reminded him of when he cut up a bear with a chainsaw and fried him in a pan for dinner.

These callers were children. David was appearing on "Kids America" on WNYC. At the close of the show, host Kathy O'Connel asked David what inspired the music. David said nothing about *chinoiserie* or "dink-dink-dink-dink-dink . . ." Instead he answered, "It's about a lot of germs attacked by a bear and then they all chase a frog down the railroad tracks."

During the fall, Basquiat could be seen pedaling his small red bike through Alphabet City looking like a grade-school refugee. He was there to score horse. In November, Andy Warhol's piss paintings were exhibited at the Gagosian. He called them *Oxidations*. Several months before, art critic Paul Taylor had declared that Warhol's piss paintings were "exceptional works in the cannon of this saint of twentieth century art." Yoko Ono showed up at the opening. Warhol reported in his diary that a number of dowagers asked him how he created the paintings. He didn't have the heart to tell them because their noses were right up against the canvas.

This is the same month that the Securities and Exchange Commission imposed a record $100 million penalty against the Darth Vader of Wall Street, Ivan Boesky.

David Byrne spent the holiday in Tokyo with Adelle.

In the New Year, Andy Warhol ran into Yoko Ono again at the opening of a Keith Haring show. This was their last chance meeting. In the middle of the night on February 22, 1986, Andy Warhol lay on a hospital bed

312

after having his gallbladder removed the afternoon before. According to Warhol historian Paul Alexander, the night nurse was too busy reading her Bible to notice the pop artist had begun turning blue. When she finally noticed Andy had the blues, it was too late. The pop artist was pronounced dead at 6:31 A.M. It was a Sunday morning. "Sunday Morning" is, of course, one of the Velvet Underground's truly tender songs.

voodoo days

True Stories had not put Talking Heads over the top, only David. Chris and Tina aired their disappointment publicly in the January 15, 1987, issue of *Rolling Stone*. The band posed for the article in CBGBs, the dive where they first blossomed all those years ago. Everyone but David slouches on a black couch. David stands on the couch, looking—as the reporter said—like George Washington in a rowboat crossing the Delaware. General Byrne looked as if "he had not forgotten who had taken him to the river and steered him through those swirling murky waters."

Tina's first words to the reporter were, "Where's your hatchet?" She and Chris both used this vessel of the press to tell David that it was their own fault the public perceived General Byrne as rowing across the Delaware by himself. He had been given credit for everything Talking Heads did because no one else in the band ever objected. Chris told David in the public pages of *Rolling Stone* what he felt he could not say in private, "When you get on the cover of *Time*, and there's that much promotion, you slowly but surely begin to lose your grassroots flowering. If a politician is on the cover of *Time*, you stop believing him. And *True Stories* has sold less than *Little Creatures. . . .*"

Chris then predicted that on the next record, he and his wife would assert themselves. Tina agreed. She'd even write some songs for the band. Everything she wrote would be completely credited to her. She wasn't going to throw David any freebies. As for singing, Chris mused about doing lead vocals for a tune just like Ringo did on "With a Little Help from My Friends."

Chris and Tina's biggest issue was touring. David didn't want to return to the stage unless the band could come up with a show that topped the Big Suit tour (now referred to as the *Stop Making Sense* tour). He even half-heartedly suggested they have actors appear between songs.

My God, no. Why not have children and old women play our instruments like the video for "Burning Down the House"!

Chris and Tina weren't going to share the stage with extra Heads again. They couldn't afford to. They needed to make some money. They had an expensive house in the Connecticut suburbs on a piece of land with a pond the locals called Talking Heads Lake.

"We're gonna lose our whole audience if we don't tour," Tina lamented. *Goddamn it, David. Wise up!*

David's reasons for not touring were a little more complex than not wanting to repeat history. First, he privately saw himself more as a film-maker then a musician. Then he read something about R. Crumb—the old sixties underground comic book artist, creator of *Fritz the Cat*. Crumb said that he *had* to draw all those perverse big-butted women. It was the only way to exorcise them. Drawing underground comics wasn't a job. It was a necessity. Those big-butted women were a matter of physical and mental survival. David compared himself to Crumb and realized, "That's how I used to feel about performing."

Used to feel.

He didn't feel that way now. He could remember his old need. Standing onstage was like burying your face in the big butt of an R. Crumb gal. Thank God he was free of that old jones. He'd even found religion. Not Jesus or Scientology, but that African-originated faith called voudoun or vodun—aka voodoo. Because this vulgarization has been used by Americans as diverse as Joseph Campbell and Miles Davis, we'll call it voodoo, too. Most Americans first became aware of voodoo in the 1950s at drive-ins where spooky flicks like *I Walked with a Zombie* first screened. Hollywood had portrayed voodoo as Negroid witchery from Haiti. Several years earlier in 1947, avant-garde filmmaker Maya Deren went down to Haiti to shoot her documentary about the religion, *Divine Horsemen*. She discovered the theological differences between voodoo sects were as complex and diverse as those found in American Protestantism. Voodoo was a blanket term for West African religions fragmented by slavery. Voodoo/voudoun was practiced in Haiti and New Orleans, but it was called Santería in the Caribbean. In Brazil there were three cults—Macumba, Umbanda, and Candomblé.

Haitian-style voodoo was old hat to Chris and Tina, but David had been mainly interested in voodoo roots music. In the late 1970s, he and Mary Clarke would go dancing to salsa bands at the Corso Ballroom in Yorkville. In San Francisco the previous summer, David had spent his nights at Caesar's Latin Palace in the Mission District, grooving to salsa once again. David picked up enough voodoo theology to sing an invocation to the deity Papa Legba in *True Stories*. More recently, David went down to the Rio de Janeiro film festival with Edward Pressman to screen *True Stories*. David heard about all this heavy voodoo activity in the hills of Bahia—a region with a climate and vegetation very similar to West Africa.

David nosed around and found the citizens practiced Candomblé and honored a multiple of gods—*orishas*—with names like Ogún and Yemanja and Oshun. In Candomblé, women are the link between God and the cult. And men are the link between the cult and the outer world. According to voodoo-ologist Luc Sante, men do this through pop music.

Ha! David recalled seeing a photo of a man being possessed by a Candomblé force named Ogían. The man was smoking a cigar, half slouched, half playing an air guitar. The epitome of *rock 'n' roll body attitude*.

Music for God. Hmm. David realized he had been a practicing Candomblé for most of his life.

Jerry was in Milwaukee awaiting the birth of his first son. The pregnancy had been a surprise. It was a good and sobering thing. Carol and Jerry loved each other very much. There was no question they would have the kid. But this new life changed the context of everything, the way the death of Jerry's first band, the Modern Lovers, and the death of his parents had. Jerry felt himself getting more and more serious about things. He and Carol were in Milwaukee because it was a much easier town for a baby than New York. But maybe they should move here permanently. New York was an expensive place to live. As for marriage, Jerry wanted to tie the knot, but not right now. "This was a real busy time," he remembered. "I didn't want to interrupt that just because we ought to get married."

Jerry's "creature of love," Griffin, was born March 12, 1987.

The *Rolling Stone* article two months earlier had begun with Chris raging about the time that David "tricked" the *New York Times Magazine* into substituting the band shot with a portrait of himself for the cover, an event that had happened a year and a half earlier back in 1985. The media loved referring to itself almost as much as it loved to let celebrities trash each other. The March '87 issue of *Esquire* did a story on bruised egos of the SoHo art world starring Robert Longo along with fellow paint dribblers Julian Schnabel, David Salle, and Eric Fischl. In 1987 there were few prominent art critics left who thought that the works of Robert Longo, Julian Schnabel, David Salle, and Eric Fischl were important. The collectors who bought those four's work had much money and no taste. After the *Esquire* writer paid tribute to each young painter's ego and insecurities, readers learned David Salle burned the Longo cover to a Glenn Branca record because Salle hated Longo's work. Schnabel, in turn, hated Fischl. The latter didn't care for Schnabel's work but really hated Longo. Longo himself respected Salle, but disliked Schnabel and Fischl.

All four liked to eat at a restaurant called Indochine.

The article was illustrated with an energetic Robert Longo drawing of two businessmen fighting; a Julian Schnabel painting of an ugly impressionistic realism via blotches; David Salle doing harmless magazine photograph realism; and finally, a typical Eric Fischl depiction of naked bourgeois. There were photos of all four artists. Julian Schnabel and Robert Longo posed with celebrities—Schnabel with over-the-hill actress Sylvia Miles, and Longo with his "good friend" David Byrne beside him laughing.

By spring, Longo's pal, David, was back in the States. David began talking with Ed Pressman about doing another film titled *Shango*. It would be a dramatic love story about Santería that would take place in Haiti and San Francisco. David also hooked up with one of his favorite writers, Robert Farris Thompson. Together they visited a *canzo*, a kind of voodoo initiation ceremony in the Bronx. David joyfully drank a potion of rum, chicken blood, and gunpowder with Thompson at a voodoo ceremony in New Haven. The two traveled to various Afro-Latin clubs in New York where David rocked out to a one-note bamboo Haitian trumpet as naturally as if he had grown up dancing to such music—which in a way he had, all those ethnographic records he checked out from the library as a kid.

In late spring, David agreed to record again with Talking Heads. Not that he had any songs. Neither did Tina. Under David's influence the band returned to a global pop vibe. In particular, David wanted to experience voodoo music influences—the salsa beat—along with the tried-and-true African rhythms and funk. No one seriously objected. The other Heads were grateful that David was still considering Talking Heads as one of his creative outputs.

The group met in a studio in New York and began improvising. They came up with forty grooves, which they distilled down to a dozen to take to . . . Paris. The band wanted to record in new terrain. Sigma Studios had too much *True Stories* vibe. And Compass Point was Tom Tom Club. "It just came to 'Why don't we go somewhere different?' " Gary Kurfirst remembered. "Maybe if we go somewhere different we could lock ourselves away and not have all the exterior interference and become a real band again."

They chose the City of Light.

Of course, both Jerry and Tina felt at home here. But in the late 1980s, many felt that Paris was becoming as much an African city as a French one. The cream of African, or at least Franco-African, talent had relocated to this old colonial capitol. David had heard about all those incredible shows, restaurants, nightclubs, musicians, producers, and radio stations.

Talking Heads would record at Studio Davout, a former Parisian movie theater. Originally, the "Chief Inspector" Wally Badarou was going to produce the album, but he had a scheduling conflict. He did assemble the African musicians that he thought Talking Heads would get along with, like percussionist Abdou M'Boup, guitarist Yves N'Djock, and Jose 'Ie' Jerez on trumpet.

Steve Lillywhite produced the sessions. This thirty-something Brit's major production accomplishments involved Simple Minds, Big Country, and Peter Gabriel's third album. More recently, Lillywhite had mixed several songs on U2's *Joshua Tree* and produced *If I Should Fall from Grace with God* for the Pogues. For the Talking Heads album, Gary Kurfirst saw Lillywhite as a referee, not a producer. Kurfirst's own job was a perpetual state of walking on eggs. "When Steve came in and got involved with this band," Kurfirst recalled, "they were already probably the biggest band in America, the most popular band in America—the greatest band in America. I think that his job at that point really was to sort of make sure they didn't kill each other."

Jerry saw Lillywhite's function differently. Not only had each member of Talking Heads produced their own music, they'd produced other people's. "When you've already done it yourself, what you look for in a producer is different." There was never the sense that Talking Heads couldn't have made a good record even if Lillywhite hadn't been there. "That being said, Steve was enthusiastic and a delight to work with. He had ideas. He added things. He was great."

Life in Paris was better than great. Jerry had rented an apartment with Carol and the baby in the Sixth Arrondissement on rue Bonaparte, just up from the famous cafe where Verlaine and Rimbaud used to hang out.

Tina loved Paris. She could speak French all day.

The group adopted European work habits. They would start recording in the morning, then break for lunch. Go to the corner cafe for a one-hour lunch—none of this take-out food like in the States.

Jerry remembers the relaxed working schedule with mixed feelings. "There's a whole thing about getting back to work. Some days this process is better than others. Sometimes a musician needs that time to clear his mind. Other times, if one is in the middle of something, it's better not to have a fresh thought and just keep hammering at what it was you were doing. And not have a new idea but complete the one that you started."

Lillywhite didn't always agree with the band. He would be the one to listen to the run-through tape of the songs. He could tell right away what sections worked and what didn't. He made concrete suggestions and pushed things along. He wasn't moody like Eno. He was more conservative in the studio, but that had hidden blessings. The song that would eventually be called "Mommy Daddy You and I" happened very serendipitously because Lillywhite wasn't always monkeying with the mixer. As Jerry explained,

"You have a multitracked tape and you set the levels for each track. When you're doing a rough mix, a lot of people tear the whole thing down and start from scratch. Steve said, 'No, no. Don't tear the whole thing down. Leave the last mix and let's see what happens.' We heard this whole thing where the accordion comes in, we thought, 'That's fantastic. We would never have got that without the accentual mix.' "

There were few overdubs on the new songs. On many of the cuts, the band played in the same room together. This almost always results in better playing than when musicians are stuck in separate booths. But playing in the same room also makes for a certain amount of leakage. If David's guitar is picked up by the microphone recording Tina's bass, it may eliminate the producer's option to erase David's part and have him redo it because the erased guitar part is permanently affixed to the bass track.

"Hermetically sealed is great," Jerry said. "But it's harder to get a performance with a lot of feeling."

Various other Brits, including the Smiths' guitarist Johnny Marr, played on the record. The band got along best with the Franco-African players. An African percussionist named Brie pulled out a pair of Western chaps covered with bean pods. After he put them on, these musical pants rattled like huge shakers when he walked.

Chris asked him, "Do you know the Bo Diddley beat?"

He said, "No."

So Chris played an example and Brie said, "Oh, yeah! That we know!"

The song with the musical pants would be "Ruby Dear." What sounds like shakers is actually Brie in his bean pants dancing the Bo Diddley beat.

When drummer Moussa Cissokano needed to tighten the heads of his drums, he took them down into a bathroom underneath the control room and started a fire. Then he took the drum and set it down over the flame—the heat would tighten the skins. Smoke began billowing up through the control booth. After that, Talking Heads got him an electric heater.

• • •

Jerry knew Fela's manager, who heard of a great guitarist named So. Jerry told Francis to send the guy over. A little later, a fellow showed up at the Davout. But there was a language problem.

"Are you the guitarist?" asked Jerry.

"Yes," he said.

"Where's your guitar?" David asked.

"I don't have my guitar," the man answered.

"Here," David said, holding out an instrument. "Use one of ours. You can plug in over here."

The visitor did. The band began to play. What the guitarist was playing didn't work with anyone else's performance.

Jerry finally said, "I like what you're playing but I don't think it fits with the other music."

"Change the other music," the guitarist answered.

Just then another fellow showed up at the studio. He had a guitar. This was the real So. The first guy was a delivery person. But So refused to take his place. That would be rude.

David wanted to try writing lyrics in the studio. He wore a suit to the session and a pair of fat black horn-rims with clear glass lenses. He set up the studio room at Davout like a theater piece. He sat at a large bureau with a tiny desk lamp shining down on a piece of paper covered with indecipherable squiggles. As a particular track played, he took suggestions from Tina and others in the control room.

Tina looked through the glass and thought to herself how small David looked sitting there screaming out the chorus, "Blind." Pause. "Blind." Pause. "Blind, blind, blind, blind, blind"—David pronouncing the word *Blahnd!*

Blahnd!?

Blahnd, blahnd, blahnd, blahnd, blahnd.

The tracks were all recorded. David had one more thing to do before he returned to New York. He was going to marry Adelle Lutz. As Adelle tells the story: "I had been in Paris a few times before DB and I wanted to get married. Eloping in a foreign country was very hard work. In retrospect, it took too much planning to be a proper 'elopement.' David

321

Seidner, my old friend, was then living in Paris and came as DB's witness and another friend, Gabrielle Forte, flew in from Milan to be my witness. DB was as cool as a cucumber. He was steady, cheerful, and I was a train wreck inside."

The ceremony was held on July 18 at the town hall at St. Sulpice. "The mayor of that arrondissement was a small thin man in a brown suit with a Miss America–style band cutting from shoulder to opposite hip quite loaded with medals," Adelle continues. "I understood very little of what he said. The guard at the door would bow and stretch his jaw at me each time I was to say 'oui.' "

Adelle had to return to the States for a JoAnne Akalaitis production at the Guthrie Theater in Minneapolis. Jo Harvey Allen (the *True Stories* Lying Woman) was in it, as well as her honky-tonk husband, Terry, who was writing some neo-panhandle art songs for the piece. "There were a lot of pals in Minneapolis," David said. "I thought, 'Why not go there to work on my lyrics for a week?' I wrote the words for '(Nothing but) Flowers' and 'Totally Nude' while I was there. The former while driving aimlessly in the suburbs . . . singing into a little tape recorder."

All the other lyrics were written in New York. The words were sparklingly dissociative. David intended "Big Daddy" to be a woman's version of a Tennessee Williams scenario. "Ruby Dear" concerned midnight radio, being hounded from the bedroom to the kitchen, and someone named Johnny Jones spinning down a hole like Alice in Wonderland. "Cool Water" was literally about working stiffs (as in dead people). David also wrote a song that seems biographical—about leaving Baltimore with his mother and father and sister, heading north (to Canada?)—everyone wearing "our grandfather's clothes."

When David was asked about the autobiography in that song, he answered, "We took some road trips as a family. And I sort of remember moving from Hamilton, Ontario, to Baltimore when I was seven or eight."

David's sister Celia went public once or twice after David had been declared a Renaissance Man. "We weren't your typical American family." She and her brother did a lot of things together, "but we rarely talked about it. So it's hard to know whether to call us 'close.' David is a very private person and is still pretty shy at times."

She told no one about sitting out on the neighbor's front porches naked in the moonlight. No one from the press encouraged her to talk about the time she was sick and David bought her a copy of *The Phantom Toll Booth*. Or the times that he helped her with her homework. Normal stuff. Big brother stuff.

The most curious new song was "Bill"—a short Hawaiian-sounding song with vibes and steel guitar whose lyrics merge the big dumb lummox in *Of Mice and Men* with James M. Cain seediness. "My Randy Newman tendencies surface in a song about a child molester," David said.

Tina saw David's new lyrics differently. "The lyrics are all a cry for help," she said. "They're all, 'I'm just a little boat. I'm floating adrift. I don't have an anchor. I'm in water too deep for my anchor to reach. A boat adrift.'"

Jerry knew Talking Heads was for all practical purposes David Byrne and Talking Heads, just as it was Mick Jagger and the Rolling Stones. They were never going to make real money unless David concentrated on the band. And he wasn't. Jerry decided to devote all his energy to cutting a second record, *Man with a Gun*. Not a *solo* album exactly. Alex and Bernie were playing on it. Jerry wanted to form a second band like Chris and Tina had done. The group would be called Casual Gods, a name suggested by a friend of a friend who lived in Chris's European home, Paris.

323

Great name, but Jerry wasn't kidding himself. He knew very well this new band would always be considered Jerry Harrison *and* Casual Gods.

Once a year, a European city became the cultural capital of the Old World—that old mostly white world of Lisbon, Antwerp, London. Berlin was to be the art capital in 1988. The year before, Robert Wilson had been chosen to do a theatrical performance that would be turned into a movie in Berlin. David wanted to make the movie, but he was only scheduled to write the music. The filming would be done by forty-two-year-old German filmmaker Wim Wenders.

Robert Wilson, David Byrne, Wim Wenders. Three of the most creative people on the planet! Wenders, especially, was a kindred spirit.

Wenders's *American Friend* (containing Dennis Hopper's immortal line, "A little older. A little more confused") and the film he was completing called *Der Himmel Über Berlin (Wings of Desire)* were both quirky homages to American culture merged with a Germanic poetic flare worthy of Rilke. Best of all, Wim loved rock 'n' roll.

They all met in the fall in Berlin where Wilson showed them squiggles on a piece of paper—his first step toward actually writing a dramatic script. This play would be a retelling of the story of Gilgamesh, hero of Sumerian legend. As Wilson explained it, that ancient epic confronted the same issues that came up during the Industrial Revolution. "It deals with what it means to be in the city. What it means to be civilized versus nature." It made sense to set the work in the nineteenth century. Gilgamesh would be an industrial tycoon. The work would be called *The Forest*.

What one actor involved in the production remembers most about David was that he arrived wearing beautiful shoes. David was very quiet and discreet. In terms of star power, he was bigger than Robert Wilson, but he was careful not to upstage the Texan.

Wilson wrote plays based on workshop improvisations. The first thing he cared about was movement, not a script. The second most important thing was lighting. About a third of any Wilson production budget was spent on lighting.

Wim Wenders showed up at one or two workshops. Then he quite sensibly left. David soon followed.

The apocalypse/tycoon theme of *The Forest* proved to be timely. After David returned to New York, the Big Money days of the 1980s officially ended when the stock market crashed on October 19, 1987.

Near the end of the year, Jerry approved the cover of the first Casual Gods album, *Man with a Gun*. Hugh Brown designed it. "I had found this poster called the Thug in a gun shop in New York," Jerry said. "It was on newsprint of a guy pointing a gun at you with a bull's-eye." An artist took a photo of Jerry and, using flat and glossy lacquer (similar to the original Velvet Underground cover for *White Light/White Heat*), the poster was put over his face. At a certain reflection, you see Jerry's face turn into a guy pointing a gun at you.

Then a psycho killer in England went into a schoolyard and shot a bunch of children. Jerry had just two weeks to change the cover and the album title.

The new Talking Heads album was released in the late winter of '88 and was called *Naked*. Jerry believes it is the group's most unappreciated album. He's right. *Naked* is marvelous. John Chernoff felt the record was the apotheosis of the journey Talking Heads had started with *Remain in Light*. "The band had mastered the idioms," he said. "This is not easy to do. A lot of people tried it—you know the names. I'm sure Paul Simon's *Graceland* sold a zillion times more than *Naked*, but *Graceland* isn't unified and true to its idioms like *Naked* is. David Byrne can create things that have the integrity of the idiom and yet still have a kind of modernized edge."

As good as it was, *Naked* didn't fare well in the market due to several factors. First, the band didn't tour to support the record. Second, Americans had grown blasé about the Caucasian musical pillaging of the Third World. David Byrne may have mastered African idioms, but he seemed like one more white guy poaching on people of color. The *Washington Post* was particularly pissy about everything related to Talking Heads. Writer Mark Jenkins called "(Nothing but) Flowers"—David Byrne's sci-fi complaint about a world where technology has fallen apart and nature has covered over the Pizza Huts and shopping malls—an "ecological protest song about the opposite of the actual threat." The singer misses his microwave oven. Going to the 7-Eleven. "In his quest for irony," Jenkins wrote, "David Byrne rushes to the brink of irrelevance."

The *Post* correctly identifies the other unsuccessful song as "Mr. Jones." This was David's "Bizarro World" reinterpretation of Bob Dylan's "Ballad of a Thin Man." But David's lyrics didn't match the music. The happy horn parts and steel guitars are not the right Siamese twin for Dylan's blowsy drunken piano put-down of Mr. Jones.

As for the qualities of Mr. Jones himself—Mr. Dylan's Jones is a surreal Everyman oppressed by sword swallowers and one-eyed midgets. Jones's only sociological identification is that he hangs out with college professors and great lawyers (an oxymoron) as well. He also loves the oeuvre of F. Scott Fitzgerald. Mr. Jones is obviously not Joe Six-Pack.

325

Mr. Byrne's Jones is a salesman at some convention whose tight ventilated slacks keep falling down. Mr. Byrne appears to be sincere in embracing Jonesness, but who is kidding whom? Mr. Jones was the one who read *Bright Lights, Big City* for kicks. He thought *Ishtar* was a gas. His cash greased the SoHo art world. "There used to be a sharp demarcation between the bourgeois world and the art world," art critic Barbara Rose lamented to *The New Yorker*'s Janet Maslin. "The bourgeois world was Other. . . ."

"Its values were Other. . . ."

This was the world of Mr. Jones. Long ago artists didn't want to have anything to do with him. Artists didn't see Mr. Jones socially, let alone have dinner with the guy. Sadly, that's all everyone wanted to do in the 1980s. Artists wanted to be invited to fancy restaurants and discothèques with Mr. Jones.

Mr. Jones from the suburbs.

That guy out there in New Jersey and on Long Island collecting art to get a foothold in chi-chi Manhattan. "The people who are talking about art today are the people who twenty years ago were talking about . . . big cars," Rose said. "I'm not interested in the values of suburbia or its lifestyle or its aspirations. I left suburbia many years ago, and I don't want to go back."

The *Post*'s Mr. J (that's Jenkins, not Jones) also reviewed a book titled *What the Songs Look Like*, a collection of illustrated Talking Heads lyrics. In 1983 artist Frank Olinsky had come up with the idea of a book resembling Alan Aldridge's *The Beatles Illustrated Lyrics* from 1969.

Jenkins dismissed all the art in *What the Songs Look Like* and then used the book to skewer the whole Talking Heads aesthetic: "Inadvertently, *What the Songs Look Like* expands on Talking Heads' conceptual bankruptcy to indict the emptiness of their visual art contemporaries." This was unfair. The Basquiat contribution to "Mind" was disposable—a sloppy but elaborate line-drawing doodle of gears, spirals, and skeletons—and the Robert Longo painting of crowds and car keys and angels cohabitating (or wrestling?) beneath a white line drawing of an electric guitar was as uninspired as all of Robert Longo's post–"Men in the Cities" work. The contributions from lesser known artists, however, such as Stewart Wilson's Kabuki/Eskimo fetishes for "Making Flippy Floppy" or Geoff Spear's out-of-focus color photographs of Abraham Lincoln and George Washington beneath a flaming wheel, are in keeping with the post-psychedelic fun of the original Aldridge Beatles book.

It was David, latent Dadaist, who came up with the concept for the album art for *Naked*. On the album cover, a chimp poses before a red background, surrounded by an elaborate golden frame, holding a violet. Tibor Kalman's M&Co. created the cover by using the Yellow Pages to find someone to retouch a monkey photograph with paint. Further monkey business appeared inside the album. If you squeezed open the empty record sleeve you could read the message: "There was no Tiger in the mountains, the Monkey will be king." This Chinese proverb might be a possible reference to Brian Eno, who had released *Taking Tiger Mountain by Strategy* ten years before.

Finally, David sings about monkeys on this album. On "The Facts of Life," he sings, "Mon key see and mon key do . . ." in a song implying that we are all biological machines like our parents were before us. "Someday we'll be walking around on Venus and Mars but inside—deep inside we'll still be monkeys."

Tina publicly stated that *Naked* was the first album they had made with an attitude that she could call "kind." She said the newly married David was a more trusting man. You can't tell it from the band photograph that accompanies the album. David is hunkering down in Times Square giving a screaming laugh while holding a glass box with two banana shapes in it that resemble surrealist May Ray's painting of huge lips in the sky. Jerry stands behind laughing with David, but Chris and Tina look a bit strained. Like they're laughing at the boss's joke.

David explained the photo, "Tibor Kalman thought we should be photographed candidly, less posed and more casual. So he had a guy hang out with us for a day in the studio and out to nearby Times Square, where we ran into some folks who were taking pictures of their prize pickle (really) in famous locations. There was a photo book called *The Red Couch* that no doubt inspired them. They spotted us, and asked if I would hold it. Hearing what it was, I cracked up."

The *Post*'s Jenkins also reviewed Jerry's just-released *Casual Gods* album with *Naked*. It was released on a new label called Fly Records.

Several month's before, Talking Heads had renegotiated their Warner Bros. contract. Part of the deal was that the band now had their own boutique label. David thought of the name—a reference to fly on the wall. As for the music of *Casual Gods:* "Among Heads apologists," Jenkins wrote, "it's a given that Jerry Harrison's albums are less significant than the output of the band. That may have been the case with *The Red and the Black*, but *Casual Gods* has more memorable melodies than *Naked*." Jenkins called it "art funk" and ended by saying that *Casual Gods* was not a "great" record, but it's a "credible" one.

He was right. It is difficult to say anything about a "credible" record made so long ago except that it foreshadows a beautiful record Jerry would make several years hence.

It was during this time that Jerry finally felt like he was making money. He'd scored about $400,000 after the contract renegotiation. "I had a nice life," he recalled, "but I lived over in Long Island City, for Christ's sake." Settling down permanently in Milwaukee was looking better and better.

Jenkins finally ended his review of Talking Heads' recent product with a negative judgment (big surprise!) against *Storytelling Giant*, a collection of all the Heads videos pre-*Naked*. African-American author Hilton Als, however, wrote this amazing bit of criticism when he reviewed *Storytelling Giant* in the *Village Voice:* "Once, long ago, I used to love David Byrne more than I loved myself. I loved David Byrne more than I loved myself because I no longer wanted to be an 'interesting' black person—it was just too hard. Giving myself up to David Byrne's substantially less interesting idea of 'interesting' was a kind of momentary relief from the responsibility of carrying out that role. His aesthetic demanded surrender to a world where everyone, including myself, played white on white."

Als goes on to claim the only people who are not dull in videos are black people. It is unclear whether he is talking about all MTV fodder, or just the video enclosed in *Storytelling Giant*. Als insults three of the primary Heads by calling them "tired white people . . . who never did anything with their art degrees." He then writes, "In short, David Byrne knows how to groove and play whitey." Als claims David has become "our preeminent bridge and dissector of two anthropological curiosities—black and white, uhh, people."

The two *Naked* videos were not included in the package. The first was "(Nothing but) Flowers." M&Co. shot it. The band pantomimes and lip-synchs while the lyrics appear in various colored fonts around them. It is America's first typological rock video. A second video was made for

"Blind." No one can see it today. Apparently it was such a failure that all copies have been destroyed or hidden. Jerry explained that it was supposed to be about a fighting robot, but all the budget got eaten up before the robot was designed. In the end, he said the robot looked like a giant wrench.

So much for Hollywood . . .

David had integrated himself into a black voodoo community in Brazil, as well as multiracial Hollywood, yet he remained a visitor to both. He had only been in Hollywood a scant forty months and was already up for an Academy Award for the music to *The Last Emperor*.

For many years, the Academy Awards had been held at that Republicanesque structure, the Dorothy Chandler Pavilion. The 1987 Oscars moved to the exotic Shrine Auditorium—a Moorish double-domed temple built in 1920's *fake à la Turk*. The building served as the headquarters of the Al-Malaikah Temple, a division of the Ancient Arabic Order of Nobles of the Mystic Shrine, the same organization whose smiling drivers in matching fezzes rode their miniature red Mustang convertibles down the Main Street of Virgil, Texas, in *True Stories*.

In the spirit of the Shriners, David decided to drive himself to the Oscars. Although citizens of Los Angeles live in their cars, it is traditional to pull up to the Oscars in a limo. That wasn't David's style. He drove his Citroën. "I never had a car in high school," he says as if this was the secret explaining his relationship to automobiles. "I had seen the Citroën parked on a street with a for sale sign. It was a couple hundred bucks." It didn't take David long to figure out how to drive it.

On this particular Academy Awards afternoon there was an ungodly traffic snarl on every street and freeway surrounding the Shrine Auditorium. Dozens and dozens of stars and starlets and studio hacks had to abandon their limos and hoof it down the pavement in their gowns and tuxes. *Look, there goes Olivia de Havilland! There's Glenn Close—my God, she's so pregnant!* David blithely drove through this automotive chaos like an innocent Buster Keaton.

"My driving my Citroën to the Academy Awards created problems," David confessed. "It was very unorthodox. The parking valet guys didn't know how to work it. All the buttons functioned in a different way. It was like jumping into some kind of spaceship."

After David oversaw the parking of his Citroën, he entered the auditorium and was shown to his assigned seat near the stage beside his conominee, Japanese composer Ryuichi Sakamoto. David sat half listening to host Chevy Chase's opening monologue (he was funnier back in the days when he skewered Gerald Ford) and found himself thinking, "I have no chance of winning."

"The other nominees were John Williams and Jerry Goldsmith," David recalled. "Those were the Hollywood guys. If one of them didn't win one year, they won the next. They just trade places. And they do all the blockbuster movies. I felt, 'Well, wait a minute. This is only the second one I've done. I don't deserve to get the prize yet. You're supposed to do more.' "

So rather than worry, David sat there like a voodoo anthropologist observing the logistics of the ceremony. Nominees sat close to the stage. Then he noticed the strange tuxedoed zombies, the "chair fillers." Anytime someone left their seat, attendants would wag a little flag and a guy in a tux would come sit in the empty spot so when the television cameras panned the audience there would never be an empty seat. It was hard to imagine that anyone would get up from the ceremonies, but lots of people did. "Everyone was going off to the bathroom," David said. "It being the eighties, they were doin' drugs."

The seat zombies became an issue during the presentation of the award for animated short. Minnie Mouse was supposed to suddenly appear on camera seated in the audience, a feat accomplished by an animator "dropping" Minnie into the empty space on the empty seat, but an overeager seat filler ended up sitting in the seat and screwed up the special effect.

The Last Emperor won just about everything it was nominated for—Screenplay. Cinematography. Art direction. Costume design. Sound. No acting awards because it wasn't nominated for any.

The upcoming presidential election was evoked when Best Supporting Actress Olympia Dukakis shouted into the microphone, "Okay, Michael, let's go!" to her cousin Michael Dukakis, a man who hoped to prevent the Reagan Era from being extended any longer by that Skull and Bones Yale man, George Bush.

Finally, the Oscar for original score was up. David had been mistaken about his competition. John Williams was indeed nominated, but not Jerry Goldsmith. David was competing with filmmaking legend Ennio Morricone. Who could forget his "whistling" score for *The Good, The Bad, and the Ugly*? Morricone was up for his recent work on *The Untouchables*.

As for John Williams, he hadn't been nominated for just one Oscar, but two—he'd scored both *Empire of the Sun* and *The Witches of Eastwick*, and he must have been sitting in his seat figuring the deck was surely stacked in his favor. But David Byrne and Ryuichi Sakamoto and Gong Su's names were read instead.

"When you get announced, they zoom in on you," David remembered. "You're close enough to quickly trot up there." David found himself on the stage, girls screaming in the audience. He was wearing a neo-Nehru jacket getup. "There are three of us," David thought to the little gold man in his hand. "I guess we can't say much."

"This is a lot of fun," David said into the microphone. "But it's more fun doin' it."

Then David and Ryuichi Sakamoto and Gong Su were ushered through a series of rooms: Foreign press. Domestic press. "You get herded in," David said. "Put on a little riser. You get your fifteen minutes in here and then they take you to the next station of the cross. Then you get to go back to your seat."

As David was sitting back in his chair he was unaware that the auditorium was swarming with L.A. plainclothes cops. Stanley Kubrick's *Full Metal Jacket* was up for an Oscar for best screenplay based on material from another medium. The three writers were Kubrick himself, the great Vietnam correspondent Michael Herr, and author Gustav Hasford.

Hasford was the one wanted by the cops. He had stolen a shitload of library books. Hasford was wanted for grand theft.

The soundtrack to *The Last Emperor* took many different awards that year. A Grammy, Golden Globe, and Hollywood Foreign Press Association Award. David was asked by a reporter, "Do you prefer working alone or with a group?" "There's a time and a place for everything," he answered. "A piece of shit in the right place was fertilizer, but in your pants it's an embarrassment."

Bertolucci made dozens of acceptance speeches for *The Last Emperor* on Oscar night. In one of them he declared, "New York is a big apple, but Hollywood is a big nipple." After winning an Oscar, David realized he had finally tired of the earthquake tit. He missed New York. Hollywood was America. New York City was somewhere else. When David had lived in New York, he used to tell people he met traveling that he lived on a little island off the coast of America.

During that summer, David Byrne played with David Bowie, who had just been filmed by Martin Scorsese as Pontius Pilate in *The Last Temptation of Christ*. Basquiat had wintered in Paris, doing so many drugs he reportedly bragged, "Man, I take a hundred bags a day. That's more than Keith Richards, man, I'm strong." On August 12, Basquiat OD'ed and died at 57 Great Jones Street in New York. In September, Adelle came with David to Berlin to work on *The Forest* again.

Wilson was excited to hear what David had come up with.

"It's symphonic?" Wilson said. "You know how to score for a symphony? Or did you use a synthesizer like *Knee Plays*?"

"More or less," David answered. He had used a device called a Photon—a guitar hooked up to a synth that mimicked orchestral sounds. Then David gave a print out of the notes to L.A. arranger Jimmie Haskell. "He then wrote out scores for real instruments."

"Play it," Wilson said.

David did. But Wilson was disappointed. This was a pastiche symphony with violins and accordions. Some vocals. Pseudo-Mahler with one song that sounded like an Indian powwow chant from a John Wayne movie. Wilson could have hired the quirky orchestra Penguin Cafe and gotten the same result.

At this late date, the music would have to do. But Wilson had been hoping for something more rock 'n' roll. David was the biggest name left on the production. Wenders had dropped out. He wanted to film the movie in forests throughout the world, but he couldn't raise enough money.

David was happy to hear this news. This would be an opportunity for him to make the film.

Money and art. What an old story. Robert Wilson was a master at finding deep pockets. But it was like gambling—the house usually won. In Europe, the house was the government. More and more, Wilson relied on European money. "In Europe the government supports culture," he says. "In the U.S., the private sector makes the decisions. It's not some minister of culture in some central government deciding what is going to be supported. Often I think art and culture are too linked to commercial products. Art and culture often have nothing to do with how many products you sell. Very few people may see or understand a work, but maybe fifty years from now they'll see it in a completely different way and it will influence the number of people who are affected by it."

On the other hand, Wilson remembered growing up in Waco. There were no museums in that dusty town. No symphony or ballet. Nothing but honky-tonks and loaded Texans like George Bush. If Wilson had grown up in a comparable town in Germany like Dingolfing or Horn-Bad Meinberg, there would have been at least two or three theaters to go to. One theater would put on contemporary plays. Another would have classical German plays. Or maybe a Russian director would be an artist-in-residence. There would be more balance in the German venue. This was because of the Marshall Plan. Yes. Go back to just after the war. The art of all nations had to be protected. "If the Marshall Plan had been established in Texas," Wilson said, "we in Waco would have been interested in what was going on, culturally speaking, in the jungle or Yugoslavia."

The music rehearsals for *The Forest* took place at a theater near an old hotel containing the Red Saloon, where Kaiser Wilhelm used to play cards. David and Adelle spent four weeks in Berlin. It would end up being a depressing time. His wife said, "DB is an easy traveler. He likes to carry a fold-up bicycle on tour and a stack of city maps. He doesn't mind getting lost and he doesn't mind going the distance." So David took solitary bicycle trips around Berlin listening to Mahler on his earphones.

In one of Wilson's earlier pieces, when he couldn't find an actor to play Sigmund Freud, he chose a stranger he passed at Penn Station in New York. The man was a doctor. He accepted the role, but later complained because Wilson kept making last-minute changes.

"Is Wilson on drugs?" the sawbones demanded. In this same vein, Wilson kept changing *The Forest*. He threw out a forty-five-minute scene set in the jungle. David's music went with it.

David took it stoically. He bicycled with Mahler. This was the second time that Wilson had the opportunity to stage an event as culturally triumphant as *Einstein on the Beach*, but the chance slipped out of his hands.

The Forest was eventually performed. There were scenes influenced by Fritz Lang's *Metropolis*—factory workers with ladders and monstrous gears. This wasn't so off the wall. Wilson realized that Lang's silent masterpiece was superficially about a city in the future populated by robots. In reality, the film was concerned with the same nineteenth-century working conditions that influenced Karl Marx.

In the play, rocks bleed. Lizards turn into trees. Elegant women float with ravens perched on their wrists. The tycoon has a pet lion. Gilgamesh falls asleep one night and the moon itself sits on his chest.

The play was presented in Hamburg. During this time, David still thought he would do the movie. He drove around the West German countryside scouting for locations.

The forest was thick in Bavaria. The drive made David remember his childhood. When he was a boy the most magical place was not the library, nor the sandlot baseball field. It was an acre of Maryland pine down the road. A forest. He walked by himself among the trees. The foliage would muffle the freeway traffic. He'd snap the branches with his tennis shoes. He knew there were animals in the forest. David hoped that he would not be eaten.

The Forest was a critical success in Germany, but a financial sinkhole. Just as *CIVIL warS* was too expensive to mount in Los Angeles, there was no way this production could be done around the world. It did manage to play at the Brooklyn Academy of Music that December, but not with a full orchestra. Only on tape. David forked out his own cash to have a screenplay written, but without an international performance to back it up, his film plans failed as thoroughly as Wenders's.

During this time, the Tom Tom Club was playing the Borderline in London. Busta Jones turned up at the performance. "He was as high as a kite," Tina remembered. "He was way, way out there. He was begging for work. I couldn't give it to him. I said, 'Give me your address.' He told me, 'I don't have a permanent address right now.'"

She later heard the news that Jones had died. "I might have heard about it through *Rolling Stone*. I know that he was waiting for a bus and had kidney failure. And then I heard that he died. He was happily married finally. Supposedly kicked drugs and then was in Montreal. He had a child there."

Back in the summer of '87, the engineer of *Speaking in Tongues*, Alex Sadkin, was killed in a Jamaican car crash. He had been about to begin recording Ziggy Marley and the Melody Makers' next album. Ziggy's label, Virgin, proposed that Chris and Tina replace the dead man as producer.

Chris, of course, had a fifteen-year mad love affair with reggae, so he was game beyond belief. When Chris and Tina first met Ziggy at a recording studio, the eternal son said, "Why-a Chris bring 'im *wife* inta de studio?"

Tina set the lad straight.

The record they made, *Conscious Party*, was a top 30 hit for most of the summer of '88. The married couple and Ziggy would get together again to record *One Bright Day*, which would be a modest hit in 1989. Tina believed the sessions had been supernaturally guided by the ganja spirit of Bob Marley.

On September 1988, the Tom Tom Club played with Lou Reed and Debbie Harry. Shortly afterward, the group covered the old Velvet Underground song "Femme Fatale." Tina asked Lou to play with them.

"I felt really badly that, in a sense, I had inadvertently snubbed poor John Cale," Tina says. "Because why didn't I ask John Cale to play on it, too, you know? That was because I thought he was living in England and I was scared that he was high on coke. Because the last time I saw him was in Tucson. We were staying in the same hotel, and he came banging on our door real late at night saying, 'I know you're holding. I know you're holding.' I was afraid of him for awhile after that. It was with the big band. I can't remember cocaine before the big band. Nobody was doing it."

In 1989 the Fly label was discontinued when it was discovered that a Fly Records already existed. Simultaneously, David signed a solo deal with Warner Bros. "Part of that deal was that he would have his own label," Jerry remembered. David called it Luaka Bop after a brand of tea, because he liked the sound of the words.

During this time David hadn't forgotten about voodoo. He saw its influence everywhere. He'd see an old episode of *I Love Lucy*, and Ricky Ricardo called out "Omoolu!" as he conducted his club band. Omoolu is the god of earth. He controls health and sickness.

David just had to make an all-out voodoo album. In the spring, he had written a "Brazilian" song, "Coco De Amor," for Jonathan Demme's *Something Wild*. He had great fun with that musical genre. Soon, David was writing more songs in a voodoo vein with musicians like Johnny Pacheco and Willie Colon. Sometimes as they worked, David would even break into Spanish or Portuguese.

On June 6, Carson Harrison was born to Jerry and Carol in Milwaukee. Three days later, a daughter, Malu Valentine, was born to David and Adelle in New York City. *More creatures of love.*

336

After the birth of Malu Valentine, David asked for the placenta, which was usually tossed away. The nurse said sure. She put it in a vacuum-sealed container. David took it home and put it in the refrigerator.

Back in 1987, a producer named Kiki Miyake had challenged David to make a film on a foreign culture that would be entirely visual and not translate the experience into Western terms, so David spent a month in Bahia shooting a documentary about Candomblé. During the first week of July '89, his Brazilian documentary called *Ilé Aiyé (House of Life)* was shown on PBS's *Alive from off Center*. David's film was exciting. He used split-screen and fast-forwarding technique to compress real life into MTV moments. Ed Siegel, television critic for the *Boston Globe*, declared that Bob Dylan was the last figure to balance eclectic artistry with popular acceptance until David Byrne. Siegel then took an observant jab:

> David Byrne shows none of the humor and irony that he
> has shown toward American evangelicals. Is Zeze [a
> Candombléan] any different from Tammy Faye Bakker,
> and is Candombléan culture any less an opiate that
> Western religions?

It's unlikely any of the voodooites were soliciting money on television like Tammy Faye, but David's blatant acceptance of tropical religion and visions of God put him in the same trap that he observed in the Sex Pistols' phenomenon: The other is always more holy than the known. Perhaps if the followers of Candomblé came to America, they might have found Tammy Faye's eyelashes the most extreme example of feminine delicacy and proof of the woman's holiness.

• • •

Coinciding with the showing of David's documentary, the four Heads appeared on the same stage for the last time in the twentieth century to play music.

The Tom Tom Club had a gig at the new Ritz, a nightclub that had taken over the old Studio 54. Chris and Tina had invited both David and Jerry to come onstage. Both said yes. But only Jerry came to rehearsal. On the night of the actual show, when David joined his bandmates for the encore, Tina asked him which song he'd like to do. And David replied, "Sing a verse of 'Under the Boardwalk.' "

The band started the intro. David learned into the microphone, but didn't sing.

The band ran through the intro again. David didn't sing.

He just stood there.

Tina then walked up to the mike and sang the verse. She set him up for the next verse. He started to sing. He sang two words. That was all he remembered. He stayed silent on the stage.

The decade ended with an exhibition of Robert Longo's work at the Los Angeles County Museum of Art. The Longo show was poorly received. At the time of the exhibition, Longo was being called the John Travolta of eighties art.

On October 2, 1989, Luaka Bop released David Byrne's solo album, *Rei Momo* ("King of Carnival"). It gathered some good reviews in nonrock venues like *Newsweek,* but generally it was treated as just another bit of white-guys-ripping-off-brown-people. David Byrne's cultural chameleonism. A Drew Friedman cartoon appeared in *Spy* depicting David and Paul Simon peeking out of tropical bushes and discovering each other.

Just more borrowing. David even listed the proper dance for each song—a Cumbia, Orïsa, Merengue, Mapeyé, Bomba/Mozambique, Salsa/Reggae, Cha cha cha, Samba, Charanga, Rumba/Lles, another Merengue and Samba, a Bolero, and finally another Mapeyé. It appears such listings are common courtesies so people know what dances are coming. Jon Pareles gently dismissed *Rei Momo* in the *New York Times,* identifying as the problem that the music was cut like a Talking Heads record, in layers. "The band sounds subdued and studied."

When David played these songs live, it was a different story. In early October, he returned to the stage of *Stop Making Sense,* the Pantages

Theater in Los Angeles. He now had fourteen band members, including trumpeters, trombonists, sax men, plus percussionists as well as the usual guitar players. The band was bigger, but David had no Big Suit. He didn't even sing all the songs. Instead, he had reincarnated himself as Ricky Ricardo. Who knows, he may have even yelled "Omoolu!" at the start of the show.

David was a band leader now, not a psycho killer. A singer from Bahia, Margareth Menezes, opened the show and did a showpiece in the middle of David's set.

338

David didn't make any postmodern Robert Wilson gestures during the show. Occasionally, he'd take a step forward and shake his ass the way a good American shakes it. He danced with his arms outstretched while his band stomped out the insanely named dances.

Bomba, Rumba, Mapeyé, and finally a Brazilian Pagode.

The audience was somewhat inert until David encouraged them to leave their seats. Shake their asses along with him. This created some conflicts with theater security. David then ended the show with only the second Talking Heads tune of the night. The first had been "Mr. Jones"—the brass arrangement so dynamic that the misshapened lyrics no longer mattered. The last song was "Papa Legba."

David was completely enraptured in Candomblé voodoo. He was speakin' words to God through pop songs.

Just before David went on the *Rei Momo* tour, Jerry had a serious talk with him. "It looks like this is going to be a long separation," he said. "My feeling is it's stupid."

David didn't look at him.

"David, you get all the credit for the success of Talking Heads," Jerry said. "Because you get that credit, you can record trumpet players in New Orleans for *Knee Plays* and if John Rockwell gives it a good review in the *New York Times*, Warner Bros. doesn't look at how much it cost you to make that record. They go, 'David Byrne's a genius. Look at all the things he can do.'" Jerry paused. "The minute you stop Talking Heads, the solo records and all the things you are doing will be judged on a commercial basis. I don't think you'll like it. You have the best of both worlds now. For a six-month commitment every two years, you can continue to make great records. Do a continual tour. You will make enough money that you will be able to do whatever you want without worrying about money. I don't have that. When I put out a solo record, I still have to sell. You don't have that worry because you get the credit for our success. I can't imagine being in a better position. When a band like Talking Heads have been together this long no one likes the person breaking up the band. It's going to be bad for your career. It's not like we're dead—creatively dead. It's not like we're repeating ourselves."

David finally looked at him and said, "Well, maybe. I have to come to that conclusion myself."

We should have left that band a long time ago. We should have never stuck it out.

Tina Weymouth

Ah, we were troopers. We still are.

Chris Frantz

shrunken heads

BOOK FOUR

wicked little doll

In 1990 Jerry released a second Casual Gods record, *Walk on Water*, recorded with longtime buddy Ernie Brooks. For this album, Jerry had even taken singing lessons. He wasn't a Caruso or anything, but his voice now had command. The usual suspects helped him on drums and guitars, including Adrian Belew's electric menagerie on a few cuts.

Walk on Water is not a brilliant pop album. It is a totally *swell* pop album containing maybe a dozen moments of immortality. Three funky prog songs that sound like *Speaking in Tongues* with an impostor singing David Byrne's parts begin the record. It's the fourth song, "Sleep Angel," that anchors the album in the realm of the unforgettable. Jerry had this gorgeous melody for years, but was never able to complete it. The melody is as seductive as "Ruby Tuesday" or "Michelle." The narrator of the song is watching someone—a child, or maybe a woman—sleeping in the moonlight. There's something so ethereal about the melody, it's as if God is singing to himself as he watches over creation at night. Then some sassy angel starts telling him to "take it back."

"Sleep Angel" is followed by a funky, psychedelic-cum-Prince song that describes God crying for both love and for . . . Iran.

Had the Ayatollah not been dead when Jerry put this song out, the Talking Heads' keyboard player might have had a fatwa put on his head. The lyrical premise of this song is dead silly, but so are most Prince songs. Jerry's cry for Iran is still a great pop song.

The album contains other standout cuts, including a cowboy tune that has been mysteriously adapted from a biography of Jackson Pollock. Many of these new songs have a majestic stance reminiscent of "The Overload," the cut Jerry initiated on *Remain in Light*. Considering his knowledge of music theory, his ability to sculpt the previously mentioned "contrapuntal and harmonic relationships" in Talking Heads songs, one suspects that Jerry's musical knowledge surpasses David's. Unfortunately, Jerry has no edge. David, of course, is nothing but edge. During their tenure as Talking Heads, Jerry had been the perfect Tonto to David's Lone Ranger.

344

In his heart, Jerry knew Talking Heads was dead. If asked, he'd only publicly say Talking Heads was in "hibernation."

"It's been a long winter," he'd say.

Casual Gods toured that summer on a double bill with Tom Tom Club. Tina reported that she was hoping Talking Heads would do an album that year. "But I didn't get my way."

Later in 1990, Jerry and Chris and Tina played together in L.A. as part of a homage to Roy Orbison at the Universal Amphitheater. They worked up a bizarre version of "Sweet Dreams," with Tina singing lead, backups by Bonnie Raitt, k. d. lang, and Wendy and Lisa.

Jerry and Chris and Tina billed themselves as the Shrunken Heads.

David began 1991 by sharing the bill at Town Hall with John Cale and Glenn Branca for an evening of orchestra music. The Orchestra of St. Luke's played David's score of *The Forest*. The *New York Times* called the piece "a stylistic circus, with bits of jazz, comic-book matches, film score gestures, and Mr. Byrne's idiosyncratic yodeling, set against nineteenth-century figuration shorn of its emotional heft."

Mr. Byrne finally gave up on *Shango*, the Santería love story screenplay. Ed Pressman had managed to partner the project with Zoetrope. "We tried to get the script to the point where David was ready to commit to doing it," Pressman said. "We went with a couple of writers, but the script was never satisfactory to David. When a more conventional writer's approach was brought to it that made it read as a script and Zoetrope liked it, David shied away. He kept trying to break the narrative."

• • •

On June 12, 1991, the Harrisons' second son, Dylan, was born.

In October, Talking Heads met at Jimi Hendrix's old Electric Lady Studio to assemble a double-CD compilation package. David, for one, didn't want to put out such a product. "Who will I hurt if I say I don't want this album to be released?" he asked.

"Yourself for one," Tina answered. "The record company is going to put it out whether they have our cooperation or not."

David wasn't the only one who was dragging his heels about the project. Gary Kurfirst hated the fact the suits were demanding a greatest hits record. "I just felt 'greatest hits' was like putting a lid on the coffin," Kurfirst remembered. "I always felt as long as they were still alive, Talking Heads best work was yet to come."

During the late 1980s, the retail space in Tower Records down in the Village was dominated by record bins. By 1990 they'd all been ripped out. Tower now only stocked CDs and tapes. The CD market was hungry for compilation packages that contained outtakes, alternate cuts, new songs, forgotten songs, covered songs. Bob Dylan had just released a monster three-CD box set of all his previously bootlegged unreleased tracks. Unfortunately, Talking Heads was not as prolific as Mr. Zimmerman. The band unearthed only four early tracks and demos that predated *Talking Heads '77*. They then unspooled four unused instrumental tapes from various *Remain in Light, Speaking in Tongues,* and *Naked* sessions and used these to "create" four new songs.

"Popsicle" had the clearest history. This electric strut was recorded during *Speaking in Tongues*. David's 1991 lyrics begin with his declaration that he's hanging out at the airport and it's summertime and he wants something to eat. How about a Popsicle? A Popsicle of love. The theological bent of 1990s America was *dumbing down*. Around this time, R.E.M.'s Michael Stipe could renounce the Beatles in *Rolling Stone*, saying, "Yummy yummy yummy/I got love in my tummy" had been of more importance, culturally speaking, than any song on *Revolver*. From the beginning of their career, Talking Heads had to defend themselves against being typed as a college band. A bunch of "smarty-pants." As if going to "Hahvard" (as in Jerry's case) made one less authentic than an unschooled intellectual barbarian. "Smart people can be just as sincere as stupid people!" David once insisted.

With "Popsicle," the fight was over. David would never have to defend Talking Heads' smart quotient again. "Popsicle" is almost as dumb as Stipe's "yummy yummy" statement.

"Gangster of Love" is a combination of a sampled drum track from *Remain in Light* mixed with a track that had been recorded eight years later in Paris. David's new 1991 lyrics for this slow-sliding funk hybrid sound as authentic as if he had put on blackface and strutted around the 'hood in a white fringe *Superfly* saddle coat.

"Sax and Violins," another cut recorded during the *Naked* sessions, had recently appeared on the soundtrack *Until the End of the World*, a Wim Wenders film shot in different locations around the world (fulfilling the global bee Wenders got in his bonnet while working on Robert Wilson's *The Forest*). This is more like it. The play off the phrase "sex and violence" is dumb, but dumb in a Talking Heads way, especially with its reduction of twentieth-century psychology in the line "Mom and pop will . . . fuck you up . . . for sure."

The final "new" cut, "Lifetime Piling Up," was the band being brilliant again. This is the *Naked* sessions song that the Parisian delivery man had played on, although you can't hear his contributions. Apparently he was erased, or else this is a version recorded before his arrival. The cut has a nice edgy melody with ultra-prog arrangements. David sings about his "lifetime piling up." About seeing the house where he was born. He confesses that when he was a kid he could never keep his trousers up. Then he sings about a driver spinning out of control.

Although his band was also out of control, David remained fodder for celebrity culture. "*People* magazine has become the national dream book," David said at the time. He was right. America had never been hotter about celebrities. Ex–MTV czar Robert Pittman even shortened Andy Warhol's maxim "everyone will be famous for fifteen minutes" to "everyone will be famous for five minutes." *Why the lost ten minutes?*

"Demand," Pittman answered. "Almost everyone wants to be famous, or if not famous, to have some tenuous connection to celebrity."

David showed up sporadically in *People* magazine, as well as Page Six of the *New York Post*. He was photographed going to the circus or street fairs. A photo of his refrigerator even appeared in Tina Brown's *Vanity Fair*. His icebox contained:

Hot Cha Cha All Natural Chunky Taco Sauce; seltzer;
600 feet of Kodak 16mm color film; 1 Fuji disposable
camera; Stolichnaya Crystal vodka; homemade iced tea;
2½ lemons wrapped in ScotTowels; Golden Key New
Orleans roast chicory beans; homemade pickles; decaf
mocha java blend; Fox's U-bet chocolate flavor syrup;
Ohsawa organic salt plums; corn relish; sprouts; half a
moldy grapefruit in foil; Acidophilus capsules; Zaru soba
and Cha soba noodles; Tofu Nugget; veggie patties

As well as a container with his kid's placenta awaiting a ritual burial.

In the fall of 1991, the *New York Post* reported that David was renovating a town house near Fifth Avenue in Greenwich Village. In December, the
Los Angeles Times announced that David had officially ended Talking Heads.

For years, Tina had sent David messages in the press—*You and
Eno are egomaniacs. Hey, we owe it to our fans to go on tour*. Now David was
using the press to send his obituary to the band. Pretty Arctic, but David felt
he had no other choice.

One of the tasks of the early 1990s was to reevaluate the previous decade.
"The 1980s were about selfishness," Jerry recalled. "The most generous
ideas of the 1960s were discredited by the lives of the yuppies."

The younger, newly emerging hip culture decided to define themselves by reneging on the icons of the eighties. Talking Heads was a good
target. A new music magazine called *Blast* began by bragging, "Our magazine is for the generation that doesn't think Talking Heads and David Byrne
is the coolest thing."

Music critics began comparing David to Woody Allen, a cat whose
earlier work was better than his latest. *Time* magazine "praised" David's
second post-Heads pop record, *Uh-Oh*—a collection of playful Pan-
American pop songs, but no great shakes—by stating that David is "no
longer a potential psycho killer. . . . David Byrne is now the guy who tells
poo-poo jokes to the kids."

This kind of slippage was not limited to David. Prince was a hiero-
glyph. Michael Jackson hung out with prepubescent boys and adolescent
monkeys. Even Bruce Springsteen seemed washed up and insignificant.

David would never admit that he cared. He thought it was flattering that Talking Heads was "some sort of line of demarcation or a Mason-Dixon Line." He concentrated on the music, not the spin.

When the decade started, David's old friend Lee Blake coordinated the first major AIDS benefit album, *Red Hot & Blue*—rock 'n' roll interpretations of Cole Porter. "David was the first person I went to," Blake remembered. " 'Dave, if I asked you to reinvent a Cole Porter song in your own style, and do it for me for an AIDS benefit, would you do it?' And he said absolutely. And I went away with his consent, and of course when David Byrne consents to something, especially in 1990, everyone thinks, 'Whoa, that's desperately hip. I gotta do that.' And so everyone followed quickly."

"Everyone" included the Neville Brothers, k.d. lang, Annie Lennox of the Eurythmics (also Gary Kurfirst clients), and U2.

The AIDS crisis continued to consume America's consciousness. David passed out condoms to the audience during a 1992 tour to promote *Uh-Oh*. "Sometimes audience members would blow them up like balloons," he said. "We had a little problem when we came into Israel because we had a road case filled with about a thousand condoms. They wondered what we were doing."

David's sister-in-law Tina Chow died of AIDS in the winter of 1992—a public death. Liz Smith's gossip column revealed that five years earlier, Tina had fallen in love with actor Richard Gere and her marriage to Michael Chow ended in divorce. As far as Gere was concerned, according to Smith, "Tina was just another notch in his belt." As for her husband, "Michael Chow was a dozen years her senior and dominated her." Tina Chow then became involved with "bachelor-journalist-sportsman" Kim D'Estainville. He died of AIDS in the early 1990s. *New York* magazine found it relevant to print the private fact that Tina Chow had "slept with four people in her entire life."

David responded directly to his sister-in-law's death by writing a new song, "Buck Naked." He said, "I just started singing it to our daughter. I realized that it was a song that I didn't sit down to write, it just kinda came out."

During the summer of 1992, David began performing Talking Heads songs live with his voodoo band. He'd do "Mr. Jones." "Burning Down the House." "Life During Wartime." And "Psycho Killer."

Always "Psycho Killer."

He yodeled and yipped the old songs. In New York, the audience of Heads freaks applauded and went crazy. But it was different when he played Los Angeles. The *L.A. Times* compared David to "Xavier Cugat doing the funky chicken for Merv Griffin."

During all these shows David covered, "Sympathy for the Devil." Was there another song more inappropriate for this man to sing? David was no Robert Johnson. He didn't even believe in the Devil. When he sang the Devil's dialogue line in the song that goes, "I'm in need of some restraint," he'd sing it in a squeaky falsetto like a certain billionaire cartoon mouse. In Los Angeles, David even squeaked out, "Mickey!" after he sang the line.

David reduced the Devil to a harmless Disney character. Perhaps his inherent innocence was enough to make Satan insignificant. Probably not. In towns besides New York, David found that he was considered an oldies act.

Talking Heads reconvened as a group in October 1992 to file a group suit in a New York federal court charging that EMI Records (who owned the foreign rights to Talking Heads) owned them $750,000.

The band had to go to court because David had done a dumb thing. That summer he'd wisecracked to a Brit music reporter, "We knew we were going to break up, but we signed with EMI to get a lot of money out of them."

David was just horsing around. He had forgotten the media was the media. "When EMI got wind of what I said," David recalled, "they said, 'Fuck you. We're not going to pay you for this record. You smart-asses think you're going to get a lot of money. You want the money, sue us.' "

So they did. Talking Heads had only to present a united front. They didn't have to hang out together. They met a few times to talk about legal strategy. As David later said, "It's thrilling that that's what it comes down to. These stories of creative collaborations end up in the offices of lawyers." His thoughts were reminiscent of earlier words about money: "People will do odd things if you give them money. When everything was worth money, then money was worth nothing."

In court, Talking Heads said that they did have intentions of "making more stuff" but they couldn't solve their differences. The lawyers stressed that Talking Heads hadn't planned to deceive anybody.

In the end, they got half of what they were owed.

Talking Heads' obligatory "greatest hits" double CD, *Sand in the Vaseline,* named after a work by Ed Ruscha, was released on Halloween 1992. In one of the two CD booklets, each of the Heads gave a reminiscence about the now defunct group.

The first, David's, was a callow and curious documentation of the drugs he took in the 1970s and 1980s—giving a blow-by-blow account of his experience with marijuana, quaaludes, bennies, speed, meth, angel dust, cocaine, and heroin.

What did it have to do with Talking Heads?

"I think I wanted to make it clear that, *yes, we did do drugs,*" David explained. "I wanted to be very honest. We were part of the rock 'n' roll lifestyle. For the most part we didn't do it to excess, but it was part of the lifestyle for awhile. It was hard to escape. We didn't go completely off the deep end."

The remaining Heads' bits read like self-epitaphs. Both Chris and Jerry gave accounts of the band's history; Tina thanked, but didn't name, "our artistic friends" who kept the band from believing the hype—"Who smiled for our success when it would still be years before they would be recognized for their own."

Following her usual public pattern of carrot and whip and stick, Tina gave David backhanded praise by thanking him for his "great lyrics" because "they were cool cues to let me know where I was in a song." Then she wrote a gushy love letter to David about his guitar playing. "I always wished more writers would pay as much attention to your guitar as to your words, but I guess some listeners did. I've met some of them. They're all grown and have bands of their own, now." Her words were a play off of the oft-repeated Brian Eno quip, "Everyone who bought an original copy of the first Velvet Underground record went out and started their own band."

Much later, Tina said, "David Byrne's eyes are like O. J. Simpson's. They're so full of guilt. I used to think, 'Give David a break. Give this guy a chance.' But I was ill-advised in my Christian thinking. I once thought that 'turn the other cheek' meant be really meek and mild and take crap from people. I didn't realize it meant 'look in a new direction,' because when somebody slaps you real hard it turns your head, doesn't it? 'Turn the other cheek' means it's time to turn your face in a new direction and look elsewhere and start marching. I didn't know that. I was brought up a nice little Catholic girl—'Be really nice.' " Then Tina laughed and said, "I'm not a good Catholic girl anymore, I'll have you know."

At the end of Tina's piece in the CD booklet, she thanked her husband for introducing her to "that unwieldy instrument," the bass. Also, for "demonstrating that the leader was the servant to all"—a sly acknowledgment that Chris was the founder of Talking Heads and the one who held the group together.

Chris was surely the one Talking Head who felt the demise of his band the greatest. You could transplant a recent interview with the drummer into those of an old man on his deathbed: "What a great time Talking Heads was for me. It was my dream come true. To have a band rocking the house and really getting over worldwide. Being with all kinds of elements and excitement. And in a very artistic way." See him shake his head and add, "As soon as we stopped, Peter Gabriel jumped right in there. Paul Simon, too."

It is dumb and tragic and ironic that Chris was responsible for the method David had chosen to break up the band.

After Talking Heads had finished the *Sand in the Vaseline* sessions in the fall of '91, David wanted to call a meeting and just "say it." Say they had broken up.

David believed that Talking Heads was not like the Rolling Stones. Mick and the boys could just get together as a kind of business, but Talking Heads was more than just a money pot. David explained his decision by talking about movies: "I just read this book about a bunch of filmmakers from the 1970s [*Easy Riders, Raging Bulls* by Peter Biskind]. These guys wanted to reinvent Hollywood and bring a different flavor to American filmmaking. Each film had to be a passionate personal thing. They had to live it so they couldn't do the kind of businesslike thing, 'This is a good script. I know how to make a movie. I know what actors would be right in here.' That wasn't enough. To make a movie about excess or obsession, they had to be excessive or obsessed. Some of 'em went crazy. Some just burned out. But they did great stuff. There's not many of these kind of films being made now. As musicians, we felt the same way. Our kind of band was the result of camaraderie and the music emerged out of that—when we were hanging out, we were all in it together. When that stops, you might as well be making music with anybody. Which is what happened—with me any-

351

way." Talking Heads hadn't hung out since 1980, so they'd made a good go of it, all things considering.

It's likely Chris sensed what David had on his mind. Chris said, "I don't want to meet with you unless you have good news."

"Chris refused to hear what I was about to say," David remembered. "He didn't want to hear it. Chris refused to let me say it to his face, so it came out in another way. In the press. I thought, 'Well, he turned me down. He refused to let me do the honorable thing of sayin' it to their faces.' So what do you expect?"

In 1994 David released a filmed concert called *Between the Teeth*. It was shot on Halloween 1992 at the Count Basie Theater in Red Bank, New Jersey. Codirected by David Byrne and David Wild, the film was a poor man's *Stop Making Sense*. One song is all head-level closeups of David and his Brazilian band. Another, a continuous shot. David meant the film to be a good-bye to fronting his Pan-American dance band.

Or so he said at the time. It was also good press to promote his new solo album called, simply, *David Byrne*. This was David's sensitive singer/songwriter album. David being Jackson Browne. Most of the songs are sparse rock songs with nutty Byrne-ish lines like "fruit of salty lubricant" peppered with sensitive-school-of-songwriting confessions like "I can barely touch my own self/how could I touch someone else?" Lest you think David had become too sensitive, he offered up this take on romance: "Sometimes dear/You tell me I'm an asshole/Sometimes you're an asshole too. . . ."

Once the 1990s were rolling, Jerry knew it was time to get out of New York. Talking Heads was dead. Sire abandoned the second Casual Gods album. Jerry moved with his wife and kids to Milwaukee.

In 1994 Jerry produced an album by a group called Live, *Throwing Copper*. He recorded it at Cannon Falls, Minnesota. It sold well. Really well. Picture one of those community chest cards in Monopoly that show the tycoon rolling a wheelbarrow full of money bags.

Two years earlier Tom Tom Club had made a tight little pop album called *Dark Sneak Love Action*. No one much cared. Next they were going to produce a U.K. band called Happy Mondays in the West Indies, but the project was abandoned because of drug freakouts. "In the end," Tina said, "we were lucky nobody died."

"Tom Tom Club left Sire," Seymour Stein remembered. "They went over to Island, but were dropped. I had a meeting with Tina and told her, 'I don't think it's necessarily the best idea, but if you have any problems getting another label, please come back to Sire.' I meant it very sincerely. In reference to the fact that I had worked for Redbird records, she said, 'Seymour, you worked for the Shangri-las. You know you can never go home anymore'—which is one of the titles of one of their songs. I thought that was very mean."

In 1996 Tina wrote David a letter. It agitated David terribly. "I'd get these bizarre letters from Tina. They'd say what a 'fucking dumb jerk' and 'asshole piece of shit' I was. It would go into detail how *badly* I'd behaved. What a *terrible person* I was. How 'hard I was to work with.' How 'unfair' I was. It was this thing meant to make me feel real terrible and how much 'I hate you. I hate you. I hate you.' And then in the end she'd go, 'Why don't you want to work with us? Why in the world don't you want to work with us? What's the matter?' You've answered the question. Look at the beginning of your letter, look at the end. You've answered it. There is some kind of weird denial going on."

In 1996 Chris and Tina talked Jerry into cutting another Talking Heads record using a number of different singers like Debbie Harry from Blondie. Tina wanted this to be a real Talking Heads record. To hell with David.

Jerry nixed using their complete moniker. He knew the critics would kill any Talking Heads project that didn't have David on it.

"I wished we had called ourselves the Shrunken Heads," Jerry remembered. "Chris and Tina didn't want to do that. I came up with the name of the album, *No Talking, Just Head*. I said, 'Why not put the album out with no group name, just a title? People can figure it out from there.' 'You can't do that,' Tina said. 'You have to print a name on the side.' It just annoyed me so much. 'Well, let's call ourselves the Heads.' I knew we could get killed in the press if it looked like we were trying to take over the name Talking Heads. On the other hand, I wanted to thread the needle so people would know we had been in Talking Heads. So I thought the title adequately did that. The Shrunken Heads would have been far more amusing. But I think just using the title would have been the best bet."

When David heard about the Heads, he filed suit against his former bandmates and Gary Kurfirst in U.S. District Court in New York.

For the trial, Tina tried to get John Rockwell as a witness. He declined. He was not going to take sides. "David Byrne is a shy self-centered guy," Rockwell said. "He clearly regarded Talking Heads as an expression of himself. And originally they were. As I understand, he taught Tina how to play the bass. It's a classic situation, where one person in the band thinks the band is an expression of him or herself, and the others who have some desire for fame and glory and sixties cooperative effort think of it as a shared effort. David did not think of it as a shared effort. He thought of it as his thing. When they wanted it to stop being his thing, he bailed. I don't find this too shocking. The fact that he might have been secretive or embarrassed. I bet he was more embarrassed than shy about his plots. I bet he was never deliberately and cruelly indifferent to their feelings. But who knows. It's like a marriage. When things have gone south everyone acts like a jerk. There are no rights or wrongs anymore."

Then he said, "The Tom Tom Club was never interesting. Jerry's band was never interesting. They were okay. But the brilliance in that band came from David. Anybody could see that. I'm afraid that deep down Chris and Tina could see that and didn't like it. And the fact that he was weird and uncommunicative and downright duplicitous, what do I know? That's why I didn't get involved in this lawsuit."

The trial started. David argued in his brief, "Critics and the public used to call us the Heads. And like it or not, the band was identified with my voice and my style. People will get confused." Later David told *Billboard,* "It's like being with a wife-beater who won't divorce you."

Tina told *Bass Player* magazine: "People originally said we weren't going to make it *with* David. They told us he was awful, but that just made us love him and back him even more. Now, many people's first response was 'What? You're going to try it without David?' It's silly and absurd. We were never just drones surrounding the queen bee—it was always a team. I mean, it if took only one person to make a band, wouldn't Ric Ocasek have had a great solo career?"

Tina elaborated her theory. After all, the Duke Ellington Band remained basically the same, but one time they would be fronted by Ella Fitzgerald and another time Louis Armstrong. Then she revealed to the

Boston Globe how she had suffered all the pangs of blaming, forgiving, wishing revenge, all those things. Praying. Becoming sick. Depressed to the point that she and Chris did not touch their instruments for eight months. "It was our forty days in the desert."

The case was settled out of court. All four band members owned the name jointly, and the three could use the name as long as certain conditions, which were not made public, were agreed upon. Internet rumors stated that the terms were David's control over Talking Heads' archival material.

No Talking, Just Head contains twelve harshly produced high-tech songs that in no way resemble the work of Talking Heads. The grafted-on singers are Debbie Harry (Blondie), Johnette Napolitano (Concrete Blonde), Richard Hell (Television/Voidoids), Shaun Ryder (Black Grape), Ed Kowalcyzk (Live), Gordon Gano (Violent Femmes), Michael Hutchence (INXS), Maria McKee (Lone Justice), Andy Partridge (XTC), and Gavin Friday.

With the exception of Harry, the singers wrote their own lyrics. "Rock me, lady! Tell, baby! Sleazy lady! You're with me, lady! You drive me crazy!" goes one verse. Another tells how a woman installs a video camera over her bed. The singer makes a point of letting us know her "bed" is in the "bedroom." Finally, Tina sings one cut about a punk Lolita at CBGBs. Apparently, her alter ego.

No Talking, Just Head is awful, but it didn't have to be.

The situation Talking Heads found themselves in had a precedent in Peter Gabriel—definitely David's kind of oddball. After Gabriel left Genesis in 1975, the four remaining band members auditioned a slew of different singers, but finally decided that drummer Phil Collins had a sweet enough voice. This decision made music critics rub their hands anticipating a real plane crash. To everyone's surprise, the first Gabriel-less Genesis album turned out to be a respectable little pop album. It was, of all people, Princess Diana's favorite record. Phil Collins and Genesis kept making records, records that got radio play and made money.

Rock bands *are* their singers. They are the front men. David had always been the head Head. The only way Chris and Tina and Jerry could play together without David and hope for any legitimacy would have been to follow Genesis's example and have another band member fill the role of singer. In Talking Heads' case, Jerry should have sung the bulk of the vocals. After all, he proved he could sing on *Walk on Water*.

Talking Heads fans would have been suspicious, but curious as well. Jerry was an original member of the band (as far as vinyl evidence went). In tribal terms, it would have been similar to the dead husband's brother taking the dead man's place in the marriage bed.

Hell, the bride could sing a few tunes as well! Tina does have a "very, very small voice" that in no way resembles Liza Minnelli or Barbra Streisand, but on "Punk Lolita," her voice is teched up and she sounds fine.

Instead, Chris and Tina and Jerry chose to release an embarrassment. Their record is as awful as the Doors' post–Jim Morrison release, *Full Circle,* and the Velvet Underground's post-everyone album, *Squeeze.* Worse, the Heads went on the road with Johnette Napolitano squealing out Talking Heads songs.

And then there was the voodoo doll.

The back of the CD booklet of *No Talking, Just Head* contained a photograph of a voodoo doll strewn on a heart-shaped cake. The cake is skewered with knives and the doll's arms and legs are bound. Little tags on the doll read ARROGANCE, EGOTISM, LIES, ENVY, ADULTERY, HATE, CRUELTY, BETRAYAL, THEFT, RACISM, IGNORANCE, GREED, MEANNESS, and MURDER.

"I had seen a very funny documentary about old women sewing voodoo dolls in New York," Tina said. "Voodoo is fascinating. It's not a religion. It doesn't have a Ten Commandments." When Tina did a mini video for the promotion of the Heads album, this cake and doll appeared. "You know David is going to think this song is about him," Tina said.

Sure enough, David's next solo project, *Feelings,* pictured dolls on the cover. Not voodoo dolls. Little David dolls done in realistic plastic—like Ken (of Ken and Barbie). They are tagged with labels concerning the "cardinal emotions": ANGER, SADNESS, HAPPINESS, and NUMBNESS.

If David felt anger, sadness, and numbness about the Heads, it fueled him to create the first David Byrne solo album that has an edge to it. *Feelings* also brings a technical brilliance to the production that David hadn't found since *Fear of Music.* Even an Appalachian mountain song is so high-teched it sounds like flying saucers have landed in Johnson City, Tennessee.

The lyrics are typically whacked out, but David Byrne isn't repeating himself with ditties about monkeys and being naked. In a song that sounds like a Kurt Weill tango, David sings, "He took her cocaine when she was asleep/Friends say he gave half away/And friends say that . . . they . . . are . . . in love."

On another cut, over a chamber music arrangement that's reminiscent of "She's Leaving Home" from *Sgt. Pepper*, David states miscellaneous facts like "There are thirty teeth inside of our head" and "There is only one record in the whole wide world where Jimi Hendrix sings 'House Burning Down.' " These are examples of the fact that "everything is finite." David takes great comfort in the fact that things are finite. This is David's anti-God song—he confronts the mystery of existence and discovers the concept of finitude. David is exploring a philosophy of mathematics developed by L. E. J. Brouver, who rejected the concept of infinite numbers such as pi. For Brouver everything was finite—pi was merely *undecidable*, not infinite.

Finally, David may or may not be addressing Talking Heads when he sings the line "Rock bands died when amateurs won."

John Lennon wrote "How Do You Sleep?" for Paul McCartney. Surely David wrote "Wicked Little Doll" for Tina. He croons to the "wicked little doll" that he is not her victim. The wicked little doll needs him, too. He will be her partner. He is just like her. Anyone can see that she loves him, too. "Wicked little doll," he ends the song, "I will always be in love with you."

Around this time, Tina told the *Boston Globe* that David was surrounded by greedy people. That Talking Heads had written everything together—they just let David put his name on it. When Mariah Carey sampled Tina's "Genius of Love" for Carey's hit "Fantasy," Adrian Belew's name was finally listed as a cowriter.

As for Tina's love for David, Lee Blake, that old witness of Byrnian unhingement, says, "People ask me over and over, 'What's the matter with the two of them?' I'd say, 'Tina's always been in love with David.' Maybe now she wants to destroy him rather than have him not be hers."

Mary Clarke never bought Blake's love angle. At first Mary believed the conflict was one of sex, not love. Tina was one of the most attractive women in the CBGBs scene, but David ignored her beauty. "But after some thought, I don't believe that anymore," Clarke says. "I think Tina's 'obsession' was just a control issue. She saw a loss of her own power the more powerful David became."

In the end, it really doesn't matter whether the wicked little doll was in love with David or not. As Lee Blake says, "The thing is, Tina ended up really resenting him. She tried to get out of his shadow, and that was a mistake. She should have embraced him."

Tina and David equaled each other in ambition. They followed through on every aspect of their careers. They were going to create records that sounded like no one else. They were going to dress like no one else. They were going to have complete control over their records, from the sound to the jacket.

And everything they did was going to be art.

Ambition needs to be tempered with luck. Talking Heads was lucky. Certainly Robert Wilson was even more ambitious than David and Tina, but his two great "shots for the moon"—the twelve-hour production of *CIVIL warS* at the 1984 Olympics and the global production of *The Forest*—both went bust. Compared to him, Talking Heads had a long and lucky go of it.

As artful as David was, he found himself more or less a record executive at century's end. His small record company, Luaka Bop, released several Latin, Brazilian, and Cuban pop records per year out of offices in David's Greenwich Village townhouse. David himself hated the term "world music." He felt someone like the sweet neo-*fado* Portuguese singer Paulo Bragança would surely be scooped up by American/Euro ears. Paulo wasn't. On the other hand, Luaka Bop's collections of miscellaneous international Latin music sells nicely. In the end, Luaka Bop is a nice mom 'n' pop record house.

David might well have woken up one morning to find himself wearing Seymour Stein's shoes and asked himself, "Well, how did I get here?"

As an artist, David seemed to accept his decline into marginal status. He was never going to be on the cover of *Time* magazine again. "There's no sense in me trying to compete with youth, because a young fresh face will win out every time." But he was still committed to the bread-and-butter job of songwriting. In the first year of the new century, he put most of his Luaka Bop business on hold and flew out to Los Angeles to record what felt to him to be the record of his career.

We'll see.

From the vantage point of the twenty-first century, we can look back at the eighties and nineties and see that in the eighties perhaps the wrong people made money while the nineties was when the *right* people got the dough.

Jerry Harrison made his money in the nineties. "The year I had Crash Test Dummies and Live was an extraordinary year," he says. He has been more successful as a producer than he ever was as a member of Talking Heads. "As far as record sales go, as a producer I've sold probably four times as many records as the Talking Heads' catalog—in fewer years, too. But if they're writing about me fifty years from now, I'll be remembered for Talking Heads."

In 1995 Jerry became an architect again. He began building his own house in Marin County near Sausalito, California. The idea was to reconstruct a SoHo loft in the land of the Golden Bear. "One of the reasons I moved here," he later said, "is that it's one of the last places around where you can have a good idea and affect something and still make some money."

At the end of the twentieth century, Jerry partnered with a Silicon Valley entrepreneur, Tom Zito, and Amanda Welsh, Ph.D., and created a website for garage bands to win recording contracts. Jerry convinced old cohorts Brian Eno and Steve Lillywhite to sit on the advisory board chaired by the "fifth" Beatle, Sir George Martin. Jerry's site was launched during the fall of 1999 and christened Garageband.com.

The *San Francisco Examiner* asked Jerry, "If Talking Heads was just starting out right now, would all this new technology have changed the way you approached music?"

"Yeah," he answered. "Although what's difficult about that is the same thing as the problem with making videos. It's not enough anymore to be a good musician. You have to have a great website and also make exciting videos, although Talking Heads were poised to make videos from the start because we were all in visual arts. Beauty is now more of a criterion than ever before. It's almost like Hollywood. I'd hate to think that the only way to get ahead now is to be a great musician and have a great website and be good-looking."

Six months into the new century, Jerry—still a devilishly handsome man—sat in his transplanted-to-California SoHo loft and reflected on Talking Heads' lost opportunities in the 1980s. Walking away from Live Aid was just the beginning. "We were offered, a long time ago, a chance to go on tour: 'You can make fifteen million net.' But David said no. Another offer came two years after we'd stopped touring—'Go to Australia for two weeks and two million dollars.' These were opportunities that we could have done easily. Second of all, it's fun to play together. And third of all, we got to the point where we could have been set for life." He paused. "That's a bitter pill to swallow. I see why Tina and Chris feel betrayed. They feel like they nur-tured David in the earlier days."

Then Jerry said, "I found as a solo act that you're trying to jump-start your career, you do things that you wouldn't have done with Talking Heads. I see David doing stuff like that all the time. I just think it's sad."

The last chronological moment in Talking Heads history occurred in 1999 with the DVD reissue of *Stop Making Sense*. The new remixed *Stop Making Sense* was then shown at the 1999 San Francisco Film Festival. Tina would not shake David's hand at the press conference. As the all-the-news-that's-fit-to-print grilling began, David believed the reporters were only interested in getting the band to throw dirt at one another. Or they asked over and over, "Okay, why don't you get back together?"

"They just keep hammering at you," David recounted. " 'So why don't you get along?' Which was like you've had a real painful divorce and they want you to relive that pain for them. 'Let me see you bleed again. Do it for me!' No one has the right to do that to another person. You volunteer to go to a therapist."

In a newspaper interview for the *Stop Making Sense* DVD, Tina Weymouth, citizen of Connecticut, claimed her old wounds have healed. "The scars are smooth now. I can run my fingers over them and it's not like putting your hands in the holes anymore."

Chris Frantz's final public words spoken in the twentieth century about Talking Heads occurred right after he saw the revamped *Stop Making Sense*. "It just reminds me of how good we were. I really just want to remember the good times."

And Talking Heads really was good. Viewing *Stop Making Sense* so many years later is to see a band at the height of its powers. David Byrne's coolness factor is too unique and peculiar to be obsolete. That said, the Robert Wilson touches in the *Stop Making Sense* stage production have worn thin, but for more than a dozen songs it's the band that completely dominates the stage. Talking Heads still sound like the Next New Thing even while transcending their youth. They all retain the goofy energy of a young Jerry Harrison frowning on camera over the shoulders of Doctor Bop on local Milwaukee TV, while simultaneously exhibiting the swagger of a seasoned gunslinger, a Jackson Pollock, a Gertrude Stein.

In this light, it's not necessarily a bad thing that the band broke up before they had to confront the dilemma of copying themselves or retreating into a dignified musical idiom like the elderly Buena Vista Social Club.

The 1960s whetted our appetites for rock music that would surprise us. The *Sgt. Pepper* factor. Music that could loop into our ears and do something that's never been done before. Talking Heads did that album after album. They gave us high tech and dirty tribal primitive. Songs led us into an America that is one part whirling dervish and one part post-apocalypse *Blade Runner*.

The art of Talking Heads is one thing, but their overt cultural influence is something else. Radiohead may have taken their name from a song off *True Stories*, but it's hard to imagine a slouching teenage boy wanting to become the next David Byrne, and even harder to imagine that kid wanting to be the next Sting or Prince. Bob Dylan seems like a simple, simple man compared to the 1980s array of icons.

Certainly an oddball like Michael Stipe of R.E.M. would have had a harder time becoming a pop star if David Byrne had not paved the way. To give Tina Weymouth her due as well, millions of girls who've never heard the name Suzi Quatro know that Tina tamed her large unwieldy instrument and brought it into the realm of womanhood.

Musicologist William Thalbitzer describes Inuit (Eskimo) enemies settling disputes in poetic form by drumming and singing against each other. An Eskimo who felt injured by another Eskimo would face his opponent and beat a drum. Vent anger in singing. Then the other would slam on his or her drum and howl right back at the attacker. "The songs were constantly renewed, and the hostility between the two opponents only in rare instance resulted in homicide," reports Thalbitzer.

Picture Tina Weymouth and David Byrne as Inuits.

One of David's lines in his homesick poem "This Must Be the Place" was specifically influenced by Inuit culture. "Sing into my mouth," he wrote.

This sounds vaguely pornographic at first, but David wrote that line after seeing a photograph of two Eskimos, furry hood to furry hood, lips locked, literally singing into each other's mouths.

Sing into my mouth.
Give me holy resuscitation.
Beat me like a drum.

A group like the Rolling Stones sang into our hips. The Supremes sang into our hearts. God knows where Dylan and the Band were singing in 1966. But from 1974 to the early 1990s, Talking Heads sang into our mouths like Eskimos.

Like Inuits.

Welcome home.

bibliography and
source notes

Bibliography

Books devoted to Talking Heads listed in chronological order:

1981 *Talking Heads* by Miles (New York: Omnibus Press)
1982 *The Name of This Book Is Talking Heads* by Krista Reese (New York: Proteus
     Books)
1985 *Talking Heads: The Band and Their Music* by David Gans (New York: Avon)
1986 *Talking Heads: The Vintage/Musician Series* by Jerome Davis (New York: Vintage
     Books)
     True Stories by David Byrne (New York: Penguin Books)
1987 *What the Songs Look Like: Contemporary Artists Interpret Talking Heads Songs* by
     Talking Heads and Frank Olinsky, introduction by David Byrne (New York:
     Harper & Row)
1992 *David Byrne: American Originals Series* by John Howell (New York: Thunder's
     Mouth Press)

Miscellaneous books by David Byrne:

1995 *Strange Ritual* (San Francisco: Chronicle Books). **Note:** This is a collection of
     Byrne's photographs of kitsch, curious monotony, and demons transfiguring into
     flesh.
1998 *Your Action World* (Trieste, Italy: Lipanje Puntin). **Note:** This is another collection
     of kitsch photos, along with surveillance-style photographs and questionnaires
     similar to the kinds handed out by David Byrne back in his RISD days.

Source Notes

The Usual Suspects: I interviewed many people for *This Must Be the Place*, including the four Talking Heads: David Byrne, Tina Weymouth, Chris Frantz, and Jerry Harrison. (Grateful thanks to Girl Fridays, Kara Finaly and Rachel Levin.) Others I interviewed include: Terry Allen, David Anderson, Adrian Belew, Lee Blake, Brian Breger, Celia Byrne, John Cale, John Miller Chernoff, Mary Clarke, Neil Cooper, "Jerome Davis," Mary Delahoyd, Jean De Segonzac, John Douglas, Danny Fields, Philip Glass, Al Green, Deborah Harry, Nona Hendryx, Frank Hentschker, Ann Keating, Peter Kooper, Catherine Kpew, Hilly Kristal, Ken Kushnick, Ed Lochlan, Adelle Lutz, Patty Martin, Anne McEnroe, Bob Merlis, Edmund Morris, Andy Paly, Bradley Paul, Edward Pressman, Lou Reed, John Rockwell, Susan Sontag, Linda Stein, Seymour Stein, Richard Thompson, Gus Van Sant, Tom Verlaine, Chuck Wachtel, John Waters, Robert Wilson, Neal Wiseman, Bernie Worrell, and Paul Zolo. Thanks to Cat Curry for the title of this book.

Photograph Note: Stephanie Chernikowski, one of the photographers who provided photographs for this book, is known for (1) having been kissed by Elvis when she was a Bayou teen growing up in East Texas, and (2) compiling the photo documentary *Dream Baby Dream: Images from the Blank Generation* (Los Angeles: 2.13.61. Press, 1996).

Abbreviations: The four principal Talking Heads are designated by their initials: DB = David Byrne; CF = Chris Frantz; JH = Jerry Harrison; TW = Tina Weymouth. The following publications appear as initials as well: *AF = Art Forum; CSM = Christian Science Monitor; LAT = Los Angeles Times; MM = Melody Maker; NYDN = New York Daily News; NYP = New York Post; NYT = New York Times; RS = Rolling Stone; TP = Trouser Press; VV = Village Voice; WSJ = Wall Street Journal; WP = Washington Post.*

Introduction

Conversations: DB, TW, John Cale (grateful thanks to novelist Lynne Tillman for snagging this ex-Velvet). **Carlos Fuentes's quote:** *Diana: The Goddess Who Hunts Alone* (New York: Farrar, Straus and Giroux, 1995); **David Byrne, photogenic devil:** "The whole thing of being onstage and presenting yourself—being this adjunct to the music—I didn't have a grasp of it in the beginning. It's artificial in the same way that any acting or stage performances are artificial. But if you know how to do it, it's telling the same story as your other work. . . . As for Richard Avedon, I just thought, 'I'm going to get my picture taken by Richard Avedon so I'm going to look as good as I possibly can.' I was totally so bowled over that I probably lost all sense of my own personal direction. . . . Helmet Newton didn't seem like anything. He's known for pictures that to me are elaborate setups, but when he was doing my portrait it was like, 'David, the light is very nice. Just stand there for a second. Click. That's great.' What was it like being photographed by Mapplethorpe? Like being an object, really."

1: The Secret Life of Tina Weymouth

Note: This title is taken from one of the first Talking Heads bootlegs (see Selected Bootlegs, page 382: *An Annotated Discography*); **young Tina's story:** Conversations: TW, CF, Gary Kurfirst, Jamie Dalglish, Jean De Segonzac; Printed Sources: "Elizabeth Morris Graham Is

Married," *NYT*, 11/29/64; Lally Weymouth, "A False Picture of My Family," *Women's Wear Daily*, 4/30/75; Katherine Graham, *Personal History* (New York: Knopf, 1997); **Chris and Tina's paintings:** Conversations: Jean De Segonzac, David Anderson; **Frantz's childhood:** Primary Source: Jerome Davis's *Talking Heads:* I discovered that "Jerome Davis" is the pseudonym of a well-known journalist/author who does not want his identity made public. He did the primary research/writing for the book for a flat fee back in 1986. The manuscript was then taken away from him for reasons he won't divulge. The published book was the result of several additional writers. "The book was almost an extended magazine article," he said. "I haven't looked at it in fifteen years. I regretted being involved. I naively believed the project had the cooperation of the band. By the time I found out it didn't, I was on the hook. I thought I did a good job. It was a kind of *Rashomon* thing—people who knew the band giving their very different perspectives. That could have been the basis for a good book. But it wasn't." **Details about Providence:** Conversations: TW, David Anderson, Gus Van Sant.

2: *Byrned to a Crisp*

Young Byrne: Conversations: DB, Mark Kehoe, Mary Clarke, David Anderson, Gus Van Sant, Jean De Segonzac; Printed Sources: Jim Beloff, *The Ukulele: A Visual History* (San Francisco: Miller Freeman Books, 1997); John Waters, *Shock Value* (New York: Thunder's Mouth Press, 1981); Timothy White, "Inside Talking Heads: Seventeen Years of Popular Favorites and Naked Truths," *Goldmine 25*, 12/92; Christopher Connelly, "Byrne in Love," *RS*, 10/27/83; "David Byrne: Thinking Man's Rock Star," *NYT Magazine*, 5/5/85; **conceptual performance art:** Sources: Lucrezia De Domizio Durini, *The Felt Hat: Joseph Beuys a Life Told* (Milano: Charta, 1997); Dominique de Menil et al, *Yves Klein 1928–1962 (A Retrospective)* (Houston: Institute for the Arts, Rice University, in association with the Arts Publisher, Inc., New York, 1982); Robert Horvitz, "Chris Burden," *AF*, 5/76; **Bradley Paul's description of Baltimore:** "It may be confusing that I mention Baltimore County and Baltimore as separate entities," he wrote. "It's actually a rare situation. Baltimore is what's known as an 'independent city'—that is, a city that politically is not part of a county. There are only two other independent cities in the U.S., St. Louis, Missouri, and Carson City, Nevada. This situation causes a sort of very strange hostility between city and county dwellers. The Baltimore city line is well-demarcated, and people in the county—in Lansdowne, for example—are frequently quite defiant about their non-citiness. Lansdownians would be more likely to go further south into the county—it's easier to drive to. City dwellers are considered uppity or peregrine—in Baltimore City, of all places!" **Edgar Allen Poe in Baltimore:** Sources: Thomas Dwight and David K. Jackson, *The Poe Log: A Documentary Life of Edgar Allan Poe 1809–1849* (New York: G. K. Hall & Co., 1987); "Poe's Death Is Rewritten as Case of Rabies, Not Telltale Alcohol," *NYT*, 9/15/96; **David Byrne and the draft:** Can a Scottish citizen be eligible for the draft? "Yes," Byrne wrote in an e-mail. "As a green-card holder I have all the privileges and responsibilities of all you Yanks, except I can't vote for president . . . and one other thing: If I'm deemed undesirable, I can be harassed or kicked out (see John Lennon's immigration case and his FBI file)." Byrne's draft board was in Catonsville, a community "slightly more well-to-do" than Arbutus. This was the place where Daniel Berrigan and other peaceniks poured blood over the records. "This effectively delayed my draft decision for a few years until the lottery went into effect"; **Gus Van Sant** went to RISD on a student deferment; **Byrne's "working**

class" roots: David's sister Celia says, "Financially our family was middle class, but we were raised in a working-class mentality. Everybody in the family had to pull their weight. I mean, you didn't get to walk away from the dinner table and just say 'bye.' My mom wasn't going to be our servant, kind of thing. . . . Both David and I hated me having to sell Girl Scout cookies. I hated that with a passion. I don't think either of us are really good salesmen." **Byrne and the monkeys:** Jerome Davis dug this one up, quoting the primate researcher, David Brown, claiming that "David [Byrne] got along better with my research animals than anyone before ever had. . . . They loved him. . . . He became best friends with a female named Jerome. Couldn't separate the two of them." Although David Byrne denies this monkey business, I trust Davis's research. I have no clue why Byrne would deny Jerome (the monkey, not the author); **Camp:** <u>Sources</u>: Clement Greenberg, *Art and Culture: Critical Essays* (Boston: Beacon Press, 1961); Susan Sontag's "Notes on Camp" included in *Against Interpretation* (NY: Anchor Books edition, 1990); Fabio Cleto, editor, *Camp: Queer Aesthetics and the Performing Subject, A Reader* (Ann Arbor: University of Michigan Press, 1999). **Byrne and (1) Joan LaBelle, (2) San Francisco, (3) Edith the Egg Lady:** <u>Source</u>: Mark Kehoe; **Byrne as a correspondent:** Whenever Byrne and Kehoe were separated, they would write each other as faithfully as Emerson corresponded with Thomas Carlyle. It's curious to think of Byrne as some nineteenth-century epistolarite, but then *Billboard* honcho Timothy White once quoted Byrne revealing that when he was a kid he wanted to be a mailman so he could read people's postcards as he made his rounds.

3: Down Normal

Providence narration: <u>Sources</u>: All interviewees from previous chapters, plus FBI profiler John Douglas; **cybernetics:** <u>Conversation</u>: DB; <u>Printed Sources</u>: Norbert Wiener, *Cybernetics, or Control and Communication in the Animal and the Machine* (New York: Wiley, 1949); G. T. Guilbaud, *What Is Cybernetics?* (New York: Grove Press, 1960). **David Byrne on performing "Psycho Killer" throughout his career:** E-mail Q&A: *Was there ever a concert that the Talking Heads DID NOT play "Psycho Killer"?* "Probably I dropped it once or twice out of spite. But this would have been rare." *How about "David Byrne" solo concerts?* "Didn't do it at first on the *Rei Momo* [big Latin band] tour . . . but then after a while I thought it would be a laugh to do a version using berimbaus [Brazilian bowed instruments], so it ended up as part of this tour set as well. And yes, my first tour of South America [Talking Heads had never been there]. I felt I should do as many of the obvious favorites as musically feasible with that band . . . so 'Psycho Killer,' 'Burning Down the House,' etc., were all added to the Latin band's set"; **David Anderson on "Psycho Killer":** "David [Byrne] had all the words and chords written. The song is mostly his. You know how the music goes, *Psycho killer qu'est-ce que c'est?* then it goes, *bum bum bum bum-bum.* I wrote the *bum bum bum bum-bum* part"; **"Sick Boy":** I met David Anderson in person at a recent (summer of 2000) art opening for Jamie Dalglish, and Anderson sang for me an early unrecorded David Byrne Artistics composition called "Sick Boy": "Sick boy, I don't feel well/City streets/A little confused/Tore up/Guess there's no answers/Maybe I'm wasting my time . . ." Another verse went, "Sick boy, I'm just wasting my time/Sick boy, I want to be someone special/But maybe I'm just wasting my time/Maybe I'm just wasting my time"; **Barbara Conway's murder:** Mark Kehoe remembers the story this way: "Barbara married a guy in Providence. He had an affair with a woman he worked with. Someone knocked on the door. A woman was there, saying, 'I was riding my bike and the chain broke. Can I come in and call someone?' Barbara said, 'Sure.' The woman came in and shot Barbara." Mary Clarke heard a different story: "Barbara's husband met this woman elsewhere (California?), on a conference of some sort. The woman developed a crush on him, and followed him stalker-like back to Barrington, Rhode Island. . . ."

4: Find Yourself a City to Live In

Descriptions of New York: <u>Conversations</u>: DB, TW, Jamie Dalglish, David Anderson, Mark Kehoe, Gus Van Sant, Hilly Kristal, Philip Glass; <u>Printed Sources</u>: Concert advertisements in the *Village Voice* (thanks to *VV* librarian Hervay Petion); **History of New York in the mid-1970s:** Personal recollections, along with <u>Printed Sources</u>: Jack Newfield, *The Abuse of Power: The Permanent Government and the Fall of New York* (New York: Viking Press, 1977); Ronald Sukenick, *Down and In: Life in the Underground* (New York: Beech Tree Books, William Morrow, 1987); George J. Lankevich, *American Metropolis: A History of New York City* (New York: New York University Press, 1998); Yvonne Sewall-Ruskin, *High on Rebellion: Inside the Underground at Max's Kansas City* (New York: Thunder's Mouth Press, 1998); Ric Burns and James Sanders, with Lisa Ade, *New York: An Illustrated History* (New York: Knopf, 1999); **Don DeLillo:** *Great Jones Street* (New York: Houghton Mifflin, 1973); **Dalglish's eight-hour David Byrne video:** This video disappeared years ago and has become the Holy Grail of Talking Heads research. Dalglish is convinced that Talking Heads manager Gary Kurfirst has it. Kurfirst says he doesn't know what Dalglish is talking about.

5: Uh-Oh, Love Comes to Town

Chris, Tina, David in Manhattan: <u>Conversations</u>: CF, TW, DB, Jamie Dalglish, Brian Breger, Patty Martin; <u>Printed Sources</u>: Clinton Heylin, *From the Velvets to the Voidoids: Pre-Punk History for a Post-Punk World* (New York: Penguin Books, 1993); Legs McNeil and Gillian McCain, *Please Kill Me: The Uncensored Oral History of Punk* (New York: Grove Press, 1996); "SoHo Scene May Include Pollock Pl." *NYT*, 2/7/72; David Shirey, "Soho [sic] Artists Are Divided on Jackson Pollock Place," *NYT*, 2/17/72; **Chris and Tina didn't make the cut at Yale:** "We made the first cut out of thousands," Tina remembers. "It was down to the last 100 people, but they could only take eight. Even before we did our interview, they'd already made their selection. We asked, 'Why did you have us come down and do the interview if you already made the selection?' They said, 'I dunno. Beats us.' It was based on something other than merit at that point"; **Jeff Turtletaub:** Tina is convinced that Susan kicked Dave Byrne out of Dalglish's loft so the young man had to camp out at the loft of ex-RISD student Jeff Turtletaub. Turtletaub is unable to confirm this because he died of AIDS in the mid-eighties. After consulting Jamie Dalglish and Mark Kehoe, I can find no evidence that David lived with anyone else during his first year in NYC other than Dalglish, and then the loft on Chrystie Street; **Gerald Ford:** <u>Sources</u>: Richard Reeves, *A Ford, Not a Lincoln* (New York: Harcourt Brace Jovanovich, 1975); Gerald R. Ford, *A Time to Heal: The Autobiography of Gerald R. Ford* (New York: Harper & Row Publishers and The Reader's Digest Association, Inc., 1979); **Brice Martin:** Dalglish reported that Brice Martin would show up when Talking Heads played CBGBs; **Tina learns the bass:** To write these passages, I consulted Peter Pickow's *Beginning Bass Guitar* (New York: Amsco Publications, 1986) as well as Dana Ball, beer salesman and bass player; **Gertrude Stein:** In 1984 David Byrne declared, "I've been reading quite a bit of Gertrude Stein lately. . . . Although many of her most discussed books are surprisingly out of print, from those that remain one gets the impression of a character whose curiosity and sense of wonder never diminished—someone who, weeks away from graduating from medical school, could change direction and become involved in a completely different activity, and do it again and again. And have a great hairdo to boot" (*NYT*, 12/2/84).

6: In Vogue at CBGBs

<u>Conversations</u>: All the usual suspects, including John Cale, Tom Verlaine, and Anne McEnroe; <u>Printed Sources</u>: John Rockwell in the *NYT*: "Talking Heads: Cool in Glare of Hot Rock," 3/24/75; "A Trio That Shows Art's Effect on Rock," 9/16/75; *VV* articles: Richard Mortifoglio, "Watch Television," 7/11/75; James Wolcott, "Dylan Calls on Patti Smith," 7/7/75; **how Talking Heads got their name:** De Segonzac says: "I worked at a television station in Providence my junior year at school. Talking heads was the first bit of lingo I learned—*We're going to shoot a talking head*. That's when we interviewed a guy, and framed up the head and shoulders. I had to earn my green card to stay in the country and ended up in Columbus, Ohio. And they had never heard of a talking head. It was something that was just used at that station in Providence. I later ran into Tina and she asked me what I was doing. 'I'm working at a TV station.' I told her about *talking heads*. 'Hey, that'd be a great name for a band,' she said." More than ten years later in 1986, the mystery of the name deepens: David Byrne made this chance comment to a reporter, "The band name came from a B-grade movie that somebody saw advertised in *TV Guide*. I *think* [italics mine] it was called *The Talking Head*." I can find no reference to such a film ever being made; **tape of Talking Heads' first CBGBs show:** TW: "Of course, no one had a tape of our first show. Nobody taped us. People didn't even have tape recorders back then except those massive things. We did nine songs for each set. No one has a list of the song list. There's nothing that exists. There's no set list. There's zilch"; **"Living in a cabin in the woods building bombs":** After David Byrne made this historical reference to the Unabomber, he said. "I think he had a really interesting take on technology"; **"They shrank up real small":** Detail from Miles's *Talking Heads*.

7: Seymour Stein

<u>Conversations</u>: TW, DB, Seymour Stein, Ken Kushnick; <u>Printed Sources</u>: William Duckworth, *Talking Music: Conversations with John Cage, Philip Glass, Laurie Anderson, and Five Generations of American Experimental Composers* (New York: Da Capo Press, 1999). ***Saturday Night Live:*** <u>Source</u>: Doug Hill and Jeff Weingrad, *Saturday Night: A Backstage History of Saturday Night Live* (New York: William Morrow, 1986); **Andy Warhol:** <u>Sources</u>: Ingrid Schaffner, *The Essential Andy Warhol* (New York: Harry N. Abrams, 1999); Trewin Copplestone, *The Life and Works of Andy Warhol* (Avonmonth, England: Siena 1994); Victor Bockris, *The Life and Death of Andy Warhol* (New York: Bantam, 1989); unless otherwise notated, all remaining references to Warhol are from *The Andy Warhol Diaries*, Pat Hackett, editor (New York: Warner Books, 1991); **Lou Reed's album *Nomad*:** <u>Source</u>: Peter

Doggett, *Growing Up in Public* (New York: Omnibus Press, 1992). **Johnny Podell:** Conversation: TW; Printed Source: Victor Bockris, *Transformer: The Lou Reed Story* (New York: Simon & Schuster, 1994); **Phil Kaufman:** Conversation: JH; Printed Sources: Sid Griffin, *Gram Parsons: A Music Biography* (Pasadena: Sierra Records & Books, 1985); Ben Fong-Torres, *Hickory Wind: The Life and Times of Gram Parsons* (New York: Pocket Books, 1991).

8: A Former Modern Lover

Conversations: JH, DB, TW, Seymour Stein, Danny Fields, Philip Glass, John Cale; Printed Sources: Tim Mitchell, *There's Something About Jonathan: Jonathan Richman and the Modern Lovers* (London: Peter Own Publishers, 1999); John Cale and Victor Bockris, *What's Welsh for Zen: The Autobiography of John Cale* (London: Bloomsbury, 1999); Richard Goldstein, "Talking Heads Hyperventilate Some Clichés," *VV*, 2/2/76. **Dear Mr. Rockwell:** Xerox of original letter given to me by John Rockwell; **John Cale on Modern Lovers:** "What I recall, sitting in my office listening to the Modern Lovers, was the music started from a very weak-kneed supposition, but by the end it had won you over. The weakness had become a strength. A kind of magic in human personalities that really pays off. Both the Modern Lovers and Talking Heads had this urban sensibility and a great deal of naïveté. Their lyrics were conversational. Bus depot conversations. Things you'd hear in malls across America." *When the band self-destructed, did Warner Bros. blame John Cale?* "I don't know. Look, if I was blamed for that, I was blamed for my own solo career. I had kept fighting for Warner to keep Bob Seger on the label until finally Bob Seger left. Then the minute he left, he had a top 10 album. There was a meeting about David Bowie when *Hunky Dory* came out and we turned down *Hunky Dory* for other than artistic reasons."

9: These Are the Days My Friend: Summer '76

Conversations: DB, TW, Seymour Stein, Philip Glass, Robert Wilson, Mary Clarke. **Byrne's first television:** In *AF*, 10/99, David Robbins proclaimed, "We were . . . the first generation of American artists not to regard TV as an enemy . . . for whom it was authentic to feel that TV wasn't the demise of civilization but instead the linchpin of a contemporary information infrastructure, unnamed, and still forming, perhaps, but by which we did not feel at all intimidated, from which we derived joy, and in which we even took pride"; **first date and a mystery:** Mary and David's first date was seeing the Jerry-less Modern Lovers at Town Hall. Also that Fall: Talking Heads played their only gig at Max's and covered Jonathan Richman's "Pablo Picasso" for apparently the first and only time. Twenty-five years later, David told me they played the song to seduce Jerry into joining the band. Jerry, however, wasn't in NYC that night. Nor does he ever remember hearing Talking Heads cover the song; **$15,000 advance:** David doesn't remember what Talking Heads' first advance was. "It was the kind of money that we give to Luaka Bop now. Sadly it hasn't changed that much." Jerry told me when he joined the band, he negotiated a separate contract for $5,000. I'm guessing that makes the first advance $15,000. I ran this figure by Gary Kurfirst: "The first advance was . . . less than $25,000. I don't know the exact figure, but it was less than $25,000." ***Einstein on the Beach:*** According to Glass, he and Wilson also considered scenes in a cowboy saloon as well as Japanese war monsters fighting in tanks of water ("That proved impractical: Tanks of water are very heavy"); <u>Printed Sources</u>: Philip Glass and Robert T. Jones, *Music by Philip Glass* (New York: Da Capo Press, 1995); Richard Kostelanetz, editor, *Writings of Glass: Essays, Interviews, Criticism* (Berkeley: University of California Press, 1997); John Rockwell, "Philip Glass's Decline," *The New Republic*, 4/10/00. **Robert Wilson:** <u>Conversations</u>: DB, Philip Glass, Robert Wilson; <u>Printed Sources</u>: Franco Quadri, "It's About Time," *AF*, 10/84; Trevor Fairbrother, *Robert Wilson's Vision* (New York: Henry Abrams, 1991); Franco Quadri, Franco Bertoni, Robert Stearns, *Robert Wilson* (New York: Rizzoli International Publications, 1998); **Funkanauts:** Rickey Vincent's *Funk: The Music, the People and the Rhythm of the One* (New York: St. Martin's Press, 1996) and Nelson George's *The Death of Rhythm & Blues* (New York: Penguin, 1988) contain perhaps the most important writing on funk in the twentieth century—seconded by Craig Werner's *A Change Is Gonna Come: Music, Race & the Soul of America* (New York: Plume, 1999); Larry Muhammed searched this chapter for "racial profiling"; **Bongiovi and Jimi Hendrix:** <u>Source</u>: John McDermott with Eddie Kramer, *Hendrix: Setting the Record Straight* (New York: Warner Books, 1992); **Patti Smith's broken neck:** <u>Sources</u>: Victor Bockris and Roberta Bayley, *Patti Smith: An Unauthorized Biography* (New York: Simon & Schuster, 1999); Nick Johnstone, *Patti Smith: A Biography* (London: Omnibus Press, 1997); **Cale drinking:** <u>Conversation</u>: JH.

10: 3-2-4

<u>Conversations</u>: DB, JH, John Rockwell, Ken Kushnik, Seymour Stein.

11: Before and After Eno

Heads in Europe: <u>Conversations</u>: Linda Stein, JH, DB, John Cale, Lee Blake; <u>Printed Source</u>: Jim Bessman, *Ramones: An American Band* (New York: St. Martin's Press, 1993); **Eno details:** <u>Conversations</u>: DB, JH; <u>Printed Sources</u>: Eric Tamm Brain, *Eno: His Music and the Vertical Color of Sound*, Updated Edition (New York: Da Capo Press, 1995); Jon Savage, "Eno's No Bounds," *The Guardian*, 11/26/93; John Rockwell, "Report from New York's Rock Underground," *NYT*, 2/20/77; "The Odyssey of Two British Rockers," *NYT*, 5/23/78; In Rockwell's collection of essays *All American Music: Composition in the Late Twentieth Century* (New York: Vintage, 1984) he makes the provocative and astute comparison that after Eno left Roxy Music, he worked almost exclusively in a studio "rather like Glenn Gould"; **after the European tour:** Linda Stein considered managing Talking Heads. When the Ramones found out, they went "ballistic." Their manager, Danny Fields, hated both David Byrne and Tina Weymouth (for undisclosed reasons). He told Linda to forget the idea. And she did.

12: Talking Heads '77

<u>Conversations</u>: DB, TW, JH, Lee Blake, Mary Clarke, Seymour Stein, Gary Kurfirst; <u>Printed Sources</u>: John Rockwell, "The Artistic Success of Talking Heads," *NYT*, 9/11/77; Robert Palmer, "Rock: New Theater Opens with Punk," *NYT*, 12/29/77; **Che's beard:** Gary Kurfirst insists he resembled Che, yet no one seems to remember his legendary beard; **Eno and Bowie:** <u>Sources</u>: Eric Tamm's *Eno*; David Buckley, *Strange Fascination: David Bowie,*

The Definitive Story (London: Virgin, 1999); Henry Edwards and Tony Zanetta, *Stardust: The David Bowie Story* (New York: McGraw-Hill, 1986); George Tremlett, *David Bowie: Living on the Brink* (New York: Carroll & Graf Publishers, Inc., 1996); Christopher Sandford, *Bowie, Loving the Alien* (New York: De Capo Press, 1998), **Lally Weymouth's dinner party:** (unsigned) "Still Feuding After All These Years, Gore and Norman Stage Fight Night at Lally's," *People*, 11/14/77; **Sex Pistols, performing:** <u>Conversations</u>: DB, Ken Kushnik; <u>Printed Source</u>: *TP*, 11/79; **tour locations:** Miles's *Talking Heads* book.

13: Aspects of Byrne

<u>Conversations</u>: DB, JH, TW, Mary Clarke, Lee Blake, Gary Kurfirst; **Weldon Kees:** (1914–55) was a minor American poet who either disappeared in Mexico or—more likely—jumped off the Golden Gate Bridge. His fine New York poem "Aspects of Robinson" is collected in Philip Lopate's *Writing New York* (New York: Library of America, 1998); **New York literati:** <u>Source</u>: Susan Edmiston and Linda D. Cirino, *Literary New York: A History and Guide* (Boston: Houghton Mifflin Co., 1976).

14: More Songs About Buildings and Food

<u>Conversation</u>: DB; <u>Printed Sources</u>: "Straight Talk," *Newsweek*, 8/21/78; Harry Sumrall, "Talking Heads: Living Up to Punk's Premise," *WP*, 9/13/78; Robert Palmer, "Talking Heads and Grooves," *NYT*, 11/10/78; Barbara Charone, "More Songs About Typing and Vacuuming," *Creem*, 10/79; Lester Bangs, *VV*, 8/20/79—Bangs referred to "Big Country" in this review of *Fear of Music*; **Eno as stud:** <u>Conversations</u>: DB, CF, JH, TW; <u>Printed Sources</u>: Paul Stump, *Unknown Pleasures: A Cultural Biography of Roxy Music* (London: Quartet Books, 1998); Brian Eno, *A Year with Swollen Appendices: Brian Eno's Diary* (London: Faber and Faber, 1996); Chrissie Hynde, "Everything You'd Rather Not Have Known About Brian Eno," *New Musical Express*, 2/2/74; **other Eno-esque matters:** <u>Sources</u>: Mitchell Schneider, "Brave New Eno," *Crawdaddy*, 5/78; Anthony Korner, "Aurora Musicalis," *AF*, Summer 1986; Greg Allen, "Enologue," *TP*, 10/78; Stanley Mieses, "Eno, Before and After," unidentified article from Eno website; **NO NEW YORK:** Recorded in New York City, Spring 1978. (Side One) Contortions: "Dish It Out," "Flip Your Face," "Jaded," "I Can't Stand Myself"; Teenage Jesus and the Jerks: "Burning Rubber," "The Closet," "Red Alert," "I Woke Up Dreaming." (Side Two) Mars: "Helen Fordsdale," "Hairwaves," "Tunnel," "Puerto Rican Ghost"; DNA: "Egomaniac's Kiss," "Lionel," "Not Moving," "Size"; Noir historian Glenn O'Brien believes that the term "no wave" came from French New Wave film director Jean-Luc Godard's comment, "There are no new waves, there is only the ocean" ("Style Makes the Band," *AF*, 10/99); **Chris Blackwell:** <u>Conversation</u>: TW; <u>Printed Sources</u>: Joanie McDonell, "Chris Blackwell," *Interview*, 9/85; "Hypnotic Sound of Reggae Floats Far from the Slums of Jamaica," *WSJ*, 8/10/81; Timothy White, *Catch a Fire: The Life of Bob Marley*, the Definitive Edition (New York: Owl, 1998); **Glass making money:** <u>Source</u>: Robert Palmer, "Philip Glass Comes to Carnegie Hall—At Last," *NYT*, 5/28/78; **Girls in Europe:** <u>Conversations</u>: DB, JH, Mary Clarke. "Remember when you asked me if I had gone to Europe and driven around with Jerry and David?" Clarke asked me. "That got me to thinking—maybe it was Lisa S. [last name suppressed] he saw there. This is kind of conjecture on my part, but it makes some of the pieces fall into

place. Lisa S. was a girl-about-town who was Brian Eno's girlfriend for awhile. I remember driving out to see Talking Heads in Long Island and being in the car with Brian Eno and her. She was very pretty. She's half-black and half-white. She looks like Lena Horne but with a real baby face." Mary remembered that somebody even said that Lisa S. went over to Europe because she was going after Jerry, but Jerry rebuffed her, so she "settled" for David; **Some guys pick up girls and get called an asshole—did this ever happen to David Byrne?:** "I tried to chase women and do rock star stuff. In my own bumbling way I did it a little bit. But Jerry"—long pause—"I shouldn't talk about other people"; **The barking dogs:** These were the work of subway graffiti artist Keith Haring. **SAMO:** Author remembrance; Printed Source: Phoebe Hoban, *Basquiat: A Quick Killing in Art* (New York: Viking, 1998); **Eno Is God:** Author remembrance and conversation with longtime Manhattan hipster and Eno freak, Michael Curry; Printed Source: Bill Wilkowski, "Brian Eno: Excursion in the Electronic Environment," *DownBeat*, 6/83; **Eno in Chinatown:** Personal observation and what Eno reported in *MM*, 2/14/80; **I wouldn't live there if you paid me:** I asked David Byrne, *Wouldn't you love to hear someone praising suburbia?* "I'd love to hear from some kid hanging out at the mall, 'Yeah, didn't we have great times there.' I haven't heard that. Maybe that generation hasn't found their voice yet. When that voice starts to be heard it will start to say, 'Yeah, we grew up in a mall and we liked it' "; **movies Byrne saw:** E-mail from Mary Clarke; **New Year's Eve concert:** Ken Emerson wrote in the *NYT* (1/2/79) that David Byrne was both "polished" and "burnt out" on the Beacon stage. Emerson was particularly taken with "Martina Weymouth," writing, "Where she used to seem to be demurely trying to be one of the boys, now she asserted herself not only musically, but also by wearing a vivid magenta dress over flaming orange jeans."

15: Hoovering

Conversations: TW, JH; Printed Sources: Alan Platt, "Third Degree Byrne," *Soho Weekly News*, 8/23/79; Galen Brandt, "Talking Heads," *TP*, 11/79; **Seymour Stein's sexuality:** Conversations: CF, TW, DB, Mary Clarke; Printed Sources: Legs McNeil's *Please Kill Me* history; Angela Bowie with Patric Carr, *Backstage Passes: Life on the Wild Side with David Bowie* (New York: G. P. Putnam's Sons, 1993); ***American Bandstand:*** Conversations: TW, DB; Printed Sources: Steven D. Stark, *Glued to the Set: The 60 Television Shows and Events That Made Us Who We Are Today* (New York: The Free Press, 1997); Note: All television data checked against Alex McNeil's *Total Television: A Comprehensive Guide to Programming from 1948 to the Present*, 3rd ed. (New York: Penguin, 1991); **doing the dishes:** Tina often complained that Chris just let dishes stack up; **chords in "Heaven":** All musical information from conversations with Paul Zollo, author of *Songwriters on Songwriting: Expanded Edition* (New York: Da Capo Press, 1997): **Harrison in relation to Byrne's songwriting:** *How did Harrison's addition to the band effect your songwriting?* "My writing didn't change immediately, but sure, I realized I had a larger, more extensive sound palette to work with—so I began to write with that in mind. These changes in writing probably didn't start to show up till the second album, and then only on a couple of songs, as much of that album was material we had been performing live for awhile. But from then on it was obvious that with the addition of Jerry we became a real 'band' as opposed to a sketch for the idea of a band"; **singing styles:** Conversation: DB; Printed Sources: Scott Cohen, "Eno," Stephen Demorest [unidentified and undated magazine clipping]; "The

372

Discreet Charm of Brian Eno" [unidentified magazine clipping], 6/78; Calvin Ahlgren, Robert Walsh, "Mr. Zoon," *Interview*, 6/89.

16: Fear of Music

Conversations: DB, JH, TW, Ken Kushnick, Seymour Stein, Mary Clarke, Mark Kehoe; Printed Sources: John Rockwell, "Talking Heads and B-52's Finally Get Together in Concert," *NYT*, 8/13/79; "Talking Heads Strikes Again," *NYT*, 8/?/79; **Drugs:** Conversations: DB, TW, Linda Stein; Printed Source: Liner notes to *Sand in the Vaseline*. (In an article in *TP*, 5/81, Eno said, "There's no point in saying, 'I don't have an idea today, so I'll just do some drugs.' You should stay alert for the moment when a number of things are just ready to collide with one another."); **Timothy Leary's dead . . . :** On the Talking Heads official Website appears an undated interview of Timothy Leary by David Byrne apparently conducted in the early 1990s. Ironically, the two *do not* discuss drugs. They do have this exchange: TL: "You said . . . that you're gradually emerging from racism. Do you want to comment on that?" DB: "After years of telling myself, 'I'm not a racist, I'm a liberal, I'm free-thinking,' I started to acknowledge that I have these reactions that I'm not aware of, that I didn't look at before, things that have been bred into me, not necessarily by my parents—maybe by society, by the system, by television—and that's a real job to get rid of it. You can't just blissfully say, 'Everybody's equal, everybody's nice.' The conditioning is so powerful that you have to work all the time." TL: "It's invisible; racism is the water through which we swim." DB: "And you have to tread water to stay up there; otherwise you're in it. You have to go against the flow to rise above it. . . . I'm trying to deal with it, but it's not going to happen overnight. It's not something you can announce to yourself and all of a sudden you're clean and pure"; **Tina on her sister Laura:** "Laura was a brilliant girl. She could have gone to Harvard, but she wanted to split home as soon as possible. She should have waited. Another year, she would have gone to Harvard. Instead, she went to some little college in upstate New York . . . film school. . . . Back then she was a playgirl." **Sony Tape Recorder:** Sources: Genryu: SONY 40th Anniversary, 1986, Management Newsletter (Tokyo: Dai Nippon Printing Co., 1986); "Sony Founder, Hospitalized," *NYT*, 12/3/93; **Dada:** Source: Ruth Brandon, *Surreal Lives: The Surrealists 1917–1945* (New York: Grove Press, 1999); **Chris Frantz in Hawaii:** According to Jerome Davis, some kid approached Chris on the beach in Maui and offered to share a joint. The drummer smiled and said, "Sure." Chris then ended up getting mugged. Later in California, Hawaii Five-O notified him to say that they nabbed the kid when he tried to use the drummer's American Express card; **Byrne getting robbed:** David doesn't remember exactly when he was robbed. After much detective work, I deduced it was the summer of '79; **Mudd Club history:** Printed Sources: Anthony Haden-Guest, *The Last Party: Studio 54, Disco, and the Culture of the Night* (New York: William Morrow, 1997); Hoban's biography on Basquiat; JH on Mudd: "I thought the social life was really fun in the 1980s. Mainly downtown—the Mudd Club. It was a small club that had a hip crowd really late at night. In that time period, I was in the go-to-bed-at-five-in-the-morning phase"; **$9.75 a square yard:** Source: Suzanne Slesin, "Homage to the Ultimate Late '50's Backyard," *NYT*, 8/16/79; **Why did Belew live in Springfield?:** "Springfield, Illinois, is kind of a wacky place to live," he said. "The whole collection of people that I had befriended in Nashville moved to Springfield, Illinois. When I came off the David Bowie tour, I was looking for another place to live because I had no reason to stay in Nashville. My friend,

'RD,' said, 'Well, we got a studio and everything—why don't you come and take up residence here?' As awkward as it seemed, it really was a good decision at the time because it allowed me to do a lot of preparation toward making my own record"; **a Czech reporter:** <u>Source</u>: TW. She claimed that David later told Gary Kurfirst that he was going to quit Talking Heads, and Kurfirst should just manage him. Gary apparently talked him out of it. "Gary didn't tell us until later. He didn't want to break up the band. He knew David wouldn't succeed without us." David Byrne denies this happened. Gary Kurfirst just passed on the question.

17: Remain in Light

<u>Conversations</u>: DB, TW, JH, John Rockwell, Seymour Stein, Adrian Belew; <u>Printed Sources</u>: *Sand in the Vaseline* booklet; John Rockwell, "New Territory for the Talking Heads," *NYT*, 10/5/80; Ira Mayer, "10 Heads Better Than 4," *NYP*, 8/28/80; "Rock Music: Talking Heads with the Accent of Africa," *NYT*, 10/30/80; Clint Roswell, "The Talking—and Listening—Heads," *NYDN*, 10/30/80; James Kaplan, *Esquire*, 1/86; John Miller Chernoff, *African Rhythm and African Sensibility* (Chicago: The University of Chicago Press, 1979); **Beuys's fat and felt:** <u>Source</u>: Benjamin H. D. Buchloh, "Beuys: The Twilight of the Idol," *AF*, 1/80; **Byrne drifting into things:** Chris and Tina never required David to account for his whereabouts—thus David felt free to pursue other recording projects. "I just drifted into things, instead of comin' to the band and telling them," he said. "It was all left really vague. I just disappeared with no particular day comin' back. The same way with *The Catherine Wheel*. I just started doing a project. That took its toll." Byrne's sister, Celia, reveals that her brother's drifting is likely an extension of his upbringing. "Some families are very close," she said. "They do everything together. They travel together. Talk to each other every day. That's not us. It never was. We're both independent, and I think our parents maybe taught us to be overly independent in some ways. There were times when we wanted more guidance, but our parents were, 'Nope, you've got to decide for yourself. That's your decision. We're not saying anything.' So independence was always pushed as the ideal." **Jerry making records:** <u>Conversations</u>: JH, Nona Hendryx; **voudun:** "Voudun, not voodoo, is the respectful way to refer to this much-maligned African-rooted religion," wrote Robert Farris Thompson, professor of African and Afro-American art at Yale University, in *RS*, 4/21/88; **David's dream:** <u>Source</u>: TW; **details about Jon Hassell:** <u>Conversation</u>: DB; <u>Printed Sources</u>: Frederic Joignot and JeanPierre Lentin, "Musical Explorers in Africa," *Actuel*, 12/81; David Toop, *Ocean of Sound: Aether Talk, Ambient Sound and Imaginary Worlds* (New York: Serpent's Tail, 1996); **Byrne and the Great Mother:** "The world moves on a woman's hips . . ." *Does Byrne remember where he was when that great line came to him?* "No. Some words were written in California and some in NYC. . . . I do know that many of the lines in that song were inspired by having read Robert Farris Thompson's *African Art in Motion*. I included this book in the 'bibliography' section of the press release for this record—a pretty damned pretentious thing to do [including a bibliography] and one which made everyone think it was an African record. It was actually a psychedelic funk record. (I got to know Dr. Bob later on. Jonathan Demme and I are making a film about him this year.)"; **Byrne on God:** <u>Conversation</u>: DB; <u>Printed Source</u>: Robert Farris Thompson, *Macleans*, 6/13/83; **Tibor Kalman:** <u>Printed Sources</u>: Liz Farrelly, *tibor kalman design and undersign* (New York: Watson-Guptill Publications, 1998); Peter Hall and Michael Bierut, editors, *Tibor Kalman: Perverse Optimist* (New York: Princeton Architectural Press, 1998); Steven Heller, "Tibor Kalman, 'Bad Boy'

of Graphic Design, 49, Dies," *NYT*, 5/5/99; **Jon Hassell upset?:** Whatever misgivings Hassell had about the Byrne/Eno project in California, he showed up at the New York *Remain in Light* sessions. Afterward, the three men went to some carnival in Brooklyn. Unfortunately, Byrne was again afflicted by the demonic pattern of writer's block being followed by robbery—"They jumped me," Byrne said. "They put me in a choke hold and lifted my wallet—it was probably sticking out of my pocket. Jon and Brian and I chased the guys and they eventually threw the wallet toward us somewhere near Grand Army Plaza. . . . It was now empty of cash." **Chris and Tina designing the cover:** <u>Source</u>: TW; **Eno's alleged stage fright (A):** Seymour told me that Tina phoned him up in a panic: "She was worried about Eno telling David that really great artists don't have to tour—'If people make good records, people will buy them.' I don't hold to that philosophy. I remember calling Gary Kurfirst and saying to him, 'I'm a little concerned about this.' He told me not to worry." **Eno's alleged stage fright (B):** Nona Hendryx: "Eno might have said, 'The old mold of artist write/record/tour syndrome is done with.' He might have seen the future of video and there being no need to tour"; **Expanded Heads:** <u>Conversations</u>: DB, JH, Nona Hendryx, Bernie Worrell, Seymour Stein, Ken Kushnik; **my marching band analogy:** Songwriter Paul Zollo thinks my metaphor is concise. But David Byrne adds, "Well, usually the dancers who are following the music choose one rhythm to hold them all together . . . but different body parts—feet, butts, arms—may be moving to different, interior rhythms. It's part of so much North American and Latin music now that we take it for granted, but you can hear it in James Brown easily, or in the implied subrhythms in a lot of funk"; **Rising Moon:** <u>Conversations</u>: JH, Ken Kushnik, Bernie Worrell; **doctored credits:** TW told me, "David went to the printer and took our names off. He had to do it in cahoots with Tibor"; **Tina reauditioning for band:** TW: "It had nothing to do with Seymour. It had to do with David's paranoia. David made me reaudition time and time again. Anytime David felt insecure I was his whipping boy. Everytime he couldn't come up with something he'd beat me up about it. My God, if it were really true. I had to go through the motions of an audition, but it was a complete joke. The whole time it was so painful for me. It was like a mock trial. I had to do it over and over again. . . . I'm going to become a hysterical woman if you keep me running these complete patterns over and over again." *When David Byrne was asked about Tina reauditioning, he looked quizzical and said:* "Tina had to reaudition? I don't remember that. You mean Seymour said, 'I don't think she's good enough?'" *No. You made her reaudition.* "I don't remember that. That sounds like a Tina story to me. What a horrible tyrant I was. At some point I was a tyrant, but I don't think I did that. I may have asked, 'Are you sure you want to do this? We're getting a road here and it looks like it's going to go for a ways. Are you sure you want to do it? Reconsider things.'"

375

18: Expanded Heads

<u>Conversations</u>: DB, JH, TW, CF, Nona Hendryx, Bernie Worrell, Adrian Belew; **John Lennon's death:** Personal observations; <u>Conversation</u>: Adrian Belew; **Eno in Ghana:** *MM*, 2/14/80; *TP*, 5/81; **Adrian Belew on Gary Kurfirst:** "He and I never hit it off great. . . . I always thought Gary Kurfirst was a little hard to pin down. I never knew just exactly how honest, straight-forward he was as a manager, but I had to respect the fact that he surely got a lot of things done for a lot of people. . ." **Gary Kurfirst on Belew joining Talking Heads:** "I don't think Tina had the right to ask him. . . . Maybe Adrian is getting mixed up about joining the tour as a guitar player. I never heard that anybody was thinking of asking

Adrian to become a full-blooded member of Talking Heads. I can't believe that it's true. . . . [*Jerry confirms what Adrian says.*] I'm not saying Adrian is not telling the truth, because Tina may have said this to him. You get drunk one night and you say, 'Why don't you join our band?' You know, and those things happen all the time between musicians, but it never gets down to real business." **Basquiat/John Lurie/pancakes:** In December 1980 Glenn O'Brien selected Basquiat to play a starving downtown artist in his film *New York Beat*. In *King for a Decade: Jean-Michel Basquiat,* edited by Taka Kawachi (Japan: Korinsha Press, 1997), perennial downtown citizen John Lurie is interviewed and claims that he was going to be in the film as well, but walked after O'Brien demanded Lurie's African-American girlfriend "make him some pancakes." According to Mary Clarke, Lurie's girlfriend was none other than Lisa S.—the chick David Byrne was involved with in Paris two years before; **Belew on: Byrne, Tina and Zappa and Bowie:** <u>Source</u>: Adrian Belew.

19: *Twyla Tharp*

Twyla Tharp: <u>Conversations</u>: DB, TW; <u>Primary Printed Source</u>: Tharp's engrossing autobiography *Push Comes to Shove* (New York: Bantam, 1992). I asked Byrne if Tharp sent him a manuscript of the book before it was published: "No. I wondered if she was going to say something about me in there. I thought the things she said were discreet and even-tempered. Very understanding. Because our relationship crossed over the line from professional into personal. That's just sometimes inevitable. And sometimes it's not always good." <u>Other Printed Sources</u>: Angela Taylor, "It's Called the 'Wedge' and It Goes to Their Heads," *NYT*, 4/2/76; "The Dorothy Do," *Time*, 4/76; William E. Geist, "Magoos: Last Bastion," *NYT*, 3/20/85; France Herridge, *NYP*, 2/4/69; Clive Barnes, *NYT*, 11/1/66 and 2/16/69; "Supercool Twyla Tharp Is Hot Stuff" (Barne's castration mention), *NYT*, 4/4/76; Deborah Jowitt, *NYT Magazine*, 12/4/76; Anna Kisselgoff, *NYT*, 11/17/76; Barbara Rows, *People*, 4/4/77; John Rockwell, *NYT*, 5/7/77; Linda Winter, *NYDN*, 9/24/81; Steven Henry Madoff, *CSM*, 4/6/84; Margo Jefferson, *NYT Book Review*, 12/13/92; Sasha Anawalt, *The Joffrey Ballet: Robert Joffrey and the Making of an American Dance Company* (New York: Scribner, 1996); **Dolly Parton:** John Rockwell, "Rock Is Edging into Video," *NYT*, 7/20/79.

20: *Cheaper Than Dancing Lessons*

<u>Conversations</u>: DB, TW, Seymour Stein; <u>Printed Sources</u>: Jack Anderson, "Dance: from the Sidewalks of Los Angeles," *NYT*, 10/24/81; Dawn Seay, "Pom-Pom and Circumstances Turn Choreographer Toni Basil into an Overnight Pop Star," *People*, 1/10/83; Chrysalis press release biography, 1984; **Byrne on Basil:** "Most people think Michael Jackson invented the moonwalk. Hell, his whole dance style was from those Electric Boogaloo guys, those guys Toni Basil was working with—Poppin' Pete, Shabadoo, a few others"; **Miming "Mustang Sally":** <u>Source</u>: Gus Van Sant; **"the Liberace of televangelists":** <u>Source</u>: Howell's book on David Byrne.

21: *My Life in the Bush of Ghosts*

<u>Conversation</u>: DB; <u>Printed Sources</u>: John Orme, "Brian Eno Explains 'My Life in the Bush of Ghosts,' " *MM*, 2/14/81; Kurt Loder, "Squawking Heads: Byrne and Eno in the Bush of

Ghosts," *RS*, 4/5/81; Anne Ominous (pseudonym of Lucy R. Lippard), "Sex and Death and Shock and Schlock: A Long Review of the Times Square Show," *AF*, 10/80; Axel Gross, "Brian Eno: Freedom Without Form Isn't Freedom," *Aquarian Weekly*, 3/25/81; In *Bat Chain Puller: Rock & Roll in the Age of Celebrity* (New York: St. Martin's Press, 1990), Kurt Loder reports that at one point Eno took the basic *Ghosts* tracks to L.A. and played them for members of the band Tubes, and their encouragement influenced the great domed one to continue work on the project; **found instruments:** Eno has a lifelong tradition of using found instruments. Young Eno's (age seventeen) first recording was a slowed-down tape of a metal lamp stand being struck while someone recited poetry (*LAT*, 9/27/92); **Post-Christian:** Harold Blood invented this term in his discussion of *Macbeth* in *Shakespeare: The Invention of the Human* (New York: Riverhead Books, 1998); **Jean-Michael Basquiat:** Conversation: DB; Printed Sources: Hoban's biography and Kawachi's *King for a Decade* were both well-thumbed. **"Slouching Toward Avenue D":** *Art in America*, 6/84; **Lofts in Soho:** John Rockwell says: "There are two kinds of lofts in New York. One that is below the roof line of the adjacent building and one that is above. The difference is that the ones that are above the adjacent rooftops can have windows on the long sides. Those below cannot. Often lofts only had light in the front. My loft on Broome Street has light in the back. It has no windows on the side." As for Byrne's loft, Byrne wrote me: "It had windows on Greene and Houston, so there was a lot of light, but not much of a view." **Tina's loft:** Source: TW (their loft was on West Broadway between Prince and Spring); **Jerry Harrison in Milwaukee:** Conversation: JH; Printed Source: *Musician*, 11/85; **TW on *My Life in the Bush of Ghosts:*** Tina entered the www.talking-heads.net chatroom on Monday, October 26 (no year given). She fielded this question from "Jamie": *Tina, was Brian Eno like Yoko Ono—a "bad influence" that pulled DB and the rest of the band apart?* "Eno is blamed by our manager for the breakup of the band," Tina answered. "But Chris and I are still very friendly with him. It was our idea for him to produce us, and I still think he was great. But something happened to DB when he and Eno went in to do *Bush of Ghosts*. . . . Did you know that Holget Czukay from Can was the inventor of *Bush of Ghosts*? He felt really ripped off when DB and Eno did that to him."

22: Dysfunctional Family Dance

Conversations: DB, JH, John Chernoff; Printed Source: James George Frazer, *The Golden Bough* (New York: Macmillan, 1922); **The structure of female "gut":** I asked Byrne if Tharp's comment was true. He shrugged. "The bass/guts theory might be accurate. I dunno."

23: The Genius of Tina

Conversations: TW, CF, Gary Kurfirst, Adrian Belew.

24: Pagan TV Babies

Conversations: DB, TW, JH; Printed Sources: Robert Palmer, "A 'Talking Head' Collaborates with Twyla Tharp," *NYT*, 9/20/81; "After Solos, the Heads Are Together Again," *NYT*, 11/18/81; Anna Kisselgoff, "Dance: Twyla Tharp's New 'Wheel,'" *NYT*, 9/23/81; **MTV information:** Sources: Amy Harmon, "A Bridge Builder for Corporate

Culture," *NYT*, 1/12/00; Jack Banks, *Monopoly Television: MTV's Quest to Control the Music* (Boulder, Colo.: Westview Press, 1996); David Buxton, *The Avengers to Miami Vice: Form and Ideology in Television Series* (New York: Manchester University Press, 1990); R. Serge Denisoff, *Inside MTV* (New Brunswick, N.J.: Transaction Publishers, 1991); Andrew Goodwin, *Dancing in the Distraction Factory: Music Television and Popular Culture* (Minneapolis: University of Minnesota Press, 1987); Scott Nance, *Music You Can See: The MTV Story* (Las Vegas: Pioneer Books, 1993); Tom McGrath, *MTV: The Making of a Revolution* (Philadelphia: Running Press, 1996); **Frog reporter:** Source: Frederic Joignot, JeanPierre Lentin, "Musical Explorers in Africa," *Actuel*, 12/81; **B-52's:** David Byrne's production of the B-52's album had been a disaster. When Gary Kurfirst first heard the tapes, his stomach bottomed out. "I expected more. I expected better. But at the end of the day, it just wasn't there." He felt perhaps six of the ten tracks were usable. They'd release an EP, *Mesopotamia*, instead of an LP; **The Tharp Sisters at Studio 54:** Sources: "Notes on People," *NYT*, 10/25/81; *NYP*, Page Six, 10/10/81.

Book Three: The Big Suit

Sherrie Levine quote: Source: *Art Talk: The Early 80s*, edited by Jeanne Siegel (New York: Da Capo Press, 1988).

25: Speaking in Tongues

Conversations: DB, JH, TW, Adrian Belew, Bernie Worrell, Seymour Stein, Susan Sontag, Gary Kurfirst; Printed Sources: E-mail from Adelle Lutz; Lynn Van Matre, "Rock Eccentric Brian Eno Likes High Finance . . . ," *Chicago Tribune*, 4/25/82; *Entertainment Weekly*, 12/28/00; Norman King, *Madonna: The Book* (New York: William Morrow, 1991); *Madonna: The Rolling Stone Files* (New York: Hyperion, 1997); Marc Silag, "David Byrne in the Studio," *Musician*, 4/82; Robert Palmer, "Talking Heads Sum Up Sounds of 5-Year Career," *NYT*, 4/14/82; Rob Baker, "A Talking Head Speaks Out," *NYDN*, 8/15/82; Christopher Connelly's article in *RS*, 10/27/83; Robert Palmer, " 'Speaking in Tongues' Proves New Hit for Talking Heads," *NYT*, 6/22/83; John Rockwell, "Rock-and-Roll: Talking Heads in Forest Hills," *NYT*, 8/21/83; Jim Fusilli, "Talking Heads Speak in Tongues and Everyone Listens," *WSJ*, 9/2/83; Gregory Isola, "Tina Weymouth Heads Up," *Bass Player*, sometime in '96 . **"Turn of the Screw":** A similar controversy concerning credits à la Tina/Chris and Adrian Belew occurred between Paul Simon and the L.A. Mexican-American group Los Lobos. According to Paul Zollo, Paul Simon created the *Graceland* tracks by having musicians (mostly African players, and for one track, Los Lobos) just jam and come up with riffs. Simon then put a melody and lyrics (traditionally what the songwriter is credited with creating) over each of the tracks. Although the African tracks and the Los Lobos track were created the same way, Simon only gave songwriting credit to the African players, a slight that made the members of Los Lobos feel like "a National Geographic animal studied in the wild by Paul Simon." After they made their complaint public through Zollo, Paul Simon accosted the writer and said, "Los Lobos shouldn't have said that. I paid them triple-scale. I got them national exposure." Apparently songwriting credits are often based on charity and whim; **Robert Longo:** Sources: Hal Foster, "The Art of Spectacle," *Art in America*, 4/83; Carter Ratcliff, "Robert Longo," *Interview*, 4/83

(This interview deftly sums up the scene in '83. Longo said, "The thing that's so great about the Odeon [located in downtown Manhattan] is that when it first opened, they accommodated artists, so you always felt comfortable there. . . . Two friends of mine, rock and rollers, were walking through the door of the Odeon . . . and all of a sudden these limos pulled up and all these people in fur coats started getting out. One of the rock and rollers turns to the other and says something to the effect of, 'We're never going to get in.' The bouncer turned away the people in mink [and let the rock 'n' rollers in]"); Michael Brenson, "Artists Grapple with New Realities, *NYT*, 5/15/83; Paul Gardner, "Longo: Making Art for Brave Eyes," *ARTnews*, 5/85; Michael Small, "Already a Big Man on Canvas, Robert Longo Goes Multimedia," *People*, 11/10/86; Richard Price, introduction and interview, *Robert Longo: Men in the Cities* (New York: Harry Abrams, 1986); Howard N. Fox, *Robert Longo* (New York: Rizzoli, 1989); **George Clinton scaring the child out of Tina:** Conversation: Bernie Worrell. Worrell has no better sense of Tom Tom Club history than Tina. "After George touched her, the next day she had Robin," he told me. "After that, they *started* [italics mine] Tom Tom Club. And the rest is history." **Adelle Lutz information:** Sources: Caroline Rennolds Milbank, "Tina Chow in Balenciaga," *Interview*, 6/86; Nicholas Colerdige, "Chow Bella," undated Xerox of interview; **Robert Rauschenberg:** Conversation: JH; Printed Sources: Leo Steinberg, *Encounters with Rauschenberg* (Chicago: University of Chicago Press, 2000); Barbara Rose, *Rauschenberg* (New York: Vintage Books, 1987); **David Byrne on sumo wrestling:** "For every sumo wrestling match, at least half the time is spent in Shinto ritual. The actual wrestling is just *boom boom boom boom boom* it's over—fifteen seconds or so. But there is all this elaborate ritual beforehand—the salt being thrown up in the air. The priest coming in with this huge conical hat. The wrestling match is just the entertainment portion of the ritual. . . . Sumo is also a dining experience. You sit on the floor in little stalls with teeny tiny mats and order all kinds of food. Eel. And rice. It's not just beer and popcorn." **Pantages theaters:** Sources: Charles Moore, Peter Becker, Regula Campbell, *The City Observed: Los Angeles* (New York: Vintage Books, 1984); Leonard and Dale Pitt, *Los Angeles A to Z: An Encyclopedia of the City and County* (Los Angeles: University of California Press, 1997); Patrick McGrew and Robert Julian, *Landmarks of Los Angeles* (New York: Harry Abrams, 1994).

26: Stop Making Sense

Conversations: DB, JH, TW, Bernie Worrell; Printed Sources: E-mail from Adelle Lutz; Jack Kroll, "A Strong Dash of the Showman," *Newsweek*, 10/6/86; John Rockwell, "Pageant: Portion of Robert Wilson's 'Civil Wars,'" *NYT*, 4/29/84; Jim Farber, ". . . talk up their film . . ." [Xerox cut off headline] *NYDN*, 10/14/84; **"A spaniel on LSA":** Pam Lambert, "A Rock Film That's Heads Above the Rest," *WSJ*, 1/15/85; Other Sources: DVD alternate soundtrack to *Stop Making Sense*.

27: We Begin Bombing in Five Minutes

Conversations: DB, JH, TW, Mark Kehoe, Jamie Dalglish, Philip Glass, Robert Wilson, Neal Wiseman; Printed Sources: Ken Emerson's cover profile in *NYT Magazine*, 5/5/85; *Sand in the Vaseline* booklet, 1992; Peter Biskin, *Easy Riders, Raging Bulls: How the Sex-Drugs-and-Rock 'n' Roll Generation Saved Hollywood* (New York: Simon & Schuster, 1998); **Longo/**

Basquiat: <u>Sources</u>: Jeanne Siegel's *Art Talk*; Kim Foltz and Maggie Malone, "Golden Paintbushes," *Newsweek*, 10/15/84; Grace Glueck, "The Very Timely Art of Robert Longo," *NYT*, 3/10/85; **Was David Byrne buddies with Longo?** "Not really," he said. "I went over to his house-slash-studio a couple times. It was more because he had originally used an image from *Stop Making Sense* in one of his pieces. And drawing. So he invited us over. I think we went out once. And that was about it." **Ronald Reagan's bomb:** <u>Conversation</u>: JH. "I hated Reagan's gutting of people's civil rights," Harrison said. "I thought everything he stood for was awful. They say what a great job he did with the economy. He drove us into debt. He bankrupted the Soviet Union. He almost bankrupted us as well. . . . You know it's a very interesting thing—the people who seem the most inflexible can almost create real change. I found the whole Contra Irangate just America becoming a big play. It's not something I'm very proud of"; <u>Printed Source</u>: Greil Marcus *VV* quote is from an undated Xerox; **Nan Graham runs into David Byrne:** <u>Source</u>: *Publishers Weekly*, 2/7/86; *New York*, 9/8/86.

28: Little Creatures

<u>Conversations</u>: DB, JH; <u>Printed Sources</u>: Howard Finster (as told to Tom Patterson), *Howard Finster, Stranger from Another World: Man of Visions Now on This Earth* (New York: Abbeville Press, 1989); Robert Peacock with Annibel Jenkins, *Paradise Garden: A Trip Through Howard Finster's Visionary World* (San Francisco: Chronicle Books, 1996); *Sand in the Vaseline* booklet; David Byrne/Maira Kalman, *Stay Up Late* (New York: Viking Kestrel, 1987); Philip Norman, *Shout! The Beatles in Their Generation* (New York: Simon & Schuster, 1981); Carter Ratcliff, "David Byrne and the Modern Self: 'How Do I Word This?' " *AF*, 5/85; "Questions and Answers with Talking Heads," Sire press information; John Rockwell, "The Talking Heads Produce an Unabashed Pop Album," *NYT*, 7/14/85; Jay Cocks, "The Heads Are Rolling," *Time*, 9/2/85; *RS*, 4/11/85; Scott Isler, "Talking Heads: To Be or Not to Be," *Musician*, 11/85.

29: True Stories from the Mid-Eighties

<u>Conversations</u>: DB, JH, Lee Blake, Ann Keating, Gus Van Sant, Edward Pressman; <u>Printed Sources</u>: Dick Hebdige, *Hiding in the Light* (New York: Routledge, 1996); Thomas Lawson, "Toward Another Laocoon or, The Snake Pit," *AF*, 3/86; Jack Kroll, "The Eyes of Virgil Are Upon You," *Newsweek*, 10/27/86; Janet Maslin, "David Byrne in 'True Stories,' " *NYT*, 10/4/86; Michiko Kakutani, "David Byrne Turns His Head to Movies,"*NYT*, 10/5/86; Robert Ebert, "David Byrne: A True Story," *NYP*, 11/10/86; Hillary DeVries, " 'Who, Me? A Renaissance Man?,' " *CSM*, 11/17/86; Michele Abruzzi, "Homage to Middle America," *Philadelphia Inquirer*, 11/18/86; Chip Brown, "True Stories of David Byrne," *WP*, 11/20/86; "David Byrne," *People*, 12/22/86: **one night in Texas . . . :** David Byrne and Ed Pressman are driving around looking at shopping malls. On a dark panhandle road, the fuses blow out in the rental car. It rolls to the shoulder. Remember that David Byrne's father once fixed a submarine with a coat hanger—see his son open the glove compartment and take out the car's manual and read it by flashlight. Within an hour, David Byrne has fixed the car and the two men tool back into Dallas; **David eating:** *one-inch squares*—Susan Shapiro, "A Head of His Time," *Daily News Magazine*, 9/28/86; *lining nuts along the spine of a leaf of lettuce—*

Adelle-Marie Stan, "Making Sense of Rock's Renaissance Man," *Ms.*, 9/86; *"Nobody eat it yet!"*—Phoebe Hoban, "Head Trip," *New York*, 9/8/86. **Other David Byrne eating stories:** Printed Sources: In Ron Givens's "Making Sense by Not Making Sense" (*Newsweek on Campus*, 4/85), David Byrne orders coffee, a Bloody Mary, a plate of cooked spinach, and slices of Muenster cheese. He then melts the cheese over the spinach and creates "a dish that looks like Martian baked Alaska." In James Kaplan's "Who Is David Byrne? What is David Byrne? Does David Byrne Matter? Yes" (*Esquire*, 1/86), Byrne is interviewed in a Japanese restaurant and is described ordering noodles, beer, sake, Scotch "as if he were trying on clothes. . . ." In Mark Muro's "David Byrne: Talking with the Head Head" (*NYT*, 9/21/86), Byrne enters Bar Lui in SoHo and shouts, "Big pizza!" Then this "sick figure . . . rips through his lunch like a feeding animal." Other Sources: Mark Kehoe remembers: "When we'd go out to eat at RISD, Byrne would always order a grilled cheese sandwich and a glass of water. I'd say to him, '*David*, we *have* money.' " Seymour Stein told me of taking David to expensive restaurants where the young man would impulsively stick discarded bread and other food from other tables into his pockets. I, myself, ate with David Byrne at the Ear Inn in New York City one Saturday in late summer. He had catfish and customized his arugula and watercress salad—he asked the waitress to hold the turkey and eggs in a voice reminiscent of the preacher cadence of "Once in a Lifetime"—"You may find yourself living in a shotgun shack . . . *eating arugula and catfish* . . ."); *Time* **magazine cover:** Conversation: DB; Printed Source: *CSM*, 12/17/86; John K. Jessup, editor, *Henry Luce: The Idea of Henry Luce* (New York: Atheneum, 1969); **Byrne's alternative covers:** Byrne submitted two other covers. One was a cubist portrait that divided his face up more abstractly into large planes with alternating yellow and violet rectangles. The other was a self-portrait of the artist's face in a mirror printed with the *Time* magazine logo; **Sneaking in the Time Life Building:** There will be readers in places far from Manhattan who may think it's possible for a man to sneak into the *Time* magazine offices. I've had reason to be in the Time/Life Building for twenty years (Little, Brown publishers, HBO, and Book of the Month Club are all housed there). It would be easier sneaking into a bank afterhours. . . . **Tina's dream:** Source: David Handelman, "Are Four Heads Better Than One?" *RS*, 1/15/87; **Talking Heads at the drive-in:** David's drive-in idea went nowhere because "drive-ins don't have any kind of sound system other those little crappy speakers. Or you tune to an FM station. . . ." **Andy Warhol, piss paintings and death of:** Sources: Paul Taylor, *After Andy: SoHo in the Eighties* (Melbourne, Australia: Schwartz City, 1995); Paul Alexander, *Death and Disaster: The Rise of the Warhol Empire and the Race for Andy's Millions* (New York: Villard Books, 1994).

30: Voodoo Days

Conversations: DB, JH, TW, Mary Clarke, Ed Pressman, Gary Kurfirst, John Chernoff, Robert Wilson; Printed Sources: Alan Aldridge, editor, *The Beatles Illustrated Lyrics* (New York: Black Dog & Leventhal Publishers, first published 1969); Susan Dentzer, et al, "Is the Party Almost Over?" *Newsweek*, 10/26/87; David Handelman, "Are Four Heads Better Than One?" *RS*, 1/15/87; Jon Pareles, ". . . the 80's, Money Can Buy Love" [title missing on Xerox], *NYT*, 3/8/87; Pam Lambert, "New Music for Tiny Ears," *WSJ*, 11/4/87; Mark Jenkins, "The Naked Ego of Talking Heads," *WP*, 4/3/88; Hilton Als, "Tall Tales," *VV*, 5/31/88; Ron Givens, "Blame It on the Bossa Nova," *Newsweek*, 3/20/89; Richard Hilburn,

"Byrning Up the Music World (cont'd)," *LAT*, 10/8/89; Richard Cromelin, "Byrne Heads in New Direction with Latin Beat," *LAT*, 10/13/89; Stephen Holden, "David Byrne's Rhythms," *NYT*, 10/25/89; Jon Pareles, "Pop Musical Cultures Mined and Mingled," *NYT*, 10/22/89; "Dancing Along with David Byrne," *NYT*, circa 11/89; Janet Malcolm, "A Girl of the Zeitgeist," originally printed in 1986 and collected in *The Purloined Clinic* (New York: Knopf, 1992); **in Paris:** JH was telling the story about the delivery man whom the band assumed was a guitarist: "So we give him a guitar and he plays something that just doesn't go with anything anyone else is playing. One of us—I think it was Eno—says, 'I like what you're playing but I don't think it fits with the other music . . .'" *Eno wasn't at the Paris sessions, was he?* "No." *Do you realize you just made a Freudian slip and said, "Eno was there"?* "I meant Steve Lillywhite. . . . I don't know if saying *Eno* was Freudian . . ."; **Byrne getting married:** E-mail from Adelle Lutz; **Tina on David and his sister:** "Twyla Tharp said something about David Byrne being fascinated with my pregnancy. David was worried that he wouldn't get all the attention again. That's what 'Stay Up Late' is all about. It's about him revisiting his baby sister's birth. . . . Ever since his sister was born, he's been so jealous of other people getting attention. He hates his sister. He absolutely despises her"; **Celia Byrne** discounts Tina's view: "David was the only brother I knew. So, I mean, what am I supposed to tell him? 'Excuse me, I'd like to trade you in?' I mean, obviously I wanted somebody closer to my own age who I could play with. A nine-year-old boy doesn't necessarily play with a four-year-old girl. But we would take chairs and put them on their backs on the floor. Then put the dining room chairs on the floor in the back and under the table. Turn it into a rocket ship. He'd probably be the pilot. We had one pilot's helmet, and so we'd fight over that for a little bit. . . . In elementary school, I was doing this project on communication—you'd write something, and then you'd cut out a picture in a magazine. I knew what I wanted—a picture of primitive people communicating by beating on drums or logs, but we weren't allowed to cut up the *National Geographic*s. So David drew a picture of two people drumming back and forth for me. I can remember that"; **David Byrne in Germany:** <u>Conversation</u>: Frank Hentschker (an actor in *The Forest*); **Fly Records:** <u>Conversation</u>: JH; **David Byrne's Citroën:** Celia Byrne lived with her brother and Adelle in Los Angeles. "The car was part of my responsibilities when I was there," she said. "They'd call me from New York, and say, 'We're coming out.' They had two old cars, and I was supposed to charge up the batteries." *Is it true that your brother is a terrible driver?* "Yeah. He always accuses me of being a backseat driver when I'm with him. Driving was a terrifying experience when he was younger. More than one person has said this. But maybe living in L.A. got him on track. . . . I actually helped him learn to drive, because he didn't bother taking driver's ed in high school. When he was twenty-one, instead of getting a New York license, he came to Maryland because that would be easier. There was a high school near where we lived where you could practice your three-point turn and your parallel parking—stuff like that. So I took him back there, and taught him what I had learned in driver's ed"; **Voodoo details:** <u>Sources</u>: Maya Deren (foreword by Joseph Campbell), *Divine Horsemen: The Voodoo Gods of Haiti* (New York: Delta, 1972); Robert Farris Thompson, "David Byrne," *RS*, 4/21/88; "Talking Godheads," *RS*, 7/13/89; Luc Sante, "Byrne's Brazil," *Another View*, 7/89; John J. O'Connor, "Where Avant-Garde and Pop Meet," *NYT*, 7/5/89; **Byrne forgot the words:** <u>Source</u>: TW. I later asked JH about this. "I don't remember the details," he said quietly. "I'm sure Tina had a more vivid relationship." **Robert Longo:** <u>Conversation</u>: Artist/historian Mary Delahoyd; <u>Printed Sources</u>: Lynn Hirshberg, "The Four Bushmen of the Apocalypse," *Esquire*, 3/87; Roberta Smith, "Once a Wunderkind, Now Robert 'Long Ago'?," *NYT*, 10/29/89; William Wilson, "Robert Longo: Too Much Too Soon?" *LAT*, 10/1/89;

Book Four: Shrunken Heads

Tina and Chris quotes: <u>Conversation</u>: TW, CF.

31: Wicked Little Doll

<u>Conversations</u>: DB, TW, JH, CF, Gary Kurfirst, Lee Blake, Seymour Stein, John Rockwell; <u>Printed Sources</u>: Peter Castro, "Sleep Talk," *People*, 8/6/90; Page Six, "David Byrne's Baby Daughter . . . ," *NYP*, 9/5/90; "Very Moving . . . ," *NYP*, 11/29/90; "Occasional Talking Head David Byrne, Along with His Wife . . . ," *People*, 11/11/91; Jon Pareles, "David Byrne Finds a Groove Closer to Home," *NYT*, 3/22/92; "David Byrne Marks Another Phase Ended," *NYT*, 2/2/94; "David Byrne Is Still Not Decided," *NYT*, 6/18/94; Jim Sulivan, "Talking Byrne," *Boston Globe*, 8/14/92; Peter Watrous, "David Byrne Tries to Stop Making a Spectacle of Himself," *NYT*, 6/19/92; Chris Willman, "Byrne-ing Down the Wiltern," *LAT*, 9/16/92; Ken Tucker, "For David Byrne There's Joyousness in Melancholy," *NYT*, 6/19/94; Jeff Salamon, "Making Fuzzy Wuzzy," *VV*, 6/28/94; Jancee Dunn, "David Byrne," *RS*, 8/11/94; "David Byrne's Luaka Bop," *Inside Borders* catalog (undated); Marty Lipp, "David Byrne: Luaka Bopper," *Rhythm*, 1/99; David Byrne, "I Hate World Music," *NYT*, 10/3/99; Vassilis Stathopoulos, "What's This Green Button?," undated interview on www.talking-heads.net. **"Sleep Angel":** Harrison was justifiably proud of this piece. "Beautiful song don't you think?" **"Lifetime Piling Up" video:** The only video from *Sand in the Vaseline*, this four-minute piece was a compilation of previous videos; **poo poo jokes:** John Leland, *Time*, 4/9/92; **death of Tina Chow:** <u>Conversations</u>: DB, Linda Stein; <u>Printed Sources</u>: Jill Newman and Constance C.R. White, "Tina Chow, 41, Won Acclaim as a Designer of Jewelry," *Women's Wear Daily*, 2/2/92; Liz Smith, "A Giant Do for Brooke," *New York Newsday*, 2/23/92; Robert Hilburn, "Something from the Heart," *LAT*, 6/1/94; Timothy White, "David Byrne: Songs of a Self-Made Man," interview contained in *Music to My Ears: The Billboard Essays* (New York: Owl Books, 1997); Jerry Adler and Tara Weingarten, "Performance Cuisine," *Newsweek*, 8/16/99; **Byrne and the Devil:** <u>Conversation</u>: DB; **court case:** Craig Rosen, "Byrne Goes Head to Head in Suit with Ex-Bandmates," *Billboard*, 9/2/96; **David Byrne's refrigerator:** The *Vanity Fair* photo is reproduced and referred to in a 1997 interview with Christa Wessel on www.talking-heads.net; **Byrne on marriage:** *How has marriage changed your life?* "It's wonderful, but I'm also consistently conflicted about it. I see myself as this free creative spirit and my image of married life was something boring and conservative, so all those mental pictures are in conflict." **Harrison's house:** <u>Conversation</u>: JH; <u>Printed Source</u>: Elaine Louie, "In Redwoods, on the Far Western Fringe of SoHo," *NYT*, 1/21/99; **Tina's parting thoughts on the twentieth century:** "Talking Heads did some festivals where we played in front of huge crowds—you can't imagine having that much power over that many people. It seemed unnatural. It seemed anti-artistic. So when David said, 'I want to go on sabbatical,' that was fine. But then it got beyond what Jerry Harrison would describe as 'sensible.' We could all do solo things, but David thought that *Stop Making Sense* would do the job of touring for us. Or that recycling old records of ours would do the job of giving people what for us was an ongoing dialectic with

the end of the twentieth century. I thought Talking Heads was something bigger than all of us. We could have gone in the direction of the Grateful Dead—be a small-world model." **Tina Weymouth on writers:** "Writers are liars. That's why I say these [rock] books all lie. They're all wrong and they all lie. Because they're based on lies put out by David Byrne and other journalists. Music magazines are rubbish. You can't believe anything that you read. You don't have to believe me either. . . . You've got to be so careful. I watched what happened to Albert Goldman after his Elvis book. It's like Truman Capote. People won't talk to you. They won't trust you. Is that what you want to do with the rest of your life, David? It's sad . . ."; **Eskimo logic:** <u>Source</u>: Alan P. Merrian, *The Anthropology of Music* (Evanston, Ill.: Northwestern University Press, 1964); *Secrets of Elvis*, Yung Kim.

discography

Official Releases

This discography reflects the inconsistent vinyl designations of Side I/II, Side 1/2, and Side A/B.

"Love→Building on Fire"/"New Feeling" (Sire) *7-inch single*. Released early '77.

"Uh-Oh, Love Comes to Town"/"I Wish You Wouldn't Say That" (Sire) *7-inch single*. Released late August '77.

Talking Heads '77. Talking Heads (Sire). Released mid-September '77. Produced by Tony Bongiovi, Lance Quinn, and Talking Heads. All selections written by David Byrne except where indicated. (Side I) "Uh-Oh, Love Come to Town"; "New Feeling"; "Tentative Decisions"; "Happy Day"; "Who Is It"; "No Compassion." (Side II) "The Book I Read"; "Don't Worry About the Government"; "First Week/Last Week . . . Carefree"; "Psycho Killer" (David Byrne, Martina Weymouth, Christopher Frantz); "Pulled Up." (*7-inch single:* "Psycho Killer"/"Psycho Killer (acoustic)"—this is the version in which Bongiovi added strings.) **Notes:** No session musicians are credited on this record (such as the saxophonist on "First Week, Last Week/Carefree"), but Jerry Harrison reported that Bongiovi spent most of the recording budget on "some triple-scale players who were buddies of his."

More Songs About Buildings and Food. Talking Heads (Sire). Released mid-July '78. Produced by Brian Eno and Talking Heads. All selections written by David Byrne except where indicated. (Side I) "Thank You for Sending Me an Angel"; "With Our Love"; "The Good Thing"; "Warning Sign"; "The Girls Want to Be with the Girls"; "Found a Job." (Side II) "Artists Only" (David Byrne/Wayne Zieve); "I'm Not in Love"; "Stay Hungry" (David Byrne/Chris Frantz); "Take Me to the River" (Al Green/M. Hodges); "The Big Country." (*7-inch single:* "Take Me to the River"/"Thank You for Sending Me an Angel.") **Notes:** Mary

Clarke remembered hearing the demo pressing of *More Songs About Buildings and Food*. "That blew me away more than the first album. Eno did an amazing job. I was hearing songs that I already heard, but hearing them produced in this way they were still the same songs, but they were so fabulous."

Talking Heads Live on Tour. Talking Heads (Warner Bros.). Released to radio stations in '79. Recorded at the Agora in Cleveland on March 15, 1979. Only 600 copies were pressed. The band played: "The Big Country"; "Warning Sign"; "Artists Only"; "The Girls Want to Be with the Girls"; "The Good Thing"; "Electricity"; "New Feeling"; "Found a Job"; "Psycho Killer"; "Take Me to the River."

Fear of Music. Talking Heads (Sire). Released early August '79. Produced by Brian Eno and Talking Heads. All selections written by David Byrne except where indicated. (Side 1) "I Zimbra" (David Byrne, Brian Eno, Hugo Ball); "Mind"; "Paper"; "Cities"; "Life During Wartime"; "Memories Can't Wait." (Side 2) "Air"; "Heaven"; "Animals"; "Electric Guitar"; "Drugs." (*7-inch single:* "Life During Wartime"/"Electric Guitar.")

Remain in Light. Talking Heads (Sire). Released early October '80. Produced by Brian Eno. *On the vinyl release this note appeared:* "Selections written by David Byrne & Brian Eno except where indicated." (When any of the *Remain in Light* songs appear on either *The Name of This Band Is Talking Heads* or *Sand in the Vaseline*, the songwriting credits now read: "Written by David Byrne, Brian Eno, Chris Frantz, Jerry Harrison, and Tina Weymouth.") (Side 1) "Born Under Punches (The Heat Goes On)"; "Crosseyed and Painless"; "The Great Curve." (Side 2) "Once in a Lifetime"; "Houses in Motion" (David Byrne/Brian Eno/Jerry Harrison); "Seen and Not Seen"; "Listening Wind"; "The Overload" (David Byrne/Brian Eno/Jerry Harrison). (*7-inch single:* "Once in a Lifetime"/"Seen and Not Seen"; "Houses in Motion"/"The Overload.") **Notes:** Mitchell Cohen in his *Creem* review of this record, "Play That Funky Music White Boy," playfully called David Byrne and Brian Eno "the Leopold and Loeb of fascinatin' rhythm."

My Life in the Bush of Ghosts. Brian Eno and David Byrne (Sire). Released February '81. Produced by Brian Eno and David Byrne. **Notes:** Eno's website contains a curious mention that this record was delayed because Warner Bros. wanted *Remain in Light* to be released first. As absurd as the website claim seems (what about the trouble with the recording of Kathryn Kuhlman, Mr. Eno?), Seymour Stein said, "I don't think that's true, Warner delaying *My Life*. I couldn't swear to you, though. I would like to say this is preposterous, but you know I could see people being worried at Warner. . . ."

The Red and the Black. Jerry Harrison (Sire). Released early June '81. Produced by Jerry Harrison with Dave Jerden.

Tom Tom Club. Tom Tom Club (Sire). Released fall '81. Produced by Stephen Stanley, Tina Weymouth, and Chris Frantz.

The Catherine Wheel. David Byrne (Sire). Released fall '81. Produced by David Byrne. **Notes:** The album contains eleven cuts; the CD, twenty-three.

The Name of This Band Is Talking Heads. Live 2-LP set (1977–79). Talking Heads (Sire). Released late March '82. Produced by Talking Heads. Side 1 recorded live at Northern Studio, Maynard, Massachusetts, 11/17/77. Side 2 recorded live at the Capitol Theater, Passaic, New Jersey, 11/17/79. Sides 3 and 4 recorded at Emerald City, Cherry Hill, New Jersey, 11/8–9/80; Central Park, New York City, 8/27/80; Sun Plaza Concert Hall, Tokyo, Japan, 2/27/81. (Note: The second album captures the '81–'82 Expanded Heads, including Busta Jones, Adrian Belew, and Nona Hendryx.) (Side 1) "New Feeling"; "A Clean Break"; "Don't Worry About the Government"; "Pulled Up"; "Psycho Killer" (David Byrne/Martina Weymouth/Christopher Frantz). (Side 2) "Artists Only" (David Byrne/Wayne Zieve); "Stay Hungry" (David Byrne/Chris Frantz); "Air"; "Building on Fire"; "Memories Can't Wait." (Side 3) "I Zimbra" (David Byrne/Brian Eno/Hugo Ball); "Drugs" (David Byrne); "Houses in Motion" (words by David Byrne; initial music by David Byrne, Chris Frantz, Jerry Harrison, Tina Weymouth, Brian Eno; additional music by David Byrne and Brian Eno; musical and vocal arrangements by David Byrne and Brian Eno); "Life During Wartime" (David Byrne). (Side 4) "The Great Curve" (words by David Byrne); "Crosseyed and Painless" (words by David Byrne and Brian Eno); "Take Me to the River" (Al Green/M. Hodges). For all songs on Side 4: Initial music by David Byrne, Chris Frantz, Jerry Harrison, Tina Weymouth, Brian Eno; additional music by David Byrne and Brian Eno; musical and vocal arrangements by David Byrne and Brian Eno. **Notes:** Scott Isler in *TP*, 7/82, writes, "This package . . . is not the typical live 'stall' release. If nothing else, it provides crucial documentation of the bygone Expanded Heads onstage in full cry—one of rock's finer moments in the '80s."

Under the Boardwalk. Mini album. Tom Tom Club (Sire). Released summer '82. Produced by Chris Frantz, Tina Weymouth, and Stephen Stanley.

SP EAK IN GI N TO NGU ES. TA LKI N GHE ADS. Talking Heads (Sire). Standard package released early June '83. Limited edition Robert Rauschenberg package released June 29, 1983. Produced by Talking Heads. (Side A) "Burning Down the House"; "Making Flippy Floppy"; "Girlfriend Is Better"; "Slippery People"; "I Get Wild/Wild Gravity." (Side B) "Swamp"; "Moon Rocks"; "Pull Up the Roots"; "This Must Be the Place (Naive Melody)." (*7-inch single:* "Burning Down the House"/"I Get Wild/Wild Gravity"; "This Must Be the Place (Naive Melody)"/"Moon Rocks.") **Notes:** David Fricke in *RS*, 6/9/83, praised the record—"The Heads have never cut the funk into finer, more fluent pieces"—by specifically saying it evolved the freedom of band member's solo efforts: *Tom Tom Club, The Red and the Black*, and *The Catherine Wheel*. Unfortunately, Fricke closes his review by dismissing *My Life in the Bush of Ghosts* as an "academic safari [that flaunts] its cleverness."

387

Close to the Bone. Tom Tom Club (Sire). Released summer '83. Produced by Chris Frantz, Tina Weymouth, and Stephen Stanley.

Stop Making Sense. Talking Heads (Sire). Released early September '84. No producer listed. Consult original albums for complete songwriting credits. (Side One) "Psycho Killer"; "Swamp"; "Slippery People"; "Burning Down the House"; "Girlfriend Is Better." (Side Two) "Once in a Lifetime"; "What a Day That Was"; "Life During Wartime"; "Take Me to the River." (*7-inch single:* "Stop Making Sense (Girlfriend Is Better)"/"Heaven.")

5 Minutes. Bonzo Goes to Washington (Jerry Harrison) (Sleeping Bag). Released fall '84. Produced by Jerry Harrison and Daniel Lazerus.

Music for the Knee Plays. David Byrne (ECM). Released late April '85. Produced by David Byrne.

Little Creatures. Talking Heads (Sire). Released early summer '85. Produced and performed by Talking Heads. All songs by David Byrne except where indicated. (a) "And She Was"; "Give Me Back My Name"; "Creatures of Love"; "The Lady Don't Mind" (lyrics by David Byrne, music by David Byrne, Chris Frantz, Jerry Harrison, Tina Weymouth); "Perfect World" (lyrics by David Byrne and Chris Frantz). (b) "Stay Up Late"; "Walk it Down"; "Television Man"; "Road to Nowhere." Bonus track on CD version: "The Lady Don't Mind (extended mix)." (*7-inch single:* "Road to Nowhere"/"Give Me Back My Name.")

True Stories. Talking Heads (Sire). Released July '86. Produced and performed by Talking Heads. Songs by David Byrne. (Other Side) "Love for Sale"; "Puzzlin' Evidence"; "Hey Now"; "Papa Legba." (This Side) "Wild Wild Life"; "Radio Head"; "Dream Operator"; "People Like Us"; "City of Dreams." The CD also contains "Wild Wild Life (long E.T. mix)."

Sounds from True Stories. (Sire). Released July '86. Background music from David Byrne's motion picture *True Stories*.

Casual Gods. Jerry Harrison: Casual Gods (Sire). Released '88. Produced by Jerry Harrison; assistant producer, Ernie Brooks. **Notes:** Although Casual Gods was to be presented as a full-fledged band, Jerry Harrison's name appears on the spine and label of the LP.

Naked. Talking Heads (Sire). Released April '88. Produced by Steve Lillywhite and Talking Heads. Lyrics by David Byrne. Music by David Byrne, Chris Frantz, Jerry Harrison, and Tina Weymouth. (A) "Blind"; "Mr. Jones"; "Totally Nude"; "Ruby Dear." (B) "(Nothing but) Flowers"; "The Democratic Circus"; "The Facts of Life"; "Mommy"; "Daddy You and I"; "Big Daddy"; "Bill" (not available on the vinyl version); "Cool Water."

Boom Boom Chi Boom Boom. Tom Tom Club (Sire). Released '89. Produced by Chris Frantz and Tina Weymouth (additional production, Arthur Baker).

Rei Mono. David Byrne (Luaka Bop). Released fall '89. Produced by Steve Lillywhite with David Byrne.

Walk on Water. Jerry Harrison: Casual Gods (Fly). Released '90. Produced by Jerry Harrison, Dan Hartman, Ernie Brooks, Alex Weir, and Bernie Worrell.

The Forest. David Byrne (Luaka Bop). Released winter '91. No producer listed. Composed by David Byrne. Orchestrated and conducted by Jimmie Haskell.

Dark Sneak Love Action. Tom Tom Club (Sire). Released '92. Produced by Chris Frantz, Tina Weymouth, Mark Roule, and Bruce Martin.

Popular Favorites: Sand in the Vaseline. Talking Heads (Sire/Warner Bros.). Released Halloween '92. (Disc 1) "Sugar on My Tongue"; "I Want to Live"; "Love→ Building on Fire"; "I Wish You Wouldn't Say That"; "Psycho Killer"; "Don't Worry About the Government"; "No Compassion"; "Warning Sign"; "The Big Country"; "Take Me to the River"; "Heaven"; "Memories Can't Wait"; "I Zimbra"; "Once in a Lifetime"; "Crosseyed and Painless"; "Burning Down the House"; "Swamp"; "This Must Be the Place (Naive Melody)." (Disc 2) "Life During Wartime (Live)"; "Girlfriend Is Better (Live)"; "And She Was"; "Stay Up Late"; "Road to Nowhere"; "Wild Wild Life"; "Love for Sale"; "City of Dreams"; "Mr. Jones"; "Blind"; "(Nothing but) Flowers"; "Sax and Violins"; "Gangster of Love"; "Lifetime Piling Up"; "Popsicle." (*Sand in the Vaseline* was also released as a limited edition triple LP.)

389

Once in a Lifetime. Talking Heads (Sire/Warner Bros.). Scaled down single CD of *Sand in the Vaseline,* including one bonus track—the live version of "Slippery People." Tracks: "Psycho Killer"; "Take Me to the River"; "Once in a Lifetime"; "Burning Down the House"; "This Must Be the Place (Naive Melody)"; "Slippery People (Live)"; "Life During Wartime (Live)"; "And She Was"; "Road to Nowhere"; "Wild Wild Life"; "Blind"; "(Nothing but) Flowers"; "Sax and Violins"; "Lifetime Piling Up."

Uh-Oh. David Byrne (Luaka Bop). Released March '92. Produced by Nick Launay.

David Byrne. David Byrne (Luaka Bop). Released summer '94. Produced by Susan Rogers, Arto Lindsay, and David Byrne.

No Talking, Just Head. The Heads (MCA). Released '96. Produced by Chris Frantz, Jerry Harrison, and Tina Weymouth.

Feelings. David Byrne (Luaka Bop). Released May '97. Produced by David Byrne and others.

12 x 12: original remixes. Talking Heads (EMI). Released '99. "The Lady Don't Mind (extended version)"; "Television Man (extended version)"; "And She Was (extended mix)"; "Wild Wild Life (long E.T. mix)"; "Love for Sale (extended mix)"; "Hey Now (Milwaukee mix)"; "Radio Head (extended mix)"; "Blind (extended mix)"; "(Nothing but) Flowers (Lillywhite mix)"; "Ruby Dear (Bush mix)"; "Blind (Deaf Dumb & Blind Mix)"; "Love for Sale (love dub)."

Stop Making Sense. Talking Heads (Sire). Released fall '99. Full CD track listing: "Psycho Killer"; "Heaven"; "Thank You for Sending Me an Angel"; "Found a Job"; "Slippery People"; "Burning Down the House"; "Life During Wartime"; "Making Flippy Floppy"; "Swamp"; "What a Day That Was"; "This Must Be the Place (Naive Melody)"; "Once in a Lifetime"; "Genius of Love (Tom Tom Club)"; "Girlfriend Is Better"; "Take Me to the River"; "Crosseyed and Painless."

Selected Bootlegs

The following bootlegs were chosen for audio quality and archival value.

John Cale & Friends: The Ocean Club. July 1976. John Cale, Patti Smith, Lou Reed, David Byrne, and others. (Tracks) "Ghost Story"; "Buffalo Ballet"; "You Know More Than I Know"; "Waiting for the Man"; "I Keep a Close Watch"; "The Jeweler"; "Gun"; "Pablo Picasso"; "Cable Hogue"; "Baby What You Want Me to Do." The following were recorded minus David Byrne at Max's Kansas City in October: "Pablo Picasso"; "Mary Lou"; "Nasty Gasses"; "Viola/Piano Instrumental"; "Fear"; "The Thoughtless Kind." **Notes:** The sound quality is great for what it is.

Electricity. Talking Heads, double LP (allegedly also available on CD). The first three sides are a bootlegged version of Warner Bros.' *Talking Heads Live On Tour* (Agora, Cleveland, Ohio, 1978). Tracks: "The Big Country"; "Warning Sign"; "Artists Only"; "The Girls Want to Be with the Girls"; "The Good Thing"; "Electricity"; "New Feeling"; "Found a Job"; "Psychic [sic] Killer"; "Take Me to the River." This last side allegedly contains the complete contents of the first Talking Heads bootleg: *The Secret Lives of Tina Weymouth* (that disk is worth hunting down to see the back cover photo of Tina Weymouth as an Icelandic cheerleader circa 1965). (Tracks) "Psycho Killer (demo)"; "Care Free (demo)"; "Artists Only (demo)"; "1-2-3 Red Light (live)"; "Take Me to the River" and "Artists Only" (both from *Saturday Night Live*). **Notes:** The legitimate live album *The Name of This Band Is Talking Heads* only contains cuts from 1977 and 1979, so this excellent 1978 recording fills in the missing year between. Of particular interest is the lengthy guitar solo that Byrne (presumably) ends "Psychic [sic] Killer" with. For a man who constantly renounced guitar solos to the press, he can play nasty if he wants to. The demo of "Psycho Killer" (recorded in Long Island for Beserkeley Records) documents Byrne playing around with the rhythm of "fa fa fa." Finally, "1-2-3 Red Light" was a song Talking Heads frequently covered circa 1976. Don't confuse this bootleg with another called *Electrically*, which is composed of live shows from UCLA and the Roxy in Los Angeles, 1978.

What the Songs Look Like. Talking Heads, CD only. Live radio broadcast, spring 1979. Tracks: "The Big Country"; "Warning Sign"; "Artists Only"; "Girls Want to Be with the Girls"; "The Good Thing"; "Drugs"; "Electricity" [sic, really "New Feeling"]; "Found a Job"; "Psycho Killer"; "Take Me to the River." **Notes:** This disk fills out the four 1979 cuts contained on *The Name of This Band Is Talking Heads*. It gives you a taste of how "The Big Country"—the song that closes the group's second album—now works opening a live show. It also contains an excellent dueling guitar finale between Harrison and Byrne on "Psycho Killer" (it almost sounds like Neil Young dueting with Tom Verlaine).

Emitting Diode. Talking Heads, LP only. Central Park and Heatwave Festival, Toronto, August 1980. No specific credits for tracks appear, but the bulk of this double album appears to be from the Central Park concert. Tracks: "Psycho Killer"; "Warning Sign"; "Stay Hungry"; "Cities"; "I Zimbra"; "Once in a Lifetime"; "Houses in Motion"; "Born Under Punches"; "Crosseyed and Painless"; "Life During Wartime"; "Take Me to the River"; "The Great Curve." **Notes:** This bootleg, as well as the bootleg CD *Byrned to a Crisp* (Heatwave Festival only), documents the premiere of the Expanded Heads. The Heatwave tracks are a little ragged, particularly on background vocals.

Ghosts Date. David Byrne and Brian Eno, allegedly both LP and CD. Outtakes from *My Life in the Bush of Ghosts*. **Notes:** This is another Holy Grail. I've never seen it, but supposedly this bootleg contains the original version of "The Jezebel Spirit" with the sampled voice of Kathryn Kuhlman.

Gimme Heads! Talking Heads, LP. Miscellaneous outtakes from all years. Tracks: "Love→Building on Fire (mono version)"; "And She Was (alternative version)"; "Artists Only (demo)"; "Psycho Killer (demo)"; "First Week/Last Week (demo)"; "Love Goes to Building on Fire (stereo version)"; "The Lady Don't Mind (original version from *Speaking in Tongues* sessions)"; "Cities (slow version)"; "Heaven (acoustic version)"; "Naive Melody (outtake from *Stop Making Sense*)"; "1-2-3 Red Light (live)"; "Electricity (original version of "Drugs")." **Notes:** This entry was pulled from the www.talking-heads.net. If the recording actually exists, it is of intense archival interest because of "The Lady Don't Mind" and the two *Fear of Music* outtakes.

Chicken Shack. Talking Heads, LP only. Live recording from Milan, Italy, July 1982. Tracks: "Soundcheck"; "Psycho Killer"; "Cities"; "Once in a Lifetime"; "Mind"; "Far to the Crack" ["My Big Hands" from *The Catherine Wheel*—no doubt an Italian translation of the lyric "fall through the crack"]; "Think You Had Enough" ["Big Business" from *The Catherine Wheel*]; "I Zimbra"; "Swamp"; "Take Your Time" ["Slink" from *The Red and the Black*]; "Houses in Motion"; "Great Big Room"; "Life During Wartime"; "Take Me to the River." **Notes:** This record covers the tour years between *The Name of This Band Is Talking Heads* and *Stop Making Sense*. The brief soundcheck is a reminder of how untheatrical the Expanded Heads were before the Big Suit tour. The pair of *The Catherine Wheel* covers hint at what a killer Talking Heads album that David Byrne solo album would have been. Jerry Harrison sings "Slink" and reveals that his voice sounds beefier live than in the studio.

Other Related Works

David Byrne

Unplugged. (Bootleg CD.) Live 1992 concert in Italy? **Notes:** These live cuts showcase Byrne's maturing voice. A voice that was often compared to a strangled chicken now resonates with as much Old Testament authority as Johnny Cash. Particularly touching are the three Talking Heads songs he covers as well as the hillbilly classic "Green-back Dollar." This is a beautiful recording.

An Acoustic Evening with David Byrne and Richard Thompson. (Bootleg tape.) March 24, 1992, concert at St. Ann's in Brooklyn Heights, New York. **Notes:** First there was Sinatra and Dean Martin, now Thompson and Byrne. Richard Thompson spoke to me once in a very limited fashion about Byrne: *How did you meet David Byrne?* "I can't remember the first time. I think I met him backstage somewhere." *Did you follow the Talking Heads?* "Yeah. They were great. They were fantastic. I think Talking Heads were very important in the history of popular music. Dave's a great performer and thinker." *So you just hit it off?* "Yeah. Yeah. There's common ground there, somewhere." (On *Beat the Retreat*, the '94 Richard Thompson tribute CD, David Byrne contributes a swell version of "Just the Motion.")

Jerry Harrison

Producer: (1991) Live, *Mental Jewelry*; Poi Dog Pondering, *Vole, Vole* (produced one-third of album); Pure, *Purefenalia*. (1992) Psychofunkubus, *Skin*; Billy Goat, *Bush Roaming Mammals*. (1993) Crash Test Dummies, *God Shuffled His Feet*; Live, *Throwing Copper*. (1994) Fatima Mansions, *Lost In the Former West*; Black 47, *Home of the Brave*; General Public. (1995) Verve Pipe, *Villains*; Bog Men, *Life Begins at 40 Million*; Please, *Here It Comes It Again*. (1996) Big Head Todd and the Monsters, *Beautiful World*; Rusted Root, *Remember*; Outsiders, *Neurotic Outsiders*. (1997) Mayfield 4, *Fallout*; Noella Hutton, *Noella Hutton*; Kenny Wayne Shepherd Band, *The Trouble Is*. (1988) Stoke 9, *Nasty Little Thoughts*; Foo Fighters, *Walking After You*; Bijou Phillips, *I'd Rather Eat Glass*. (1999) Live, *The Distance of Us*; Kenny Wayne Shepherd Band, *Live On*; No Doubt, *New*.

Chris Frantz and Tina Weymouth

Tom Tom Club: The Good, the Bad, and the Funky. The first Tom Tom Club album of the twenty-first century is an eclectic collection of funk, dub, and African pop songs. Half the vocals are Tina Weymouth's meager cooings; the rest of the cuts are legitimate funk sung by Charles Pettigrew. This record will no doubt linger in the collective cultural memory as strongly as *Dark Sneak Love Action* did. Saying that, the disk contains one clever song titled "Happiness Can't Buy Money." Tina would often complain to me about personal finances the way we all can do. She also promised to write her own book about her ex-band. "But a book about Talking Heads is nothing I'd do for money," she said to me. "Only for love."

Selection of Talking Heads' Covers

Living Colour: *Vivid*—includes "Memories Can't Wait"; Luna: *Bonnie and Clyde*—includes "Thank You for Sending Me an Angel"; Bonnie Raitt: *Burning Down the House*—includes "Burning Down the House"; This Mortal Coil: *Filigree & Shadow*—includes "Drugs"; Tom Jones: *Reload*—includes "Burning Down the House"; *Soundtrack to Gus Van Sant's Psycho*—includes James Hall singing "Psycho Killer"; Phish: *Remain in Light* (bootleg)—includes complete Halloween night '96 concert of the band covering every song from *Remain in Light* at the Omni in Atlanta, Georgia.

Don't Worry About the Coverband: A Tribute to Talking Heads: This is a collection of some-times intriguing, sometimes amateur sounding Euro bands covering "Once in a Lifetime," "Burning Down the House," "Television Man," "Drugs," "Love for Sale," "Road to Nowhere," "Happy Day," "Mind," "Air," "Life During Wartime," "Psycho Killer," "Girlfriend Is Better," "Sugar on My Tongue," "Puzzlin' Evidence," "And She Was," and "The Great Curve."

Talking Heads Website

Francey/Studio Zimbra's www.talking-heads.net

Notes: This Website is the definitive *source* for miscellaneous Talking Heads credits, such as various twelve-inch remixes to minor musical projects that David Byrne, Chris Frantz, Jerry Harrison, and Tina Weymouth were involved in back during the twentieth century. (Grateful thanks to Frank Francey for providing me with rare Talking Heads cuts and bootlegs.)

filmography

Videos

Crosseyed and Painless (1981), directed by Toni Basil.
Once in a Lifetime (1981), directed by David Byrne and Toni Basil.
America Is Waiting (1981), directed by Bruce Conner (for Byrne/Eno, *My Life in the Bush of Ghosts*).
Burning Down the House (1982), directed by David Byrne.
This Must be the Place (Naive Melody) (1983), directed by David Byrne.
And She Was (1985), directed by Jim Blashfield and Melissa Marsland.
The Lady Don't Mind (1985), directed by Alan Kleinberg.
Road to Nowhere (1985), directed by David Byrne and Stephen R. Johnson.
Stay Up Late (1986), directed by Ted Bufaloukos.
Wild Wild Life (1986), directed by David Byrne (won MTV Award for Best Video).
Love for Sale (1986), directed by David Byrne and Melvin Sokolsky.
Blind (1988), directed by Rocky Morton and Annabel Jankel.
(Nothing but) Flowers (1988), directed by David Byrne.
Lifetime Piling Up (1992), no director.

David Byrne Videos

Dirty Old Town (1989); *Make Believe Mambo* (1989); *Don't Fence Me In* (1990); *Girls on My Mind* (1992); *Hanging Upside Down* (1992); *She's Mad* (1992); *Angeles* (1994); *Back in the Box* (1994); *Waters of March* (with Marisa Monte) (1996); *Miss America* (1997).

Jerry Harrison Videos

Five Minutes (Bonzo Goes to Washington) (1984); *Kickstart* (date unavailable); *Man with a Gun* (1988); *Rev It Up* (1988); *Damage I've Done* (1996); *Don't Take My Kindness for Weakness* (1996).

Tom Tom Club Videos

Genius of Love (1981); *Pleasures of Love* (1982); *Don't Say No* (1989); *Subocena (Boom Boom Chi Boom Boom)* (1990); *Call of the Wild* (1992).

Movies and Full-length Videos

The Blank Generation (circa 1976), directed by Amos Poe and Ivan Kral. **Note:** This is a silent movie of Talking Heads and other groups such as Blondie and the Ramones playing on stage at CBGBs. It is as quaint an artifact as an old Tom Mix two-reeler. The most interesting thing about the Talking Heads footage is David Byrne's open mouth. His front tooth is really chipped—your eye is drawn to it immediately. I asked Lee Blake if the tooth was a prominent part of Byrne's face? His smile? "No, he's got such a beautiful smile, no one cares about a bloody chipped tooth," she replied, irritated. "When David was younger, there was this extraordinary fucking Gregory Peck thing about him. And he was just very, very handsome. Very shy, a little bit gawky, but extremely handsome. He went from being Gregory Peck to being Anthony Perkins, easily. . . ."

The Catherine Wheel for BBC (1982), directed by Twyla Tharp.

Stop Making Sense (1984), directed by Jonathan Demme.

Survival Guide for PBS (1985), directed by Jonathan Demme.

True Stories (1986), directed by David Byrne.

Ille Aiye (The House of Life) for PBS (1989), directed by David Byrne.

Red, Hot + Blue (1990), includes Byrne's video promo of "Don't Fence Me In."

Between the Teeth (1993), directed by David Byrne and David Wild.

Television Shows

Saturday Night Live: Sometime in '78 Talking Heads played "Take Me to the River" and "Artists Only"; on 2/10/79 the band played "Take Me to the River" and "I Zimbra"; on 11/18/89 David Byrne played "Dirty Old Town" and "Loco de Amor."

Late Show with David Letterman: Sometime in '83 Talking Heads played "Burning Down the House" and "I Zimbra"; on 10/28/86 David Byrne appeared to plug *True Stories*; on 10/28/96 the Heads played "Damage I've Done."

The Tonight Show: Sometime in '92 David Byrne played "The Cowboy Mambo" and "Burning Down the House."

MTV Unplugged: Sometime in '93 David Byrne joined Natalie Merchant and her band, 10,000 Maniacs, onstage.

Politically Incorrect: Sometime in '96 Tina Weymouth appeared on a panel.

Muppets Tonight: Sometime in '96 Kermit the frog donned a Big Suit and sang "Once in a Lifetime."

Sessions at West 54th Street: David Byrne hosted the show '98 through '99.

index